Desk Reference on the
STATES

BOOKS IN THE DESK REFERENCE SERIES

CQ's Desk Reference on American Courts

CQ's Desk Reference on American Criminal Justice

CQ's Desk Reference on American Government

CQ's Desk Reference on the Economy

CQ's Desk Reference on the Federal Budget

CQ's Desk Reference on the Presidency

CQ's Desk Reference on the States

CONGRESSIONAL QUARTERLY'S

Desk Reference on the
STATES

BRUCE WETTERAU

Congressional Quarterly Inc.
Washington, D.C.

CQ Press
A Division of Congressional Quarterly Inc.
1414 22nd St. N.W.
Washington, DC 20037

(202) 822-1475; (800) 638-1710

www.cqpress.com

Printed in the United States of America

05   04   03   02   01   6   5   4   3   2

Cover and interior design: Anne Masters Design, Inc., Washington, D.C.

Library of Congress Cataloging-in-Publication Data

Wetterau, Bruce.
    CQ's desk reference on the States / Bruce Wetterau.
        p.   cm.
    Includes bibliographical references and index.
    ISBN: 1-56802-444-4 (cloth)
    1. State governments--United States--Handbooks, manuals, etc. 2. Legislative bodies--United States--States--Handbooks, manuals, etc.--I. Congressional Quarterly. II. Title. III. Title: Congressional Quarterly's desk reference on the states.
JK2408.W48 1999   99-19293
320.473--dc21

CONTENTS

Preface vii

I The States 1
The States in History **1**
Statehood **12**
State Constitutions **16**
States and the Union **20**
District of Columbia **27**
For the Record **29**
Where Can I Find . . . **32**

II Governorship 34
In General **34**
Powers and Privileges **37**
Getting Into and Out of Office **44**
For the Record **49**
Governors' Backgrounds **56**
Lieutenant Governors **58**
Attorneys General **60**
Cabinet and Executive Branch **60**
Where Can I Find . . . **65**

III Legislatures 68
In General **68**
Making Laws and Debating **76**
Sessions and Votes **87**
Committees and Caucuses **88**
Members' Backgrounds **90**
Arrivals and Departures **91**
For the Record **94**
Senate **99**

House of Representatives **100**
Lobbyists: The "Third" House **102**
Where Can I Find . . . **104**

IV Campaigns and Elections 107
In General **107**
States and National Politics **113**
State Parties and State Primaries **116**
Gubernatorial Races **127**
Legislative Races **133**
Judicial Elections **135**
For the Record **137**
Petitions and Propositions **141**
Campaign Finance **144**
Where Can I Find . . . **146**

V State Courts 150
In General **150**
State and Federal Court
    Jurisdictions **154**
State Supreme Court and
    Other Appellate Courts **155**
Lower Courts **157**
Stepping Up and Stepping Down
    from the Bench **158**
Legal Terms and Procedures **163**
For the Record **165**
Supreme Court Tests of States'
    Powers **166**
Where Can I Find . . . **175**

VI State of the States   179

In General **179**

Business and Labor **185**

Crime and Criminal Justice **192**

Education **201**

Environment **206**

Federal Aid to States **213**

Health and Welfare **217**

State Aid to Localities **226**

Taxes and Spending **229**

Transportation—Highways and
Mass Transit **239**

Where Can I Find . . . **243**

**VII What About My State?
——The State Profiles 246**

Subject Index 305

Name Index 320

PREFACE

Anyone who has tried to find information on state government has encountered this basic research problem: there may be fifty different right answers to the same question—one for each state. The dilemma made writing a question-and-answer book about state government, already a formidable task, that much more challenging. Organizing the answers and framing them in clear, uncomplicated terms also presented their own difficulties. But the result is a book that will be all the more useful to those who need a ready reference on the states, including librarians, students, writers, editors, and others.

CQ's Desk Reference on the States is the third title in the Desk Reference series of books, which provide readers with quick and easy access to broad and otherwise unwieldy subject areas. In the following pages readers will find answers to questions on subjects ranging from constitutional matters and the origins of the states, to the length of a governor's term, legislative procedures, voter turnout, and the organization of state court systems. But while textbook definitions of terms and concise explanations of the general aspects of state government are important features of this book, they represent only one facet of its coverage.

Complementing the book's broad perspective on state government is its focus on the individual states. More than half the answers in the *Desk Reference* provide current statistics or other facts and figures on specific states (including more than sixty tables and lists), and an additional 20 percent of the book is devoted entirely to such data (see Chapter 7, "What About My State?—The State Profiles"). In many cases readers will need to look no further than this book for up-to-date information on the states. But when additional research is necessary, readers may consult the lists of other useful, recently published sources that appear at the end of each chapter. The Web address of the home page for every state in the Union appears in Chapter 7.

The question-and-answer format presents a wealth of information in brief, clearly written answers that can be easily understood, even by someone with little or no knowledge of state government. As in the other books in the series, readers can use this *Desk Reference* in two ways. They can look up a specific fact, figure, procedure, term, event, or other piece of information relating to the states. Or they can read through the questions in a chapter sequentially to get a quick but thorough introduction to any one of the book's five main subject areas: state history and government, the office of governor, state legislatures, campaigns and elections, and state courts.

This two-books-in-one quality—combining the depth of a ready reference with the breadth of a subject area guide—is an important feature of all volumes in the Desk Reference series. So, too, are the extensive cross-references, which help readers find related entries to supplement their research. For example, many of the answers are followed by cross-references to other, related entries. There are also free-standing cross-references alerting readers to questions that appear in other sections but that might have been included under the current heading as well. The detailed index makes it easy to locate such reference information as definitions, important firsts, and noteworthy events. It also lists all entries mentioning a particular state. Readers need not skim entire sections of the book, or even whole pages, to locate detailed information. The index identifies the entry or entries providing the answers, allowing direct access to the desired information.

Reference books are not made by authors alone. I want to thank all those who contributed their time and expertise to this latest volume in the Desk Reference series. Dave Tarr, my editor at CQ Press, oversaw the book from its beginning as a promising idea and provided me with valuable guidance throughout the publication process. A good library is a resource too often taken for granted. The sizable collections of the University of Virginia's Alderman and Clemons Libraries helped make this and other books in the series possible. And when it came to the knotty research questions, the government information resources staff at Alderman, notably Jon Rice, Barbara Selby, and staff director Walter Newsome, always provided helpful suggestions. And finally, CQ senior editor Christopher Karlsten deserves thanks for his work in editing the book and preparing it for publication.

—Bruce Wetterau

THE STATES

Q 1. What were the largest and smallest states when the country was formed? Today?

A Surprisingly, in 1790, a year after the U.S. Constitution was ratified, Georgia ranked first among the original thirteen states in land area—145,196 square miles. At that time Georgia's western border was fixed at the Mississippi River, however, and in 1802 the state ceded its western lands (which later became Alabama and Mississippi) to the federal government. That shrank Georgia to its present-day 58,000 square miles.

Virginia ranked second at 64,284 square miles in 1790, but at the time it included what is now West Virginia. When West Virginia broke away from the state at the beginning of the Civil War, Virginia lost some 24,000 square miles. Meanwhile, Rhode Island (just over 1,000 square miles) and Delaware (just under 2,000 square miles) were the smallest states in 1790, and remain so today.

Texas, of course, became the biggest state once it joined the Union in 1845. At some 260,000 square miles, it was well ahead of its closest rivals, California and Montana. That changed in 1959, however, when Alaska entered the Union. At just over 570,000 square miles, Alaska now ranks first and is over twice the size of Texas. *(See also Chapter 7 for land areas of the individual states.)*

Q 2. Which states had the largest and smallest populations in 1790? 1990?

A According to the nation's first official census in 1790, Virginia was the most heavily populated of the thirteen original states—a total of 692,000 people lived there. Pennsylvania (434,000), North Carolina (394,000), and Massachusetts (379,000) followed, and New York came in fifth with 340,000 residents. Delaware had the smallest population, just 59,000 people.

The 1990 census two hundred years later put California at the top of the list with over 29.7 million people. That was well ahead of the next two most heavily populated states, New York (17.9 million) and Texas (16.9 million). By 1996 Texas had moved ahead of New York, based on Census Bureau estimates of population growth.

In 1990 the state with the smallest population was Wyoming, which had just 453,588 residents. Arkansas was next to last with 550,043. Other states with fewer than 1 million residents include Alaska, North Dakota, Delaware, South Dakota, Montana, and Rhode Island.

See 62 Which of the original thirteen states was most heavily populated in 1790?

Q **3. Which of the original thirteen states had the largest urban population?**

A Massachusetts ranked first with 51,000 city dwellers in 1790, most of whom lived in the bustling port city of Boston. Pennsylvania had 44,000 people living in urban areas, and New York, 39,000. Delaware, Georgia, New Jersey, North Carolina, and Vermont all had fewer than 1,000 city dwellers.

See 62 Which of the original thirteen states was most heavily populated in 1790?

Q **4. When did California become our most populous state?**

A The 1970 census made it official—California replaced New York as our most populous state, based on a population of over 19.9 million residents. California had been growing by leaps and bounds for decades, and by the 1960 census it had closed to within about a million of New York's population, the longtime population leader. Continued growth in the 1960s finally pushed California into the top spot, and today it has an estimated population of some 31 million people. New York had held the record as the most populous state since the 1810 census. Its population today is about 18 million.

See 62 Which of the original thirteen states was most heavily populated in 1790?

Q **5. What were the original thirteen states?**

A The thirteen colonies that formed the United States at the outset of the Revolutionary War were Connecticut, Delaware, Georgia, Maryland, Massachusetts, New Hampshire, New Jersey, New York, North Carolina, Pennsylvania, Rhode Island, South Carolina, and Virginia.

6. Which of the original thirteen states was settled first and when were the others established?

A English settlers established the first permanent settlement in Virginia, followed a few years later by the arrival of the pilgrims in Massachusetts. Of the original thirteen colonies, all but Connecticut and Rhode Island began as chartered colonies, which were governed by companies formed to colonize the region or by individuals named as proprietors. During the 1600s, though, British kings began trying to assert direct control over the colonies by establishing them as royal colonies and appointing governors to oversee them.

The original thirteen colonies were established as follows:

Virginia. It was first explored in 1584 and became the site of the first permanent British settlement in North America in 1607. Virginia became England's first royal colony in 1624.

Massachusetts. Settlement of this chartered colony began in 1620 with the landing of the first colonists, led by the Pilgrims, at Plymouth Colony. It became a royal colony (including Maine) in 1691.

New Hampshire. The first settlers arrived in 1623. Captain John Mason, who had gained control of the colony, established Portsmouth the following year. New Hampshire became a royal colony in 1679.

New York. It was first settled by the Dutch as New Netherland in 1624. The British took control in 1664, dividing New Netherland into the colonies of New York and New Jersey.

New Jersey. The Dutch settled this area as part of New Netherland in 1630. New Jersey was divided in two after the British gained control of New Netherland in 1664, but was reunited when it became a crown colony in 1702.

Delaware. Dutch settlers arrived in 1631, and the Swedes who followed soon after introduced the log cabin in North America. The British took control of the region after 1664, and in 1682 Delaware became the self-governing "Lower Counties" of Pennsylvania. In 1776 Delaware broke away from Pennsylvania and became an independent entity.

Connecticut. Emigrés from nearby Plymouth Colony first settled the area in 1633. Connecticut was chartered as a colony in 1662 by King Charles II. Connecticut and Rhode Island were the only two colonies allowed to elect their own governors.

Maryland. It was originally settled in 1634 as a refuge for Catholics seeking the freedom to practice their religion. Maryland became a royal colony in 1691.

Rhode Island. It was originally settled in 1636 by Roger Williams, a religious dissenter from Plymouth Colony. Settlements were organized as a colony in 1644 and received a royal charter in 1663.

Pennsylvania. The British gained control over the area in 1664 when they seized New Netherland (New York) from the Dutch. In 1681 King Charles II gave the charter for Pennsylvania to William Penn, son of Admiral William Penn, in gratitude for the admiral's service. Penn sought to establish a haven of religious freedom for Quakers, and after he founded Philadelphia the following year, the colony grew rapidly. By 1723 Philadelphia had become the second-largest city in the British empire.

North Carolina. After the ill-fated attempt to establish a colony on Roanoke Island in 1585, colonization efforts moved northward to the Virginia coast. England's King Charles I granted the first land patent in 1629 for what would become North Carolina, but settlement did not begin until the 1650s. North Carolina finally became a royal colony in 1729.

South Carolina. English colonists arrived in the area from 1670 onward, but the colony of South Carolina was not organized until 1712. It became a royal colony in 1719.

Georgia. Long the subject of dispute between Spain and England, Georgia was originally part of the grant to proprietors of Carolina. King George II chartered Georgia as an independent colony in 1732, making it the last of the original thirteen colonies to be formed. The first settlers arrived in 1733.

Q 7. Where did the other states come from?

A The thirty-seven other states that now make up the United States came to the Union in a variety of ways. Dividing up some of the original colonies created a number of new states. Maine was once part of Massachusetts, for example, and western lands that some colonies had claimed led to the creation of four midwestern states—Illinois, Indiana, Michigan, and Ohio—as well as several southern states, including Kentucky, Tennessee, and Alabama.

The Louisiana Purchase, arranged by President Thomas Jefferson, effectively doubled the size of the United States and eventually added all or part of fifteen new states to the Union (Louisiana, Iowa, Missouri, Nebraska, and Montana among them). Later in the 1800s, treaties with Spain and Britain gave the United States other valuable territories, including lands that became Florida (1819), parts of Wisconsin (1842), North Dakota (1818), and Oregon, Washington, Idaho, and part of Wyoming (1846). Another land purchase in 1867 added the Alaska territory.

Texas revolted against Mexican rule and, after spending a few years as an independent republic, joined the Union in the 1840s. California, Nevada, Utah, Arizona, and parts of New Mexico, Wyoming, and Colorado were carved out of the territory captured by the United States during the Mexican War (1846–1848). And finally, the expanding United States presence in the Pacific during the late 1800s and early 1900s led to the acquisition of Hawaii, first as a territory and then as a state. *(See also 27 How did West Virginia come to be a state?)*

See 14 When did the states join the Union? 30 What other territories besides Puerto Rico are United States possessions?

Q 8. What was the Dominion of New England?

A For a time during the colonial period, the separate colonies (or territories) of Massachusetts, Connecticut, Maine, New Hampshire, New Jersey, New York, and Rhode Island ceased to exist. Between 1686 and 1688 England's King James consolidated them all into a single province called the Dominion of New England. His plan was to strengthen his control over the colonies, but the king's governor, Sir Edmund Andros, only succeeded in generating widespread resentment. When King James was overthrown in England in 1688–1689, Americans arrested Governor Andros, and the separate colonial governments were restored.

See 18 What are the New England and Middle Atlantic States?

Q 9. Which state names are based on Native American words?

A Twenty-seven state names are believed to derive from words in languages of Native Americans (or native peoples). They are:

Alabama. "Alba ayamule" (Choctaw: I open the thicket).

Alaska. "Alayeksa" (Eskimo: great land).

Arizona. "Aleh-zon" (Papago: place of the small spring).

Arkansas. From the French for "Kansas," the Algonquian name for the Quapaw tribe.

Connecticut. "Quinnehtukqut" (Mohican: beside the long tidal river).

Hawaii. "Hawaiki" (Hawaiian: homeland).

Idaho. Artificial Indian name, made up by George M. Willing.

Illinois. "Illini" (Illinois tribe: man or warrior).

Iowa. "Ayuxwa" (Iowa tribe: one who puts to sleep).

Kansas. "Kanze" (Kansas tribal name: south wind).

Kentucky. "Kentake" (Iroquois: meadowland).

Massachusetts. Algonquian for "big hill place," apparently in reference to Great Blue Hill, near Milton.

Michigan. "Majigan" (Chipewa: clearing).

Minnesota. "Mnishota" (Dakota Sioux: sky-tinted water).

Mississippi. "Mici sibi" (Chipewa: large river).

Missouri. Algonquian, possibly the word for "big canoe people" or another for "muddy water."

Nebraska. "Niboathka" (Omaha tribe: river, or flat).

North Dakota. "Dakota" (Dakota tribal name: friends, allies).

Ohio. "Oheo" (Iroquois: beautiful river).

Oklahoma. Choctaw words "ukla" and "huma" (person red, or red people).

Oregon. Uncertain origins, possibly from the Algonquian "wauregan" (beautiful river); the Spanish name for a tribe, "orejon" (big ear); or other sources.

South Dakota. "Dakota" (Dakota tribal name: friends, allies).

Tennessee. "Tanasi," the name of two Cherokee villages.

Texas. "Teysha" (Caddo: Hello, friend), or the Spanish "tejas" (allies).

Utah. From the tribal name of the Ute Indians, or possibly the Apache "yuttahih" (higher up).

Wisconsin. Possibly the Chipewa word for "grassy place."

Wyoming. "Meacheweaming" (Delaware Indian: at the big flats).

See 14 When did the states join the Union?

🅠 10. Where did the other state names come from?

🅐 Twenty-three state names are thought to have origins in words other than those of native peoples. They are:

California, from the Spanish for "an earthly paradise."

Colorado, from the Spanish for "red," meaning "red land."

Delaware, named for Virginia governor Thomas West, Baron De la Warr.

Florida, from the Spanish for "land of the flowers."

Georgia, named for England's King George II.

Indiana, coined by Congress in 1800 (by adding an "a" to Indian, for "land of the Indians").

Louisiana, named for French King Louis XIV (in 1681).

Maine, named after the French province of Mayne.

Maryland, named by Lord Baltimore for England's Queen Mary (Henrietta Maria).

Montana, from the Spanish for "mountainous."

Nevada, from the Spanish for "snowy."

New Hampshire. Named after Hampshire County in England (in 1622).

New Jersey, named after England's Isle of Jersey.

New Mexico, named by Spanish explorers (in 1562).

New York, named after the Duke of York.

North Carolina, from the Latinized version of Charles ("Carolina"), after England's King Charles II.

Pennsylvania, named after William Penn, founder of the colony.

Rhode Island, from the Dutch "roodt eylandt" (red island).

South Carolina, from the Latinized version of Charles ("Carolina"), after England's King Charles II.

Vermont, from the French "vert" and "mont" (green mountain).

Virginia, named after England's Queen Elizabeth, who was known as the Virgin Queen, in 1607.

Washington, named in 1853 after President George Washington.

West Virginia, after the state of Virginia, of which it was once a part.

See 14 When did the states join the Union?

Q 11. Why did North Dakota consider changing its name?

A Freezing temperatures, cold winds, and blinding snowstorms may be a fact of life during North Dakota's winters, but for a time in 1989 the state government seriously considered changing its name to just plain Dakota. The "North" in North Dakota, supporters of the name change argued, made the place seem colder. The state's tourism director weighed in with surveys showing visitors commonly thought the state was cold and flat, and even state residents reportedly were affected by the word "north." The state senate actually took up the question of dropping "North," but resoundingly defeated the measure in a 36 to 15 vote.

Q 12. Which state was first to join the Union?

A Although the Constitution did not take effect until nine states had ratified it (on June 21, 1788), the first state to approve ratification was Delaware, on December 7, 1787. Pennsylvania completed its ratification of the Constitution just a few days later.

See 70 Who was the first governor?

Q 13. What was the fourteenth state—the first new state created after the Constitution was adopted?

A Vermont became the first new state on March 4, 1791, less than a year after the last of the original thirteen colonies, Rhode Island, ratified the Constitution. Although other colonies had claims to the region, Vermont declared itself an independent commonwealth in 1777, while the Revolution was still being fought. Claims to the territory were not resolved until 1790, well after the war.

Q 14. When did the states join the Union?

A The dates on which each of the fifty states joined the Union are listed below. Dates for the first nine are based on the dates they ratified the Constitution, although the Constitution (and so the Union) technically was not in effect until nine states had ratified it.

	State	*Date joined Union*
1.	Delaware	December 7, 1787
2.	Pennsylvania	December 12, 1787
3.	New Jersey	December 18, 1787
4.	Georgia	January 2, 1788
5.	Connecticut	January 9, 1788

State	Date joined Union
6. Massachusetts	February 6, 1788
7. Maryland	April 28, 1788
8. South Carolina	May 23, 1788
9. New Hampshire	June 21, 1788

(Constitution ratified and in force)

10. Virginia	June 25, 1788
11. New York	July 26, 1788
12. North Carolina	November 21, 1789
13. Rhode Island	May 29, 1790
14. Vermont	March 4, 1791
15. Kentucky	June 1, 1792
16. Tennessee	June 1, 1796
17. Ohio	March 1, 1803
18. Louisiana	April 30, 1812
19. Indiana	December 11, 1816
20. Mississippi	December 10, 1817
21. Illinois	December 3, 1818
22. Alabama	December 14, 1819
23. Maine	March 15, 1820
24. Missouri	August 10, 1821
25. Arkansas	June 15, 1836
26. Michigan	January 26, 1837
27. Florida	March 3, 1845
28. Texas	December 29, 1845
29. Iowa	December 28, 1846
30. Wisconsin	May 29, 1848
31. California	September 9, 1850
32. Minnesota	May 11, 1858
33. Oregon	February 14, 1859
34. Kansas	January 29, 1861
35. West Virginia	June 20, 1863
36. Nevada	October 31, 1864
37. Nebraska	March 1, 1867
38. Colorado	August 1, 1876

(table continues)

State	Date joined Union
39. North Dakota	November 2, 1889
40. South Dakota	November 2, 1889
41. Montana	November 8, 1889
42. Washington	November 11, 1889
43. Idaho	July 3, 1890
44. Wyoming	July 10, 1890
45. Utah	January 4, 1896
46. Oklahoma	November 16, 1907
47. New Mexico	January 6, 1912
48. Arizona	February 14, 1912
49. Alaska	January 3, 1959
50. Hawaii	August 21, 1959

Q **15. What has been the longest the United States has gone without admitting a new state?**

A Just under forty-seven years. That was the span between the admission of Arizona, the last of the western states (February 14, 1912), and that of Alaska, the first of two noncontiguous states (January 3, 1959). It has been thirty-nine years since the last state, Hawaii, was admitted.

Q **16. Does the Constitution allow states to change their borders?**

A Yes, but Article IV, Section 3, of the Constitution forbids the joining of states or the creation of new ones from their territories, unless Congress and the legislatures involved approve. Section 3 also empowers Congress to admit new states to the Union.

See 27 How did West Virginia come to be a state?

Q **17. Why was the Mason-Dixon line drawn?**

A Now famous as a symbolic dividing line between the North and South, the Mason-Dixon line was originally surveyed in the 1700s to resolve border disputes between the colonies of Pennsylvania and Maryland. Between 1763 and 1767 surveyors Charles Mason and Jeremiah Dixon led a party of skilled woodsmen westward along the boundary, clearing a corridor through the wilderness to allow them to survey the line. Ultimately they charted 233 miles of the boundary before being forced to turn back by hostile Indians. Though the line became a symbolic border between northern and southern states, it did not reflect the actual division of states during the Civil War. For example, Maryland is below the line but did not secede with other southern states; so, too, is the District of Columbia, which remained the seat of the federal government.

See 27 How did West Virginia come to be a state?

Q 18. What are the New England and Middle Atlantic states?

A Captain John Smith gave New England its name while exploring the region's coastline in 1614. Eventually Connecticut, Maine, Massachusetts, New Hampshire, Rhode Island, and Vermont were carved out of this region. The states immediately south of it—New York, New Jersey, and Pennsylvania—make up the Middle Atlantic states.

Q 19. Which states are considered part of the "Deep South"? The Sunbelt?

A Alabama, Georgia, Louisiana, Mississippi, and South Carolina are the Deep South states. Many other nearby states are counted among the states of the South, however, including North Carolina, Virginia, Tennessee, Kentucky, Arkansas, Texas, and Florida.

The Sunbelt includes the southern states (especially Florida and Texas) but extends westward across the entire southern tier of states to California. The Sunbelt is named for the generally sunny and more favorable climate found in these states, one reason why they have experienced such high growth in recent decades.

See 17 Why was the Mason-Dixon line drawn?

Q 20. Where did the name Dixie come from?

A Louisiana originally was settled by the French, and even after statehood there remained a strong French influence there. For that reason, when the Citizens' Bank in New Orleans decided to issue $10 notes some years before the Civil War, it made them bilingual by including the French word for ten, *dix*, on the back. Because of the notes, people began calling New Orleans the "Land of Dixie." The expression caught on. Soon it was applied to all of Louisiana and then more generally to the South.

Dixie's place in the language was assured in 1859 when minstrel Daniel Decatur Emmett wrote the now-famous song "Dixie" for a traveling minstrel show. Both the song and the expression became popular in the North and South. When the Civil War broke out, the Confederacy adopted "Dixie" as its unofficial anthem. The song was even played at Jefferson Davis's inauguration as president of the Confederacy.

21. What states belong to the Midwest and West regions?

A The term *Midwest* refers to the north central region of the United States and usually includes Illinois, Indiana, Iowa, Kansas, Michigan, Minnesota, Missouri, Nebraska, Ohio, and Wisconsin.

The Plains states, a region named for the vast plain covering it, also include some of these states. The nine Plains states are Iowa, Kansas, Minnesota, Missouri, Nebraska, North Dakota, Oklahoma, South Dakota, and Texas.

The West includes all states west of the Mississippi River. The Southwest region encompasses a smaller region within the West and is generally taken to include Arizona, California, Colorado, southern Nevada, New Mexico, Oklahoma, Texas, and Utah.

STATEHOOD

Q **22. How do states become states?**

A The Constitution gives Congress the power to admit new states to the Union (Article IV, Section 3). The procedure itself involves the following steps: Congress must first receive a petition for statehood from the legislature of the territory or independent state. If Congress approves the petition, the legislature then must draft a proposed state constitution. Once Congress has accepted the constitution, it can then enact a bill to admit the state. But statehood does not actually become official until the president has signed the bill into law.

See 12 Which state was first to join the Union? 14 When did the states join the Union? 16 Does the Constitution allow states to change their borders? 27 How did West Virginia come to be a state?

Q **23. What was the state of Franklin?**

A Efforts to make this proposed state part of the Union failed, although the territory itself eventually was included in a state that did join.

Settlers in western North Carolina formed Franklin, named for Benjamin Franklin, after North Carolina ceded the territory to the federal government in 1784. Congress ignored their petition for statehood, but the settlers elected a governor (John Sevier) and established a government that lasted until the end of Sevier's term in 1788. North Carolina once again took control of the area and in 1796 turned the territory over to the new state of Tennessee.

Q 24. Who proposed the state of Deseret?

A Mormons who had settled in what is now Utah proposed a state named Deseret, which is the Mormon word for "honeybee." When Congress ignored their petition for statehood in 1849, Mormon leader Brigham Young established a Mormon government and claimed for Deseret a huge territory stretching as far west as the California coast and as far south as New Mexico.

Congress responded in 1850 by creating a much smaller state, Utah, and named Young the governor. That avoided for the time being any direct conflict with the Mormon leader. But President James Buchanan eventually did send troops when Young refused to step down as governor in 1857.

Q 25. What effect did the Missouri Compromise have on the admission of states to the Union?

A The Missouri Compromise, established in 1820, sought to maintain the balance between states where slaveholding was legal and those where it was not. The idea was to admit states in pairs—one slaveholding and one free state—at roughly the same time. The compromise sidestepped the heated controversy over ending slavery but did nothing to resolve it.

The question first arose in 1819 when Missouri, acquired as part of the Louisiana Purchase, applied for statehood as a slaveholding state. Antislavery forces opposed any further spread of slavery and held up Missouri's admission, but the following year proslavery senators were in a position to hold up the admission of Maine, a free state. By the compromise, Maine was admitted as a free state in 1820, Missouri's entrance as a slave state was authorized the same year, and slavery was forever barred from territories in the Louisiana Purchase north of 36 degrees, 30 minutes.

Other states admitted while the Missouri Compromise remained in effect were Arkansas, Michigan, Florida, Texas, Iowa, and Wisconsin. The Missouri Compromise remained in effect until the Compromise of 1850 gave residents of prospective states the right to decide the slavery issue.

Q 26. Which states seceded during the Civil War?

A Eleven southern states seceded at the outset of the Civil War. South Carolina broke away from the Union first on December 20, 1860, soon after Abraham Lincoln won the presidential election but before hostilities had actually started. Mississippi joined South Carolina on January 9, 1861, followed by Florida (January 10), Alabama

(January 11), Georgia (January 19), Louisiana (January 26), Texas (February 1), Virginia (April 17), Arkansas (May 6), North Carolina (May 20), and Tennessee (June 8).

After the Civil War the Confederate states were all readmitted to the Union, beginning in 1866 with Tennessee. In 1868 Alabama, Arkansas, Florida, Louisiana, North Carolina, and South Carolina all were readmitted. Two years later the last of the Confederate states—Georgia, Mississippi, Texas, and Virginia—rejoined the Union.

Q 27. How did West Virginia come to be a state?

A Originally the western part of Virginia, this mountainous region was geographically isolated from the state's political and economic center, the eastern tidewater region. Western Virginia was populated by owners of small farms, who did not use slaves and who otherwise had little in common with large plantation owners. For many years they paid proportionally higher taxes than the plantation owners, received less than their share of public money for roads and schools, and were underrepresented in the state legislature.

The long-standing tensions finally came to a head when Virginia seceded from the Union on April 17, 1861, at the outset of the Civil War. Protected by federal troops, delegates from western Virginia counties declared the government of Virginia reconstituted at Wheeling in western Virginia, and by October western Virginia's voters had approved a referendum creating the new state of West Virginia.

Reconstituting the Virginia government was necessary because the U.S. Constitution requires approval by both the state legislature and Congress before a state can divide itself. Once a new state constitution had been drafted and received congressional approval, West Virginia formally entered the Union on June 20, 1863, as the 35th state.

See 16 Does the Constitution allow states to change their borders?

Q 28. Was the Civil War the first time states considered seceding from the Union?

A No, opposition to the War of 1812 was very strong in Massachusetts and some other New England states. By 1814 newspapers and even some politicians in the region were calling on New England states to protest the war by seceding and forming an independent republic. Later in 1814 Massachusetts legislators organized the Hartford Convention, at which delegates from New England states were to discuss the war and secession.

Only Massachusetts, Connecticut, and Rhode Island sent official delegates, though, and moderate leaders quickly took control of the convention. That stifled any further movement toward secession, and the convention's final report contained no mention of it. Instead it proposed such amendments to the Constitution as federal funding for state-controlled militias and a new system of apportionment for the House of Representatives that would have benefited northern states at the expense of the South.

See 51 What was the nullification controversy?

▶ When were the last states admitted to the Union? *See 14 When did the states join the Union?*

Q **29. Why has Puerto Rico not become a state?**

A Most Puerto Ricans appear to favor commonwealth status over either statehood or outright independence. Puerto Rico became a U.S. territory in 1898, and all Puerto Ricans are U.S. citizens. They do not pay income taxes (but do pay Social Security taxes), receive certain welfare benefits (some 60 percent get food stamps), and can travel and work on the U.S. mainland at will.

Commonwealth status would basically maintain things as they are, while independence would mean an end to welfare benefits, an increase in poverty, and probably also a mass migration of Puerto Ricans to the U.S. mainland. Statehood, on the other hand, could spell the end of Puerto Rico's Spanish culture, would mean Puerto Ricans would have to start paying federal income taxes, and would probably spark a mass migration of Puerto Ricans from the U.S. mainland to their home island. But poverty on the island might be eased, because Puerto Ricans would be eligible for full social welfare benefits.

Statehood was not an option when Puerto Ricans voted three to one in favor of commonwealth status in 1951 and 1967. Puerto Ricans again voted to keep the commonwealth status in 1993, but the vote was close—48.6 percent voted for commonwealth, 46.3 percent for statehood, and 4.4 percent for independence. In 1998, 46.5 percent voted for statehood, while 50.2 percent chose the "none of the above" option.

Q **30. What other territories besides Puerto Rico are United States possessions?**

A Four small island nations are also United States territories—American Samoa (a group of seven small Pacific islands), Guam (largest of the Mariana Islands), the Northern Marianas (the six inhabited Pacific islands are a U.S. commonwealth), and the U.S. Virgin Islands (a group of over fifty Caribbean islands). Other tiny island possessions include the Caribbean island of Navassa, as well as Wake Atoll, Midway Atoll, Johnston Atoll, Palmyra Atoll, and Howland, Jarvis, and Baker Islands, all in the Pacific.

American Samoa, Guam, and the Virgin Islands each send a nonvoting delegate to the U.S. House of Representatives.

See 61 Does the District elect members of Congress the way states do?

STATE CONSTITUTIONS

Q 31. Which state was first to adopt a constitution?

 Massachusetts enacted its constitution first on May 16, 1775, shortly after the Revolution began. Adopted by the Provincial Congress of Massachusetts, it served as an interim constitution until a new one was drawn up and ratified in 1780.

See 12 Which state was first to join the Union?

Q 32. Can state constitutions be changed?

A Yes, there are four formal methods of constitutional change, though not all states allow all of them. *Legislative proposals* are passed by the state legislature and usually are ratified by voters (in what is called a constitutional or general referendum). All fifty states permit this type of constitutional change, as well as change by *constitutional convention.* A convention can be called to consider major revisions or the drafting of an entirely new constitution.

Constitutional commissions may also propose amendments, but they act only as an advisory body for the governor or legislature. Similarly, petitions can lead to a *citizen initiative,* in which a proposed constitutional amendment appears on the ballot for approval by the voters.

Interpretation of a specific provision is another, informal means of constitutional change. The most direct route for interpreting the constitution is through *judicial review* by state courts—the court decision in a specific case can determine how a provision will be enforced in the future. Both the legislature and executive branch may also influence the way specific constitutional provisions are interpreted.

See 35 How many states permit voters to decide constitutional questions by citizen initiatives? 36 What does a constitutional convention do? 38 What can a constitutional commission do?

Q 33. What is the most common way state constitutions are changed?

A State constitutions are most often changed by legislative proposal. All but about 10 percent of changes to constitutions have been accomplished by this method, and since 1970 voters have approved some 70 percent of all the legislative proposals put on the ballot.

Most states require approval by only a simple majority of voters, but procedures for getting the proposed change through the legislature vary from state to state. Many states require that both houses of the legislature pass the measure by either a two-thirds or three-fifths vote. But others have more complex procedures, including voting approval in more than one legislative session.

Q 34. In which state have voters approved the largest number of constitutional amendments?

A Alabama voters have approved 582 of 818 proposed amendments to their various constitutions over the years (six constitutions, including the latest). These include "local" amendments, however, which affect only one county and require voter approval only in that county. Local amendments also brought to 465 the approved amendments in South Carolina (of 650 proposed). California voters, in a state without local amendments, approved 491 of 823 proposed amendments.

See 66 Which state has replaced its constitution the most times?

Q 35. How many states permit voters to decide constitutional questions by citizen initiatives?

A Voters in seventeen states have the right to vote on constitutional questions put on the ballot by petition. This method of constitutional reform was an outgrowth of the Progressive reform movement of the early 1900s. The minimum number of signatures required to put an initiative on the ballot varies from state to state (from 3 percent to 15 percent of all votes cast for governor in the previous election). The seventeen states permitting citizen-backed constitutional initiatives are:

Arizona	Florida	Missouri
Arkansas	Illinois	Montana
California	Massachusetts	Nebraska
Colorado	Michigan	Nevada

| North Dakota | Oklahoma | South Dakota |
| Ohio | Oregon | |

See 344 Where were the first citizen initiatives approved?

Q 36. What does a constitutional convention do?

A A constitutional convention is an assembly of delegates called to consider revisions to the state constitution or even the drafting of a completely new one. All fifty states provide for the calling of a convention and over 230 conventions have been held since the United States was formed. In every state except Delaware, any proposed changes to a state's constitution must be approved by the voters, however, and the success rate for convention proposals is less than that for legislative proposals.

See 32 Can state constitutions be changed? 33 What is the most common way state constitutions are changed?

Q 37. How is a constitutional convention called?

A Only the state's legislature has the power to call a convention, but it may either decide to call the convention on its own or submit the question to voters for a decision. Fourteen states require that the question of calling a constitutional convention be regularly put before voters. In Maryland and New York, for example, the question of calling a convention must appear on the ballot at least once every twenty years. Iowa and Alaska vote on it at ten-year intervals.

Q 38. What can a constitutional commission do?

A Usually commissions of this type are organized to recommend changes or additions to state constitutions. They may be called on to rework a single provision or section, to decide what revisions are needed in the entire document, or to write an entirely new constitution. A commission may also be asked to do the preliminary work for an upcoming constitutional convention.

A constitutional commission can be called in all fifty states by a governor or the legislature, but the commission's findings are not binding. Florida allows a constitutional commission to submit proposed amendments directly to the voters, but in all other states the governor or the legislature decides whether voters will have the chance to approve them. Governors and legislators often use commissions to defuse political pressure generated by an issue, and for that reason commission recommendations, which may come one and a half years later, are routinely ignored.

Q 39. Did the Kestnbaum Commission influence the movement to reform state constitutions?

A The 1955 Commission on Intergovernmental Relations, a federal commission popularly known as the Kestnbaum Commission, sharply criticized what was then the disorganized and overly detailed condition of most state constitutions. Its final report concluded that ". . . most states would benefit from a fundamental review of their constitutions to make sure that they provide for vigorous and responsible government, not forbid it."

While the commission was not the only group calling for wide-ranging reform of state constitutions, it was among the most influential. And beginning in the 1960s reform movements within the various states resulted in fundamental reviews of state constitutions. Since then over half the states have either heavily revised or enacted completely new constitutions.

Q 40. What is the Model State Constitution?

A To promote effective constitutional reform, the National Municipal League has developed a standard model for state constitutions that contains twelve basic articles. To one degree or another all state constitutions today incorporate elements of the Model State Constitution.

The model has been revised several times since the league first published it in 1921. The revisions largely came in response to changing circumstances confronting the states. But the basic premises remain the same: to make the document brief, logical, and readable, so that even an average citizen can understand it; to include fundamental principles needed to make a sound constitution; and to promote stability while also allowing the flexibility to meet changing circumstances.

The twelve basic articles include a bill of rights similar to that found in the U.S. Constitution, and separate articles on powers held by the states, voting and elections, the legislative, executive, and judicial branches, state finances, empowerment of local governments, public education, civil service, relations between states and between states and localities, and procedures for revising the constitution.

See 32 Can state constitutions be changed?

Q **41. What are the functions of state government?**

A Much of what state government does involves providing basic services to the public, either on its own or in conjunction with local governments or the federal government. For example, the state oversees public education; administers Medicaid and other health care programs; administers welfare, unemployment insurance, and other social programs; builds and maintains state highways; promotes economic development within state borders; maintains a court system and prisons to try and punish persons who commit major crimes; and plays an important role in monitoring environmental regulations. And of course the government also collects state revenues, including taxes and license fees.

Q **42. Do states have any powers under the U.S. Constitution?**

A The Constitution allows states the right to maintain a militia—what today is the National Guard—and to exercise various powers within their borders, including the power to make the state's laws and to tax its citizens, administer justice, and regulate commerce. Of course, where federal and state laws conflict, federal law takes precedence, but in many areas either there are no federal laws or states and the federal government share the powers (concurrent powers). For example, federal and state governments exercise the concurrent power to tax.

The Tenth Amendment to the Constitution grants states (or the people) powers not specifically delegated to the federal government. But laws passed by Congress, and related federal court decisions upholding them, have vastly expanded the federal government's implied powers (those not specifically delegated in the Constitution). They have effectively undermined the Tenth Amendment.

But the Constitution also guarantees states a key role in the federal government itself. Each state sends two senators and a number of representatives (based on population) to Congress, which makes the federal laws. Each state participates in presidential elections by sending delegates to the Electoral College, and the states hold the final authority when it comes to amending the Constitution itself. Three-quarters of the states must ratify a proposed amendment before it can become the law of the land.

See 46 What is federalism? 48 Can states alter the U.S. Constitution? 50 Why was the Tenth Amendment to the U.S. Constitution important to states? 54 What effect did the Fourteenth Amendment have? 55 How did the Sixteenth Amendment bolster the federal government's power over states? 56 What is federal preemption?

Q **43. What limits does the Constitution impose on states?**

A Article I, Section 10, of the Constitution covers a series of broad prohibitions that bar states from entering into treaties, declaring war, granting titles of nobility, coining money, imposing import and export duties (without the consent of Congress), or passing bills of attainder, ex post facto laws, or laws limiting contractual obligations.

The Constitution also mandates that all federal laws take precedence over state laws (Article VI, Section 2) and requires that all criminal trials, except for treason, be tried by jury (Article III, Section 2). It also specifies that states cannot merge or subdivide themselves without the consent of Congress (Article IV, Section 3).

Lastly, the Fourteenth Amendment expressly forbids states from passing laws that restrict the "privileges and immunities" of American citizens or deny them equal protection under the laws. This amendment figured prominently in Supreme Court decisions that dismantled segregation in the South during the 1960s and furthered the rights of criminal defendants.

See 54 What effect did the Fourteenth Amendment have? 56 What is federal preemption?

Q **44. Are there rules concerning relations between the states?**

A The Constitution addresses two aspects of how states deal with each other in Article IV (Sections 1 and 2). Section 1 requires that the various states give the laws, records, and court decisions of other states "full faith and credit." But differences between state laws on such matters as divorce have frequently complicated legal cases. Section 2 specifies that states cannot treat people from another state differently under the law than their own citizens. It also requires that fugitives who flee across state lines be extradited to the state where the crime occurred.

Q **45. Can states leave the Union?**

A Before the Civil War some opponents of a strong federal government believed states had the basic right to secede from the Union, should fundamental disagreements between states and the national government arise. The heated debate over continuing slavery during the first half of the 1800s proved to be just such a controversy. Proslavery states in the South argued that they had, after all, voluntarily joined the Union and should be able to leave it as well. But their critics, notably President Abraham Lincoln, said states had surrendered such rights when they accepted the Constitution.

The Civil War finally decided the question of a state's right to secede (and put an end to slavery), but only after four years of bloody warfare between Union and Confederate armies.

See 25 What effect did the Missouri Compromise have on the admission of states to the Union? 26 Which states seceded during the Civil War? 27 How did West Virginia come to be a state? 28 Was the Civil War the first time states considered seceding from the Union? 51 What was the nullification controversy?

Q 46. What is federalism?

A Federalism is a system of government in which the national and state governments share powers and responsibilities. The United States Constitution established federalism as our system of government—a compromise between confederacy, in which states hold the power, and unitary government, in which the national government is all-powerful. The Constitution defined various federal powers, such as providing for the national defense and negotiating treaties, and protected states by reserving for them the unenumerated powers (in the Tenth Amendment).

According to early ideas about federalism, the national government and the states were each to reign supreme in their own spheres. *(See 47 What are dual federalism and cooperative federalism?)* But the gray areas between boundaries of federal and state spheres led to inevitable disputes.

Many disputes have been decided in the Supreme Court, but the most serious conflict over states' rights and federal powers was decided on the battlefield during the Civil War. The federal government's victory settled the basic issue of the national government's primacy over the states and ended slavery as well. During the twentieth century, a more activist government and favorable Supreme Court decisions greatly expanded federal government powers. So too did the states' dependency on vast sums of money the federal government sent them in the form of grants.

See 42 Do states have any powers under the Constitution? 51 What was the nullification controversy? 54 What effect did the Fourteenth Amendment have? 57 How has the federal government used grants to increase its control over the states? 182 What are federal mandates? 494 How do federal grants affect state budgets?

Q 47. What are dual federalism and cooperative federalism?

A Dual federalism was the dominant view of federalism in this country until the 1930s. Dual federalism meant that federal and state governments each operated as the sovereign power within their own areas of authority, but that they had an essentially competitive relationship with each other where their powers overlapped. Until the Civil War, states were the dominant power in the arrangement, and the federal government largely confined itself to functions specifically delegated to it by the U.S. Constitution.

The federal government's victory in the Civil War effectively ended the notion of state-centered federalism, but it was not until the Great Depression that a new scheme of federalism came into being—*cooperative federalism.* To counter the effects of the depression, President Franklin D. Roosevelt greatly expanded the powers of the federal government and gave it a greater role in what were once considered state responsibilities (such as job programs and social welfare plans). Increasingly federal government authority overlapped state authority and the two powers tended more and more to share responsibilities. The new relationship was based on cooperation rather than competition, although there could be no question about the federal government's dominant role in this form of federalism.

Other more recent versions of federalism include *creative federalism,* a view promoted by President Lyndon Johnson to explain huge increases in federal grants to states for his Great Society programs. Presidents Richard Nixon and Ronald Reagan each pointed to their own versions of *new federalism,* which basically sought to return powers and responsibilities to the states.

Q **48. Can states alter the U.S. Constitution?**

A Yes, states have the option of calling a constitutional convention for the purpose of proposing new amendments or even rewriting the whole document. Article V of the Constitution states that Congress must convene a constitutional convention if two-thirds of the state legislatures request it. Today that would be thirty-four states.

No constitutional convention has ever been called, but twice in this century one nearly was. The drive for an amendment establishing direct election of U.S. senators in the early 1900s (instead of by legislative appointment as the Constitution originally specified) nearly resulted in the first ever constitutional convention. But the threat of a convention helped push the proposed amendment through Congress instead. Then in the late 1980s, the push for a convention to write a balanced budget amendment failed after winning the support of thirty-two states (just shy of the necessary thirty-four).

Q 49. How many states are required to ratify a constitutional amendment?

A Once a proposed amendment has been drafted and approved by Congress or a constitutional convention, it is then submitted to the states for ratification. Three-quarters of the states (thirty-eight of the fifty states) must ratify the amendment before it becomes part of the Constitution.

Congress decides whether ratification is to be by the state legislatures or ratification conventions within each state, however. The only amendment ever ratified by convention was the Eighteenth Amendment (Prohibition Amendment).

Q 50. Why was the Tenth Amendment to the U.S. Constitution important to states?

A Because it reserved for the states (or the people) all powers not specifically withheld from them or delegated to the federal government by the Constitution, the Tenth Amendment was intended to define the original division of power between states and the federal government. During the first half of the 1800s it provided a basis for supporters of states' rights against the national government. But over the years since then, laws passed by Congress and Supreme Court decisions upholding them have vastly expanded federal powers and effectively undermined the Tenth Amendment.

See 46 What is federalism? 56 What is federal preemption? 430 What did the Court rule in National League of Cities v. Usery? *433 What did the Court rule in* South Carolina v. Baker?

Q 51. What was the nullification controversy?

A During the late 1700s and early 1800s many people believed states had the power to "nullify" within their borders any federal laws thought to be unconstitutional. Thomas Jefferson and James Madison first proposed the idea of states nullifying federal laws in 1798, after the federal government passed the controversial Alien and Sedition Acts.

Nullification again became an issue when the federal government passed a tariff that hurt southern states (1828, the "Tariff of Abominations"). South Carolina actually adopted an Ordinance of Nullification to void the tariff law within its borders. Congress responded by passing the Force Act in 1833, which allowed the president to use the military to uphold federal laws, but avoided armed conflict by also reducing the tariff.

Nullification later figured in the debates over slavery, and southern states claimed it gave them the right to secede at the outset of the Civil War. The federal government victory in the war effectively ended the debate over nullification (as well as slavery)—thereafter, states had no choice but to obey federal laws.

See 56 What is federal preemption?

Q 52. Do states lobby the federal government?

A States promote their interests by lobbying the federal government through a variety of channels. Three major national groups that represent the states in Washington, D.C., are the Council of State Governments, the National Governors' Association, and the National Conference of State Legislatures. Other organizations represent the interests of specific state agencies, such as the Association of State Development Agencies, or of particular state officials, such as the National Association of Attorneys General. In addition, over thirty-two states maintain their own offices in the nation's capital, both to provide information and to lobby federal agencies, Congress, and the White House on matters of interest to them.

Q 53. How does the Council of State Governments work to help promote better state government?

A A nonpartisan organization, the council works with state officials to promote more effective government through education, research, and information services. It provides assistance to all three branches of state government, including identifying common policy problems and acting as a clearinghouse for solutions developed in other states. The CSG also publishes *The Book of the States,* a useful collection of current information on the states.

See 78 What does the National Governors' Association (NGA) do? 184 What is the National Conference of State Legislatures (NCSL)?

Q 54. What effect did the Fourteenth Amendment have?

A Written after the Civil War, this amendment affirmed the rights of former slaves, specifically granting them citizenship. At the same time, however, the amendment also guaranteed all citizens "due process" and "equal protection" under the law, and barred states from abridging those rights. From the 1950s onward, Supreme Court decisions based on the Fourteenth Amendment have increased federal powers over the states in such areas as voting rights, civil rights, and rights of criminals.

Q 55. How did the Sixteenth Amendment bolster the federal government's power over states?

A When the Sixteenth Amendment established the federal income tax in 1913, it opened up a huge new source of revenue—and financial power—for the federal government. Tax rates and total revenues rose dramatically from World War I onward, and from the 1930s onward the number of federally financed programs in the states multiplied rapidly.

While much of the federal tax money was and continues to be spent in the states for the public good, it also serves as a way for the federal government to control the states. Congress can and does pass spending bills that benefit a particular state or group of them, and the federal government routinely lays down rules on how the money is to be spent. States that depend heavily on federal dollars have little choice but to comply.

See 57 How has the federal government used grants to increase its control over the states?

Q 56. What is federal preemption?

A The supremacy of federal over state laws is mandated by Article VI, Section 2, of the U.S. Constitution. Where federal legislation and legal codes conflict with state laws, the federal statutes always take precedence. This is called federal preemption of the state legislation or legal code.

The Founding Fathers wrote the Constitution's supremacy clause to create a strong national government, even though it meant reducing the power of the states. In fact, the supremacy clause has been a legal basis since the 1930s for the rapid expansion of federal control over commerce and other activities once regulated by the states. For example, the federal government's Air Quality Act set minimum standards nationwide, preempting state regulations on levels of air pollution within their borders.

See 422 What did the Court rule in Gibbons v. Ogden?

Q 57. How has the federal government used grants to increase its control over the states?

A Between 1960 and 1998 federal spending for grants to state and local governments doubled, rising from 7.6 percent to over 15 percent. While states benefit from the many billions in federal dollars, the grant money comes with a variety of strings attached. States are forced to comply with various federal regulations if they want to get the money in the first place. For example, states that receive federal highway grants must not only build the roads according to federal specifications, but they must also agree to federal rules on things like speed limits and minimum drinking age. In addition, there are also so-called cross-cutting regulations that apply to all federal grants, such as guidelines for assessing environmental impact, protecting civil rights, guaranteeing accessibility for people with disabilities, and maintaining fair labor practices.

See 182 What are federal mandates? 489 What is the primary way states get money from the federal government? 492 How do the basic types of grants differ?

DISTRICT OF COLUMBIA

Q 58. Is the District a state?

A No. The need for a symbolic center of the national government was clear to the Framers of the Constitution, and in Article I, Section 8, they provided for creation of a small district to serve as the nation's capital. Congress got full control over this district, which was to be separate from any other state. But the idea was not to create a new state with representation in Congress, a federally controlled state that could compete with other states. Instead it was to be both a symbolic center and a place where Congress could function free from outside intimidation.

Q 59. Who decided where to locate the capitol?

A President George Washington picked the exact spot, once Congress resolved a protracted struggle over the general location. Article I, Section 8, of the United States Constitution had authorized Congress to create a ten-square-mile district for the nation's capital, but did not specify where. Members of Congress from the North wanted it located near the business centers of New York City or Philadelphia, but southerners bitterly opposed any location that would give northern business interests an easy opportunity to influence the government.

Treasury Secretary Alexander Hamilton finally broke the deadlock in 1790 by arranging a tradeoff: southerners in Congress agreed to support a bill allowing the federal government to assume state debts incurred during the Revolutionary War. The bill favored the northern states, but in return, northern members of Congress agreed to support a bill locating the capital district in the South, between Virginia and Maryland.

In 1791 President Washington then personally selected the site along the Potomac, not far from his estate at Mount Vernon. Construction of the capital proceeded slowly, and when the government officially moved to Washington in 1800, construction of federal buildings was far from complete.

Q 60. What is home rule?

A Though the Constitution gave Congress complete control over the District, people living within its borders have from time to time sought a greater role in the government, what has come to be called home rule. Congress has in fact allowed the District limited self-rule in the past, notably from 1800 to 1874 and from 1974 onward, when District voters won the right to elect their own mayor. In recent years supporters of home rule have also pushed to make the District a state, complete with representation in Congress.

But in the mid-1990s, corruption, mismanagement, and deterioration of services within the elected government prompted Congress to sharply curtail the District government's powers. A financial control board was created to reform the government. Given wide-ranging powers, it eventually stripped the elected mayor of most of his powers. After the election of a new mayor, Anthony Williams, in 1998, the board restored virtually all of them, however.

See 30 What other territories besides Puerto Rico are United States possessions?

Q 61. Does the District elect members of the U.S. Congress the way states do?

A District voters elect a nonvoting delegate and one "shadow" representative to the House, and two "shadow" senators to the Senate. The shadow members are so called because the District is not a state and so is not entitled to full representation in Congress. (If the District did become a state, it would have two senators and one representative.)

The two shadow senators and one shadow representative are not members of Congress. The District delegate—since 1990, Eleanor Holmes Norton—is, though her powers are limited. She can take part in House committee votes and make speeches on the House floor, but does not have the right to take part in floor votes. A principal task of the shadow members is to lobby for District statehood. Shadow senators also provide testimony before congressional committees on various other issues affecting the District (including appropriations) and play a role in nominations for District judicial appointments.

The idea of "shadow" members to Congress is not new. Shadow representatives and senators have attended sessions of Congress from time to time since the early 1800s, when territories first began sending them in preparation for statehood.

The congressional committees that oversee District affairs are the House Government Reform Committee, the Senate Governmental Affairs Committee, and the appropriations subcommittees on the District of Columbia in both the House and Senate.

See 285 Do District of Columbia votes count in presidential elections?

FOR THE RECORD

▶ What were the first and last states to become states? *See 12 Which state was first to join the Union?*

▶ When was the first state constitution adopted? *See 31 Which state was first to adopt a constitution?*

Q 62. Which of the original thirteen states was most heavily populated in 1790?

A Surprisingly, Rhode Island, the smallest of the states, turned out to be the most heavily populated. According to the 1790 census, there were 64.5 people for every square mile of land area in Rhode Island. Connecticut and Massachusetts were next in line with 49.4 and 47.1, respectively. The state with the sparsest population was Georgia, which in 1790 had just 0.6 per square mile.

Q 63. Which state was first to adopt an official state sport?

A Maryland became the first in 1962 when it adopted the medieval contest of jousting as its state sport. Maryland also has an official state boat—the skipjack. See also individual state entries in Chapter 7 for official state emblems and other related items.

See 69 Which state decided to make the bolo tie its official neckwear?

Q **64. When did the federal government begin funneling money to states through grant programs?**

A Grants-in-aid actually pre-date the Constitution. The U.S. government under the Articles of Confederation established the first in 1785—grants of federal land for establishing public schools in the Old West (the Land Ordinance Act). But the federal government did not begin sending significant amounts of money to states (fiscal federalism) until the era of the Great Depression.

Under President Franklin Roosevelt the number of federal grant programs rose significantly for the first time—from 12 in 1932 (worth $193 million) to 26 in 1937 (worth $2.66 billion). World War II and the 1950s saw further expansions, so that by 1960 the number of programs had hit 132 (worth almost $7.02 billion a year). Federal grants to state and local governments mushroomed during the 1960s and in 1998 totaled over $250 billion.

See 491 Has the portion of federal grant money in state budgets been rising or falling? 494 How do federal grants affect state budgets? 505 Where do states get their revenue from?

Q **65. How many amendments to the U.S. Constitution has Congress submitted to the states?**

A Congress has considered over twenty-five hundred proposed amendments since the U.S. Constitution was drafted in 1789, and it has sent over one thousand of them to the states for ratification.

Of these the states finally approved only twenty-seven, the most recent being in 1992.

Q **66. Which state has replaced its constitution the most times?**

A As of 1996, Louisiana leads all other states with eleven new constitutions, the latest having been adopted in 1975. Georgia is close behind with ten constitutions (the latest in 1983). South Carolina has put in place seven constitutions, but its last went into effect in 1896.

See 34 In which state have voters approved the largest number of constitutional amendments?

Q 67. Which state has the longest constitution?

A Alabama is far and away the leader in this department, having a constitution that runs 220,000 words. That is nearly three times the next longest, the 80,000-word Texas constitution. One reason why the Alabama constitution has so many words is that it includes "local" amendments that apply to only one county (an estimated 70 percent of the amendments). By Alabama law, once the legislature has put a local amendment on the ballot, it takes only approval by voters in the affected county to add it to the state constitution.

Q 68. Which state constitution has a provision concerning the length of wrestling matches?

A California's, and it is not the only state with seemingly out-of-place constitutional provisions like this one. Oklahoma's constitution specifies the flash point of kerosene used for illumination, and Maryland's goes so far as to specify matters of off-street parking in Baltimore. New Hampshire's gives its citizens the right to a revolution.

For the most part, provisions like these are remnants of earlier times, when state constitutions tended to be long, rambling documents weighted down with hordes of overly detailed amendments.

See 40 What is the Model State Constitution?

Q 69. Which state decided to make the bolo tie its official neckwear?

A Arizona has officially adopted this stringlike necktie, which is fastened at the neck with an ornamental clasp. The tie is reminiscent of the bola, a piece of rope with weights on each end. Gauchos in the Southwest once used bolas to ensnare the legs of cattle.

Most state legislatures have used their legislative powers to adopt such fairly standard items as a state motto, state flower, state tree, state fish, and the like. But a few have made more unusual selections on the order of Arizona's. Massachusetts, for example, has adopted cranberry juice as the official state beverage (Mississippi and Vermont picked milk).

North Dakota named the "Spirit of the Land" as its state march, and Alaska designated dog mushing as the official state sport. South Dakota and Oklahoma have official state grasses (Western Wheat grass and Indian grass, respectively), and eleven states actually have official fossils—Alaska, California, Colorado, Kentucky, Missouri, Montana, Nevada, New Mexico, New York, North Dakota, and Pennsylvania.

See Chapter 7 for lists of the official emblems for each state.

WHERE CAN I FIND. . .

Sources listed below contain additional information on topics covered in this chapter.

Almanac of the 50 States. Edith R. Hornor, ed. Palo Alto, Calif.: Information Publications, 1994.

   A book of tables, it contains both state-by-state profiles and comparative tables on various topics. Has recent past, current, and projected statistics on population and various other topics.

The Book of the States, 1996–1997. Lexington, Ky.: Council of State Governments, 1997.

   A compilation of tables with useful footnotes, this book has a section on state constitutions that includes state-by-state listings of current practices and other data. There is also a section ("State Pages") containing both historical and current data on each state.

CQ's State Fact Finder 1999: Rankings Across America. Kendra A. Hovey and Harold A. Hovey. Washington, D.C.: Congressional Quarterly Inc., 1999.

   Up-to-date rankings and lists of other comparative data on the fifty states are included for a wide array of topics, including government and population. The bulk of the book is arranged by subject, but there is an index in the back listing references state-by-state.

Facts About the States, 2d ed. Joseph Kane. New York: H. W. Wilson Company, 1993.

   The book primarily offers state-by-state coverage, including sections on key dates in the state's history, demographic statistics, and other information. Has useful lists of books written about the state at the end of each state's entry.

Historical Statistics of the United States, Colonial Times to 1970. U.S. Department of Commerce. Washington, D.C.: Government Printing Office, 1975.

   This two-volume set is a collection of tables of historical data. Though most of the statistics are national or regional, some tables do break down the data by state. Two hard-to-find statistics they contain are land area by states and population of states, decade by decade and by sex, age, race, and urban/rural residence.

Politics in the American States, A Comparative Analysis, 7th ed. Virginia Gray, Russell Hanson, and Herbert Jacob. Washington, D.C.: Congressional Quarterly Inc., 1999.

  The book draws on a variety of surveys and other sources of interest to political scientists. The first chapter offers a perceptive comparison of the states, and the second analyzes federal-state relations.

State & Local Government, 2d ed. Ann Bowman and Richard Kearney. Boston: Houghton Mifflin Company, 1993.

  A textbook on state and local government, it is a valuable basic source of information on the history and mechanics of state constitutions, state and federal interactions, and the like. It is clearly written and accessible to general readers.

The State and Local Government Political Dictionary. Jeffrey Elliot and Sheikh R. Ali. San Bernardino, Calif.: Borgo Press, 1995.

  Arranged by topic, the entries in this book provide brief definitions of terms relating to the topic. There are sections on constitutions and intergovernmental relations, and entries provide both a brief definition and a discussion of the significance of the term being covered.

Worldmark Encyclopedia of the States. Ed. Timothy and Susan Gall. Detroit: Gale, 1997.

  The state-by-state treatment in this standard reference includes a fairly detailed narrative of each state's history, as well as shorter overviews of its government, population history, and other reference topics.

GOVERNORSHIP

IN GENERAL

Q 70. Who was the first governor?

A When Delaware became the first state to ratify the Constitution on December 6, 1787, it officially became the first state in the Union. Delaware's governor at the time, Thomas Collins—whose official title was president of Delaware—thus won the honor of serving as the first state governor.

Collins, who had entered office in 1786, died in 1789 before finishing his term. Delaware governors were called "president" until a new constitution was enacted in 1792.

See 12 Which state was first to join the Union?

Q 71. How long do governors serve?

A For all but two states, governors serve four-year terms. Only New Hampshire and Vermont have two-year terms, but neither state imposes term limits.

See 102 Which states do not have term limits for their governors? 103 Do any states bar their governors from serving consecutive terms?

Q 72. Who is the longest serving governor in this century?

A Iowa's governor Terry Branstad (R) served sixteen consecutive years, a record for this century. Having begun his first term in 1983, Governor Branstad completed his final term in January 1999.

Previously, Illinois governor James Thompson (R) held the record, having served fourteen consecutive years from 1977 to 1991. Thompson served an unprecedented four terms in Illinois before declining to run again in 1990 (due to a changeover in Illinois, his first term was only two years; the rest were four).

See 103 Do any states bar their governors from serving consecutive terms?

Q 73. What are a governor's duties?

A The governor wears many "hats" while in office. He or she is the state's chief administrator and so is responsible for the operation of all the agencies, departments, commissions, and other divisions of the executive branch, as well as for taking charge during major emergencies, such as floods and urban unrest. As the state's single most influential policy maker, the governor also spends considerable time as a legislative leader, shepherding bills through the legislature to advance policy goals.

The position of top-ranking official in the state means the governor must take on the duties of ceremonial leader at state functions, while also serving as the unofficial leader of his or her political party. Governors are responsible for promoting economic development and coordinating state interests in grant programs with federal agencies, Congress, and the president. In addition, the governor serves as the civilian commander-in-chief of the state's National Guard.

See 86 Why is the governor's role as coordinator between the state and the federal government important? 138 What does the lieutenant governor do? 157 Does the governor control the bureaucracy?

Q 74. How do "caretaker" and "managerial" governors differ?

A Various external factors may affect how a governor approaches his or her job—for example, the governor's margin of victory at the polls, voter expectations, and even constitutional limitations on the governor's powers. But the governor's personal style and leadership ability also enter into the equation, and this is often what helps determine the difference between caretaker and managerial governors.

On the one hand, caretaker governors respond to crises as they arise and try to keep the government running smoothly. But they avoid the considerable risks of trying to promote major policies and programs that might move the state government in new directions. Managerial governors, however, take those risks and use the office to become policy leaders. They set goals and strive to change the way the government operates. Perhaps most important of all, managerial governors have the ability to convince the government bureaucracy to follow their lead in these policy initiatives.

▶ Who has served as governor in the various states? *See individual state entries in Chapter 7 for complete lists of governors.*

75. What does the governor's staff do?

Staff personnel are hand-picked assistants who work closely with the governor. They help in many different ways, including acting as liaisons with legislators, the media, and federal, state, and local agencies; writing speeches, press releases, and handling correspondence; and providing research and recommendations on political and legal matters.

Among the staffers governors typically have are a chief of staff, legislative liaison, press secretary, legal adviser, budget director, speechwriter, and intergovernmental coordinator.

See 89 Which governors have the smallest and largest staff allowances?

76. How much of a governor's time is spent on ceremonial functions?

Some governors have reported spending more than half their time on such ceremonial duties as ribbon-cutting ceremonies for highways and buildings, meeting visiting dignitaries, handing out awards and college diplomas, and welcoming new industries to the state. Though many governors see these duties as keeping them from more important state business, the largely ceremonial events usually do result in favorable media coverage and help keep up contact with constituents. Both are important pluses for any politician who wants to be reelected.

77. What has been the chief goal of state government reforms that began in the mid-1960s?

The powers of governors' offices throughout the states have been significantly increased as a result of the ongoing reform efforts. In addition to creating a stronger chief executive, the reforms have also reorganized the bureaucratic machinery of the executive branch. The reforms became necessary as states shouldered increasing responsibilities for providing public services, such as health care, from the 1960s onward.

See 179 What basic problems confronted state legislators until the reforms of the 1960s?

78. What does the National Governors' Association (NGA) do?

A nonpartisan lobbying and research organization, the NGA serves state governors by providing analyses of major issues of concern to states, by helping them formulate solutions to these problems, and by offering other types of technical assistance. It lobbies the federal government on behalf of the states and sponsors meetings of the governors twice a year to discuss common problems and policy options.

See 53 How does the Council of State Governments work to help promote better state government? 184 What is the National Conference of State Legislatures (NCSL)? 254 What are the most influential lobbying groups?

Q **79. Who prepares the state budget?**

A The governors are responsible for preparing the states' annual proposed budgets. Nearly all governors have the power to appoint their budget directors and otherwise exercise considerable control during the process of preparing their state's fiscal agenda.

The proposed budget must be approved by the state's legislature, however, and at times the legislature may make major changes or scrap the governor's budget altogether. This is more often the case when the legislature is dominated by a party other than the governor's, or when state agencies and the governor have conflicting priorities. Usually, though, the governor's proposed budget will at least set the agenda for the budgetary debate in the legislature.

POWERS AND PRIVILEGES

Q **80. What is the difference between the governor's formal and informal powers?**

A *Formal powers* are those granted to the governor by the state's constitution. They include such things as the right to appoint heads of state agencies, recommend (but not introduce) legislation, veto legislation, prepare the state's proposed budget, and serve the prescribed term of office. Not all governors have all these powers or the right to exercise them to the same degree, however, which makes some governorships more powerful than others.

Informal powers are not specifically granted by law and usually have much to do with the governor's personality and abilities. For example, some governors are skilled at communicating through the media (and maintaining good relations with the media), which means they will have a better chance of gaining publicity and promoting policies. Another valuable skill is the ability to bargain successfully with legislators and interest groups in order to win passage of bills promoting the governor's policies. Other aspects of the governor's personality and image, such as ambition, experience, youth, and energy, also can contribute to a strong governorship. A governor with strong informal powers is often able to use them to take greater advantage of his or her formal powers.

See 84 Which states have the strongest governorships?

81. Are there limits on a governor's powers?

Though the governor is the chief executive, the separation of powers between the executive, legislative, and judicial branches puts important limitations on the governor's powers. The legislature often must approve the governor's appointees, for example, when the governor has the power to appoint. Many governors have the power to veto bills, but the legislature can override the veto with the necessary number of votes. Revamping an agency or changing a program's priorities may also require legislative approval. Changes like these could also result in a court challenge, involving the judicial branch.

Another major limitation arises in states where other top executive branch officials are elected, instead of being appointed by the governor. These officials owe their jobs to the voters and not the governor, so that the governor has much less influence over them. For that matter, most state employees are hired under the state's merit system and are protected by rules, regulations, and collective bargaining agreements. Because they remain in their jobs long after the governor's term ends, entrenched bureaucrats can sometimes successfully resist policy changes sought by the governor.

82. How do governors influence the legislative agenda in their states?

Though they do not always get all they want, governors tend to dominate the legislative agenda, even though it is the legislature that actually passes or rejects the legislation. In the first place, governors have an extra measure of political clout because they are the single most powerful individuals in the government. That clout can be used to sway individual legislators, or it can help the governor appeal directly to the public on policy issues, and so put pressure on the legislature to act.

But their duties as governors also give them opportunities to control the agenda. For example, the governor is expected to lay out policy issues in the state-of-the-state address, which opens each legislative session. And the governor must deliver a proposed budget to the legislature, giving him or her an important role in deciding how state funds are to be spent (and what programs are to be emphasized).

During the legislative session, the governor's legislative liaisons lobby legislators on behalf of bills on the governor's agenda, while members of the governor's staff may testify at hearings and consult with committees. Where bills face crucial votes, the governor may offer behind-the-scenes deals, trading favors such as judgeships and other appointments or pork barrel projects to win votes from key legislators. Then, too, the governor usually can win important concessions on bills by threatening to veto them, or by actually doing so.

Q 83. Can governors themselves introduce bills into the legislature?

A The governor does not have the authority to introduce a bill directly. Instead, a member of the state's legislature who is either a member of the governor's party or who is a policy supporter must introduce the measure. Because the only way to put the governor's policies into effect is to pass legislation, governors are forced to work closely with state senators and house members.

See 189 Who can introduce a bill?

Q 84. Which states have the strongest governorships?

A Hawaii, Maryland, New York, New Jersey, and West Virginia had the strongest governorships as of the mid-1990s, based on a rating system for governors' formal powers and other factors (including whether the governor's party held the majority in the legislature). Compiled by Thad Beyle, an expert in the field, the study gave Maryland the highest rating (4.3). The other leading governorships scored 4.0 or better on a 5-point scale, while the weakest governorships, those of North and South Carolina, each scored 2.5. Nevada, Texas, and Vermont were the only other states with governorships that came in under 3.0.

See 80 What is the difference between the governor's formal and informal powers?

Q 85. What role do governors play in relations between the states?

A The governor's responsibility for coordinating state-to-state relations has become more important in recent decades because some problems, such as water pollution and hazardous waste disposal, involve more than one state. States also have found that working together proves advantageous when dealing with the federal government on such national concerns as welfare reform and health care.

Q 86. Why is the governor's role as coordinator between the state and the federal government important?

A Federal grant programs to states for such things as highway funds and welfare payments not only affect the well-being of state residents, but they also have a major impact on state finances. The amount of money provided by the federal government, how it is to be spent, and what matching funds the state must supply are all important questions that require coordination between individual states and the federal government.

The governor's office serves as the main point of contact between the federal government and the state agencies responsible for disbursing the federal money. Such matters as funding needs, program adjustments, and the ever-increasing responsibilities being taken on by state governments are all important questions relating to federal grant programs. Governors must take up issues like these with federal agencies, Congress, and even the president.

See 57 How has the federal government used grants to increase its control over the states?

Q 87. What is the governor's salary?

A Governors generally are well paid, with most receiving annual salaries ranging from $75,000 to $100,000 plus. New York's governor receives the highest salary, $130,000, and California, Michigan, Maryland, and Washington all pay their governors $120,000 or more. Montana's governor gets the least, $59,310, while Arkansas runs a close second at $60,000.

See 129 How much do top elected officials get paid in my state? 141 How much do lieutenant governors get paid?

Q 88. What other perks do governors get?

A Most but not all governors enjoy such perks as free housing in the official governor's mansion, state-supplied automobiles, free travel aboard state airplanes and helicopters, a travel allowance, and an allowance for an office staff. Only Arizona, Massachusetts, Rhode Island, and Vermont do not have official governor's residences, while Indiana is the only state that does not provide its governor with a separate travel allowance. Ten states do not give their governors access to state airplanes, but every state supplies automobile transportation and an allowance for office staffs.

Q 89. Which governors have the smallest and largest staff allowances?

A Wyoming's staff allowance is the stingiest, paying salaries for only eight full-time and one half-time staffer in the governor's office. Iowa comes in a close second with an allowance for ten staffers. On the high side is Florida with 264 staffers (as of the mid-1990s), but the larger number can be misleading. Definitions of the governor's office staff differ among states, with some including more executive office functions in the governor's staff than others.

New York's governor also has a large staff (203), as does the governor of Texas (190).

See 75 What does the governor's staff do?

Q 90. How important is the governor's power to appoint?

A While electing officials to high state government posts makes them directly responsible to voters, allowing the governor to appoint them instead increases the governor's control over the bureaucracy and, many reformers think, makes for more effective government. When the governor appoints heads of state agencies and other top executive branch posts, these officials are more likely to support the governor's policies.

Where voters can elect a member of another party as commissioner of education, for example, partisan politics between the governor and commissioner could stall even urgently needed reform. In some cases, such as the attorney general's post, electing the official provides a useful counterbalance to the governor's powers, however. Though the number varies from state to state, governors usually can appoint some four hundred high-level officials to posts in the executive branch.

See 266 Which state elects the largest number of state officials?

Q 91. How does the veto work?

A Once a bill has passed both houses of the legislature, it is sent to the governor to be signed into law or vetoed. To veto the whole bill, the governor simply returns it to the legislature unsigned, with an explanation of what is objectionable. The legislature then must either override the governor's veto (by a two-thirds vote in each house in most states) or pass a revised bill.

Most states also have *line-item vetoes,* which means the governor does not have to veto the whole bill. Instead, specific sections can be vetoed, while the rest of the bill can be signed into law. A number of states also allow the governor to reduce specific amounts in funding bills, rather than requiring him or her to strike out the item altogether. (The legislature can of course override the governor on specific item vetoes.) About a third of the states also allow *executive amendments.* Here, the governor actually recommends changes needed to make a vetoed bill acceptable. The legislature then votes for or against the proposed changes. Fifteen states also allow governors to *pocket veto* bills. When the legislature is in session, the governor must sign or veto a bill within a specified number of days or the bill automatically becomes law (usually between three and ten days, but up to sixty in some states). However, once the legislature adjourns, governors in the fifteen states have the power to pocket veto the bill by simply not signing it within a specified period, which runs anywhere from three to sixty days.

See 124 Which states were first to give their governors the power to veto bills? 125 Which two states were first to adopt the line-item veto? 204 Can a bill become law without the governor's signature?

Q 92. About how many bills on average do governors veto and how many vetoes are overridden?

A Governors generally use their veto power sparingly, vetoing on average only about 5 percent of the bills passed by the legislature. Veto overrides, on the other hand, have increased markedly in recent years. Where governors' vetoes were once overridden somewhat less than 2 percent of the time on average, the rate has climbed to 8 percent or more in some years.

Part of the increase can be explained by the greater frequency of divided state governments. But legislatures have also become more assertive in recent years, leading to a greater willingness to confront governors through a veto override.

See 128 What year saw the largest number of divided state governments? 203 How many vetoes and veto overrides were there in a recent year?

Q 93. What state governor become notorious in recent years for his frequent use of the veto?

A Wisconsin governor Tommy Thompson (R) earned the nickname "Dr. No" because of his frequent use of his veto powers. By one count in 1990 he had used his line-item veto 615 times on just three budget bills (Wisconsin's constitution allows him to veto single words and even punctuation marks). After eight years in office, Thompson reportedly had issued a staggering 1,500 vetoes.

See 91 How does the veto work?

Q **94. Does any state governor not have the veto power?**

Q **94. Does any state governor not have the veto power?**

A Up until 1996, North Carolina's governor was the only one who had no power at all to veto legislation. The state's governors persisted in asking for veto power for years, however, and finally, in 1996, voters passed a referendum giving it to them.

Q **95. How many governors do not have line-item veto powers?**

A Seven states do not allow their governors the line-item veto—Indiana, Maine, Nevada, New Hampshire, North Carolina, Rhode Island, and Vermont. Governors in eleven states that do allow the line-item veto have the option of simply reducing the amount of funding for a particular program, rather than eliminating it altogether. And in Alabama, Massachusetts, and Virginia the governors can avoid using the veto altogether. They have the option of amending a bill and returning it to the legislature for approval or disapproval.

See also 125 Which two states were first to adopt the line-item veto?

Q **96. What purpose do executive orders serve?**

A Governors may use executive orders to reorganize the government bureaucracy and to issue special directives during natural disasters and other emergencies. Forty-four states give their governors this power by statute or constitutional provision, and the six others do so by custom.

Organizational changes are a different matter, however. Just twenty-four states give their governors the power to reorganize by executive order. For the rest, that power remains with the legislature.

Q **97. Are pardon, reprieve, and commutation of a sentence the same?**

A State governors have the power to pardon convicted criminals. About three-quarters of the governors have the power to do so on their own authority. The rest have the option of issuing pardons that have been recommended by the state's board of pardons. The pardon can be *absolute,* which in effect wipes the slate clean immediately, or *conditional,* which becomes effective when specified conditions have been met.

A *reprieve* is quite different from a pardon. It only delays a scheduled execution of a prisoner—it does not rescind the sentence. Neither does *commutation,* which is a reduction in a sentence. When commuting a convicted criminal's sentence, the governor can decide to reduce it, say, from execution to a life sentence, or eliminate any further jail time altogether.

See 113 How many governors have been impeached and removed from office?

Q 98. Do the governors or the president of the United States command the state National Guard units?

A Most of the time the governors have overall control of the state National Guard units, but during times of national emergency, the president can call up the units. The president, as commander-in-chief of all U.S. military forces, then controls the guard units until the emergency is declared over.

For their part, state governors have regularly called out the guard to help with disaster relief during such emergencies as floods and earthquakes. They have also used guard units to restore order during urban riots and mass protests. *(See also the next question.)*

Q 99. Who pays for state National Guard units?

A Congress foots the bill for these state militia units, which serve as an auxiliary of the regular army. Congress also determines how they are organized and even supplies the munitions they use. But the guard units are a cooperative venture between the federal government and states. The state adjutant general acts as their commander (the governor is their civilian commander-in-chief), and states have the authority to appoint officers of their guard units.

GETTING INTO AND OUT OF OFFICE

Q 100. What are the basic requirements for becoming governor?

A Qualifications for the office vary considerably from state to state. Most states have a minimum age (usually between twenty-five and thirty years of age) and require the candidate to have been a state resident for a specified number of years (usually five to seven years). United States citizenship is usually but not always required, and some states specify state citizenship, as opposed to state residency. Status as a qualified voter may also be required.

States impose these qualifications in different combinations, though, and no state imposes all of them. Kentucky, Maryland, Montana, and Nebraska each have four of the five requirements, for example, and Kansas has none whatsoever.

Q **101. Which states have the lowest legal age for governor?**

A Four states do not even have age restrictions—Kansas, Massachusetts, South Dakota, and Vermont—and two others require the governor to be a qualified voter (Ohio and Rhode Island), which means he or she would have to be at least eighteen years old. Three states actually specify age eighteen as the governor's minimum age: California, Washington, and Wisconsin. To date none has had a governor that young.

Q **102. Which states do not have term limits for their governors?**

A Only fifteen states do not limit their governors' terms in some way or other. Of those that do, most allow governors to serve two additional terms, if the governors can win reelection. Some states impose slightly different restrictions, such as making the governor eligible for office for up to eight out of twelve years or imposing a four-year waiting period after two consecutive terms.

The fifteen states that have no term limits are:

Connecticut	Minnesota	Utah
Idaho	New Hampshire	Vermont
Illinois	New York	Washington
Iowa	North Carolina	Wisconsin
Massachusetts	North Dakota	Wyoming

See 71 How long do governors serve?

Q **103. Do any states bar their governors from serving consecutive terms?**

A Both Mississippi and Virginia do not allow their governors to serve consecutive terms. Governors in both states can run for reelection four years later, though.

Q **104. Are there advantages to a longer term of office?**

A Yes, the current standard of four-year terms (for most all states) has several pluses. Alfred E. Smith, the governor of New York during the 1920s, summed up his experience with two-year terms when he quipped, "One hardly has time to locate the knob on the Statehouse door."

In fact, new governors usually spend their first year setting up their administrative machinery and learning the ropes. Even four-year governors tend to accomplish little during their last year in office, because the upcoming election campaign relegates them to lame duck status. But the middle two years usually provide them with the best opportunities for promoting their policies and programs. Two-year governors, on the other hand, not only have to learn the ropes, but they must also begin working for reelection as soon as they take office. They are forced to make do with the previous administration's budget for their first year and are elected to such a short term that entrenched bureaucrats can easily resist policy changes with stalling tactics.

See 71 How long do governors serve? 102 Which states do not have term limits for their governors?

Q 105. What governors have become president of the United States?

A Sixteen former state governors went on to become president of the United States, beginning with Thomas Jefferson and including our most recent president to date, Bill Clinton. Three served as governor of Virginia before becoming president—Jefferson, James Monroe, and John Tyler. Four were New York governors—Martin Van Buren, Grover Cleveland, Theodore Roosevelt, and Franklin D. Roosevelt. Tennessee and Ohio each sent two former governors to the White House: James Polk and Andrew Johnson, and Rutherford Hayes and William McKinley, respectively. The other former governors were Woodrow Wilson (New Jersey), Calvin Coolidge (Massachusetts), Jimmy Carter (Georgia), Ronald Reagan (California), and Bill Clinton (Arkansas).

Q 106. What do most governors do after leaving office?

A Governors have followed a variety of paths after serving out their terms. Some remain in public life, using their years in the governor's mansion as a stepping stone to national politics. They often run for office as a United States senator or representative, and some have gone on to become the vice president or president of the United States. Other fortunate ex-governors have been appointed to high-level positions in the federal government.

Many governors also return to private life, however, seeking out high-level positions in the corporate world or in higher education. Or they may return to lucrative law practices in which they can offer clients the advantage of their many contacts in the state government.

See 103 Do any states bar their governors from serving consecutive terms?

> *". . . [There] are two important climaxes in political life: rising to power and falling from it."*
>
> —Madeleine Kunin, former governor of Vermont,
> in her book *Living a Political Life* (1994)

Q 107. How many governors have resigned from office?

A To date 161 governors have resigned from office. Many have left to take a higher office after winning election to the U.S. Senate, for example, or in the case of New Jersey governor Woodrow Wilson, to become president of the United States. (Wilson resigned as governor in 1913.) And New York governor Daniel D. Tompkins resigned in 1817 after being elected vice president of the United States in the Monroe administration.

Not all the resignations were a step up, however. Some governors have been forced to resign in the face of scandal or criminal charges. Among those governors in recent times who have been forced to resign from office because of criminal allegations are Illinois governor Otto Kerner, Maryland governors Spiro Agnew and Marvin Mandel, Louisiana governor Edwin Edwards, Oklahoma governor David Hall, and Arkansas governor Jim Guy Tucker.

Q 108. What is a recall?

A Recall allows voters to remove a governor or other elected official from office for any reason, even though his or her term is far from over and even if no crime has been committed. Not all states have this provision, and specific procedures vary.

Typically, starting the recall begins with petitioners collecting the large number of required signatures, often 25 percent or more of eligible voters (or 25 percent of the number of votes cast in the election for the official). This makes it difficult to start a recall, but if enough voters sign the petition, the state must hold a recall election. Then if a majority of voters cast ballots for recall, the official is removed from office. The election for the governor's or other official's replacement may be held separately or on the recall ballot.

See 126 Who is the only governor ever recalled? 228 Why did Michigan voters recall several legislators?

Q 109. Which states allow recall of the governor and other officials?

A Seventeen states have recall provisions for governors and nearly all other state officials. Most include all elected and appointed state officials, but some states do not allow recall of judicial officers. Rhode Island limits recalls to the governor, lieutenant governor, secretary of state, attorney general, and treasurer. States allowing recalls of state officials are:

Alaska	Kansas	New Jersey
Arizona	Louisiana	North Dakota
California	Michigan	Oregon
Colorado	Montana	Rhode Island
Georgia	Nevada	Washington
Idaho	Wisconsin	

Q 110. Who was the first governor removed from office by a state supreme court order?

A Wisconsin governor William Augustus Barstow, in March of 1856. Governor Barstow, a Democrat, had served out a first term (1854–1856) and was just beginning his second in 1856. But in March of that year the Wisconsin supreme court ruled that there had been election irregularities and that Barstow's opponent, Republican Coles Bashford, should therefore occupy the governor's mansion. Barstow resigned the following day and Bashford was installed soon after.

Q 111. Have any governors been assassinated?

A No governors have been killed, but in recent decades two governors have been wounded in assassination attempts. Texas governor John Connally apparently was not an intended target, but was wounded during the assassination of President John F. Kennedy in Dallas in 1963. Less than a decade later, in 1972, Alabama governor George C. Wallace was shot and seriously wounded by a would-be assassin in Laurel, Maryland. Wallace was left permanently paralyzed below the waist.

Q 112. How many governors have died in office?

A To date ninety-nine governors have died while still in office. And in at least one case the governor's replacement also died soon after taking office. Delaware's governor, Thomas Stockton, had died March 2, 1846, after serving one year of his term. Joseph

Maull succeeded him as acting governor, but survived just two months before dying in office, too. Maull's successor, William Temple, served out the rest of the term.

Meanwhile, three governors-elect had the misfortune of dying before even taking the oath of office, so they never officially became governors. The three were Delaware's Henry Molleston (died 1820), Georgia's Eugene Talmadge (died 1947), and Wisconsin's Orland S. Loomis (died 1943).

▶ Can a governor be impeached? *See 178 What is the procedure in the legislature for impeachment?*

Q 113. How many governors have been impeached and removed from office in this century?

A Just six governors have been impeached and removed from office since 1900. The first was New York governor William Sulzer, who was removed from office in 1913. Texas governor James E. Ferguson was next in 1917, followed by John Walton (Oklahoma, 1923), Henry S. Johnston (Oklahoma, 1929), Evan Mecham (Arizona, 1988), and Guy Hunt (Alabama, 1993).

See 127 Who were the first governors to be impeached? Impeached and removed from office?

FOR THE RECORD

Q 114. When did the first woman governor take office?

 In 1924, the year in which the first two women served as state governors. Wyoming voters elected Nellie Tayloe Ross as governor that year to complete her husband's term. He had died after just two years in office.

Miriam Amanda Ferguson of Texas also succeeded her husband into office, but under somewhat unusual circumstances. Mr. Ferguson had been impeached and prohibited from serving as Texas's governor again. The couple campaigned together, with Mrs. Ferguson running successfully as the proxy candidate for her husband. Tayloe Ross is officially the first woman governor, since she took office earlier in 1924 than Ferguson.

See 118 Has a black woman ever served as state governor? 131 Which women governors took office after their husbands' death?

Q **115. How many women have served as governor?**

A To date sixteen women have served as state governor (or acting governor). They are:

Nellie Tayloe Ross	Wyoming	1925–1927
Miriam Amanda Ferguson (D)	Texas	1925–1927, 1933–1935
Lurleen Wallace (D)	Alabama	1967–1968
Ella Grasso (D)	Connecticut	1974–1980
Dixy Lee Ray (D)	Washington	1977–1981
Vesta Roy (R, acting)	New Hampshire	1982–1993
Martha Layne Collins (D)	Kentucky	1984–1987
Madeleine Kunin (D)	Vermont	1985–1991
Kay Orr (R)	Nebraska	1987–1991
Rose Mofford (D) (succeeded to office)	Arizona	1988–1991
Joan M. Finney (D)	Kansas	1991–1994
Barbara Roberts (D)	Oregon	1991–1994
Ann W. Richards (D)	Texas	1991–1994
Christine Todd Whitman (R)	New Jersey	1994–
Jeanne Shaheen (D)	New Hampshire	1996–
Jane Dee Hull (R)	Arizona	1997–

See 118 Has a black woman ever served as state governor?

Q **116. Who was the first black to serve as governor?**

A Louisiana's lieutenant governor, Pinckney Benton Stewart Pinchback, became the first in 1872, when he succeeded to office during Reconstruction. The elected governor, Henry Clay Warmoth, was forced out of the governorship when he refused to acknowledge impeachment proceedings against him. Pinchback then finished Warmoth's term, serving as acting governor from December 9, 1872, to January 13, 1873.

See 236 What percentage of state legislators are black? 237 When was the first black elected to a state legislature?

Q **117. Who was the first black governor elected to office?**

A In 1989 Douglas Wilder, a Democrat and former lieutenant governor in Virginia, become the first black elected governor. He served a four-year term as governor from 1990 to 1994. (Virginia law prohibits governors from serving consecutive terms.)

See 236 What percentage of state legislators are black? 237 When was the first black elected to a state legislature?

Q 118. Has a black woman ever served as state governor?

A Technically, yes. Democrat Barbara Jordan served as governor of Texas for one day in 1972, becoming the first black woman to ever hold the office. She was appointed to the post as part of the state's traditional "governor for a day" program.

Q 119. Has there ever been a Hispanic governor? An Asian?

A Yes, as California's lieutenant governor, Romualdo Pacheco succeeded to the governorship when the elected governor, Newton Booth, resigned early in 1875. Governor Pacheco served out the remainder of Booth's term to December 9, 1875. New Mexico governor Ezequiel C. de Baca was elected in his own right in 1916, but died just six weeks after taking office in 1917. Octaviano Larrazolo was elected governor of New Mexico in 1918, however, and served out a two-year term. Since then other Hispanic governors have held office in New Mexico (Jerry Apodaca, 1975–1979; Toney Anaya, 1983–1987), Arizona (Raul Castro, 1975–1977), and Florida (Bob Martinez, 1987–1991).

The first Asian American governor was Hawaii's George R. Ariyoshi, who was elected in 1973 and served from 1974 to 1986.

The first Asian American governor elected on the mainland was Washington's governor, Gary Locke, a Chinese American elected in 1996.

Q 120. Who was the first Italian American governor?

A Rhode Island's governor John Pastore became the first in 1945, after being elected to office earlier that year. He served until 1950, resigning just weeks before the end of his term to take office as the first Italian American U.S. senator.

Q 121. Has any governor ever switched parties?

A Yes, Washington governor John R. Rogers was elected as a Populist in 1896 and after serving one term, won another as a Democrat in 1900. More recently Louisiana governor Charles Roemer won election in 1987 as a Democrat. Just before his reelection campaign in 1991, he switched to the Republican party, but lost to his Democratic challenger that fall. Alabama's Fob James fared better in 1994. A Democrat, he had served as governor from 1979 to 1983. He switched to the Republican party in 1994 and won the gubernatorial race that fall.

Q 122. Do Republicans or Democrats control more governorships?

A As of February 1999, Republicans led Democrats by a significant margin—31 state governors were Republican and 17 were Democrats. (Maine's governor is an independent, and Minnesota's is a member of the Reform party.) As always, the situation could change drastically at the next big election cycle.

See 128 What year saw the largest number of divided state governments? 233 Do Republicans or Democrats control more state governments?

Q 123. Which southern states became the first to elect Republican governors since Reconstruction?

A Resentment in the South—over its loss in the Civil War and the role of Republican extremists during Reconstruction of the South in the years after—resulted in the election of a solid succession of Democratic governors in southern states during the late 1800s and through much of the 1900s. North Carolina, South Carolina, and Texas became the first southern states to break the long streak of Democratic governors, and all did so in the 1970s.

Q 124. Which states were first to give their governors the power to veto bills?

A Massachusetts and New York included the power to veto entire bills in their original constitutions. Thus it is the oldest form of veto in use in this country.

See 91 How does the veto work?

Q 125. Which two states were first to adopt the line-item veto?

A Georgia and Texas adopted the line-item veto in 1868, becoming the first states to do so. But it was not long before many other states joined their ranks, and today only a few deny their governors this power of vetoing specific items within a bill.

See 91 How does the veto work? 95 How many governors do not have line-item veto powers?

Q 126. Who is the only governor ever recalled?

A North Dakota's Lynn Frazier is to date the only governor ever forced out of office by a recall. A progressive Republican who had been elected to his third term in 1920, Frazier became the target of a recall drive in 1921 as opposition to his progressive policies mounted. A central issue was the state bank—in which all state and local money had to be deposited—that Governor Frazier had created during his second term. Independent Republican Ragnvald Nestos won the recall election in October 1921 and took office the following month. Frazier had not entirely fallen out of favor with North Dakota voters, however. In 1922 they elected him to the U.S. Senate.

Q 127. Who were the first governors to be impeached? Impeached and removed from office?

A Kansas impeached its first governor, antislavery party leader Charles Robinson, on charges of treason and conspiracy in 1862, shortly after he had entered office. The charges had been brought by the proslavery party, however, and Robinson was acquitted by a federal grand jury later that year. He served out his term, which ended in 1863.

The first governor actually removed from office by impeachment proceedings was William Woods Holden, governor of North Carolina between 1868 and his impeachment in late 1870. Governor Holden was found guilty of "high crimes and misdemeanors" following a senate trial in early 1871 and officially removed from office.

See 113 How many governors have been impeached and removed from office?

Q 128. What year saw the largest number of divided state governments?

A In 1996 there were thirty-two state governments in which the governor and legislature were not under the control of the same party. That set a record for most number of "divided" governments in recent years.

Just prior to the 1997 elections, Republicans claimed control of both the governor's office and both houses of the legislature in twelve states, the Democrats in five.

See 187 How can a strong legislative majority work against the party in power?

129. How much do top elected officials get paid in my state?

A New York's governor earned more than any other state official in 1998—$130,000—while the governors of Illinois and Michigan took home comparable annual salaries of $126,590 and $124,195, respectively. No governor earned less than Nebraska's, who was paid $65,000. Following are the annual salaries of the top elected officials in each state.

State	Governor	Lieutenant governor	Secretary of state	Attorney general	Treasurer
Alabama	$87,643	$90,720 [1]	$61,780	$115,695	$61,780
Alaska	81,648	$76,176	—	83,292	—
Arizona	75,000	—	54,600	76,440	54,600
Arkansas	65,182	31,505	40,739	54,318	40,739
California	114,286	94,500	94,500	107,100	94,500
Colorado	70,000	48,500	48,500	60,000	48,500
Connecticut	78,000	55,000	50,000	60,000	50,000
Delaware	107,000	44,600	89,900	99,100	79,700
Florida	107,961	103,415	106,870	106,461	106,870
Georgia	111,480	72,812	89,538	102,211	96,804
Hawaii	94,780	90,041	—	85,302	—
Idaho	85,000	22,500	67,500	75,000	67,500
Illinois	126,590	89,357	111,697	111,697	96,804
Indiana	77,199	64,000	45,999	59,202	45,994
Iowa	101,313	70,919	80,524	94,485	80,524
Kansas	85,225	96,661	66,206	76,144	66,206
Kentucky	93,905	79,832	79,832	79,832	79,832
Louisiana	95,000	85,000	85,000	85,000	85,000
Maine	70,000	—	60,154	69,347	66,144
Maryland	120,000	100,000	70,000	100,000	100,000
Massachusetts [2]	75,000	60,000	85,000	62,500	60,000
Michigan	124,195	91,686	112,439	112,439	99,994
Minnesota	114,506	62,980	62,980	89,454	62,980
Mississippi	83,160	40,800	75,000	90,800	75,000

State	Governor	Lieutenant governor	Secretary of state	Attorney general	Treasurer
Missouri	$107,268	$64,823	$86,046	$93,120	$86,046
Montana	78,246	53,407	62,848	66,756	70,420
Nebraska	65,000	47,000	52,000	64,500	49,500
Nevada	90,000	20,000	62,500	85,000	62,500
New Hampshire	86,235	—	68,768	76,983	68,768
New Jersey	85,000	—	100,225	100,225	100,225
New Mexico	90,000	65,000	65,000	72,500	65,000
New York	130,000	110,000	90,832	110,000	80,000
North Carolina	107,132	94,552	94,552	94,552	94,552
North Dakota	73,176	60,132	55,464	62,592	55,464
Ohio	111,467	57,637	82,347	85,509	82,347
Oklahoma	70,000	62,500	42,500	75,000	70,000
Oregon	88,300	—	67,900	72,800	67,900
Pennsylvania	105,035	83,027	72,024	107,016	107,016
Rhode Island [2]	69,900	52,000	52,000	55,000	52,000
South Carolina [2]	106,078	46,545	92,007	92,007	92,007
South Dakota	84,740	30,766	57,576	71,973	57,576
Tennessee	85,000	—	86,484	107,820	86,484
Texas	99,122	99,122	76,966	79,247	79,247
Utah	87,600	68,100	—	73,700	68,100
Vermont	80,725	40,289	60,825	61,027	60,825
Virginia [2]	110,000	32,000	76,346	97,500	93,573
Washington	121,000	62,700	64,300	92,000	84,100
West Virginia	99,000	—	65,000	75,000	65,000
Wisconsin	101,861	54,795	49,719	97,756	49,719
Wyoming	95,000	—	77,000	80,000	77,000

Source: Council of State Governments, *The Book of the States, 1998–99* (Lexington, Ky.: Council of State Governments, 1998).

Notes: — indicates state does not have post, or duties are fulfilled by another official.

[1] Alabama's lieutenant governor receives $50 per day when legislature is in session.

[2] Salary figures are from 1996.

130. What is the average age of today's governors?

A The average age of governors has declined by about five years since the 1940s, and most governors today are in their late forties.

See 100 What are the basic requirements for becoming governor?

 131. Which women governors took office after the husbands' death?

A The first woman to serve as state governor, Wyoming governor Nellie Tayloe Ross, was the only one to date. When her husband died after two years in office, voters elected her to serve out the remainder of her dead husband's term (1925–1927).

Two other women governors were elected as stand-ins for their husbands, however. Miriam Amanda Ferguson was elected governor of Texas in place of her husband in 1924. A former Texas governor, he had been impeached and barred from running. Lurleen Wallace became Alabama's first woman governor in 1967. She also had been elected as a stand-in for her husband, former governor George Wallace, who was barred by state law from running for a third term. She died in office in 1968. The first woman governor elected to office in her own right was Connecticut governor Ella Grasso, who served from 1974–1980.

See 115 How many women have served as governor?

 132. Which two brothers were first to serve as governor at the same time?

A Between 1827 and 1829 brothers Levi Lincoln, Jr., and Enoch Lincoln both held office as governor in their respective states. Levi, Jr., was governor of Massachusetts (from 1825) and Enoch the governor of Maine (beginning in 1827). The two brothers remained in office simultaneously until October 8, 1829, when Enoch died.

More recently, in 1999, Texas governor George W. Bush and his brother Jeb, the newly elected governor of Florida, both held the office of governor.

 133. How many years of education do governors have on average?

A Governors generally have earned their bachelor's degree and a post-graduate degree by the time they reach office. They are substantially better educated than is the general population, which averages about eleven years of education, just under what is needed for a high school diploma.

Q 134. About what percentage of governors earned law degrees?

A Some 66 percent of all governors who took office between 1960 and the mid-1990s had law degrees.

Q 135. Have any governors taken office without ever having held a previous government job?

A By far the great majority of governors taking office in recent decades have had at least some previous experience in government, but occasionally voters do elect candidates without any. One survey of governors taking office between 1970 and 1987 showed that only 8 percent had no prior government experience.

Q 136. How many served in state legislatures before becoming governor?

A The state legislature is by far the most common springboard to the governor's mansion. A recent survey of sitting governors showed over half had served in the upper or lower house before being elected governor. Serving as a lieutenant governor or other elected executive branch official also provides key experience for would-be governors—about 28 percent of the governors surveyed had held one of these posts during their careers (sometimes in addition to a term in the legislature). Among the other avenues to the governor's mansion were law enforcement (about 27 percent) and local government posts (about 14 percent).

Q 137. Who were the first Catholic and Jewish governors?

A Louisiana governor Edward Douglass White became the first Catholic governor when he took office in 1835. A former member of the U.S. House of Representatives, he remained in office as governor until 1839.

Democrat Moses Alexander became the first practicing Jew to serve as governor in 1915, when he took office in Idaho. He remained in office until 1919. Much earlier, in 1801, David A. Emanuel served eight months as governor of Georgia to finish out the unexpired term of a governor who resigned. Emanuel was of Jewish descent but was a Christian convert when he took office.

LIEUTENANT GOVERNORS

Q 138. What does the lieutenant governor do?

A The key reasons states have lieutenant governors is to provide a successor should the governor die or become permanently incapacitated, and to have someone to assume the governor's responsibilities when the governor is temporarily incapacitated or traveling outside the state. In many states the lieutenant governor also serves as presiding officer of the state senate, and in twenty-five states he or she can break a tie vote in the senate. Most of them today also receive special assignments from the governor.

The office was frequently regarded as a do-nothing job until recent years, but the increasing complexity of government has meant lieutenant governors in many states have gained greater responsibility and played a more visible role in government.

See 73 What are a governor's duties?

Q 139. Which states do not have lieutenant governors?

A While most states tend to give the lieutenant governor few real responsibilities, governments in seven states get by without even having one. Arizona, Maine, New Hampshire, New Jersey, Oregon, West Virginia, and Wyoming all operate without lieutenant governors. In Tennessee the person selected as Speaker of the state senate also holds the title of lieutenant governor.

Q 140. How many states elect their governors and lieutenant governors as a team?

A Twenty-four of the states that have lieutenant governors do so and thereby avoid the problems that can follow when voters elect governors and lieutenant governors of different parties. The states are:

Alaska	Kansas	New Mexico
Colorado	Kentucky	New York
Connecticut	Maryland	North Dakota
Florida	Massachusetts	Ohio
Hawaii	Michigan	Pennsylvania
Illinois	Minnesota	South Dakota
Indiana	Montana	Utah
Iowa	Nebraska	Wisconsin

See 142 What happens when the governor and lieutenant governor are of opposite parties?

See 142 What happens when the governor and lieutenant governor are of opposite parties?

Q **141. How much do lieutenant governors get paid?**

A Salaries of lieutenant governors vary widely from state to state depending on the importance placed upon the office. The lieutenant governor of New York receives the highest salary, $110,000, with Maryland and California not far behind at $100,000 and $90,000 a year, respectively. On the low end are Alabama (at $12 per day, plus expenses) and Texas ($7,200).

See 87 What is the governor's salary? 129 How much do top elected officials get paid in my state?

Q **142. What happens when the governor and lieutenant governor are of opposite parties?**

A Separate elections for governor and lieutenant governor do ensure that both office-holders are separately accountable to the voters. But the system can be counterproductive when the two are of opposite parties and partisan politics hampers the governor's effectiveness. For example, a lieutenant governor of the opposing party may use the post to snipe at the governor's policies. Or politically ambitious lieutenant governors may intervene more directly when they get temporary control of the government, such as during a governor's trip outside of the state. Then they may take advantage of the situation by vetoing legislation, convening special legislative sessions, or otherwise frustrating the governor's policies.

See 128 What year saw the largest number of divided state governments?

Q **143. Who succeeds the governor in states that do not have a lieutenant governor?**

A Either the president of the state senate (four states) or the secretary of state (four states) is designated as the next in line to succeed the governor, should the governor die or become incapacitated. In Tennessee the Speaker of the senate (who is also designated lieutenant governor) succeeds.

See 139 Which states do not have lieutenant governors?

ATTORNEYS GENERAL

Q **144. What does the attorney general do?**

A As the state's top legal officer and head of its justice department, the attorney general ranks among the state's top public officials—in some states the second most powerful after the governor. In addition to managing the broad policy aims of the state's justice department, he or she advises the governor, state agencies, and local government officials on all legal matters. This includes advising the legislature on the constitutionality of pending legislation. Rendering opinions concerning interpretations of existing laws is a big part of the job, and the attorney general is also responsible for representing the state in all court cases.

Q **145. In which state does the legislature select the attorney general?**

A The Maine legislature elects the state attorney general, the only state to do so. Voters elect their attorneys general in forty-two states, and seven other states fill the post through appointments.

Q **146. Why is the attorney general's office such a powerful position?**

A The power to open highly publicized criminal and civil prosecutions is probably the attorney general's most powerful weapon. Vigorous prosecution of criminals, civil cases involving environmental and consumer protection issues, and scandals involving government corruption all leave a lasting impression in voters' minds. The media exposure that comes with these sensational cases can help an ambitious attorney general gain the statewide voter recognition needed to run for the governor's office.

The attorney general's position in the legal structure offers additional advantages. In many states, the state justice department is the state's single biggest law office. And the attorney general's legal opinions concerning interpretations of state law have the force of law, unless they are overturned in a court challenge.

▶ How much do attorneys general get paid? *See 129 How much do top elected officials get paid in my state?*

CABINET AND EXECUTIVE BRANCH

Q **147. Who are cabinet members and what do they do?**

A Cabinet members are heads of the major departments or agencies within a state government, such as education, justice, labor, social services, or transportation. They meet regularly with the governor to discuss policy matters and help formulate administration policy. But they also help maintain relations with the legislature and the public by explaining and promoting the governor's policies.

Governors did not always have the cabinet system to turn to for policy advice. New York governor Alfred E. Smith introduced the idea in his state during the early 1900s. Today most cabinet members are appointed, though a few states elect some or all of them.

Q **148. Do all state governments have cabinets?**

A Most states have cabinets in one form or another. They vary widely in size, from the seven members in Vermont's cabinet to thirty in Ohio's. Alabama, Arizona, Illinois, Minnesota, Nebraska, Tennessee, and Washington all have cabinets of twenty-five or more members. Some states also organize agency heads into subcabinet working groups or task forces to develop policies for specific problems or areas of concern.

The eleven states that do not have cabinets are Georgia, Idaho, Indiana, Iowa, Mississippi, Nevada, New Hampshire, North Dakota, Oregon, Rhode Island, and Texas. Idaho and Iowa do have subcabinet systems, however.

Q **149. What are sunset laws?**

A Sunset laws are automatic expiration dates built into legislation authorizing programs or agencies. Unlike programs that were created to last indefinitely, those with sunset provisions end after the specified period—anywhere from two to twelve years. The state legislature can prevent termination of the program by reviewing its performance and passing legislation to renew it. These laws became popular in the mid-1970s as a way to make agencies more accountable to the legislature and, critics of big government hoped, to reduce the number of ineffective programs. After Colorado passed the first sunset law in 1976, thirty-five other states adopted them, but results were mixed at best, and twelve states have since repealed their sunset laws or allowed them to lapse. Few programs have been discontinued because of sunset laws and critics argue that the legislature's periodic review of agencies is both costly and time consuming. But the process does promote legislative oversight of state agencies.

See 183 How do legislatures monitor state agencies?

"I now have twenty-three good friends who want to be on the Racing Commission. [After making the appointment,] I'll have twenty-two enemies and one ingrate."

—Unnamed governor, on the pitfalls of the power to appoint.

Q 150. What does the state auditor do?

A The auditor or comptroller oversees the state's financial accounting systems and conducts postaudits—audits of agency accounts to be sure that state funds have been spent as the legislature intended. Auditors may also be responsible for the approval of spending before money is actually disbursed (preaudit), and for conducting periodic performance audits to see how well programs and agencies are meeting goals set by the legislature.

Auditors are chosen by the governor or legislature in half the states and are elected in the other half. However, they are independent of the governor and report their findings to the legislature.

Q 151. How many positions does the governor usually fill by appointment?

A Governors appoint about half the top-level positions in the executive branch of state governments, though often the legislature or a commission must approve. The method for selecting the other appointees varies from state to state and according to the position involved, but these officials may be elected, named by a board or legislative commission, or picked by agency heads.

Typically, the governor appoints administrative heads in such areas as accounting, banking, finance, agriculture, budget, corrections, environmental protection, health, human services, personnel, public works, public safety, revenue, and transportation.

Q 152. Can the governor remove appointed officials from office?

A When the governor has the power to fire an appointee, which is not always the case, actually doing so may in fact be politically impractical. Unless there is a clear case of improper behavior, firing the appointee is likely to arouse a storm of protest from the official's supporters. In the end, the political fallout may cause the governor more harm than would leaving the appointee in office.

Where the governor's appointment power is shared (such as with boards or the legislature), removing an appointed official may be all but impossible to arrange. In recent years many states have given governors the power to remove appointed officials under laws governing administrative reorganization. But U.S. Supreme Court rulings have imposed limits on a governor's power to fire appointees of previous governors—even those who belong to the opposing party.

Q 153. Which state elects, rather than appoints, the most top officials?

A North Dakota elects twelve of its top state officials, more than any other state. Elected officials are governor, lieutenant governor, secretary of state, attorney general, agricultural commissioner, chief state school officer, treasurer, labor commissioner, tax commissioner, insurance commissioners (two), and the utility commissioner.

Q 154. What is the civil service?

A Civil service is the system governments use to manage the hiring, firing, and advancement of employees who work in jobs that are not filled by political appointment or by election to office. The system is based on merit, which means hiring and advancement decisions are based on a worker's qualifications and performance. Most jobs in state government are covered by civil service rules. States began adopting civil service systems in the late 1800s to combat the ill effects of the patronage system—the hiring of unqualified workers and outright corruption in government hiring and advancement policies. New York (1883) and Massachusetts (1884) were the first states to adopt the civil service merit system. Today every state has a merit system of its own for at least part of its work force.

See 311 What is patronage?

Q 155. What is the bureaucracy?

A This broad term can be used to refer to the administrative arm of government at any level—federal, state, or local. It usually is meant to include all the government's agencies and departments, as well as the workers who staff them, from clerks and low-level administrators on up to top officials in the administration. In fact, bureaucracies do the day-to-day work of government, turning broad policies into programs that actually provide services to the public.

The individuals and groups the bureaucracy serves are called clientele. Of course, clientele benefit from the services, but they also provide support and political clout for the agencies that serve them. This power base can be an important factor in dealings between, say, the governor and specific agencies over the budget matters or procedures.

Q 156. How does bureaucratic discretion figure in the operation of state agencies?

A Because the laws that set up government programs are worded in fairly broad terms, administrators who must actually run the programs have significant leeway in how they operate. This is called *bureaucratic discretion,* and the decisions these bureaucrats make can mean the difference between a program that works and one that doesn't.

Q 157. Does the governor control the bureaucracy?

A While their formal powers may allow them to exercise considerable control over agencies in the executive branch, governors usually do not devote themselves to micromanaging the bureaucracy. For one thing, the wide array of agencies and the complex maze of regulations by which they operate makes a "hands on" approach difficult to achieve. For another, governors also have other time-consuming obligations, such as promoting their legislative agendas in the legislature.

Governors can and do focus their attention on specific agencies, however, especially where the agency is involved in the governor's policy objectives, such as improving education. Or in a time of budget cutting, the governor may decide to target the few agencies with the highest spending levels. A crisis within an agency or its area of responsibility may also prompt the governor to become more directly involved.

See 73 What are a governor's duties?

Q 158. What role does the legislature play in the bureaucracy?

A The legislature exercises considerable influence over the bureaucracy. Among the traditional powers the legislature wields are approval of agency budgets, confirmation of appointments to high-level agency posts, the right to investigate the agencies, and the power to create, abolish, or reorganize programs and even agencies themselves.

See 41 What are the functions of state government? 161 What do the state legislatures do? 165 What powers do state legislatures have?

Q 159. How do state agencies and interest groups interact?

A The government agencies and interest groups regularly work together for their mutual benefit. Agency officials get valuable information from interest groups, which ranges from technical information needed for operating the agency to recommendations on proposed regulations and feedback on the success of existing programs. Interest groups, on the other hand, get the opportunity to make their members' views on issues heard, can influence agency decisions on how regulations are carried out, and can contribute to more effective government by keeping public officials informed about the effects of proposed changes to programs. The danger in this kind of relationship arises when a well-organized interest group representing only a small segment of the general public gains undue influence over the agency. The agency in effect becomes a clientele agency, which serves the interest group's needs rather than the general public's or even those of competing interest groups. Greater concern for public representation has helped keep a focus on the public good, however. For example, consumers are now represented by *proxy advocacy* offices in about half the states when there are dealings between public utilities and the agencies that regulate them.

Q 160. What is the public interest?

A At first glance this seems obvious, but as agency administrators know from experience, it often is impossible to determine just what the general public interest is in specific cases. Instead, officials confront a host of competing interests, including contrary demands from various segments of the voting public, special interest groups, and elected officials charged with overseeing the agency. And then there are the state laws and administrative rules that also limit what action can be taken.

Nevertheless, agency officials must find a balance between the competing demands in any given case, while adhering to the laws and regulations that govern their actions.

WHERE CAN I FIND. . .

Sources described below provide more detailed information on topics discussed in this chapter.

Almanac of the 50 States. Ed. Edith R. Hornor. Burlington, Vt.: Information Publications, 1994.

A book of tables, it contains both state-by-state profiles and comparative tables on various topics. Has recent past, current, and projected statistics on population and various other topics.

American State Governors, 1776–1976. Joseph E. Kallenbach. Dobbs Ferry, N.Y.: Oceana Publications, 1977.

This three-volume set is divided into two basic sections, a state-by-state listing of governors and their terms (plus election statistics), and biographies of the governors of each state. The notes at the end of the listings of governors' terms provide valuable leads on which governors did not serve full terms, and why (death, impeachment, and so on). Kallenbach also discusses, for each state, the history of the governor's term of office, qualifications for office, state constitutions, and the like.

Biographical Directory of the Governors of the United States, 1790–1978. Ed. John W. Ramo. Westport, Conn.: Meckler Publications, 1985.

An excellent source for biographical information on the governors. Contains fairly detailed biographies, about a page long, for each governor in the listed period. Biographies are arranged by state and then by date the governor was in office.

See also other volumes for coverage of more recent governors (vol. 1978–1983, edited by John W. Ramo; vol. 1983–1988, edited by Marie Marmo Mullaney; and vol. 1988–1994, edited by Marie Marmo Mullaney).

Black Firsts, 2,000 Years of Extraordinary Achievement. Jessie Carney Smith, ed. Detroit: Visible Ink, 1994.

Contains a hard-to-find list of firsts for blacks in state and local government, organized state-by-state.

The Book of the States, 1996–1997. Lexington, Ky.: Council of State Governments, 1997.

A compilation of tables with useful footnotes, this book has a section on governors, including a list of current state governors (their term of office, birth date, and other data), qualifications for office, powers, and even a state-by-state list of procedures for impeachment. Other tables contain current information for other top officials and the bureaucracy, as well as for the legislative and judicial branches.

CQ's State Fact Finder 1999: Rankings Across America. Kendra A. Hovey and Harold A. Hovey. Washington, D.C.: Congressional Quarterly Inc., 1999.

This book contains up-to-date rankings and lists of other comparative data on the fifty states for a wide array of topics, including "Governor's Power Rating," "Term Limits," and other tables relating to the executive branch and its functions.

The book is arranged by subject, but there is an index in the back listing references state by state.

Governors and Legislatures: Contending Powers. Alan Rosenthal. Washington, D.C.: Congressional Quarterly Inc., 1990.

A detailed look at the relationship between governors and their legislatures, this book covers their respective roles in policy making, budgeting, and management of the government.

Politics in the American States: A Comparative Analysis, 7th ed. Virginia Gray, Russell Hanson, and Herbert Jacob. Washington, D.C.: Congressional Quarterly Inc., 1999

The book draws on a variety of surveys and other sources of interest to political scientists. Chapters on the governor's office and the bureaucracy provide valuable insights into the inner workings of the executive branch.

State & Local Government, 2d ed. Ann Bowman and Richard Kearney. Boston: Houghton Mifflin Company, 1993.

A textbook on state and local government, it is a valuable basic source of information on the history and mechanics of state government, including the governor's office and more generally the executive, legislative, and judicial branches. It is clearly written and accessible to general readers.

State and Local Government: Politics and Public Policies. David Saffell and Harry Basehart. Boston: McGraw-Hill, 1998.

An up-to-date and very readable textbook, it combines coverage of the basics on state and local government with current policy concerns. Among the chapters relevant here are the ones on governors and intergovernmental relations.

The State and Local Government Political Dictionary. Jeffrey Elliot and Sheikh R. Ali. San Bernardino, Calif.: Borgo Press, 1995.

Arranged by topic, the entries in this book provide brief definitions of terms relating to the topic. There are sections on the executive branch, the bureaucracy and civil service, and intergovernmental relations, as well as on other areas of government. Entries provide both a brief definition and a discussion of the significance of the term being covered.

Worldmark Encyclopedia of the States. Ed. Timothy and Susan Gall. Detroit: Gale, 1997

The state-by-state treatment in this standard reference includes a fairly detailed narrative of each state's history, as well as shorter overviews of its government, population history, and other reference topics.

|||
LEGISLATURES

IN GENERAL

Q 161. What do the state legislatures do?

A A big part of the legislature's work is policymaking, which legislators do by enacting new laws, revising old ones, raising and lowering taxes, deciding where to spend state funds, and approving the state budget. While the legislature is the dominant force in policy making, the judicial and executive branches also have a say in these matters.

The legislature is also a representative body, and legislators must identify and represent the interests of their constituents. On another level of representation, legislators help individual constituents or groups of them deal with specific government-related problems (called casework).

The legislature's oversight functions include assessing agency performance in meeting goals and holding fact-finding hearings on policy questions, corruption, and other matters. Judicial functions of the legislature include impeachment proceedings against members of the executive and judicial branches.

See 73 What are a governor's duties?

Q 162. Why do states have two legislative houses?

A The idea of checks and balances embodied in the U.S. Constitution is at work in the state legislative system as well. Just as the U.S. Congress has two houses—the House of Representatives and the Senate—the legislatures of forty-nine states also have upper and lower houses, making them *bicameral* legislatures. A *unicameral* legislature has only one house.

Because two houses must approve a bill before it can become law (in Congress and most state legislatures), passing a bad bill is less likely than if there were only a single house. The bicameral structure tends be less efficient, makes change more difficult, and favors the status quo, however.

Q 163. Which colony established the first bicameral legislature?

A Massachusetts earned that distinction in 1644 when it restructured its legislature to allow greater representation for the colonists. The Massachusetts General Court, as it was called, thereafter had two chambers, one for deputies and one for magistrates.

Q 164. Which state has a unicameral legislature?

A Nebraska has had a single-house legislature since 1934, and it remains the only state with a unicameral legislature. The Legislature, as it is called, has forty-nine members, who have the title of senator. An advantage of a unicameral legislature is greater efficiency in lawmaking. The same bill does not have to be debated and passed in two chambers. However, scrutiny by the second chamber does provide a safeguard against passage of a bad bill.

See 265 Which state holds nonpartisan elections for state offices?

Q 165. What powers do state legislatures have?

A Broadly speaking, legislatures enact the state government's programs and policies, decide how they will be funded, and oversee the operation of government agencies and departments. State laws also regulate city and county governments within the state, set legal standards for relations between residents of the state, and provide for law enforcement.

The legislature passes the state's laws (subject to the governor's veto), has the power tax and spend, approves the state budget, has investigative powers, and plays a leading role in amending the state's constitution. State legislatures also ratify amendments to the U.S. Constitution and conduct impeachment proceedings against state officials.

See 91 How does the veto work? 161 What do the state legislatures do? 178 What is the procedure in the legislature for impeachment?

Q 166. What name is most commonly used for the legislature?

A In most states it is simply called the legislature, but twenty states have named it the general assembly. In New Hampshire it is the General Court, and Oregon calls it the Legislative Assembly. The District of Columbia's legislative body is the Council of the District of Columbia. See individual state entries in Chapter 7 for the name of the legislature in your state.

Q **167. What is the average size of state legislative houses?**

A State senates typically have about forty members, while the lower houses have about one hundred on average. Those numbers vary considerably from state to state, however, with the biggest differences being in the size of their house of representatives. A number of states have fewer than fifty members in the house. See individual state entries in Chapter 7 for the number of senators and representatives in your state.

See 231 What state has the most state representatives? The least? 232 Which states have the largest and smallest number of senators?

Q **168. What states have the largest and smallest legislatures?**

A At 424 members, New Hampshire has the largest legislature by a substantial margin. Pennsylvania has 253 seats in its legislature, and only four other states have legislatures with 200 or more members (Georgia, 236; New York, 211; Minnesota, 201; and Massachusetts, 200).

Nebraska's 49-member unicameral legislature is the smallest, though the two-chambered legislative bodies in Alaska (60 members), Delaware (62), and Nevada (63) are not much bigger. Just four other states have legislatures with fewer than 100 members—Hawaii (76), Arizona (90), Oregon (90), and Wyoming (90).

See 231 What state has the most state representatives? The least? 232 Which states have the largest and smallest number of senators?

Q **169. How many state legislators are there nationwide?**

A As of the mid-1990s, legislatures of the fifty states had a grand total of 7,424 seats. Of them 5,440 were held by members of the lower house and 1,984 by senators. At any one time a small number of seats may be vacant due to members' deaths, resignations, and other causes.

See 231 What state has the most state representatives? The least? 232 Which states have the largest and smallest number of senators?

Q **170. Do Republicans or Democrats hold more seats in the state legislatures?**

A Although totals change with every election cycle, Democrats in a recent poll held a slight edge over Republicans in the total number of seats. In a survey of state senators taken in 1998, Democratic senators numbered 1,021 and Republicans 925. (One senator was an independent.) Democrats held 2,870 house seats, against 2,553 for Republicans. (Thirteen house members were not affiliated with either party.) While the total number of seats is an indicator of how well a political party is doing at the state level, the more important concern is which party holds the majority of seats in one or both legislative houses in a given state. That determines how much influence the party will have over the legislative agenda.

See 186 What happens when one party has a legislative majority? 202 Do legislatures and governors ever come into conflict? 233 Do Republicans or Democrats control more state governments?

Q 171. What is reapportionment?

A Every ten years, after the federal government's census figures are released, states *reapportion*—redraw—their legislative districts to reflect changes in the population. Large numbers of people moving into a district from another state or from an urban to a suburban district, for example, can significantly change populations in legislative districts. The districts must then be redrawn so that each one in the state is roughly equal in population.

The Supreme Court made this mandatory when it set the guideline of "one person, one vote" for apportioning districts. But variations are allowed, and differences range up to about 5 percent in some states. Usually efforts are also made to keep the districts compact and unbroken, with no isolated pockets. In recent years, courts have also mandated the drawing of districts with large minority populations to increase minority representation in government.

See 174 What is a majority-minority district? 419 What did the Court rule in Baker v. Carr? *431 What did the Court rule in* Reynolds v. Sims?

Q 172. Why is redistricting important?

A While the basic aim of redrawing districts is to ensure every person has equal representation in the state government, the political party in power at the time can gain a distinct advantage by controlling where district lines are drawn.

For example, splitting in half an area that traditionally votes Republican can dilute the party's voting strength and may cost Republicans a seat in the legislature. Or, if a district must be eliminated because the state lost population, and Republicans control the state legislature, a Democratic legislator's seat may be sacrificed. The courts generally do not object to these aspects of redistricting, so long as the district populations are roughly equal.

Q 173. What is a gerrymander?

A Gerrymandering is a name for the drawing of election district lines to favor a particular party, voter group, or politician. The word itself was first used by a *Boston Gazette* cartoonist in 1812 to describe an odd-shaped Massachusetts legislative district. Leaders of the Anti-Federalist party had drawn the strange, salamander-shaped district to contain most of the Federalist party members in Massachusetts in a single district (a gerrymandering tactic called "packing").

That assured Federalists of one seat but gave Anti-Federalists a clear majority in all the other districts. The political cartoonist called attention to the tactic, however, dubbing the odd district a "GerryMander." The cartoonist linked the last name of Massachusetts's Anti-Federalist governor, Elbridge Gerry, with the district's salamander shape.

Another tactic used in gerrymandering is called "cracking."

Here, instead of packing all members of an opposing party into one district, lines are drawn so that the party's strength is dispersed over several districts. That way the party will be unable to muster enough votes to win an election in any of them.

Q 174. What is a majority-minority district?

A Prodded by the federal government, states in the South and elsewhere sought to increase black representation in government following the 1990 census. They did so by redrawing certain districts in a way that created a majority of black voters within the district—what became known as majority-minority districts.

In some cases, however, the districts were oddly-shaped and drew court challenges, with opponents contending they amounted to racial gerrymandering (as in North Carolina, Texas, Georgia, and Florida). In *Miller v. Johnson* (1995), the Supreme Court struck down a majority-minority district in Georgia, ruling that it was unconstitutional because race had been the "predominant factor" in drawing it. While brushing aside the issue of their sometimes strange shapes, the Court refuted the basic premise of majority-minority districts. The justices concluded that maximizing black representation is not required by law and found no constitutional basis for "carving electorates into racial blocs."

See 237 When was the first black elected to a state legislature? 249 How many black representatives are there?

Q 175. Who actually draws up the districts?

A In most cases the state legislatures are responsible for redrawing the districts after each census, and that means whichever party is in power at the time will control the process. Control over redistricting falls outside the legislatures in eleven states. Impartial commissions handle the job in nine of them, and in the others, Alaska and Maryland, the governors control the process.

See 172 Why is redistricting important?

Q 176. How much do legislators get paid?

A Salaries legislators earn vary widely from state to state, although higher pay usually means legislative sessions are longer and more demanding. Some states pay a per diem rate based on days the legislature is in session. Of those that paid an annual salary (as of late 1997), New Hampshire paid the least, just $200 a year. New York paid the most, $57,500, while Michigan ($51,895), Massachusetts ($46,410), and Ohio ($42,426) were not far behind.

Compensation packages for legislators can be quite complicated, though, because many states also pay living expenses, travel and other expenses, and an additional amount for each day a legislator works on state business when the legislature is not in session. Legislative leaders in the house and senate also receive additional pay in some states.

See 87 What is the governor's salary? 129 How much do top elected officials get paid in my state? 373 How much do state court judges earn?

Q 177. Who sets the pay for legislators?

A Legislators themselves do in thirty-four states, either by their sole discretion or in conjunction with a compensation commission. In twenty-one states compensation commissions either have complete control of the process or at least provide recommendations on pay increases to the legislatures. In New Hampshire, Rhode Island, and Texas the state constitution determines legislators' pay.

Q 178. What is the procedure in the legislature for impeachment?

A Impeachment proceedings involving the governor, other elected officials, and judges generally begin in the state's house of representatives. If the house approves the impeachment measure, then the senate conducts the trial. Following the trial, the senate votes for or against conviction and removal from office. A two-thirds vote is required for conviction.

See 113 How many governors have been impeached and removed from office? 239 Which state does not have any provision for impeachment proceedings? 403 What other ways can a judge be removed from the bench?

Q 179. What basic problems confronted state legislators until the reforms of the 1960s?

A Legislatures in most states suffered from three major problems that left them unable to cope with the growing responsibilities of state government in the 1960s. The legislative bottleneck they created helped bring on much needed reforms from the mid-1960s onward, however.

For one, the lawmakers were paid so little that legislatures failed to attract highly qualified candidates. For example, New Hampshire paid its legislators only $100 a year. Furthermore, legislative sessions were short and infrequent enough up to the 1960s that a seat in the legislature was largely a part-time position. Legislators often held other jobs, and some even collected unemployment insurance when sessions ended.

The short, infrequent legislative sessions that once were the norm created another problem as well. As the demands on state government grew during the 1960s, legislators found they had too little time to study problems or the bills being proposed to solve them.

Legislators were further hampered by the lack of adequate staff. They had little or no help in researching policy problems, and in some states did not even have the staff needed for drafting legislation.

See 77 What has been the chief goal of state government reforms that began in the mid-1960s?

Q 180. What is considered the ideal size for a state legislature?

A Size affects the workings of legislatures in two important ways: Larger legislatures tend to be more representative, because individual legislators have smaller districts and a smaller segment of the population they must represent. Smaller legislatures, on the other hand, tend to be more efficient because there are fewer legislators involved in the process of making laws.

The Citizens' Conference on State Legislatures, which recommended a number of reforms in state governments during the 1960s, set the ideal size for a state legislature at somewhere between 100 and 150 members, including both senators and representatives. Eighteen of the fifty states have legislatures with over 150 members. See individual state entries in Chapter 7 for the number of legislators in your state.

See 168 What states have the largest and smallest legislatures?

Q 181. When was the first televised hearing of a state legislature?

A On April 11, 1954. Newark's WATV televised a New Jersey senate hearing, which was called to investigate Sen. Malcolm Forbes's proposed ban on further construction projects by the Port Authority of New York and New Jersey. The Senate Committee on Federal and Interstate Relations held the hearing. The proposed ban was defeated.

Q 182. What are federal mandates?

A Environmental protection regulations, health care standards, and the like may be enacted by the federal government, but it is the states that are routinely required to implement them. These federal requirements on states are called *mandates,* and in the past the federal government has helped states pay the cost of complying with the regulations. These *funded mandates* became the basic mechanism of "regulatory federalism," which channeled federal grant money to states so long as they complied with the appropriate federal regulations.

Funded mandates increased rapidly in the 1970s, but during the late 1970s and the 1980s a lagging economy and the budget crunch forced the federal government to cut back on grants to states. Meanwhile, Congress continued to impose new mandates on states during the 1980s, but without providing any funding for compliance.

The federal cutbacks and many new *unfunded mandates* helped put an increasingly severe strain on state finances, forcing states to lobby for more money or fewer mandates. While federal grants to states did increase somewhat during the early 1990s, Congress attacked the problem at its roots by passing the 1995 Unfunded Mandates Reform Act. The act made it much harder for the federal government to impose new mandates on states without paying for them.

Q 183. How do legislatures monitor state agencies?

A Legislatures have several ways of keeping tabs on and controlling the activities of agencies. They can use auditors to evaluate agency programs and policies, require extensive documentation in the agency's budget requests, review agency rules and regulations, and can control the flow of federal grant funds to them. The legislature also has the option of passing so-called sunset laws, which require legislative evaluation and approval of a program before it can continue beyond a set number of years.

See 149 What are sunset laws?

Q 184. What is the National Conference of State Legislatures (NCSL)?

A An association serving state lawmakers nationwide, the NCSL promotes interstate cooperation, conducts research, monitors state legislation and regulations, and holds seminars on problems and policies confronting legislators. The group acts on behalf of the interests of state legislatures at the federal level and publishes reports, books, and other materials on activities and concerns of state legislatures.

See 53 How does the Council of State Governments work to help promote better state government?

MAKING LAWS AND DEBATING

Q 185. What is the difference between a bill and a statute?

A A bill is a proposed law that has been introduced into the legislature. Once the bill has passed both houses in identical form and has been signed by the governor, it becomes a law, or more precisely, a statute.

Statutes are laws that have been passed by the state's legislature (instead of being made by judicial decisions or arising from accepted practice, as in common law). Statutes are either public laws or private laws. Public statutes deal with matters affecting the general public or a segment of it. Private laws concern an individual who has sought legislative help with a specific problem created by a public law.

Q 186. What happens when one party has a legislative majority?

A In the legislature, the old saying "the majority rules" is all too true. Basically, majority status concentrates legislative and policy-making power in the hands of the party with the most votes and allows it to organize the chamber. For example, because the majority party has the votes, it can prevail on procedural questions and win passage of programs it favors. Having the majority in the house or senate also means that the party captures the leadership positions—including the Speakership and all or most of the committee chairs in the house, the senate presidency (in states where the senate names the president), and committee chairs in the senate.

Q **187. How can a strong legislative majority work against the party in power?**

A Factionalism within the majority party usually increases as the size of the majority increases. That is because as the opposition decreases in numbers, there is less pressure on the majority party members to close the ranks and vote the party line. Rivalries among party members characteristically develop along ideological, geographic, and other lines after the party reaches a 60 or 70 percent majority.

See 233 Do Republicans or Democrats control more state governments?

Q **188. What are the three basic types of legislator?**

A Legislators can be divided into three broad categories based on the approach they take to their work. *Delegates* are legislators who believe they should faithfully represent their constituents and vote according to their constituents' wants.

Trustees, on the other hand, follow their judgment on issues that come before the legislature and vote accordingly, because they believe they know what will be best for their constituents. *Politicos* take one or the other approach depending on the issue. For example, if the legislator has become involved in a policy matter, he or she will rely on personal judgment when deciding how to vote. But for an issue of less personal concern, the politico votes the way his or her constituents would want.

Q **189. Who can introduce a bill?**

A The power to introduce bills into the legislature belongs solely to members of the legislature. The governor, other government officials, lobbyists, and interested parties may become involved in drafting the measure, but they cannot introduce it. A member of the house or senate must agree to sponsor the bill before it can be introduced. In most states there is no limit on the number of bills a member can introduce, however.

190. About what percentage of bills actually become law?

Thousands of bills are introduced in state legislatures each year, but most of these measures die in committees. Roughly 30 percent of the bills introduced annually in most state legislatures become law, but sometimes the rate is much lower. One year in New York only 6 percent of nearly sixteen thousand bills that had been introduced passed both houses.

Q **191. How many bills were introduced and passed in the state legislature in a recent year?**

A Just how many bills died, and how few passed, in the various state legislatures can be seen in the figures listed below. Except as noted, the following totals are for regular legislative sessions ending in 1997.

State	Bills		Resolutions	
	Introduced	Enacted	Introduced	Enacted
Alabama	1,832	387	741	385
Alaska	495	113	132	51
Arizona (1995)	957	300	70	23
Arkansas	2,041	1,362	149	NA
California	3,024	951	233	136
Colorado	598	338	113	101
Connecticut (1995)	3,226	387	256	149
Delaware	628	220	187	14
Florida (1995)	2,605	473	152	0
Georgia	1,515	511	1,176	975
Hawaii	4,287	383	961	211
Idaho	695	404	57	38
Illinois	3,484	537	293	245
Indiana (1995)	1,504	34	50	6
Iowa	1,290	217	32	2
Kansas	970	192	41	10
Kentucky (1996)	1,333	357	323	239
Louisiana	4,087	1,487	636	488
Maine (1995)	1,586	607	33	2
Maryland	2,385	759	45	8

State	Bills		Resolutions	
	Introduced	Enacted	Introduced	Enacted
Massachusetts	NA	NA	NA	NA
Michigan (1995)	2,299	291	43	2
Minnesota	4,258	235	0	4
Mississippi	NA	NA	NA	NA
Missouri (1995)	1,242	170	63	4
Montana	1,013	552	75	56
Nebraska	891	307	53	8
Nevada	1,167	691	202	158
New Hampshire	1,007	351	49	8
New Jersey	1,462	259	186	6
New Mexico	2,617	370	35	6
New York	NA	NA	NA	NA
North Carolina	2,334	528	60	33
North Dakota	881	554	116	90
Ohio	856	112	77	26
Oklahoma	1,963	421	242	151
Oregon	3,091	871	191	38
Pennsylvania (1996)	4,764	377	640	464
Rhode Island (1995)	3,708	445	[a]	522
South Carolina	1,389	257	775	553
South Dakota	557	300	13	3
Tennessee	2,044	661	987	NA
Texas	5,561	1,487	166	15
Utah	668	394	63	41
Vermont	738	74	136	120
Virginia	1,920	933	663	536
Washington	2,408	456	88	12
West Virginia (1995)	1,431	303	197	31
Wisconsin	936	27	121	38
Wyoming	463	202	20	3

Source: Council of State Governments, *The Book of the States, 1998–1999* (Lexington, Ky.: Council of State Governments, 1998).

[a] Figure for bills introduced includes resolutions as well.

NA = Figure not available.

Q 192. What is a quorum?

A Procedural rules require that at least a majority of members must be present in the state house of representatives or senate in order for the chamber to conduct legislative business. If the senate has eighty members, for example, then a minimum of forty-one members would have to be present in the senate chamber. In practice, achieving a quorum can be difficult, however. Legislators are often busy with committee meetings, talking with constituents, or taking care of other legislative duties. When enough legislators cannot be found to reach a quorum, those present may decide to conduct business until someone challenges the proceedings for lack of a quorum.

Q 193. When is a roll-call vote usually required?

A Almost all states require a roll-call vote for passage of important bills. That means every member present in the senate or assembly must individually vote either yes or no (or abstain) on the bill and have their vote recorded by name in the public record.

Roll-call votes are also taken to determine a quorum and when the legislature votes to override or sustain the governor's veto. Most state legislatures will require a roll-call vote on any question before the senate or house, if a minimum number of legislators request it.

Q 194. Which state legislature was first to use an electric tote board to record votes?

A The Wisconsin Assembly became the first to use an electric tote board on January 11, 1917. Each legislator's name appeared on the board, while green and white lights indicated a vote for or against the question being considered. The device vastly speeded up the process of taking roll-call votes, which now could be completed electronically in just eleven seconds.

Q 195. What role do committees play in the legislative process?

A Before a bill can be debated on the floor of the assembly or the senate, it must be considered by a committee. So, after a bill has been introduced into either chamber, it is referred to the appropriate committee. Ultimately, committee members read the bill, may hold hearings on it and write amendments to it, and then will decide whether to approve or reject the measure. If the committee approves, the bill will be scheduled for floor debate. A rejection usually means it dies in committee. (In thirteen states, though, committees must report out all bills whether they approve or not.)

See 211 What types of committees are there?

Q 196. Why is the rules and calendar committee so important?

A This committee in the house of representatives has charge of two key functions in the chamber's lawmaking process: it sets the rules for debate and voting on the various bills that have cleared committees, and it decides when each bill will be debated on the assembly floor. The rules committee, which is chaired by the assembly Speaker and usually dominated by members of the majority party, can block the progress of a bill by referring it back to the original committee, by delaying the rules committee's consideration of it, or by putting it so far down the list that the legislative session is sure to end before it can be debated on the assembly floor.

The rules committee thus controls which bills reach the house floor and generally gives a higher priority to bills favored by the majority party. Opposition members do have recourse to a *discharge petition,* which allows them to force a bill out of the rules committee after seven days. The problem is that a majority of members must sign the petition.

See 211 What types of committees are there?

Q 197. How does a bill typically become a state law?

A Bills may begin their journey through the legislature as nothing more than a recommendation from a state agency, the governor's office, a lobbyist, or a citizens' group. However, only a legislator can actually introduce the bill, so that one or more legislators must sponsor it once it has been put in writing.

The proposed bill is then introduced into both the house and senate. Basic steps followed by the bill are essentially the same in both houses. The bill gets a *first reading*—its title is read before the house (and senate), and it is referred to the appropriate committee. A bill to build a new bridge would go to the transportation committee, for example (and to the appropriations committee as well, since money will be spent).

The committee chair in turn refers the bill to a subcommittee. The subcommittee analyzes the bill, hears testimony, offers amendments, and finally sends the bill to the full committee. The full committee then hears testimony and offers amendments before voting to report (or not report) the bill to the full house or senate.

Bills reported out of committee go to the rules and calendar committee, which schedules them for floor action. Because state legislatures typically have fixed limits on sessions and many bills to consider, scheduling is an important concern. Once the bill has been scheduled, it is given its *second reading*—that is, it is formally introduced before the full house or senate.

During floor action, the bill is debated and amendments are offered and voted upon. Some amendments may be favorable, while others may be calculated to undermine the bill's support or otherwise attack its original intent. The amended bill is then given its *third reading,* which is the final vote for passage by the full house.

If the bill is finally approved by both the house and the senate, any differences between the two versions still must be worked out. This is done by a *conference committee,* a temporary committee composed of both the house and senate members. They work together to reconcile the differences, and their recommendations for the wording of the compromise bill are put into a *conference committee report.* Both the house and senate then vote to approve the final version. If they do, the bill is *enrolled*—that is, it is sent to the governor for his or her signature (or veto).

See 200 What happens when a bill is "enrolled"?

Q 198. What do the majority and minority leaders do?

A Both the senate and house have majority leaders. They are second in command of the organizational structures in their respective chambers. The house majority leader works closely with the Speaker, while the senate majority leader works with the president of the senate. They control the scheduling of legislation in their respective houses, lead floor debates on bills, and help develop and implement their party's legislative strategies. Majority leaders may also act as their party's spokesperson.

House and senate minority leaders have much less power in their respective chambers, because their party has fewer votes than does the majority party. The minority leaders are the top legislative officials of their party, however, and act as party spokespersons. They are in charge of developing strategies for opposing the majority party's legislative program, leading the minority opposition in floor debates, and negotiating with the majority party.

See 186 What happens when one party has a legislative majority?

Q 199. How do the whips assist in the legislative process?

A Both the majority and minority parties in the house and senate have special assistants called *whips,* who keep tabs on party members and make every effort to get members to vote the party line. Whips conduct surveys of party members' views on upcoming bills, make sure party members are present for important votes, help manage floor debates, and handle other aspects of maintaining party discipline in the legislature. When the majority leader is not present in the house or senate, majority whips serve as acting floor leaders.

Q 200. What happens when a bill is "enrolled"?

A Enrolling is a step in the process of transforming a bill into law. Often the two houses of a state's legislature pass two different versions of the same bill. In this case a conference committee usually must work out a compromise bill, because both houses must pass identical bills before the measure can be considered approved by the legislature. If legislators in the house and senate vote to approve the compromise bill, the presiding officers of both houses sign and certify it—a procedure called *enrolling* the bill. The bill then goes to the governor to be signed into law (or vetoed).

Q 201. Is there a difference between authorization and appropriation?

A Yes, authorization is the first step in the two-step funding process; appropriation is the second. An authorization bill provides the legislative approval needed to run a state program or agency. But the appropriations bill must be passed before money can be spent to fund the program or agency.

The two-step process provides greater control over spending because two different committees are involved. Standing committees in the legislature are responsible for authorization bills within their areas of responsibility (such as health care or the environment). A separate appropriations committee handles the appropriations bill, which determines actual funding levels and other matters.

See 211 What types of committees are there? 215 What does an appropriations committee do?

Q 202. Do legislatures and governors ever come into conflict?

A The system of shared responsibilities for governing the state helps prevent abuse of power by either the governor or legislature, but it also produces a tension between them that sometimes erupts into open conflict over policy matters. Both the governor and legislature have advantages in these power struggles, although in recent years legislatures generally have been gaining power, and a greater voice in how the states are run.

Often these struggles over power and policies are worked out behind the scenes. Legislators or the governor may offer compromise wording in a bill advancing environmental protection, for example, that gets the bill passed by the legislature and signed by the governor. But when tensions rise, as they have in recent years over state budgets, governors and legislators may square off. In these tests of strength, vetoes and veto overrides are only the most obvious signs of conflict.

Struggles between governors and their legislatures only intensify when the governor is of one party and the legislature is dominated by the other. This *split party control* has become a regular feature of the political landscape in the South—which was once almost uniformly controlled by the Democratic party—as well as elsewhere in the country in recent years. The competition between political parties and their policy goals only adds another source of tension to a system with a built-in element of conflict.

See 128 What year saw the largest number of divided state governments? 233 Do Republicans or Democrats control more state governments?

Q **203. How many vetoes and veto overrides were there in a recent year?**

A In 1997 governors vetoed about one thousand of the thousands of bills submitted by the legislatures for their signature. As is typically the case, legislatures managed to muster enough votes to override only a small fraction of vetoes. Vetoes and veto overrides in each state are listed below for 1997, unless otherwise noted.

	Vetoes	Vetoes overridden
Alabama	20	1
Alaska	10	6
Arizona (1995)	8	
Arkansas	9	8
California	197	
Colorado	27	
Connecticut (1995)	2	
Delaware	5	

	Vetoes	Vetoes overridden
Florida (1995)	28	
Georgia	15	
Hawaii	14	
Idaho	5	
Illinois	88	1
Indiana (1995)	11	3
Iowa	13	
Kansas	2	
Kentucky (1996)	1	
Louisiana	19	
Maine (1995)	1	
Maryland	132	
Massachusetts (1993)	53	6
Michigan (1995)	4	
Minnesota	15	
Mississippi (1993)	17	
Missouri (1995)	5	
Montana	7	3
Nebraska	5	1
Nevada	3	
New Hampshire	4	
New Jersey	18	1
New Mexico	102	
New York (1993)	93	
North Carolina	0	
North Dakota	11	2
Ohio	1	
Oklahoma	24	
Oregon	43	3
Pennsylvania (1996)	1	
Rhode Island (1995)	24	
South Carolina	19	8
South Dakota	13	1
Tennessee	0	
Texas	36	

	Vetoes	Vetoes overridden
Utah	6	
Vermont	0	
Virginia	15	
Washington	126*	
West Virginia (1995)	4	
Wisconsin (1997–1999)	1	
Wyoming	1	

Source: Council of State Governments, *The Book of the States, 1997–98* (Lexington, Ky.: Council of State Governments, 1997).

* Total includes 34 partial vetoes.

See 92 About how many bills on average do governors veto and how many vetoes are overridden? 191 How many bills were introduced and passed in the state legislature in a recent year?

Q 204. Can a bill become law without the governor's signature?

A Under certain circumstances, yes. Every state imposes a time limit for action by the governor while the legislature is in session. In most cases the governor has from five to fifteen days to either sign the bill or veto it. If the time expires before the governor has acted, the bill becomes law without the governor's signature. Then, too, if the governor vetoes the bill but the legislature successfully overrides the veto, the bill becomes law without a signature.

Legislative procedures also allow for one other situation. In all but fifteen states a bill automatically becomes law if the governor has not signed or vetoed it by the time the legislative session ends. In the other states, the governor can "pocket veto" the bill by not signing it within the specified number of days after the session has ended.

See 91 How does the veto work?

Q 205. What happens if a bill is vetoed after the regular session ends?

A In most states, governors have a specified number of days after the session ends to sign or veto last-minute bills passed by the legislature (anywhere from five to sixty days). If the governor fails to act, the bill usually will become law. But if he or she vetoes the measure, the legislature must reconvene in a special session to consider either amending the bill or overriding the veto.

See 91 How does the veto work?

SESSIONS AND VOTES

Q **206. What is a session?**

A Whenever a state legislature meets to conduct business, it is said to be in session. Legislatures routinely meet in *regular* session and sometimes in *special* session.

Most states have regular legislative sessions once a year, but seven meet every two years. Usually the regular session begins in January, although a few legislatures wait until February or April.

Special sessions may be called to deal with emergencies, with specific problems confronting the government, such as the need for budget cutbacks, or even to consider impeachment charges.

See 209 How can a special session be called? 214 Why are interim committees important?

Q **207. Which state legislatures meet only once every two years?**

A The legislatures of seven states hold regular sessions every two years (biennial sessions)—Arkansas, Kentucky, Montana, Nevada, North Carolina, Oregon, and Texas. Vermont's legislature also has biennial sessions, but regularly splits the session so that in fact it sits during both years of the biennial period.

Q **208. Which states had the shortest and longest regular legislative sessions in a recent year?**

A The New Hampshire legislature had the shortest session in 1995—just 26 legislative days. Alabama's conducted its business in 30 legislative days, while Wyoming's wound up spending a comparatively leisurely 37 legislative days in session (in 1994 it spent only 19 days in session).

A legislative day is any day one or another chamber is in session.

The Michigan legislature remained in session for 352 days, far longer than any other state except Wisconsin, which remains in continuous session for two years at a time. Nevada's legislature meets only once every two years, but it's session in 1995 lasted 169 calendar days. Connecticut's was 155 days, and Oregon's was 153.

Q 209. How can a special session be called?

A Special sessions can be convened by the governor in most states. In some states the legislature itself may request that the governor call a special session, usually if two-thirds of the members approve through a petition or vote.

COMMITTEES AND CAUCUSES

Q 210. What do committees do?

A The full house or senate is too large to closely consider each bill that comes before it. Instead, small groups of legislators are appointed to committees, which serve as the workhorses of the legislative process. Committees focus on specific areas, such as government operations, education, or transportation, and only consider bills relevant to the committee's specialization. The committee may hold hearings or receive other testimony on the bill, attach amendments or even rewrite major portions of the bill, and decide whether to accept or reject it.

Committees are also responsible for overseeing the operation of government agencies within their areas of specialization.

Q 211. What types of committees are there?

A The four basic types are standing committees, select committees, joint committees, and a type of joint committee called a conference committee.

Standing committees are permanent and consider bills within a specified area, such as the environment or banking and finance. *Select committees* are formed on a temporary basis to consider matters outside the areas covered by standing committees. Members of both the senate and house make up *joint committees,* which can be either permanent standing committees or temporary panels organized to deal with a specific issue. *Conference committees* are joint committees created for the specific task of reconciling differences between house and senate versions of bills.

The house and senate in a state legislature typically have standing committees in the following areas:

agriculture	energy	judiciary
appropriations	environment/	local affairs
banking and finance	natural resources	public employees
commerce	ethics	rules
communications	finance (senate)	human services
education	government operations	transportation
elections	health	ways and means
	insurance	(house)

See 214 Why are interim committees important?

Q 212. How many committees are there in a state legislature?

A Though legislative reform has tended to lower the number of standing committees, the number of committees in state legislatures still varies widely. New York has the most senate committees (thirty-two), while Missouri has the most house committees (forty-two). Maryland has the fewest—six senate and seven house committees. On average, state legislatures have nineteen house and fifteen senate committees. In Connecticut, Maine, and Massachusetts the substantive standing committees are all joint house-senate committees. Members of both legislative houses serve on them together.

Q 213. What powers does a committee chair have?

A Although the committee chair's powers have been limited in recent years, he or she still has tremendous influence over the fate of bills within the committee's jurisdiction. The chair usually decides when and for how long committee meetings will be held, which bills will be handled, and when to hold public hearings. These powers give the chair a significant role in the legislative process.

Q 214. Why are interim committees important?

A Interim committees, which are formed by most state legislatures, operate when the legislature is not in session. Both the house and senate use interim committees to begin work on policy and legislative matters that will be of concern in the upcoming session. This head start is especially important in states where legislative sessions are short or there are many bills to consider.

See 211 What types of committees are there?

Q **215. What does an appropriations committee do?**

A Appropriations committees in both chambers of the state legislature oversee the funding of all state agencies and programs. They have jurisdiction over spending bills only, but this power of the purse gives them substantial control over government operations.

Once a program has been authorized (by passage of an authorization bill), the appropriations committee determines how much money the program will actually get and how it will be used. The committee can make the appropriation for any amount up to the limit specified in the authorization bill, so it controls how much or how little the program will be able to accomplish.

Appropriations bills usually start in the house of representatives. The senate appropriations committee usually begins senate deliberations on the bill once it has passed the house.

Q **216. Do legislatures in all states rely on the seniority system?**

A Party leaders in legislatures of many states do use the seniority system to one degree or another when determining committee assignments and perks. But often they also take into account personal abilities and political considerations when making the decisions. Needless to say, younger members tend to criticize the seniority system, since it favors older members.

MEMBERS' BACKGROUNDS

Q **217. How many legislators hold other jobs?**

A Most state legislators are part-time lawmakers, but the number of full-timers is apparently rising. According to a survey in the mid-1980s, 89 percent of state legislators either held other jobs, were self-employed, or were retired from their occupation.

Lawyers (16 percent) and business owners (14 percent) made up the largest groups of part-time legislators. Full-timers totaled 11 percent of all state legislators. Employees of companies also totaled 11 percent, and educators 8 percent.

Q **218. What is the average age of state legislators?**

A State legislators average forty-nine years of age, according to a recent survey of nine hundred legislators. The survey also showed that, on average, they ran for their first public office at age thirty-eight.

See 130 What is the average age of today's governors?

Q **219. What percentage of legislators have college degrees?**

A A recent survey revealed that 80 percent of state legislators have at least their under-graduate college degrees.

See 133 How many years of education do governors have on average?

Q **220. What is the family background of the average legislator?**

A Most state legislators live in the state where they were born, often in the same town or city where they were raised. Many are married, and the average size of legislators' families is 2.4 children. The legislator's family income ranges on average from $60,000 to $80,000.

See 234 Has the percentage of women legislators been rising? 236 What percentage of state legislators are black?

Q **221. Who were the first husband and wife to serve simultaneously in the two chambers of the same state legislature?**

A Two Democrats, Richard and Maurine Neuberger, found themselves in opposite chambers of the Oregon legislature beginning in 1950. Oregon senator Richard Neuberger had been in office since 1948. His wife, Maurine, joined him in the legislature after winning election as a state representative in 1950.

ARRIVALS AND DEPARTURES

Q **222. What qualifications must a legislator have to be eligible for office?**

A Every state has minimum age requirements for their legislators, with the age for members of the house generally being a bit lower than that for senators. Minimum ages for house members in the various states range from eighteen to twenty-five years old, with twenty-four states having a minimum of twenty-one and seventeen allowing eighteen-year-olds to serve in the house. Minimum ages for senators range from eighteen to thirty years old, with twenty states requiring senators to be at least twenty-five. Eighteen-year-olds can become senators in fifteen states.

Other qualifications for office vary considerably between states. Twenty require senators and house members to be U.S. citizens, while some other states stipulate the candidate must be a qualified voter. Over thirty states have state citizenship requirements (from one to five years for the house; one to seven for the senate), and most also require residence in the district the candidate will represent.

See 100 What are the basic requirements for becoming governor? 392 What qualifications are required to become a judge?

Q 223. In which states is the membership turnover rate the highest and lowest?

A Leaders of political parties and legislators themselves pay close attention to the figures for membership changes in the legislature after each election. For the most part incumbents have had a good chance of winning reelection in recent years, but as always there are exceptions.

For example, in 1994 Kansas had a 55 percent change among members of the senate, and Alabama was not far behind with a 46 percent change. Maine, Maryland, and New Mexico also registered 40-plus percent changes in senate memberships. Two states, Mississippi and South Carolina, had the lowest senate turnover in 1994—just 2 percent of the membership was newly elected. Illinois, Minnesota, Oklahoma, and Wisconsin also had under 5 percent new senators.

House membership turnover also varied widely from state to state in the 1994 elections. Maine and Nevada both experienced a 45 percent change in house memberships, with Maryland and Washington also having turnovers in the 40-plus percent range. The house membership in Mississippi and Louisiana remained virtually unchanged, however. Only one new member was voted into office in these two states, amounting to a 0.08 percent and 0.09 percent change, respectively.

See 233 Do Republicans or Democrats control more state governments?

Q 224. What happened in the 1991 Arizona bribery sting?

A Seven Arizona legislators were videotaped taking bundles of cash during this sting operation organized by Phoenix police in 1991. A police informer posing as Tony "V" offered the money to a number of state senators and representatives in return for their vote on a casino gambling bill. The seven who took the money were later charged with bribery, money laundering, and filing false election statements.

Q 225. How many South Carolina legislators were convicted in Operation Lost Trust?

A Sixteen were convicted of selling their votes following an FBI undercover sting operation in 1990. With hidden videocameras rolling, a lobbyist working as an FBI informer offered cash bribes to the legislators in return for their vote to approve a pari-mutuel gambling bill. Seventeen legislators were arrested in connection with the sting, and a jury acquitted just one of them.

Q 226. Which state sparked the wave of state term limit bills that swept the country in the early 1990s?

A Oklahoma. Less than a year after Oklahoma voters approved term limits for elected state officers and legislators in 1990, legislatures in forty-two other states were considering term limit bills. Today thirty-five states impose term limits of one sort or another.

See 102 Which states do not have term limits for their governors?

Q 227. Do states have term limits for legislators?

A Yes, twenty states have adopted term limits for legislators as of the mid-1990s. They are (house/senate limits in years):

Arizona (8/8)	Maine (8/8)	Ohio (8/8)
Arkansas (6/8)	Massachusetts (8/8)	Oklahoma (12/12)
California (6/8)	Michigan (6/8)	Oregon (6/8)
Colorado (8/8)	Missouri (8/8)	South Dakota (8/8)
Florida (8/8)	Montana (8/8)	Utah (12/12)
Idaho (8/8)	Nevada (12/12)	Washington (6/8)
Louisiana (12/12)	Wyoming (12/12)	

See 102 Which states do not have term limits for their governors?

Q 228. Why did Michigan voters recall several legislators?

A When the Michigan legislature failed to heed voter opposition to a large temporary state income tax increase, opponents of the increase organized a successful campaign in 1984 to recall several legislators. Voters ultimately removed enough legislators to change party control of the legislature, which had been evenly divided.

See 126 Who is the only governor ever recalled?

Q 229. Do legislators have retirement benefits?

A Nearly all states have some sort of retirement plan for legislators. As in the case of private plans, legislators' benefits begin after they reach a certain age (or number of years of service). Benefits are calculated on the basis of the number of years served, and in seventeen states they are calculated by the same or similar formula used for other state employees. The only two states without legislative retirement plans are California and Rhode Island. In Rhode Island legislators elected after January 1995 are ineligible for the state retirement system but do receive a benefits package.

See 176 How much do legislators get paid?

FOR THE RECORD

Q 230. When was the first legislative assembly held in the colonies?

A The first legislature convened in Jamestown, Virginia, on August 9, 1619, and remained in session just a few days, until August 14. Nevertheless, the general assembly, consisting of twenty-two members (two from each borough in the colony), was the first representative body in the New World.

Q 231. What state has the most state representatives? The least?

A New Hampshire has far and away the largest with 400 representatives (but only 24 senators). Pennsylvania is next with 203 seats in its house of representatives, followed by Georgia (180), Missouri (163), and Massachusetts (160).

Alaska has the smallest number of representatives, just 40, followed by Delaware (41), Nevada (42), Hawaii (51), and Oregon (60).

See 168 What states have the largest and smallest legislatures? 169 How many state legislators are there nationwide? 170 Do Republicans or Democrats hold more seats in the state legislatures? 324 How many state legislators are not affiliated with the Democratic or Republican parties?

See 168 What states have the largest and smallest legislatures?

Q 232. Which states have the largest and smallest number of senators?

A As of the mid-1990s, Minnesota had the largest senate, with 67 seats. New York's was second with 61 seats. Alaska has the fewest number of senators, 20, followed by Delaware (21), Nevada (21), New Hampshire (24), and Hawaii (25).

See 168 What states have the largest and smallest legislatures?

Q 233. Do Republicans or Democrats control more state governments?

A As of November 1998, the Republican party controlled more state governments than the Democrats, fourteen to nine. But party control of state governments—that is, one party controls the governorship and both houses of the legislature—is a fleeting thing that can change with each election.

In the case of some divided governments, party control conceivably could change even before the elections. Where one party holds a slim legislative majority in the senate, for example, the loss of even one or two members because of medical problems, forced resignation due to a scandal, or even a defection to the minority party could cost the party its majority.

Party control of the state, the governor's party affiliation, and the legislative majority/minority in each state is listed below:

State	Party in control	Governor's party	Senate majority/ minority	House majority/ minority
Alabama	D	D	D 23/R 12	D 69/R 36
Alaska	—	D	R 14/D 6	R 23/D 17
Arizona	R	R	R 16/D 14	R 40/D 20
Arkansas	—	R	D 29/R 6	D 76/R 24
California	D	D	D 25/R 15	D 48/R 32
Colorado	R	R	R 21/D 14	R 39/D 26
Connecticut	—	R	D 20/R 16	D 96/R 55
Delaware	—	D	D 13/R 8	R 26/D 15
Florida	R	R	R 25/D 15	R 72/D 48
Georgia	D	D	D 33/R 23	D 102/R 78
Hawaii	D	D	D 23/R 2	D 39/R 12

State	Party in control	Governor's party	Senate majority/ minority	House majority/ minority
Idaho	R	R	R 31/D 4	R 59/D 11
Illinois	—	R	R 32/D 27	D 62/R 56
Indiana	—	D	R 31/D 19	D 53/R 47
Iowa	—	D	R 30/D 20	R 56/D 44
Kansas	R	R	R 27/D 13	R 77/D 48
Kentucky	D	D	D 20/R 18	D 66/R 34
Louisiana	—	R	D 25/R 14	D 78/R 27
Maine	—	I	D 20/R 14/I 1	D 79/R 71/I 1
Maryland	D	D	D 32/R 13	D 105/R 32
Massachusetts	—	R	D 33/R 7	D 131/R 28/I 1
Michigan	R	R	R 23/D 15	R 58/D 52
Minnesota	—	RP	DFL 42/R 24	R 71/DFL 63
Mississippi	—	R	D 34/R 18	D 84/R 36/I 2
Missouri	D	D	D 18/R 16	D 86/R 76/I 1
Montana	R	R	R 32/D 18	R 59/D 41
Nebraska	—	R	(nonpartisan, unicameral legilature)	
Nevada	—	R	R 12/D 9	D 28/R 14
New Hampshire	—	D	D 13/R 11	R 246/D 153/I 1
New Jersey	R	R	R 24/D 16	R 48/D 32
New Mexico	—	R	D 25/R 17	D 40/R 30
New York	—	R	R 35/D 26	D 98/R 52
North Carolina	D	D	D 35/R 15	D 65/R 55
North Dakota	R	R	R 31/D 18	R 64/D 34
Ohio	R	R	R 21/D 12	R 59/D 40
Oklahoma	—	R	D 33/R 15	D 61/R 40
Oregon	—	D	R 18/D 12	R 34/D 25/I 1
Pennsylvania	R	R	R 30/D 20	R 103/D 100
Rhode Island	—	R	D 42/R 8	D 86/R 13/I 1
South Carolina	—	D	D 25/R 21	R 68/D 56
South Dakota	R	R	R 22/D 13	R 52/D 18
Tennessee	—	R	D 18/R 15	D 59/R 40
Texas	—	R	R 16/D 15	D 79/R 71
Utah	R	R	R 18/D 11	R 54/D 21
Vermont	D	D	D 17/R 13	D 81/R 65/I 4
Virginia	—	R	R 21/D 19	D 50/R 49/I 1

State	Party in control	Governor's party	Senate majority/minority	House majority/minority
Washington	D	D	D 28/R 21	D 49/R 49
West Virginia	—	R	D 29/R 5	D 75/R 25
Wisconsin	—	R	D 17/R 16	R 55/D 44
Wyoming	R	R	R 20/D 10	R 43/D 17

Notes:

D = Democrat   RP = Reform

R = Republican   DFL = Democratic Farmer Labor

I = Independent   — = Neither party controls the state (divided government).

See 122 Do Republicans or Democrats control more governorships? 128 What year saw the largest number of divided state governments?

Q 234. Has the percentage of women legislators been rising?

A Before 1970 women were a rarity in state legislatures, but since then their numbers have grown steadily. By 1975 women held about 8 percent of all state legislative seats, and by 1998 they had captured 21.6 percent, or a total of 1,605 seats.

Women legislators had also increased their share of legislative leadership posts to 14 percent of the total. In 1998 women held the largest proportion of legislative seats (between 30 and 39.5 percent) in the following states: Arizona, Colorado, Minnesota, Nevada, New Hampshire, Vermont, and Washington.

Q 235. Which state has the most female legislators?

A As of 1996, women held 59 seats in the 147-seat legislature of Washington State, more than in any other state. Vermont had the second highest number of women legislators with 55—out of a total of 180 members in the two houses. Connecticut had 50 women in its 187-seat legislature.

See 115 How many women have served as governor? 244 What percentage of state senators are women? 250 What percentage of state representatives are women?

A Blacks hold a significantly smaller proportion of legislative seats than women, though their share rose significantly in the early 1990s. Between 1975 and 1985, the percentage of black legislators rose from 4 percent to 5 percent and remained at about 5 percent for the remainder of the 1980s. From 1992 onward, however, the percentage of blacks in state legislatures rose to about 8 percent, perhaps in response to creation of the majority-minority election districts.

See 117 Who was the first black governor elected to office? 174 What is a majority-minority district?

Q **237. When was the first black elected to a state legislature?**

A Two blacks, Charles Lewis Mitchell and Edward Garrison Walker, hold that distinction. Both were elected to the Massachusetts legislature during the same election in 1866. The first black woman legislator in state government was Crystal Bird Fauset, who served in the Pennsylvania house beginning in 1939.

See 116 Who was the first black to serve as governor? 118 Has a black woman ever served as state governor? 242 How many state senators are black? 249 How many black representatives are there?

Q **238. Who became the first black to be elected to a southern state legislature since Reconstruction?**

A Leroy Reginald Johnson earned that distinction when he was elected to the Georgia legislature in 1962. Johnson ultimately served in the legislature for twelve years.

See 116 Who was the first black to serve as governor? 118 Has a black woman ever served as state governor? 242 How many state senators are black? 249 How many black representatives are there?

Q **239. Which state does not have any provision for impeachment proceedings?**

A Only Oregon does not have any constitutional provision for impeachment of elected officials. Instead, Oregon officials can be tried in the criminal court system on such charges as delinquency in office, corruption, malfeasance, and incompetence.

See 178 What is the procedure in the legislature for impeachment? 401 Can state judges be impeached?

SENATE

 240. How long do state senators serve?

A All but twelve states have four-year terms for members of the state senate. Senators in those twelve serve two-year terms. States with two-year terms are:

Arizona	Maine	North Carolina
Connecticut	Massachusetts	Rhode Island
Georgia	New Hampshire	South Dakota
Idaho	New York	Vermont

See 227 Do states have term limits for legislators? 245 How many states have two-year terms for house members?

241. What do the president and president pro tempore of the senate do?

A The president is the presiding officer of the state senate. The president pro tempore acts in that capacity whenever the president is absent from the senate. As the presiding officer, the president has considerable influence over legislative procedures in the senate. He or she recognizes members who want to introduce bills or speak in a floor debate, decides points of order, and is in charge of enforcing decorum in the senate. The president (and the pro tempore) does not take part in floor debates and does not vote, except to break a tie.

Among the president's other powers are the power to make appointments to select and conference committees and to administer oaths of office. In twenty-seven states the lieutenant governor serves as the president of the senate. In the other states the president is elected by members of the senate. Usually the senior member of the majority party is elected to fill the post.

See 246 What does the house Speaker do?

242. How many state senators are black?

A There were ninety-eight black senators serving in state legislatures nationwide as of 1990. Both Georgia and Illinois had seven each, more than any other state. Alabama, Louisiana, Maryland, New York, and South Carolina all had five black state senators.

See 117 Who was the first black governor elected to office?

"If you need a state trooper to give you a ride somewhere, he'll get it for you. If you need a bill killed in committee, he'll help you kill it. He'll do favor after favor and won't ask anything in return. But when he needs you to vote with him, and he doesn't ask often, he'll just say, 'I need you on this one.' And you may be voting against your mother when you vote with O'Keefe, but you'll go ahead and vote with him anyway."

—A frank assessment of senate president Michael O'Keefe's modus operandi, from John Maginnis's *The Last Hayride, 1984*

249 How many black representatives are there? 397 When did the first black become chief justice of a state supreme court?

Q 243. When was the first woman elected to a state senate?

A The Utah state senate seated the first woman senator, Martha Hughes Cannon, who was elected in 1896. She was reelected after serving her first term.

See 114 When did the first woman governor take office? 247 Who was the first woman house Speaker in a state legislature?

Q 244. What percentage of state senators are women?

A As of 1998, 18.5 percent of all state senators were women. In all, 368 women were serving as senators—215 Democrats, 139 Republicans, and 14 nonpartisans or independents. Washington and Minnesota had the largest number of women senators (23 and 22, respectively), while Alabama and Utah had the fewest (one each).

See 234 Has the percentage of women legislators been rising? 250 What percentage of state representatives are women?

HOUSE OF REPRESENTATIVES

Q 245. How many states have two-year terms for house members?

A Members of the lower house in forty-five states serve two-year terms. Four other states—Alabama, Louisiana, Maryland, and Mississippi—have four-year terms. Nebraska's unicameral legislature does not have a lower house.

See 227 Do states have term limits for legislators? 240 How long do state senators serve?

Q **246. What does the house Speaker do?**

A As the presiding officer of the legislature's house of representatives, the Speaker in most states has considerable power over members and over the legislative process. The Speaker controls the assignment of bills to committee, recognizes members who want to speak during floor action, and rules on points of order, procedural questions, and motions. In addition, he or she chairs the rules committee, often the most powerful committee in the house, and handles negotiations with the governor over legislation.

Unlike presidents of the senate, Speakers have the right to take part in debates and to vote. Since they also control committee assignments, they can discipline members by withholding any of the many small favors and benefits under their control. In more drastic situations, they can even remove unruly members from committees.

House members elect the Speaker, who is usually a senior member of the majority party.

See 241 What do the president and president pro tempore of the senate do?

Q **247. Who was the first woman house Speaker in a state legislature?**

A Minnie Davenport Craig became the first woman Speaker in state government when she was elected to the post in North Dakota. She served one full session as Speaker, from January 3 to March 31, 1933.

See 114 When did the first woman governor take office? 243 When was the first woman elected to a state senate?

Q **248. What was the Revolt of the T-Bar Twelve?**

A While house Speakers wield considerable power, there are limits to their control over members of even their own party. Democrat Jim Barker, the four-term Speaker of Oklahoma's house of representatives, apparently ventured beyond them during his tenure in the 1980s. Twelve house members finally decided they had had enough. Meeting at a bar called the T-Bar in 1989, they put together a plan to oust Barker from the Speakership. Though such revolts are fairly rare, the T-Bar Twelve rounded up enough votes from dissatisfied Democrats and opposition Republicans to unseat Barker in mid-1989.

Q 249. How many black state representatives are there?

A According to a survey in 1990, 317 blacks held seats in state houses of representatives. Georgia had the largest number of any state that year, 23, while ten states had none at all—Hawaii, Idaho, Iowa, Maine, Montana, Nebraska, New Mexico, North Dakota, South Dakota, Utah, and Wyoming.

See 242 How many state senators are black?

Q 250. What percentage of state representatives are women?

A Women held 1,237 house seats, or nearly 23 percent of the total in legislatures nationwide in 1998. Of these women, 730 belonged to the Democratic party and 504 to the Republican party. The state with far and away the most women house members was New Hampshire, where they held 122 of the 400 available seats. Maryland and Vermont followed with 48 women house members each. Alaska had the fewest (4), though Arkansas came close with 5.

See 234 Has the percentage of women legislators been rising? 244 What percentage of state senators are women?

LOBBYISTS: THE "THIRD" HOUSE

Q 251. Where did the term lobbyist **come from?**

A The word *lobby* first appeared in sixteenth-century England, in reference to the corridors and halls within the House of Commons. *Lobbyist* came into use much later, though—in the early 1800s, when it was applied to agents working for special interests in Albany, the state capital of New York. The label arose from the fact that the agents often gathered in lobbies and corridors of the state legislature, waiting for a chance meeting with legislators to further their cause.

Q 252. Do lobbyists help or hinder the legislative process?

A The answer to this question often depends on which side of an issue you happen to find yourself. Lobbyists and the special interest groups they represent can and do influence legislation more than any single individual could. If you fall within a group affected by the legislation—for example, senior citizens or teachers—then you would probably say the lobbyist helped the legislative process by pushing for a bill favoring your group's interests. But if you don't belong to the group and the measure winds up increasing state spending (or raising your taxes), you might say the lobbyist has unfairly influenced the legislators.

At bottom, lobbyists are exercising important rights—to petition the government and to exercise free speech—which by their very nature sometimes help and sometimes hinder the lawmaking process. But lobbyists also prove useful to legislators in various ways, by providing information about the needs and interests of groups they represent, providing expert testimony at committee hearings, and evaluating the effectiveness of programs affecting groups they represent.

Q 253. What are the five basic types of lobbyists?

A Lobbyists can be grouped into five broad categories—contract, association, company, governmental, and cause lobbyists. *Contract lobbyists* work for various interest groups, sometimes upward of fifty to one hundred at once. *Association lobbyists* are employed by a single organization, such as a trade, professional, or business association. *Company lobbyists* are also in-house employees who work for a single company, which has interests in the state. *Governmental lobbyists* represent the interests of local government associations, county and local public employee associations (for example, the county sheriffs' association), and the county governments themselves. *Cause lobbyists* usually represent a specific nonprofit or other public interest group to promote such issues as good government (League of Women Voters) and protecting the environment (Sierra Club). This category also includes lobbyists for both liberal and conservative ideological groups, as well as informal lobbying efforts by concerned citizens.

Q 254. What are the most influential lobbying groups?

A A 1994 study of the influence of special interest groups ranked the top ten as follows:

1. teachers' groups
2. chambers of commerce and other business groups
3. electric, water, and other utility companies
4. bar associations and other lawyers' groups
5. labor groups
6. doctors' and medical associations

7. insurance companies and groups

8. manufacturing companies and groups

9. hospital and other health care groups

10. bankers' groups

WHERE CAN I FIND. . .

Sources described below provide more detailed information on topics discussed in this chapter.

The Almanac of State Legislatures: Changing Patterns 1990–1997. William Lilley III, Laurence J. DeFranco, and Mark F. Bernstein. Washington, D.C.: Congressional Quarterly Inc., 1998.

An atlas containing maps and statistical tables, this book provides basic geographic, economic, political, and sociological data for each of the 6,744 state and house senate districts nationwide.

The Book of the States, 1998–1999. Lexington, Ky.: Council of State Governments, 1998.

An annual compilation of tables presenting comparative information about each of the states, this book has sections on the legislative and other branches of state government, as well as on elections, state finances, employment, and other concerns of state governments.

Campaign Finance, Lobbying and Ethics Legislation, 1996. Denver, Colo.: National Conference of State Legislatures, 1997.

This booklet surveys recent legislative activity in campaign finance, ethics, and lobbying in thirty states. It includes useful summaries of the legislation, arranged by state.

Directory of State Legislative Leaders, 1998. Denver, Colo.: National Conference of State Legislatures, 1998.

A names and numbers book, it provides contact information for legislative presiding officers, majority and minority leaders, and key staffers.

Governors and Legislatures: Contending Powers. Alan Rosenthal. Washington, D.C.: Congressional Quarterly Inc., 1990.

A detailed look at the relationship between governors and their legislatures, this book covers their respective roles in policy making, budgeting, and management of the government.

Inside the Legislative Process. American Society of Legislative Clerks and the National Conference of State Legislatures. Denver, Colo.: National Conference of State Legislatures, 1996.

   This valuable guide to legislative practices and procedures also contains comparative data on legislative processes in the various states.

Lawmaking and the Legislative Process. Tommy Neal. Denver, Colo.: National Conference of State Legislatures, 1996.

   A very readable narrative treatment of the lawmaking process. It uses fictitious case histories to explain step by step how various types of bills finally become law. The book also contains tables and other data on the states.

Legislative Roll Call. Denver, Colo.: National Conference of State Legislatures, 1997.

   This directory of current state officials provides a useful state-by-state roster, as well as contact information, statistics, and articles on current concerns.

Mason's Manual of Legislative Procedure. Paul Mason. Denver, Colo.: National Conference of State Legislatures, 1989.

   The authoritative source for parliamentary procedure in the state legislatures, it is used by the legislators themselves.

Politics in the American States: A Comparative Analysis. 7th ed. Virginia Gray, Russell Hanson, and Herbert Jacob. Washington, D.C.: Congressional Quarterly Inc., 1999.

   The book draws on a variety of surveys and other sources of interest to political scientists. Chapters are written by individual authors and cover a wide range of subjects relating to state government, including the legislature, interest groups, and the executive and judicial branches.

State and Local Government. 2d ed. Ann Bowman and Richard Kearney. Boston: Houghton Mifflin Company, 1993.

   A textbook on state and local government, it is a valuable basic source of information on the history and mechanics of state government, including the legislative, executive, and judicial branches. It is clearly written, has a detailed index, and is very accessible to general readers.

State and Local Government: Politics and Public Policies. David Saffell and Harry Basehart. Boston: McGraw-Hill, 1998.

   An up-to-date and very readable textbook, it combines coverage of the basics on state and local government with current policy concerns. Among the chapters relevant here are the ones on legislatures and political parties and interest groups.

The State and Local Government Political Dictionary. Jeffrey Elliot and Sheikh R. Ali. San Bernardino, Calif.: Borgo Press, 1995.

    Arranged by topic, the entries in this book provide brief definitions of terms relating to the topic. There is a section on the legislative branch that includes terms relating to legislative procedures. Entries provide both a brief definition and a discussion of the significance of the term being covered.

The State Atlas of Political and Cultural Diversity. William Lilley III, Laurence J. DeFranco, and William M. Diefenderfer III. Washington, D.C.: Congressional Quarterly Inc., 1997.

    This atlas contains maps and profiles of state house and senate districts with heavy concentrations of any of the fifteen ancestral groups covered—including black, Hispanic, Native American, Asian, European, and Arab.

State Government: CQ's Guide to Current Issues and Activities, 1999–2000. Thad L. Beyle. Washington, D.C.: Congressional Quarterly Inc., 1999.

    This collection includes readings on contemporary policy and concerns in various areas of government, including the legislature.

State Government Research Checklist. Lexington, Ky.: Council of State Governments, 1979–.

    This periodical lists titles of state government publications by subject. It is an invaluable research guide to past state government publications.

The Third House: Lobbyists and Lobbying in the States. Alan Rosenthal. Washington, D.C.: Congressional Quarterly Inc., 1993.

    A very readable book about lobbyists and what they do, both for their clients and for the legislative process.

IV
CAMPAIGNS AND ELECTIONS

IN GENERAL

Q 255. Which state was first to approve the use of printed ballots?

A Pennsylvania passed the first state law allowing voters to use printed ballots for general elections in 1799. Called vest pocket tickets, the ballots were printed by political parties and listed only party candidates.

Q 256. What is the Australian ballot?

A A secret ballot, which the government provides to voters at public expense, is called an "Australian ballot." Candidates and their party affiliations are printed on the ballot, along with a place for voters to make their selections.

This type of ballot, which voters fill out and deposit in secret at polling places, did not come into use until the 1890s. Before then, voters arrived at polling places with colored sheets printed by political parties or were required to state their preferences orally. Because these methods required voters to make their choices known publicly, they allowed parties an opportunity to pressure voters.

The Australian ballot was first used in elections at Victoria, Australia, in 1857.

Q 257. How do the office block and party column ballots differ?

A Candidates' names on the Australian ballot (see previous question) are organized in two basic ways—by office and by party. The office block version lists all candidates for governor together, followed by candidates for lieutenant governor, attorney general, and so on. Party column ballots arrange all candidates' names in columns according to their party.

Twenty states use office block ballots, which tend to encourage voting based on candidates and issues. Political parties prefer the party column ballot, which is used in thirty states, because it encourages voting by party.

Q **258. Which state was first to use voting machines?**

A Thomas Edison invented the first electric voting machine in 1869, but the device proved a practical failure. It was not until April 12, 1892, that an improved version—Myers's automatic ballot cabinet—was first used at Lockport, New York. After that, voting machines began replacing the old-fashioned ballot box, and today they are used in most state and federal elections.

Q **259. Have governors always been elected to office?**

A State legislatures generally elected governors in the early years of the Republic, which meant governors were accountable to the legislature. This was what had been intended, however. At the time there was widespread distrust of governors; many Americans remembered the abuses suffered at the hands of British governors during the colonial period. So for the first years after ratification of the Constitution, governors were relatively weak and under the control of the legislature. Eventually, however, the switch to popular election of governors, as well as other changes, gradually increased the independence of the governorship, giving it the political prestige and power it enjoys today.

See 73 What are a governor's duties?

Q **260. What executive branch officials are typically chosen by voters?**

A The governor is elected in all fifty states, and all but seven also elect a lieutenant governor. Forty-three states elect their attorneys general and thirty-eight, their treasurer. The secretary of state, superintendent of schools, and auditor are also elected in over half the states.

See 266 Which state elects the largest number of state officials?

▶Which states elect the governor and lieutenant governor independently?

See 140 How many states elect their governors and lieutenant governors as a team?

Q **261. Which incumbent state official faces the greatest chance of losing a reelection bid?**

A Although incumbent governors generally have good prospects for reelection, statistically they are returned to office at the lowest rate for elected state officials. Between

1968 and 1994, incumbent governors were reelected an average of 77 percent of the time, giving them comfortable odds for winning an additional term. But other state officials do even better. During the same period state representatives won reelection 90 percent of the time; state senators returned to office 86 percent of the time. An average of 89 percent of other incumbent statewide officers were also reelected.

One reason why governors are less successful at the polls is the prestige and political importance of the office. It tends to attract highly qualified challengers, and according to studies, governors face experienced opponents in about 75 percent of the races.

See 103 Do any states bar their governors from serving consecutive terms?

Q 262. In which states have Democrats and Republicans dominated elections in recent years?

A The number of state governments controlled by any one party has declined significantly in recent years, with both parties being considered competitive in the majority of states. For example, a recent survey of party control of state elective offices between 1995 and 1998 showed the Democrats dominating in nine states and the Republicans in twelve. Both parties were competitive during that period in the other twenty-eight states (Nebraska was excluded from the survey because its state legislative elections are nonpartisan).

The nine states controlled by Democrats were Arkansas, Georgia, Hawaii, Kentucky, Louisiana, Maryland, Missouri, Rhode Island, and West Virginia.

Republican-dominated states during the period were Arizona, Idaho, Kansas, Montana, New Hampshire, New Jersey, North Dakota, Ohio, Pennsylvania, South Dakota, Utah, and Wyoming.

See 122 Do Republicans or Democrats control more governorships? 170 Do Republicans or Democrats hold more seats in the state legislatures? 233 Do Republicans or Democrats control more state governments? 321 How many votes did Democratic and Republican gubernatorial candidates get in a recent election?

Q 263. Do voters tend to split their tickets when voting for state officials?

A Yes, ticket-splitting has become increasingly common in state elections. For example, Vermont voters in 1994 elected a Democratic governor with a commanding 70 percent of the vote, a Republican U.S. senator with 50 percent, and an independent U.S. representative with 50 percent. Obviously a sizable number of Vermonters split their tickets during this election. But the number of divided state governments today is another good indicator of ticket-splitting nationwide. As of 1997, one party controlled the governor's mansion and the other controlled one or both houses of the legislature in thirty-three states.

See 128 What year saw the largest number of divided state governments? 142 What happens when the governor and lieutenant governor are of opposite parties? 233 Do Republicans or Democrats control more state governments?

Q **264. What was the voter turnout for a recent gubernatorial election?**

A Voter turnout for the 1996 elections ranged from 43 percent to over 57 percent in the states holding elections for governor that year. Generally speaking the turnout was higher than usual because 1996 was a presidential election year. Turnout in states where governors are elected in off years frequently is lower and most often runs in the 30- to 40-percent range. States ranked by turnout in their 1996 gubernatorial elections are, from lowest to highest:

State	1996 voter turnout (percent)	State	1996 voter election (percent)
West Virginia	43.9	Missouri	53.8
North Carolina	46.3	Washington	54.3
Indiana	48.3	North Dakota	55.7
Delaware	49.5	Vermont	57.2
Utah	50.8	New Hampshire	57.5
Montana	52.8		

See 270 Which groups of eligible voters are most likely to vote? 271 When is voter turnout highest? 321 How many votes did Democratic and Republican gubernatorial candidates get in a recent election?

Q **265. Which state holds nonpartisan elections for state offices?**

A Nebraska is the only state to do so. Candidates in Nebraska's nonpartisan elections are listed on ballots without party labels, and parties are not allowed to recruit candidates. These restrictions succeeded, as intended, in eliminating party control of state government. However, special interest groups gained greater influence as a result, and incumbent candidates have a greater advantage in the elections.

Q **266. Which state elects the largest number of state officials?**

A North Dakota wins that distinction with twelve elective offices: governor, lieutenant governor, attorney general, agriculture secretary, auditor, secretary of state, superintendent of public instruction, treasurer, commissioner of labor, commissioner of insurance, tax commissioner, and public service commissioner.

North Carolina is a close second with a total of ten elective offices, including all those above except the tax and public service commission posts.

See 90 How important is the governor's power to appoint?

Q **267. When do states usually hold elections?**

A Every state holds its elections in November, on the first Tuesday after the first Monday in the month (the same formula used to determine the date of federal elections). Most states schedule elections for even-numbered years, but five hold them in odd-numbered years. The five are Kentucky, Louisiana, Mississippi, New Jersey, and Virginia.

See 318 How many governorships will be up for grabs in the year 2000? 2002?

Q **268. What is the smallest unit in the election process?**

A The precinct is the smallest. Each has a polling place that serves anywhere from about two hundred to over a thousand voters. Both cities and counties are divided into precincts, and there are about 178,000 nationwide.

Precincts usually are also the smallest unit of political party organization. The parties elect or appoint precinct captains, who work at this grass-roots level and who are responsible for maintaining lists of voters, promoting voter registration, and making sure party members vote during elections. Precinct captains also serve on the party's county committee.

Q **269. What is a plurality?**

A In an election the candidate who wins the most votes is said to have a *plurality*. The "most votes" could be only 35 percent of all those cast in a three-way race, however, which means the candidate did not have a majority of the votes. A majority would be a minimum of half the votes cast, plus one.

270. Which groups of eligible voters are most likely to vote?

 Studies have shown that voter turnout tends to be higher among certain age and income groups. For example, middle-aged voters who are well educated and have a high income tend to be more likely to vote than people in other socioeconomic groups. Men and women tend to vote in about the same numbers, but white voters tend to have higher turnout rates than do either blacks or Hispanics.

Other groups of likely voters include people who have strong loyalties to one or another political party, or who otherwise have a sense of duty when it comes to participating in elections.

See 264 What was the voter turnout for a recent gubernatorial election?

 271. When is voter turnout highest?

 Years in which there is a presidential election tend to have the highest voter turnout. Gubernatorial elections held in off-years usually have voter turnouts that are several percentage points lower than those in presidential election years. But other factors affect turnout as well. States with greater competition between political parties tend to have higher voter turnout, and hotly contested races between individual candidates are sure to stimulate voter interest. *(See also next question.)*

 272. Do voter registration rules affect turnout?

 Yes, the more difficult it is to register and keep the registration current, the lower the voter turnout. For example, over half the states automatically cancel the registration if a voter fails to vote for a specified period of time (often four years or two general elections). And most states will not allow voters to register for a period of time before the election, usually from ten to fifty days. One study showed that turnout was markedly higher in states allowing voters to register ten days or fewer before the election (53 percent) than in states that closed registration thirty or more days before (45 percent).

See 337 Which state does not require voters to register?

 273. What is a poll tax?

 A poll tax is a fee, usually between $1 and $2, that a voter was once required to pay in order to vote in various southern states. The poll tax was adopted to discourage voting by blacks and poor whites in the South. First adopted by Tennessee in 1879, the poll tax spread to ten other southern states during the late 1800s and early 1900s. In 1961 the Twenty-fourth Amendment to the U.S. Constitution specifically banned poll taxes in federal elections. Five years later the U.S. Supreme Court declared them unconstitutional in state elections as well.

See 425 What did the Court rule in Harper v. Virginia State Board of Elections?

STATES AND NATIONAL POLITICS

Q **274. Which state holds the first presidential primary?**

A New Hampshire has traditionally held the first, on February 18 in the presidential election year. Winning the state does not gain many national convention delegates for party nominees, but this primary has been a reliable bellwether for many years. In the past four decades only Bill Clinton has gone on to win the presidency after losing in New Hampshire.

Q **275. What is Super Tuesday?**

A A plan to give southern states added clout in the national elections, Super Tuesday was organized as a day when a large number of states—most of them in the South— all held their primary elections. Beginning in the 1980s, Super Tuesday has been held about three weeks after the New Hampshire primary. In 1988 twenty states all held their primaries on the same day, but by 1992 the number of states participating dropped to ten.

Q **276. Which state hosted the first televised political convention?**

A Pennsylvania claims that distinction. The 1940 Republican national convention at Philadelphia, held June 24 to 29, was the first ever televised and was carried by NBC. The convention nominated Wendell Willkie, who went on to lose the election to President Franklin D. Roosevelt.

Another Republican convention, this time at Cleveland, Ohio, was the first political convention to be broadcast via radio. NBC radio carried the program on June 10, 1924, in which Republicans nominated Calvin Coolidge for president. Coolidge won the election that fall.

"Everyone knows that half the money spent in a political campaign is wasted. The trouble is that nobody knows which half."

Q 277. What did the term *Solid South* refer to?

A *Solid South* was a shorthand reference to the once solidly Democratic South. Until a few decades ago the Democratic party controlled the governments of virtually every southern state. In fact, Democrats had been unbeatable at the polls in the South since the Civil War, largely because of southerners' resentment at the antislavery stand of Republicans during the Civil War and the activities of radical Republicans during Reconstruction. Beginning slowly in the 1960s, however, Republicans began making inroads in the South. Today, the Republican party's more conservative leanings have given it a decided advantage in the once solidly Democratic South.

See 123 Which southern states became the first to elect Republican governors since Reconstruction?

Q 278. How do state and national party organizations interact?

A Efforts by leaders of both national parties in recent decades have produced a much higher level of coordination between national and state party organizations. Through large transfers of campaign funds, as well as various types of campaign support services, national party organizations have gotten a greater measure of control over their state chapters. That has made it possible to coordinate national strategies for federal elections (presidential, congressional) with state party efforts. The same is true of the states' party-building activities, such as get-out-the-vote drives. Prior to the 1970s, national organizations were much more dependent on state organizations for funding (through interparty transfers). Today that situation is reversed; the national party sends large amounts to state parties.

Q 279. Which state was first to popularly elect a United States senator?

A Georgia Democrat Augustus Octavius Bacon became the first popularly elected senator on July 15, 1913. Georgia held the special election just weeks after ratification of the Seventeenth Amendment to the U.S. Constitution, which changed the method of selecting U.S. senators from election by state legislatures to election by popular vote. Bacon was sworn in on July 28, 1913.

Q **280. Who was Bill Brock and how did he change the Republican party organization?**

A Brock served as national Republican party chairman from 1977 to 1981. During that time he vastly expanded the national party's program to assist party organizations and individual candidates in the states, in an effort to improve Republican party fortunes at the state level. His program eventually included outright grants to state parties, loans of experienced staffers, technical advice from consultants on everything from fund-raising to redistricting, and assistance with such things as voter list preparation and get-out-the-vote drives. Stung by Republican successes at the polls, Democrats began setting up a similar program in 1985.

Q **281. What was Paul Kirk's "Election Force" designed to do?**

A Noting the success of the Republican program serving state-level party organizations (see question above), Democratic national chairman Paul Kirk began extending support services to state party organizations. The DNC created the Election Force in 1986 as part of the program, sending full-time professional staffers and $1.2 million in resources to party chapters in sixteen key states. In return the state party organizations pledged their cooperation in such matters as party-building programs and national election campaigns.

Q **282. Who developed the Democrats' "Coordinated Campaign" program?**

A Ron Brown, Paul Kirk's successor as Democratic National Committee chair in 1989, expanded on the Election Force concept (see previous question) to create the Coordinated Campaign organization. It served Democratic candidates in thirty-six states, provided campaign services and professional staffers, and contributed some funding during the 1990 and 1992 elections.

Q **283. How did the Federal Election Campaign Act (FECA) benefit state political party committees?**

A Though FECA limits what Republican and Democratic national party committees can spend for federal elections, it does allow their state and local committees to spend any amount for voter registration, get-out-the-vote drives, and other party-building activities. This exception to spending limits opened the door to massive transfers of funds from national party organizations to their state and local committees.

Why? Because national committees wind up raising more than they are allowed to spend, under FECA rules, for federal candidates. But party-building activities in states can be organized to help the party's federal candidates, as well as those for state office. That way, the funds the national party sends to state committees are outside the federal spending limits, but still help elect the party's presidential, senate, and house candidates.

Q **284. What is the difference between "hard" and "soft" money?**

A These two terms are much in the news because of alleged abuses in financing federal election campaigns in 1996. *Hard money* is money political parties raise that is subject to federal limits on the size of contributions and to overall spending limits for a campaign. Hard money goes to pay direct campaign expenses of party candidates.

Soft money is not regulated by campaign finance laws, and contributors are not limited in the amount they can give. Soft money is held in separate accounts and can be channeled to state and local party organizations for such things as get-out-the-vote drives and other party-building activities, especially those that indirectly help the party's congressional and presidential candidates.

See 357 What are PACs?

Q **285. Do District of Columbia votes count in presidential elections?**

A Yes, District votes count in election totals, and it has as many electors in presidential races as it would if it were actually a state—three. District voters got the right to participate in presidential elections in 1961, following ratification of the Twenty-third Amendment to the U.S. Constitution.

See 58 Is the District a state?

STATE PARTIES AND STATE PRIMARIES

Q **286. What do political parties do?**

A Though Democratic and Republican parties no longer have the control over the political process they once had, they remain the dominant force in government. With rare exceptions, for example, governors and other state elected officials are all members of these parties. When governors make appointments to nonelective offices, they almost always appoint members of their party. And state legislatures, which make the laws and spend state funds, are for the most part organized along party lines, with the majority party controlling leadership posts and committee chairs.

The loss of control over candidate selection has forced state parties to adapt, however. Where the two parties once chose the candidates and ran their campaigns, many states have opted for direct primaries in which voters decide on the candidates. Candidates now rely on their own fund-raising and PACs, instead of party coffers, for a significant part of their campaign finances. And increasingly, campaigns have become candidate-centered, rather than party-centered, with candidates generally having their own campaign staff.

The state chapters of the two major parties have responded by becoming campaign service organizations for both candidates and local affiliates. Parties today provide fund-raising services, media services, candidate training, voter identification, and other services. Today, they also serve their national party organizations by helping carry out broad campaign strategies, as well as supporting party candidates for national offices.

See 298 What is a direct primary? 299 Have candidates for state office always won their nominations through primaries? 303 Does any state hold a nonpartisan primary? 308 Which states select party candidates through nominating conventions? 357 What are PACs?

Q 287. How are state parties organized?

A Both the Democratic and Republican parties have state party committees in all fifty states. Headed by a state committee chair, who usually serves a two- or four-year term, the state committees are made up of members usually chosen by county committees (by primary in some states). While state committees are affiliated with the national party organization, they do act independently.

The actual number of state committee members varies widely, from as few as twenty to over one thousand in a large state. State committees act as campaign service agencies for party candidates, recruit candidates, conduct party-building activities, adopt and promote party policies, publicize party positions on issues, and call state nominating conventions.

Below the state level and operating somewhat independently are the backbone of the state party organization, the county committees. Members of these committees are drawn from party precinct committees within the county, and the county chairs usually are members of the state committee.

The smallest organizational unit is the precinct committee, which is made up of volunteers who live in the precinct. Much of the drudge work of campaigns is done at the county and precinct levels, including posting signs, distributing literature, and conducting voter registration drives.

The parties also have other largely autonomous committees, including those for congressional and legislative districts. They are composed of members selected by county committees and focus on campaigns and concerns within their area of specialization.

Q 288. Who was the first woman to head the state committee of a major party?

A State representative Mary Teresa Norton became the first when she was selected to chair the New Jersey state Democratic committee in 1934.

See 247 Who was the first woman house Speaker in a state legislature?

Q 289. How do states regulate political parties?

A State laws regulate in one way or another most operations of political parties. They set the standards for recognizing a political party and placing the party's candidates on the ballot, impose rules on the party's organizational structure, establish membership requirements (for participation in primaries), determine the nominating procedure (many states require a direct primary), and in most states impose at least some rules on campaign financing. The specific rules vary considerably from state to state, however, with some regulating parties much more closely than others.

See 265 Which state holds nonpartisan elections for state offices? 272 Do voter registration rules affect turnout? 299 Have candidates for state office always won their nominations through primaries? 356 Do states allow corporations to contribute to state election campaigns? 359 How many states require campaign finance reporting?

Q 290. What are the minimum requirements for getting a party on the ballot?

A In order to have candidates listed on the ballot, a party must have polled a minimum number of votes in the past election. The number varies, from as a little as 1 percent in Wisconsin to 20 percent in Georgia.

A newly formed party that was not on the ballot in the previous election must collect signatures from a specified number of voters in the state to be eligible. Independent candidates must also produce the required number of signatures to get their names on the ballot.

Q 291. Have third parties succeeded at the state level?

A Third parties generally have not been successful, though from time to time their candidates do win at the state level.

Nineteen ninety-seven was not one of those times, however. Only 7 of the 7,343 sitting state legislators—just under 0.1 percent—did not belong to either of the two major parties. And all were independents, not members of third parties. Just 2 of the 50 state governors in 1999 were not Republicans or Democrats (Maine's Angus King, an independent, and Minnesota's Jesse Ventura, a member of the Reform party).

Third-party victories have tended to be few and far between. In the early 1900s the Socialist party did manage to win a few seats in the New York State legislature. And in the years before World War II, the Farmer Labor party and Progressive party enjoyed victories in Minnesota and Wisconsin, respectively. In recent years, third-party movements have tended to spring from splits within one or the other major party. The Conservative party in New York, for example, is an offshoot of the Republican party. (In 1996 five third parties appeared on the New York ballot: Liberal, Conservative, Right-to-Life, Independence, and Freedom.)

See 233 Do Republicans or Democrats control more state governments?

Q 292. What is the most active third-party movement today?

A The Libertarian party, which fields antigovernment candidates, is currently the most active third party. However, the party holds no governorships or seats in any of the state legislatures.

Q 293. What are the basic types of mass media campaign ads?

A Radio and television campaign spots can be divided into two broad categories, negative (attack) ads and generic ads. Negative ads remain a potent campaign weapon, in spite of widespread criticism of them. They come in several basic varieties, including "hit-and-run" (connecting the target candidate to an unpopular cause or event), "comedy" (ridiculing the target candidate), "not-on-the-job" (criticizing the candidate's work ethic), and "flip-flop" (attacking the candidate's record on issues).

Generic ads also come in several varieties. "Testimonial" spots rely on an ordinary citizen, relative, or celebrity to tell voters why they should vote for the candidate. "Feel good" ads focus on the voters' sense of place and local pride, while "sainthood" spots glorify what the candidate has done or will do in office. Lastly, "bumper-sticker" policy ads focus attention on popular themes in the campaign.

Q **294. In what state was the first major negative ad campaign conducted by political consultants?**

A The California gubernatorial campaign of 1934 saw the first, a full-scale media blitz with radio and movie attack ads, leaflets, and even negative cartoons. Concerned about the voter appeal Democratic candidate Upton Sinclair, a socialist, and his "End Poverty in California" platform would have in the middle of the depression, the Republican party hired outside media and political consultants to organize a negative campaign. The campaign put Republican candidate Frank Merriam in office by a 250,000-vote margin.

Q **295. How do the media become involved in campaigns?**

A Newspaper, magazine, radio, and television coverage of election issues and events is only one way the media get involved in political campaigns. They report on public opinion polls that help define issues and identify the popularity of candidates in the months and weeks leading up to the election. Through editorials, news commentary, and outright endorsements the media have an even more direct impact on voters' decisions. Radio and television debates sponsored by the media also can have a significant impact on election outcomes. And more recently, newspapers have begun critiquing campaign ads that appear on television, offering an assessment of the facts (or lack of them) as presented in the ad.

Q **296. How much did state parties collect in a recent election cycle?**

A Elections have become more and more expensive in recent years—the average of total spending on gubernatorial races in the early 1980s was just under $500 million, for example. By the late 1980s that average had shot up to just under $600 million. The scramble for additional funding has forced party organizations at both the state and federal levels to set ever higher goals for campaign funding. As a result, overall collections for state organizations of both parties in 1991–1992 neared the $200 million mark—Democratic state parties collected a total of $93.6 million, while their Republican counterparts took in just under $93 million.

Q **297. How many states hold primaries for statewide elections?**

A Although in-state candidates were once selected by state party conventions, all states today have provisions for primaries at one stage or another in the election process.

See 308 Which states select party candidates through nominating conventions?

Q **298. What is a direct primary?**

A This is the type of primary states use to decide which candidates will get party nominations for the general election. By casting ballots in the direct primary, voters themselves make the final selection of the candidates for each party, rather than leaving the choice to delegates at a party convention or caucus (thus the name *direct primary*).

The direct primary was intended to weaken party control of the nomination process and succeeded in doing so. Today all states include the primary as part of the nominating process, although in a few of them it can be bypassed.

See 308 Which states select party candidates through nominating conventions? 338 When was the first primary held?

Q **299. Have candidates for state office always won their nominations through primaries?**

A No, at first party members serving in the legislature gathered in what was called a party caucus to select the party's nominees. By the mid-1800s, however, party conventions had replaced the caucuses in the nominating process. Convention delegates, selected at the county level, voted for the nominees.

Party leaders tightly controlled the conventions, though, and put forward only hand-picked candidates. For that reason, Progressive reformers in the early 1900s pushed for direct primaries, in which voters would decide the party nominee. As a result, states instituted the primaries, which had largely replaced conventions by the end of World War I.

See 308 Which states select party candidates through nominating conventions? 338 When was the first primary held?

Q **300. Is voter turnout for primaries high?**

A No, far fewer voters participate in primaries than in general elections. In recent years, the average turnout for mid-term election primaries has been about 24 percent of the voting-age population. That is significantly less than the 47 percent average turnout for the mid-term general election in 1994, for example.

See 264 What was the voter turnout for a recent gubernatorial election?

Q **301. What is the difference between closed and open primaries?**

A To vote in a *closed primary* you must be a registered member of the party holding the primary. In an *open primary* you do not have to be a member of the party to vote in its primary. Primaries in seventeen states are closed, while nine states hold open primaries.

There are two variations on this basic theme of closed or open primaries, however. States with a more flexible version of the closed primary allow voters to register with a party, or even to switch their party registration, on election day. Ten states have this type of semi-closed primary. Eleven others have a slightly more restrictive version of the open primary—a semi-open primary. Here, the voter must specify at the polling place which party primary he or she will be voting in, and so can only vote for candidates of one party. But party membership is not required.

See 307 What type of primary is held in my state?

Q **302. What is a blanket primary?**

A In a blanket primary there is a single primary election for both parties, and voters can choose candidates of either party on an office-by-office basis. The only state to actually use this type of primary system is Washington. Alaska state law also provides for a blanket primary, but the Republican party allows only party members and independent voters to take part in its primary.

See 307 What type of primary is held in my state?

Q **303. Does any state hold a nonpartisan primary?**

A The only state to hold a nonpartisan primary is Louisiana. In this type of primary, which tends to favor incumbents, all candidates for state offices appear on the same ballot, and no party affiliations are given.

Any candidate who wins a majority of primary votes is automatically elected to office. The general election is reserved for cases in which there was no majority winner in the primary. The top two candidates for each of these posts run against each other, even if they are of the same party.

See 269 What is a plurality?

Q **304. How many states hold primary runoff elections?**

A Nine states hold primary runoffs when no candidate for a party's endorsement wins a majority of votes, or in some cases, wins less than a set percentage of votes. The top two contenders for each nomination that remains undecided face each other in the runoff primary, which is held soon after the initial primary. The winner then gets the party nomination for the general election.

Alabama, Arkansas, Florida, Georgia, Mississippi, North Carolina, Oklahoma, South Carolina, and Texas all hold runoff primaries. All are southern or border states, and all at one time were dominated by the Democratic party. The runoffs were believed necessary because the Democratic primary often fielded numerous candidates, and at times the contenders badly split the party vote. Without the runoff election, there was no way to be sure the winner had the support of the majority of Democrats in the state.

Louisiana also holds runoff primaries, but theirs is a nonpartisan primary system (see previous question).

Q **305. Do runoff elections tend to be divisive?**

A Yes, a bitterly contested primary battle between members of the same party can put the candidates at a disadvantage in the general election. Although incumbents tend to fare a bit better, one study found that when a Democratic gubernatorial candidate emerged from a tough primary fight, he or she could expect to poll an average of about 4.5 fewer votes per 100 cast in the general election.

Q **306. How often are runoffs necessary and how do candidates fare?**

A A single candidate usually wins a majority of votes in the primary race (or the required minimum percentage of the votes), so that no runoff is needed. Studies have shown that runoff primaries are held in only about 10 percent of the elections, and that about 70 percent of the candidates with the largest number of votes in the first primary also win the runoff primary.

Q **307. What type of primary is held in my state?**

A There are four basic types of primaries that are held to determine which candidates will get party endorsements—closed, semi-closed, open, and semi-open. In addition, there are two other variations, blanket and nonpartisan primaries, that are used in just three states. For more on the types of primaries, *see 301 What is the difference between closed and open primaries? 302 What is a blanket primary? 303 Does any state hold a nonpartisan primary?*

The type of primary held in your state is as follows:

State	Type of primary election	State	Type of primary election
Alabama	semi-open	Montana	open
Alaska	blanket	Nebraska	closed
Arizona	closed	Nevada	closed
Arkansas	semi-open	New Hampshire	semi-closed
California	closed	New Jersey	semi-closed
Colorado	semi-closed	New Mexico	closed
Connecticut	closed	New York	closed
Delaware	closed	North Carolina	closed
Florida	closed	North Dakota	open
Georgia	semi-open	Ohio	semi-closed
Hawaii	open	Oklahoma	closed
Idaho	open	Oregon	closed
Illinois	semi-open	Pennsylvania	closed
Indiana	semi-open	Rhode Island	semi-closed
Iowa	semi-closed	South Carolina	semi-open
Kansas	semi-closed	South Dakota	closed
Kentucky	closed	Tennessee	semi-open
Louisiana	nonpartisan	Texas	semi-open
Maine	semi-closed	Utah	open
Maryland	closed	Vermont	open
Massachusetts	semi-closed	Virginia	semi-open
Michigan	open	Washington	blanket
Minnesota	open	West Virginia	closed
Mississippi	semi-open	Wisconsin	open
Missouri	semi-open	Wyoming	semi-closed

Q 308. Which states select party candidates through nominating conventions?

A Conventions are a part of the nominating process in fifteen states. In some of those states, the party decides whether to nominate its candidates by convention or primary (Alabama, California, Colorado, and Virginia), while in others candidates for some offices are selected by primary and some by convention (Indiana, Michigan). Iowa and Kansas resort to party conventions only if their primaries are deemed inconclusive, and in South Carolina minority parties select their candidates by convention. Connecticut, New Mexico, New York, North Dakota, and Utah rely on conventions or party committees to endorse candidates for primary races.

Q 309. Is it possible to win a party's primary without endorsement by the convention?

A Yes, candidates can and sometimes do win their party's nomination based on the primary race alone. For example, New York governor Mario Cuomo failed to get the Democratic party's convention endorsement in 1982, but he went on to win the Democratic primary. The candidate must have a strong personal campaign organization to win the nomination in this manner, however.

Q 310. What offices are frequently filled through nonpartisan elections?

A Judges and local government officials are often, though not always, selected by nonpartisan elections. In this type of race, candidates are simply listed on the ballot and no party affiliation is given. The idea is to keep party politics out of the process of selecting these candidates, because of the nature of their work. Judges, for example, must make impartial decisions based on the law, not party politics. Likewise, local officials have charge of providing basic public services, and in many localities voters want to keep partisan politics out of the decision-making process.

See 265 Which state holds nonpartisan elections for state offices? 303 Does any state hold a nonpartisan primary?

Q 311. What is patronage?

A Making an appointment or hiring someone based on party loyalty is called *patronage*. Though patronage in state governments has been sharply reduced, governors and legislators still have ways of rewarding their personal allies and other party members. For example, the governor often controls choice appointments to state boards that oversee such activities as licensing professionals, higher education, and environmental protection. The same is true of hiring consultants and awarding certain contracts, which the governor can steer to his or her supporters.

"The unions and civil service have just about put an end to patronage. We still have a personnel office that checks with county chairmen to fill what jobs we have. But the jobs just aren't there anymore."

—Former Pennsylvania Governor Robert Casey

Patronage was much more widespread in the beginning of this century. Political parties tightly controlled the hiring of most state workers and used that power to put party members, qualified or not, in state jobs. But the growth of civil service programs (based on merit), unionization of state employees, and public criticism of patronage combined to change these practices.

Q 312. How did the Supreme Court decision in *Elrod v. Burns* affect state parties?

A By the 1970s, the number of patronage jobs—state and local government jobs given to members of the party in power as a reward for their loyalty—had already been sharply limited. But in some areas, such as Cook County, Illinois, patronage continued to be a problem.

That finally led to a U.S. Supreme Court ruling in *Elrod v. Burns,* which in 1976 barred a key practice in the patronage system. The Court ruled the Democratic party in Cook County could not fire non–civil service employees based on their party affiliation. Fourteen years later, the Court ruled against another element of the patronage system in *Rutan v. Republican Party* (1990). Here it said the Illinois Republican party could not base hiring, promotion, or transfer decisions for state jobholders on party affiliation and support, unless those considerations were "an appropriate requirement" for the job.

Q 313. Where do state parties get their funding?

A State parties raise a large part of their funds from individual contributors, from individual businesses, unions, professional groups, and other interest groups, and from political action committees (PACs). They also receive substantial amounts from their national party organizations for candidate support and for party-building activities. In addition, the state parties receive public funding for campaign expenses, in states that offer them.

In the 1991–1992 election cycle, Republican state parties received a larger percentage of their contributions from individuals than did Democrats (Republicans collected 57 percent from individuals, Democrats 38 percent).

Q 314. What is the Ranney index?

A The Ranney index provides a way of measuring the degree of control over state governments by the Republican and Democratic parties. Developed by the political scientist Austin Ranney, it takes into account three basic factors: (1) the percentage of votes for governor captured by each party and the percentage of seats in the legislature they hold, (2) how long the parties have controlled the governorship and the legislature, and (3) how much of the time the two parties have divided control of the governorship and the legislature. Ranney then uses these numbers to calculate his index of control, which ranges from 0 for complete Republican control to 1 for total Democratic control. A value of 0.5 means the two parties are highly competitive with one another.

See 122 Do Republicans or Democrats control more governorships? 233 Do Republicans or Democrats control more state governments? 262 In which states have Democrats and Republicans dominated elections in recent years?

GUBERNATORIAL RACES

Q 315. Why have governors' races become so expensive?

A Various factors have driven up the campaign costs in recent years. As states have become more important in the scheme of government during past decades, the office of governor has grown more attractive, both as an end in itself and as a stepping stone to national office. For that reason, more candidates have entered gubernatorial races, creating competition and extra expense in primary and general election races.

The business of campaigning has become more complex as well. Candidates must pay for such things as opinion polls, political consultants, direct mailings to voters, computers, and phone banks. Because the campaign is statewide, they are also forced to spend huge sums on media advertising, as well as a healthy amount for air travel and other types of transport so that they can reach voters throughout the state.

Another reason for rising costs stems from the increasing competitiveness of the two parties in state races. Democrats, for example, no longer dominate southern states as they once did. This has made a larger number of gubernatorial races more competitive, and more expensive.

See 122 Do Republicans or Democrats control more governorships? 233 Do Republicans or Democrats control more state governments? 334 What was the most expensive gubernatorial race to date?

▶ Can governors and lieutenant governors be elected from different parties?

See 140 How many states elect their governors and lieutenant governors as a team?

▶ When was the first black elected state governor?

See 117 Who was the first black governor elected to office?

Q 316. How does campaign spending vary from state to state?

A Both the average spending and the spending per vote vary considerably from state to state. Gubernatorial campaigns in recent decades have cost only an average of between $1 million and $2 million in Delaware, Idaho, New Hampshire, South Dakota, and Wyoming, for example, and less than $1 million in Vermont and North Dakota. At the high end, though, are Texas and California, where governors' races averaged $39.6 million and $28.6 million, respectively.

Based on average spending per vote, Wisconsin campaigns cost the least—only $1.12 per vote. Alaska gubernatorial campaigns are far and away the per-vote spending leaders at $23.82 per registered voter. The table below shows average costs, state by state, in 1993 dollars. Averages are based on spending for elections as far back as the 1950s for some states (from 1980 for North Dakota and West Virginia).

State	Average cost of gubernatorial elections (in millions)	Average spent per registered vote (in dollars)
Texas	$39.6	$4.69
California	28.6	1.90
New York	25.1	2.78
Louisiana	24.7	10.98
Florida	22.3	3.41

(table continues)

(continued)

State	Average cost of gubernatorial elections (in millions)	Average spent per registered vote (in dollars)
Kentucky	19.3	9.31
New Jersey	18.7	4.60
Illinois	14.9	2.25
Pennsylvania	11.9	1.99
Tennessee	11.7	4.28
Michigan	11.5	2.65
Virginia	11.5	3.77
Ohio	11.4	1.74
North Carolina	11.1	2.92
West Virginia	10.5	10.93
Alabama	10.4	4.38
Massachusetts	8.8	2.62
Missouri	8.4	2.75
Georgia	7.7	2.42
Alaska	7.3	23.82
Mississippi	7.3	4.43
Indiana	6.4	2.02
Minnesota	6.4	2.00
Hawaii	5.9	12.66
Washington	5.7	2.02
Connecticut	5.4	2.78
Oklahoma	5.4	2.36
Maryland	5.4	2.19
Arizona	5.3	2.72
Kansas	5.2	3.80
South Carolina	4.5	2.91
Nebraska	4.2	4.39
Wisconsin	4.0	1.12
Iowa	4.0	2.38
Rhode Island	3.8	6.93
Colorado	3.7	1.87
Maine	3.6	4.39
Arkansas	3.6	2.72

(table continues)

(continued)

State	Average cost of gubernatorial elections (in millions)	Average spent per registered vote (in dollars)
New Mexico	3.5	4.91
Oregon	3.3	1.86
Nevada	3.2	4.98
Utah	2.8	2.91
Montana	2.3	4.33
Wyoming	1.8	7.87
Idaho	1.8	2.99
New Hampshire	1.7	2.54
South Dakota	1.6	3.67
Delaware	1.3	3.83
Vermont	0.9	2.47
North Dakota	0.8	1.70
Overall average	8.6	3.87

Source: Virginia Gray and Herbert Jacob, *Politics in the American States,* 6th ed. (Washington, D.C.: CQ Press, 1996), 216–217.

Q 317. Are there any third-party governors today?

A Only two governors—Maine's Angus S. King, Jr., and Minnesota's Jesse Ventura—are not affiliated with either the Democratic or Republican party. Just the fourth governor elected to office as an independent since 1950, King is a rarity in state political circles. Ventura is the first Reform party member to be elected governor.

See 291 Have third parties succeeded at the state level? 324 How many state legislators are not affiliated with the Democratic or Republican parties?

Q 318. How many governorships will be up for grabs in the year 2000? 2002?

A Just eleven states will elect governors in the year 2000, which also happens to be a presidential election year. In nine of the states voters will also decide on who will be the lieutenant governor.

The year 2002 will be a year in which most states elect their governor and other top officials. Thirty-eight states will hold gubernatorial elections then. Thirty-two will also elect lieutenant governors and thirty, attorneys general. Lieutenant governor and attorney general posts are filled by appointment in the rest of the states holding elections in 2002. (*See also individual state profiles in Chapter 7 for the year in which the term of the governor in your state ends.*)

See 262 In which states have Democrats and Republicans dominated elections in recent years? 267 When do states usually hold elections?

Q 319. Do governors control the state party organization?

A No, governors generally do not try to run their state party apparatus. Instead, governors and the chair of the state party usually try to coordinate with each other on important party activities, including fund-raising, recruiting candidates, and gubernatorial appointments. Governors often seek to have a political ally named as the party chair, but they do not always succeed. Governors in some states do manage to gain considerable control over the party, but it is by no means the rule.

As for the election campaigns, most governors today bypass the state apparatus in favor of their own organizations, which of course they do control.

Q 320. Has a gubernatorial candidate ever taken office based solely on a primary victory?

A Two Democratic Louisiana governors, Edwin Edwards and Charles E. Roemer, III, took office based on primary wins alone. Louisiana's nonpartisan primary allows candidates for state posts to take office directly, if they win a majority of the primary votes. No general election is required. Edwards took office after winning the 1983 primary, and Roemer did so after his 1987 primary win.

▶Why do governors have a harder time getting reelected than other state officials?

See 261 Which incumbent state official faces the greatest chance of losing a reelection bid?

▶Who were the first brothers elected simultaneously to serve as governor?

See 132 Which two brothers were first to serve as governor at the same time?

321. How many votes did the Republican and Democratic gubernatorial candidates get in recent elections?

A The following tallies are for the 1998 gubernatorial elections, unless otherwise indicated.

State	Votes cast for Republican candidate	Votes cast for Democratic candidate	Votes cast for Independent candidate
Alabama	554,633	758,536	
Alaska	32,713	97,220	
Arizona	555,384	328,728	
Arkansas	421,376	272,622	
California	2,842,173	4,305,746	
Colorado	626,559	621,801	
Connecticut	607,672	342,011	
Delaware*	169,733	70,236	
Florida	2,181,373	1,769,233	
Georgia	790,071	944,070	
Hawaii	198,951	204,204	
Idaho	250,805	107,616	
Illinois*	1,698,462	1,561,144	
Indiana*	822,533	1,382,151	
Iowa	444,922	499,222	
Kansas	529,446	163,595	
Kentucky*	237,069	616,558	
Louisiana	—	—	
Maine	77,627	48,836	239,194
Maryland	662,554	826,609	
Massachusetts	965,008	900,171	
Michigan	1,875,501	1,136,541	
Minnesota	712,706		767,492
Mississippi*	361,500	338,435	
Missouri*	1,339,531	724,919	
Montana*	209,401	198,421	
Nebraska	289,690	246,982	
Nevada	223,798	182,238	
New Hampshire	101,475	209,851	
New Jersey*	838,553	1,379,937	

(Continued)

State	Votes cast for Republican candidate	Votes cast for Democratic candidate	Votes cast for Independent candidate
New Mexico	264,863	223,607	
New York	2,427,874	1,442,925	
North Carolina*	1,121,955	1,368,246	
North Dakota*	119,986	179,094	
Ohio	1,650,061	1,470,964	
Oklahoma	505,498	357,552	
Oregon	229,078	482,308	
Pennsylvania	1,725,744	929,198	
Rhode Island	150,787	124,435	
South Carolina	479,086	561,332	
South Dakota	166,602	85,409	
Tennessee	668,687	287,241	
Texas	2,567,898	1,156,727	
Utah*	321,713	177,181	
Vermont	86,624	116,731	
Virginia*	1,045,319	733,527	
Washington*	1,086,216	1,184,315	
West Virginia*	240,390	368,302	
Wisconsin	1,048,897	678,998	
Wyoming	97,299	70,661	

Notes:

* Vote tallies are from an earlier election

— No general election tallies available

LEGISLATIVE RACES

Q 322. How are legislative campaign committees organized and why are they necessary?

A Usually headed by party leaders in the legislative chambers, these committees, one for each house, are made up of party members in the chamber. Democratic and Republican house or senate campaign committees, or caucuses, as they are sometimes called, provide all the essential party support services to candidates, including fund-raising, polling services, media advertising services, and other logistical support for campaigns. They also recruit candidates.

These committees became increasingly important as competition for control of state legislatures intensified, legislative campaigns became more costly, and from the 1970s onward, state central committees proved unable to provide the added help state legislators needed. Today, legislative campaign committees raise millions of dollars in campaign funds and distribute them to legislators in their respective parties.

See 287 How are state parties organized?

Q **323. What are leadership PACs?**

A These PACs, or political action committees, are organized by leaders in the state legislatures—Speakers, majority and minority leaders, and other powerful legislative figures. Lawmakers who have leadership roles generally raise more campaign funds than they need for themselves, which means they often can distribute money to campaigns of other legislators in their party. The leadership PACs are generally used to transfer this extra money, which of course also increases the leader's influence over those who receive it. Leadership PAC funds are also sometimes used to further the leader's own interests.

See 357 What are PACs? 358 Do PACs contribute a large part of candidates' campaign funds?

Q **324. How many state legislators are not affiliated with the Democratic or Republican parties?**

A As of 1996 only 18 state legislators of the 7,399 in office did not belong to either of the major parties (excluding Nebraska's nonpartisan legislature). Four of the senators were elected as independents (two in California and one each in Maine and South Carolina). Thirteen house members were independents—three in Mississippi and four in South Carolina. Vermont had two independents and one Progressive party member.

See 122 Do Republicans or Democrats control more governorships? 233 Do Republicans or Democrats control more state governments? 291 Have third parties succeeded at the state level? 317 Are there any third-party governors today?

▶Who was the first elected black state legislator?

See 237 When was the first black elected to a state legislature?

▶Who became the first woman state senator?

See 243 When was the first woman elected to a state senate?

JUDICIAL ELECTIONS

 325. How many states allow partisan judicial elections?

A Thirteen states hold partisan elections for judges in the appellate and major trial courts. On the one hand, this type of election promotes accountability of judges to the voters. But judges in partisan elections must raise funds for their campaigns, leaving them open to influence by special interests and other major contributors.

The states with partisan judicial elections include:

Alabama	Mississippi	Pennsylvania
Arkansas	Missouri	Tennessee
Georgia	New York	Texas
Illinois	North Carolina	West Virginia
Indiana		

See 335 When was the first partisan judicial election?

326. How do judges become candidates on nonpartisan ballots?

A Unlike judicial candidates for partisan elections, who must secure a party nomination, candidates for nonpartisan elections have only to get a set number of signatures on petition to get on the ballot. In the election itself, the candidate who gets the largest number of votes wins the judgeship.

327. What is the Missouri plan?

A This system for appointing judges has been used in Missouri since 1940 and has been adopted (with variations) by other states. Usually a screening committee made up of lawyers and judges selects a number of qualified candidates based on merit (three candidates in Missouri), and the governor appoints one of them to an initial term. At the end of the term (one year in Missouri), voters then decide whether to retain the judge for another term (a retention election—see next question).

See 399 What are the five ways state court judges are selected? 400 Can politics influence merit plans?

Q 328. What are retention elections?

A Under the merit (Missouri) plans (see previous question), a judge appointed by the state's governor serves an initial one- or two-year term. The judge is then required to go before the voters in a retention election. The election is nonpartisan and the judge faces no challengers. Voters simply select "yes" or "no" on the question of whether the judge should serve another term. If a majority of voters say yes, the judge serves another term, often from eight to twelve years. Judges must be approved by voters again at the end of each term.

If the judge fails to get a majority of yes votes in a retention election, a commission of lawyers and judges nominates candidates for the judgeship on the basis of merit, and the governor chooses one of the nominees.

Q 329. Are nonpartisan judicial elections free from problems?

A Low voter turnout in nonpartisan (and partisan) judicial elections is a problem, because so few voters have a say in deciding which candidate wins the office. Also, the low voter interest in judicial campaigns means incumbents tend to win reelection so long as they are willing to run. Both of these factors mean that judges are not really accountable to voters, which is the purpose of holding judicial elections in the first place.

Another concern of both nonpartisan and partisan judicial elections is the fact that judges must raise funds to pay for the campaigns. As judicial campaigns have become more expensive, the prospect of judges being influenced by large campaign contributions has become a concern.

Q 330. Do judges have political party preferences?

A Although judges in most states run in nonpartisan elections and are generally able to rule impartially, the majority of them do in fact have party preferences. Past surveys have shown that 95 percent of judges prefer one party or another. Judges usually state a party preference in their official biographies.

See 394 To which party does the majority of judges belong?

Q **331. How often are incumbent judges turned out of office in retention elections?**

A Less than 3 percent of judges have failed to win retention elections in the over fifty years that these elections have been held. Part of the reason is that voters are not especially interested in judicial elections and turnout for retention elections is very low. From time to time, however, a judge's decisions will spark a major controversy and galvanize the electorate. A Florida supreme court judge only narrowly won a 1990 retention election, for example, after striking down a state law requiring parental consent for a teenager's abortion.

▶Are more judges Democrats or Republicans?

See 394 To which party does the majority of judges belong?

FOR THE RECORD

Q **332. Which state was first to lower the voting age to eighteen?**

A Georgia did so by amending its constitution in 1943, and the first election in which eighteen-year-olds could vote was held November 7, 1944. The voting age for federal elections was not lowered to eighteen until almost three decades later in 1971.

Q **333. When did the first state grant voting rights to women?**

A Women in Wyoming had been voting since the territory was formed, and when Wyoming became a state on July 10, 1890, the state became the first to grant them the vote. The state's constitution included a provision specifically allowing women the right to vote.

Q **334. What was the most expensive gubernatorial race to date?**

A The 1998 gubernatorial race in California was the most expensive to date. Based on preliminary reports, the two major party candidates, Gray Davis (D) and Daniel Lungren (R), raised just over $60 million and spent nearly that much during their hotly contested race.

California races are usually more expensive than those in most other states, because the state has a large population and covers a large territory. The competitiveness of the 1998 race only added to the campaign expenses.

Other states that, like California, are both large and heavily populated are Texas and New York. Gubernatorial races in these states also tend to be expensive.

See 315 Why have governors' races become so expensive?

Q 335. When was the first partisan judicial election?

A Mississippi became the first state to institute partisan elections for judges in 1832. The system is now in use in thirteen states for upper-level judicial posts.

See 325 How many states allow partisan judicial elections?

Do states elect all of their top government officials?

See 153 Which state elects, rather than appoints, the most top officials?

Q 336. When was the first state voter registration law passed?

A Massachusetts passed the first law requiring voters to register to vote on March 7, 1801. Massachusetts also passed the first literacy test for voters on May 1, 1857. Voters were required to be able to read the state constitution and to sign their name (the aged and people with disabilities were excepted).

Q 337. Which state does not require voters to register?

A North Dakota is the only state that does not require voter registration. Three states do allow voters to register on the day of the election, however—Maine, Minnesota, and Wisconsin.

See 272 Do voter registration rules affect turnout? 301 What is the difference between closed and open primaries?

Q 338. When was the first primary held?

A The first state to adopt the primary was Wisconsin, in 1907. Wisconsin's primary was a reform measure intended to limit party control over the nomination process, and by 1917 most states had adopted the primary.

See 297 How many states hold primaries for statewide elections? 299 Have candidates for state office always won their nominations through primaries?

Q 339. Which state was the last to adopt the primary system for selecting candidates for state elective offices?

A Connecticut was the last. It adopted a "challenge" primary system in 1955. Under this system, candidates are still selected at party conventions and caucuses. But if any contenders for the nomination receive 20 percent or more of the convention or caucus votes, a primary runoff between them must be held.

Fifteen years passed before Connecticut's first contested primary, but since then they have steadily become more frequent.

See 297 How many states hold primaries for statewide elections? 299 Have candidates for state office always won their nominations through primaries?

Q 340. What one state holds a nonpartisan primary?

A Louisiana is the only state to hold this type of primary. Ballots for state officers list all candidates for each office but do not include party identifications. When no candidate for governor (or other office) receives a majority of the votes, the two top candidates for the office run against each other in the general election. If a candidate does get a majority of primary votes, he or she is considered the winner and no general election for the office is held.

Although Nebraska has a nonpartisan government, its primary is classified as a closed primary.

See 320 Has a gubernatorial candidate ever taken office based solely on a primary victory?

▶Which party is winning more elections in the states?

See 233 Do Republicans or Democrats control more state governments?

Q 341. Where was the first state nominating convention held?

A Utica, New York, hosted the first convention to select nominees for New York governor and lieutenant governor in 1824. The now-defunct Democratic-Republican party organized the convention and chose De Witt Clinton as the party nominee. Clinton was elected governor in the fall of 1824.

Q 342. In which state was the Republican party founded?

A The Republican party got its start at Jackson, Michigan, on July 6, 1854. On that day a state convention of the new party adopted both the name *Republican party* and its first platform, and nominated its first candidates as well. Opponents of slavery had formed the party in reaction to passage of the Kansas-Nebraska Act (1854), which extended slavery into the western states. The name *Republican* was derived from Thomas Jefferson's defunct party, the Democratic-Republican party.

Q 343. When did the Democratic party adopt its name?

A The Democratic party got its name during the 1828 presidential campaign of Andrew Jackson. Jackson, a member of the faltering Democratic-Republican party formed by Thomas Jefferson, organized the wing of the party supporting him into a new populist-based party during the 1828 campaign. The new party took the name *Democrats* during the campaign. Jackson's victory in 1828 provided a solid foundation for the new Democratic party, which held its first nominating convention in 1832.

Q 344. Where were the first citizen initiatives approved?

A Voters in Oregon approved the first two in 1902. Citizen initiatives passed that year to allow localities to accept or ban liquor sales within their boundaries and to make primaries mandatory. However, Oregon was not the first state to enact the initiative process. That distinction goes to South Dakota, which did so in 1898.

See 32 Can state constitutions be changed? 35 How many states permit voters to decide constitutional questions by citizen initiatives?

Q 345. When was the first time two brothers faced each other in a gubernatorial election?

A The first brothers to run against each other were Robert and Alfred Taylor, who were candidates in the 1886 Tennessee gubernatorial race. Robert won the governorship by over fifteen thousand votes and eventually served from 1887 to 1891 and from 1897 to 1899. Alfred was not to be denied, however, and some three decades later finally won the Tennessee governorship in 1920 (but not from brother Robert). Alfred served from 1921 to 1923.

See 132 Which two brothers were first to serve as governor at the same time?

Q **346. What is the difference between an initiative and a referendum?**

A Both of these measures appear on the ballot and must be approved by voters in the state. Generally speaking, the difference lies in how the measure gets onto the ballot in the first place. An initiative goes on the ballot because a minimum number of voters have signed a petition requesting a vote on the measure.

A referendum, on the other hand, goes on the ballot because voters must approve action taken by the legislature. For example, all states except Alabama require voter approval of state constitutional amendments, once they have been passed by the legislature.

Q **347. Is there more than one type of initiative?**

A Initiatives come in two types. The first is the *legislative initiative,* in which citizens can petition to have a proposed law put on the ballot. If voters approve, the measure becomes law. In three states, however, once the required number of petition signatures have been gathered, the proposed law goes to the legislature first. If the legislature does not approve it, then the measure appears on the ballot.

The second type of initiative is the *constitutional initiative.* Here, voters can petition to have a constitutional amendment put on the ballot. *(See also the next question for discussion of petition referendums.)*

See 32 Can state constitutions be changed? 35 How many states permit voters to decide constitutional questions by citizen initiatives? 351 How many states allow initiatives?

Q **348. What types of referendums are there?**

A Though not all states have them, there are four types of referendums. The most common is the *constitutional referendum,* in which voters must approve an amendment to the state constitution that has passed the legislature. The amendment cannot take effect unless voters approve it. Another type is the *constitutionally mandated referendum,* or *general referendum,* which is used in nineteen states. Here voters are required to approve such things as bond issues and increases in state debt after the legislature has approved them, because the state constitution requires the referendum by voters. The legislature may also decide to put other measures on the ballot, and these are called *legislative referendums,* used by twenty-three states (see next question for list).

A hybrid is the *petition referendum,* in which voters petition to put legislation, passed by the legislature, on the ballot. Voters must approve the referendum before the legislation can become law. Twenty-four states have provisions for this type of referendum.

Q 349. How many states permit legislative referendums?

A Twenty-three states have provisions for legislative referendums. They are:

Arizona	Maryland	New Mexico
Arkansas	Massachusetts	North Dakota
California	Michigan	Ohio
Delaware	Missouri	Oklahoma
Idaho	Montana	Oregon
Illinois	Nebraska	South Dakota
Kentucky	Nevada	Utah
Maine		Washington

Q 350. Which states allow petition referendums?

A Twenty-four states have given voters the option of approving or rejecting laws passed by the legislature through petition referendums. The states are:

Alaska	Maryland	North Dakota
Arizona	Massachusetts	Ohio
Arkansas	Michigan	Oklahoma
California	Missouri	Oregon
Colorado	Montana	South Dakota
Idaho	Nebraska	Utah
Kentucky	Nevada	Washington
Maine	New Mexico	Wyoming

Q 351. How many states allow initiatives?

A Voters in eighteen states have the right to petition changes in their state constitutions (constitutional initiatives). Eighteen states also allow legislative initiatives, in which propositions to write or change state laws can be put on the ballot.

States allowing constitutional initiatives are:

Arizona	Massachusetts	Nevada
Arkansas	Michigan	North Dakota
California	Mississippi	Ohio
Colorado	Missouri	Oklahoma
Florida	Montana	Oregon
Illinois	Nebraska	South Dakota

States with legislative initiatives are:

Alaska	Missouri	Oklahoma
Arizona	Montana	Oregon
Arkansas	Nebraska	South Dakota
Colorado	Nevada	Utah
Idaho	North Dakota	Washington
Illinois	Ohio	Wyoming

Q 352. What factors affect the success of ballot propositions?

A According to a recent study, voters approved only about 44 percent of initiatives put on the ballot in the fifty states between 1981 and 1992. However, there are ways to improve the chances a proposition will succeed. The level of spending for media advertising and other efforts at promoting voter awareness of the issue are important. Some hotly contested propositions have involved many millions of dollars spent by supporters of both sides. Also, propositions that originate with voters (as opposed to those from the legislature) tend to fare better at the polls. Another practical concern is ballot position—listing the proposition closer to the top increases the chance voters will approve it.

Q 353. Why was California's Proposition 13 so important?

A Passed by California voters in 1978, Proposition 13 marked the beginning of a broader taxpayer revolt against high taxes. The proposition itself rolled back property taxes in California, forcing the state government to cut back spending because of the lost revenue. But Proposition 13 became the rallying cry for antitax movements in many other states as well. And it was an issue tailor made for Republican conservatives. In the hands of Ronald Reagan and others, Proposition 13 served as an effective argument against big government and the taxing and spending policies that support it.

Q 354. Are propositions more common today?

A Between 1987 and 1992, the number of propositions in states nationwide totaled 202, an increase of 40 percent over the number recorded in the early 1980s. In fact, propositions have been becoming more popular since the 1970s, when environmental, antitax, and other activists turned to voter initiatives as a means of forcing change.

During the early 1990s initiatives have centered on a number of issues. Term limits proved a potent subject, and voters in fourteen states approved them for their members of Congress in 1992 alone. Other initiatives in recent years have routinely centered on environmental issues, gambling and other questions of public morality, taxes and spending, and regulation of industry. In 1997 voters approved another controversial California proposition, which dismantled the state's affirmative action program and sparked a nationwide reevaluation of such programs.

CAMPAIGN FINANCE

Q 355. How many states provide public financing for election campaigns?

A Twenty-three states have public financing programs for political campaign expenses. States generate the funds by various means, including a checkoff system on state income tax forms, taxpayer surcharges, direct appropriations, or by diverting a particular type of state revenue, such as fees for personalized auto license plates. Some states allocate funds only to gubernatorial candidates, while others direct the money to the party designated by a taxpayer (in the checkoff system). Candidates or parties accepting the funds usually must agree to limit campaign spending. The states with public campaign financing are:

Alabama	Kentucky	North Carolina
California	Maryland	Ohio
Florida	Massachusetts	Rhode Island
Hawaii	Michigan	Utah
Idaho	Minnesota	Virginia
Indiana	Nebraska	Wisconsin
Iowa	New Jersey	

Q **356. Do states allow corporations to contribute to state election campaigns?**

A About half the states allow corporations to contribute part of their profits to election campaigns of state officials. Many states also allow labor unions to use money from their treasuries for campaign contributions.

Q **357. What are PACs?**

A Political action committees—PACs—are organizations set up to raise funds and distribute them to political parties and candidates. PACs were initially created to circumvent federal and state laws barring contributions to candidates by corporations and labor unions. They are in fact perfectly legal, and a wide range of groups have formed PACS, including business groups (financial and insurance groups, utilities), labor and employee groups, professional associations (especially health care), and single-issue activist groups (those promoting environmental causes, antigambling groups, and various others).

See 254 What are the most influential lobbying groups? 313 Where do state parties get their funding? 323 What are leadership PACs?

Q **358. Do PACs contribute a large part of candidates' campaign funds?**

A Yes, PAC funding for gubernatorial and legislative candidates accounts for a major portion of both candidate and state party contributions. In some cases PAC contributions can amount to 50 percent or more of all contributions. For example, PAC contributions accounted for over three-quarters of the $7.1 million Illinois legislative leaders raised in 1992.

Q **359. How many states require campaign finance reporting?**

A Every state requires timely reports of campaign finances, usually by the candidates themselves, political committees, and political parties. Laws in many states also require reporting from other individuals and groups involved with the election process, if they received more than a minimum amount of contributions or spent over a certain amount on campaign expenses.

Q 360. Do states have independent commissions to monitor compliance with campaign finance laws?

A Twenty-six states have election commissions that are charged with enforcing campaign finance laws. However, in all but a few states the commissions have been only partly successful in maintaining compliance.

Q 361. Which states have no limits on campaign contributions?

A Six states do not impose limits on the amount of contributions by individuals or organizations—Colorado, Idaho, Illinois, New Mexico, Utah, and Virginia. Nine other states impose limits on contributions by organizations, but not on those by individuals. These nine are Alabama, Indiana, Iowa, Mississippi, Nebraska, North Dakota, Ohio, Pennsylvania, and Texas.

See 355 How many states provide public financing for election campaigns?

Q 362. Can campaign donations be made anonymously?

A Not in most states. Campaign reporting requirements on individuals are such that most states either prohibit anonymous donations or limit them to very small amounts, such as $50 or less. The eleven states that do not prohibit or sharply restrict anonymous contributions are Alabama, Florida, Indiana, Maine, Mississippi, South Dakota, Tennessee, Utah, Vermont, Virginia, and Wyoming.

WHERE CAN I FIND. . .

Resources described below provide more information on topics discussed in this chapter.

Books

American State Governors, 1776–1976. Joseph E. Kallenbach. Dobbs Ferry, N.Y.: Oceana Publications, 1977.

In addition to providing biographies of individual governors, this book covers gubernatorial election statistics state by state back to 1776. Kallenbach also discusses, for each state, the history of the governor's term of office, qualifications for office, state constitutions, and the like.

America Votes 23: A Handbook of Contemporary American Election Statistics. Richard M. Scammon, Alice V. McGillivray, and Rhodes Cook. Washington, D.C.: Congressional Quarterly Inc., 1999.

Published every two years, it provides statistics on gubernatorial races, as well as congressional and presidential contests. The current edition covers 1997 and 1998 election results.

The Book of the States, 1996–1997. Lexington, Ky.: Council of State Governments, 1997.

An annual compilation of tables presenting comparative information about each of the states, this book has sections on campaigns and elections, as well as on the various branches of state government, state finances, employment, and other topics.

Campaign Finance, Lobbying and Ethics Legislation, 1996. Denver: National Conference of State Legislatures, 1997.

This booklet surveys recent legislative activity in campaign finance, ethics, and lobbying in thirty states. It includes useful summaries of the legislation, arranged by state.

Campaign Finance in State Legislative Elections. Joel A. Thompson and Gary F. Moncrief. Washington, D.C.: Congressional Quarterly Inc., 1997.

Based on data from over fifteen states, this book presents a broad study of campaign contributions and spending in state legislative elections.

Guide to U.S. Elections, 3d ed. Ed. John L. Moore. Washington, D.C.: Congressional Quarterly Inc., 1994.

Though the focus of this large tome is on federal elections, it has a chapter on gubernatorial elections, including a history and statistics (to 1993), as well as other sections on the history of political parties, nominating conventions, and lists of party nominees from 1832 to 1988.

Politics in the American States: A Comparative Analysis, 7th ed. Virginia Gray, Russell Hanson, and Herbert Jacob. Washington, D.C.: Congressional Quarterly Inc., 1999.

The book draws on a variety of surveys and other sources of interest to political scientists. Chapters are written by individual authors and cover a wide range of subjects relating to state government, including campaigns and elections, the legislature, interest groups, and so on.

Senate Election Law Guidebook. Senate Rules and Administration Committee. Washington, D.C.: Government Printing Office, 1998.

Federal and state laws concerning U.S. Senate elections, as well as other information on Senate campaigns.

State and Local Government, 2d ed. Ann Bowman and Richard Kearney. Boston: Houghton Mifflin Company, 1993.

A very readable textbook on state and local government, it is a valuable basic source of information on the history and mechanics of state government, including campaigns and elections.

State and Local Government: Politics and Public Policies. David Saffell and Harry Basehart. Boston: McGraw-Hill, 1998.

An up-to-date textbook, it combines coverage of the basics on state and local government with examination of current policy concerns. Among the chapters relevant here are the ones on political participation and elections, and on political parties and interest groups.

State Atlas of Political and Cultural Diversity. William Lilley, III, Laurence J. DeFranco, and William M. Diefenderfer, III. Washington, D.C.: Congressional Quarterly Inc., 1997.

This book is the first source for statistics on the states' ethnic and racial makeup by statehouse district. Maps of districts are provided for legislative districts with significant populations of fifteen ancestral groups.

State Government, 1999–2000: CQ's Guide to Current Issues and Activities. Thad Beyle. Washington, D.C.: Congressional Quarterly Inc., 1999.

This collection includes a number of readings on current issues related to campaigns and elections.

State Legislative Elections: Voting Patterns and Demographics. Michael Barone with William Lilley, III, and Laurence J. DeFranco. Washington, D.C.: Congressional Quarterly Inc., 1997.

An in-depth reference on state legislative elections, this book includes a summary treatment of each state, statistics on election-related demographics presented district by district, and maps showing the limits of each district. Every state in the Union is covered, and election results presented are for 1992 to 1996.

State Party Profiles: A 50-State Guide to Development, Organization, and Resources. Ed. Andrew M. Appleton and Daniel S. Ward. Washington, D.C.: Congressional Quarterly Inc., 1997.

A solid reference for the history of political parties at the state level, it includes information on organizational development and an assessment of party organizations today. The book also has a section on information resources on political parties for each state.

Organizations

California Voter Foundation, 2401 L St., 6th Floor, Sacramento, CA 95816. (916) 325-2120.

    This independent group collects and analyzes campaign finance information for current and past California races. It maintains a Web site at *www.calvoter.org.*

Census Bureau, Customer Service, Washington, D.C. 20233. Information: (301) 457-4100.

    The bureau disseminates census data on states, counties, and municipalities as well as on the nation as a whole.

Federal Election Commission, 999 E. St., N.W., Washington, D.C. 20463. Information: (202) 219-4155.

    The FEC Public Records division makes available campaign finance reports.

National Library on Money and Politics, 1320 19th St., N.W., Washington, D.C. 20036. Information: (202) 857-0318.

    This nonprofit organization provides the media and others with research and analysis on campaign financing.

V
STATE COURTS

IN GENERAL

Q 363. What is the highest state court?

A State supreme courts are the "courts of last resort," the highest in the state legal systems. These courts hear appeals of lower court rulings and have original jurisdiction in cases dealing with state constitutional issues and certain other matters. All but four states use the name supreme court. The others use court of appeals (Maryland and New York), supreme court of appeals (West Virginia), or supreme judicial court (Maine).

Oklahoma and Texas have two supreme courts—one for criminal cases, the court of criminal appeals, and one for civil cases, the supreme court.

See 380 In what cases do supreme courts have original jurisdiction? 382 Are there any cases in which the state supreme court is not the final authority?

Q 364. What are the three basic levels of state courts?

A The three tiers are, from lowest to highest, courts of limited jurisdiction, major trial courts, and appellate courts. Juvenile, family, and small claims courts belong in the first level because they have jurisdiction over only the cases that fall within a well-defined area. On the other hand, major trial courts (such as county or district courts) have jurisdiction over civil and criminal cases generally and usually try those that involve more serious matters. (They also hear appeals of limited jurisdiction courts.) Appellate courts, including intermediate appellate and supreme courts, are at the top of the court system. They hear appeals from the major trial courts.

See 382 Are there any cases in which the state supreme court is not the final authority? 385 How are appellate courts usually organized? 386 About what percentage of lower court rulings are appealed? 388 What types of specialized courts are there?

Q 365. How many new cases do state courts hear in a year?

A Each year state courts handle tens of millions of cases, ranging from minor infractions to multimillion-dollar class-action suits and major crimes like kidnapping and murder. A nationwide survey of state court caseloads in 1988 put the total for that year alone at 98 million new cases.

Lawsuits, which have been making news in recent years, represent only a fraction of the caseload (over a million of the cases filed during 1993 were lawsuits). Though the United States has more lawsuits per capita than any other country, experts are unsure whether the number of cases each year is actually increasing or merely keeping pace with the growing population. Criminal cases have increased significantly, however. New felony cases jumped by over 50 percent between 1984 and 1990.

Q 366. When was the first televised courtroom verdict?

A CBS televised the first, in a nationwide broadcast of the guilty verdict against Jack Ruby in a Dallas, Texas, criminal district court on March 14, 1964. Ruby had murdered President John F. Kennedy's assassin, Lee Harvey Oswald, in front of television cameras, and was himself sentenced to death while millions of television viewers across the country watched.

Q 367. Which state had the first night court?

A A magistrate's court in New York City became the first when it began night court hearings on September 1, 1907. Judge Charles Nathan Harris presided over sessions lasting between 8 P.M. and 3 A.M. (later shortened to 1 A.M.).

Q 368. What does a grand jury do?

A Grand juries have two functions. The first is to examine evidence against a person accused of a major crime, to determine whether the prosecutor has enough evidence to warrant a trial. The intent is to provide a check on prosecutorial powers, but in fact grand juries rarely refuse to indict those accused by the prosecutor. As a result, today about half the states have either done away with grand juries or only call them for capital cases. Instead, a preliminary hearing before a judge may be used to decide whether an indictment is warranted, or the prosecutor may simply file affidavits with the court.

The second function of grand juries is to investigate political corruption, organized crime, vice, and certain other crimes. Here the grand jury has the power to subpoena all the witnesses and evidence it needs to complete the investigation. It then decides by majority—not unanimous—vote of the jurors whether or not to indict.

See 412 How many people serve on a jury?

Q 369. How do civil, criminal, and administrative cases differ?

A Law suits for damages resulting from an auto accident, for defamation, or to recover property are all civil cases. Here there are grievances between individuals or organizations, but no law has been broken. Criminal cases involve an act by an individual or corporation that breaks a law. Robbery, fraud, and murder are all crimes, and in criminal cases the state usually acts as the plaintiff. Administrative cases include child custody cases, probating wills, and revocation of driver's licenses. They involve only an administrative action by the court.

Q 370. How have recent reforms improved the court systems in many states?

A In the past few decades many states have sought to make their court systems more efficient by centralizing administrative control of the various courts, and wherever possible to consolidate courts with overlapping jurisdictions. Under the ideal centralized system, budgeting, personnel management, record keeping, and other administrative duties for all courts statewide are handled by a single authority in the court system. In the past the individual courts handled these duties.

Q 371. Are there patterns to judges' decisions?

A Studies have shown that personal characteristics, such as age, sex, religion, ethnic background, and political ideology, do affect courtroom decisions. One study of state supreme court decisions showed, for example, that women judges tend to be more liberal than men. And Republican and Democratic judges have completely opposite tendencies when it comes to certain types of cases. For example, Republican judges tend to favor the landlord in landlord-tenant disputes, management in labor-management disputes, the taxpayer in tax cases, and the government prosecutor over the defendant in criminal cases.

Q 372. What is Dillon's Rule?

A This legal precedent was set in 1868 by Iowa judge John F. Dillon. In his ruling, judge Dillon held that local governments have only those powers that the state explicitly grants them, the powers implied in these explicit powers, and the powers absolutely essential to the purposes of local government. The rule effectively gives local government almost no discretionary power, and since 1868 federal and state courts have upheld the primacy of state government.

About half the states have granted local governments a range of powers, however, which allow them to take care of routine business without making special requests to the state.

Q 373. How much do state court judges earn?

A State supreme court justices generally earn about $90,000 a year, though the actual amount varies considerably from state to state. The District of Columbia, which is not a state, pays the highest salary to justices on its court of appeals, the highest court—$141,700. Of the states, New Jersey pays its supreme court justices the most, $138,000, followed closely by California at $137,400. Montana pays the least, $70,100.

Salaries of state trial court judges (district, circuit, superior) generally range about 10 to 20 percent less than those of supreme court justices.

See 87 What is the governor's salary? 129 How much do top elected officials get paid in my state? 141 How much do lieutenant governors get paid? 176 How much do legislators get paid?

Q 374. What do offices of court administration do?

A Every state has an office of court administration, but its role varies considerably from state to state. In many states these offices monitor and manage the court system and are involved with planning court operations and resource allocation. In some states, however, offices of court administration are concerned only with gathering statistics on court activities.

Q 375. Who pays for state court costs?

A Until fairly recently, municipal and county governments paid about three-quarters of the cost of running the courts. Since the 1970s, however, states have been paying an increasing share, as part of a nationwide effort at centralizing budgeting and finance for state court systems. Today over half the state governments pay all operating expenses for state and local courts. About twenty states have instituted centralized budget procedures as well.

Q 376. Why have case backlogs become such a problem?

A Courts in recent decades have been inundated with huge numbers of new cases, creating a serious case backlog and long delays in getting cases to trial. A rising crime rate was certainly part of the problem—felony filings increased by 50 percent between 1984 and 1990 alone—but experts point to a number of different causes for the excessive caseloads today. Law enforcement policy changes, for example, have led to big increases in drug arrests and drunk driving prosecutions. Appeals of lower court rulings are more likely now. Also, Americans today tend to be more litigious than in the past, and a threefold increase in the number of lawyers since the 1960s has made it much easier for them to have their day in court. But the courts themselves are also to blame, because poor caseload management systems have contributed to the backlogs.

See 365 How many new cases do state courts hear in a year?

STATE AND FEDERAL COURT JURISDICTIONS

Q 377. How does the dual system of courts work?

A Federal and state courts each have their own spheres of jurisdiction under the "dual system," and for the most part they operate separately. Federal courts take all cases involving federal law and questions concerning the U.S. Constitution. State courts, on the other hand, try cases that involve state laws and state constitutional issues.

Sometimes state and federal laws are nearly the same, such as those for dealing certain illegal drugs, and charges against a defendant could be lodged in either federal or state court. Or, the case may involve a national constitutional question as well as the breaking of a state law. Here the case might go directly to a federal court, or the state court might try the case first, with a federal court considering it on appeal. In any event, however, state courts can never rule against a federal law.

See 42 Do states have any powers under the U.S. Constitution? 56 What is federal preemption?

► Do federal laws take precedence over state laws? *See 56 What is federal preemption?*

Q **378. Have state courts ever expanded or modified U.S. Supreme Court decisions?**

A Yes. In certain areas, such as defendants' rights, the U.S. Supreme Court has set a minimum standard. But it has also encouraged states to expand on those standards, if they so choose. So, for example, courts in three states rejected a more lenient Supreme Court finding that allows evidence in court proceedings, even though it was produced by a defective search warrant. In Oregon, the state supreme court threw out the high court's guidelines on obscene materials because they limited free expression.

Overall, according to one estimate, about three hundred state supreme court rulings have expanded on high court rulings since 1970. However, the number of states with courts willing to go beyond Supreme Court guidelines is still relatively small.

STATE SUPREME COURT AND OTHER APPELLATE COURTS

Q **379. Do state supreme court trials have juries?**

A No, a panel of supreme court justices, including the chief justice, hears oral arguments presented by attorneys for both sides in the case. The justices then meet in private conference to decide the case by a majority vote.

Though the chief justice can play an influential role in the conference, he or she has only one vote to cast for the decision, the same as the other justices. Also, unlike the U.S. Supreme Court justice, the state chief justice does not assign opinions to specific justices, and therefore has limited influence over cases. Instead, the responsibility for writing an opinion automatically rotates among the justices.

Q **380. In what cases do supreme courts have original jurisdiction?**

A Many of the cases state supreme courts hear have been appealed from lower courts. However, supreme courts have original jurisdiction in cases involving state constitutional questions, as well as those in which the state is a party or when certain writs are involved.

See 363 What is the highest state court?

Q 381. Can supreme courts declare state laws unconstitutional?

A State supreme courts have the power of judicial review and can strike down laws passed by the state legislature. However, like the U.S. Supreme Court, state courts tend to use this power sparingly. And the number of state laws ruled unconstitutional can vary considerably from state to state. For example, the Georgia state supreme court struck down twenty-five state laws during a five-year period recently, while the court in North Carolina declared only one state law unconstitutional during the same period.

See 363 What is the highest state court? 378 Have state courts ever expanded or modified U.S. Supreme Court decisions?

Q 382. Are there any cases in which the state supreme court is not the final authority?

A State supreme courts do not have final authority in any case involving federal constitutional questions, even though a state law may also have been violated. The same is true of cases where federal laws are involved, even though the state may have a similar law, such as in drug dealing cases. Here the federal courts, and ultimately the U.S. Supreme Court, have final authority.

See 363 What is the highest state court?

Q 383. How many judges sit on state supreme court benches?

A The number of justices, including the chief justice, ranges from five to nine depending on the state. In nineteen states, five justices sit on the supreme court bench, while in eight states there are nine justices.

▶ How many justices sit on the supreme court in my state? *See profiles of individual states.*

Q 384. How long do state supreme court justices serve?

A Nearly all these justices have terms of fixed lengths, usually from six to fourteen years long depending on the state. All these justices may be reappointed to additional terms. In some states their first term is shorter.

Three states have lifetime (or near lifetime) appointments. After being appointed, justices in Massachusetts and New Hampshire are entitled to serve until they are seventy years of age. In Rhode Island they have life terms.

Q **385. How are appellate courts usually organized?**

A Though in twelve states the state supreme court is the only appellate court, increased caseloads have forced the other states to organize intermediate courts of appeal. Depending on the state, there may be just one appeals court, several regional courts, or separate appeals courts for criminal and civil cases. Usually, intermediate appeals courts have three-judge panels with no juries. After hearing the case, the judges decide the case by a majority vote.

See 364 What are the three basic levels of state courts?

Q **386. About what percentage of lower court rulings are appealed?**

A Usually only about 5 percent of the cases go to appellate courts. The legal expenses and the long wait for a trial, sometimes several years, tend to discourage appeals.

LOWER COURTS

Q **387. What are the general trial courts?**

A Usually called superior, district, circuit, or county court, these courts have jurisdiction over all criminal cases and also are empowered to hear all civil cases, with no upper limit on the monetary amounts involved. Cases involving serious crimes and major civil actions usually are tried for the first time in these courts. Crimes that are not felonies and suits involving no more than $500–$1,000 generally are tried first in minor trial courts (municipal courts).

With only a few exceptions, cases that come before superior courts are decided by a jury.

Q **388. What types of specialized courts are there?**

A The number and types of courts with special jurisdiction vary from state to state. The more common of them include:

Juvenile court, which has jurisdiction over cases involving delinquent children between the ages of about seven and eighteen. This court may waive jurisdiction in cases of murder and other serious felonies, so that the youth can be tried as an adult and subjected to a harsher sentence.

Municipal court is a minor trial court that tries traffic violations, infractions of local ordinances, minor crimes, and civil suits up to a specified monetary limit. Municipal courts may have special divisions, such as family court.

Probate court has jurisdiction over authentication of wills, as well as matters relating to administering estates of the deceased, disputes among heirs, and guardianship of children. About half the states have probate courts.

Small claims court handles disputes involving a limited amount of money, usually overdue debts and other claims amounting to no more than $2,000.

Traffic court hears cases involving motor vehicle laws, including misdemeanors, felony cases, and suits for damages. They can be organized as part of a state, county, or local court.

See 367 What state had the first night court? 413 In which state was the world's first juvenile court organized?

Q 389. What do magistrates and justices of the peace do?

A These low-level judicial officers have jurisdiction over minor offenses and disputes. Magistrates preside over trials for traffic violations, minor crimes, and civil suits that do not involve large sums. They usually have the power to hold both jury trials and nonjury hearings, to set bail for offenders, and to issue warrants. Magistrates also hold preliminary hearings on more serious matters to determine if filing a case with a higher court is warranted.

Justices of the peace are not so numerous as they once were, having been replaced by magistrates in many urban areas. Serving at the town or county level, they try traffic violations and minor criminal cases, often without a jury. In the past, few have had legal training, and the fact that their income is derived from the fines they impose opens the door to bias and corruption. A justice of the peace also has nonjudicial duties, including performing marriages.

STEPPING UP AND STEPPING DOWN FROM THE BENCH

Q 390. How long do judges serve?

A Judges' terms vary depending on the level of the court on which they serve and the number of years fixed by the state. Intermediate appellate court justices, for example, have terms ranging from four to twelve years, depending on the state. In most states, however, these justices serve either six- or eight-year terms.

General trial court judges serve anywhere from four years to life (in Rhode Island only), but for the most part their terms tend to be either four or six years.

See 384 How long do state supreme court justices serve?

Q 391. Is it possible to become a state court judge without being a lawyer?

A Yes, four states have no legal requirement that judges be members of the bar—Alabama, Massachusetts, New Hampshire, and Rhode Island. Two other states, Iowa and Nevada, require only appellate court judges to be members of the state bar. General trial court judges need not be. As a practical matter in these states, however, candidates who are not lawyers usually are not appointed to the bench.

Q 392. What qualifications are required to become a judge?

A Qualifications for appellate and general trial court judges tend to be about the same. In the twenty-two states that have minimum age requirements, for example, nearly all specify the same age. The required age varies widely between states, however, from as low as eighteen to thirty-five (in two states). United States citizenship is required for both appellate and general trial court judges in twenty states. Just four states do not require that judges be members of the state bar association. Thirty-seven states have a residency requirement for appellate court judges, and thirty-five impose the requirement on general trial court judges.

Q 393. What percentage of state court judges came from families with a history of serving in political office?

A According to statistics published in the 1980s, twenty percent of state court judges had a father or grandfather who had served in political office, including judgeships.

Q 394. To which party does the majority of judges belong?

A Judges, like most people, have party preferences. According to one survey, fully 95 percent were either Democratic or Republican. The majority were Democratic party members, but since the 1980s the number of judges with Republican preferences has been on the increase.

Q 395. When was the first Chinese-American judge appointed?

A In 1959, when Judge Delbert E. Wong was named to fill a vacancy in the Los Angeles, California, municipal court.

Q 396. Who was the first woman to become a state supreme court justice?

A Florence Ellinwood Allen became the first when she was elected to the Ohio supreme court in 1922. The first female chief justice of a state supreme court was Loma Elizabeth Lockwood, who assumed the post in Arizona in 1965. She served as chief justice for ten years.

See 114 When did the first woman governor take office? 243 When was the first woman elected to a state senate? 247 Who was the first woman house Speaker in a state legislature?

Q 397. When did the first black become chief justice of a state supreme court?

A James Benton Parsons became the first when he took office as Illinois Supreme Court chief justice on April 18, 1975. The first black to serve as a justice on a state supreme court was Jonathan Jasper Wright, who was a justice of the South Carolina court from 1870 to 1877.

See 117 Who was the first black governor elected to office? 237 When was the first black elected to a state legislature?

Q 398. How many judges are women or minority members?

A Though the number of women judges in state courts has been increasing, the number is still comparatively low. According to one estimate in 1991, only ten percent of state supreme court judges were women. Women hold about twelve percent of the other appellate court judgeships. As of 1990 there were just nine state supreme court judges who were black, but a total of 431 blacks held judgeships in the other state courts. That same year there were 57 Asian/Pacific Americans serving as state judges nationwide. Forty-six of them were in California.

See 115 How many women have served as governor? 116 Who was the first black to serve as governor? 234 Has the percentage of women legislators been rising? 236 What percentage of state legislators are black?

Q 399. What are the five ways state court judges are selected?

A Judges can be elected by voters in either partisan or nonpartisan elections. In other states the governor has the power to appoint the judges. The legislature elects judges in a few states. And in recent years the last method, the merit plan (also called the Missouri plan—see question 327), has been adopted in over twenty states. One or another of these methods is used for selecting all appellate and general trial court judgeships in thirty-nine states. In the other states, the selection method varies depending on the level of the court.

See 325 How many states allow partisan judicial elections? 326 How do judges become candidates on nonpartisan ballots? 327 What is the Missouri plan? 329 Are nonpartisan judicial elections free from problems?

Q 400. Can politics influence merit plans?

A Yes, studies have shown merit plans are anything but immune to politics. (In merit plans a state screening committee selects the candidates for a judgeship on the basis of merit, then submits its selections to the governor for final approval.) In the first place, the judge who is finally appointed by the governor may well have personal and judicial convictions similar to the governor's, or may be inclined to defer to the governor's preferences out of gratitude for the appointment. But often the governor also appoints the screening commission members, and so can influence the process by handpicking the appointees. In addition, lawyers usually dominate the screening process, which gives the legal profession opportunities to look after its own political interests.

See 327 What is the Missouri Plan? 329 Are nonpartisan judicial elections free from problems?

Q 401. Can state judges be impeached?

A Forty-five states have provisions for removal of judges through impeachment. Charges for impeachable offenses must be brought before the state house of representatives, which votes on whether or not to approve impeachment proceedings. If the house approves, the senate holds a trial on the charges, after which senators vote on the question of removing the judge.

Oregon, which has no provision for impeaching judges, gives the power of removing judges to its state supreme court (on recommendation of a judicial commission).

See 113 How many governors have been impeached and removed from office? 178 What is the procedure in the legislature for impeachment? 239 Which state does not have any provision for impeachment proceedings?

Q 402. How does the system of legislative address work?

A An option for removing judges in nineteen states, this system hinges on votes in both houses of the state legislature. If both houses approve the judge's ouster by a two-thirds vote, the legislature then asks the governor to remove the judge from office.

Q 403. What other ways can a judge be removed from the bench?

A The majority of states have special commissions to investigate misconduct by judges. The commission may recommend disciplining or removing the judge and, depending on the state, either makes its recommendation to the state supreme court or is empowered to take the action on its own.

Another way judges can be removed is by popular recall. This method requires a minimum number of signatures from registered voters in order to put the judge's recall on the ballot. If the voters then approve the recall, the judge is dismissed from office. Recall is an option in only seven states, and few judges have ever been recalled.

See 108 What is a recall?

Q 404. What was Operation Greylord?

A An FBI undercover operation aimed at corruption in Chicago's Cook County court system, Operation Greylord eventually resulted in dozens of convictions, including those of fifteen judges and fifty lawyers, as well as court clerks and police officers. The three-year investigation hinged on a local attorney who, working for the FBI, gave out bribes to fix cases the FBI had set up. Indicted court officials were accused of fixing cases ranging from drunken driving to serious felonies, and one lawyer was secretly recorded while bragging that it was even possible to fix a murder case.

Q 405. How many states have mandatory retirement?

A Over thirty-seven states require judges to retire, usually at age seventy, or otherwise encourage them to step down from the bench when they reach retirement age.

See 106 What do most governors do after leaving office? 229 Do legislators have retirement benefits?

LEGAL TERMS AND PROCEDURES

 406. Why is precedent important in law?

A basic principle of state and federal law, precedent helps courts apply laws equally in similar situations. Past court decisions (the precedents) provide a guide for all future judges in deciding a case, if the circumstances are the same or nearly so. But precedent also helps establish court policy. Lower state courts generally must follow legal precedents set by the state supreme court, for example.

While state supreme courts often turn to U.S. Supreme Court rulings for precedents, they do also look elsewhere. In fact, state supreme courts increasingly have relied on court decisions from other states in their region for precedents. Larger states with more prestigious court systems also serve as a source of legal precedent for states across the country.

407. What is a class-action suit?

This is a suit for damages brought by a small group of litigants who claim to represent a much larger group of people with the same legal complaint. Consumer complaints concerning faulty and unsafe products, incidents involving pollution and other environmental safety concerns, and job discrimination cases—all have at one time or another become the basis for class-action suits. Often this approach is the only practical way to present the case, because damages claimed by any one individual would be too small to justify legal action.

Proponents of class-action suits also point out that they are a far more efficient way to handle so large a number of complaints. Critics, however, argue that class-action suits often force businesses to choose between a long, expensive trial with lots of bad publicity and a multi-million-dollar out-of-court settlement. And because of the potential for huge settlements, this type of suit encourages lawyers to file even the questionable cases.

Q 408. Is common law different from statutory law?

A Yes, *common law* is that part of state law that has derived from accepted custom and judges' rulings in previous cases (precedents). *Statutory law*, on the other hand, is made up of laws (statutes) that have been written and passed by the legislature.

The source of our common law was England, and it was English colonists who brought it here. Both the concept of cross-examination of witnesses and jury trials, for example, have been borrowed from English common law. Statutes can replace common law, and much of the original common law in our present legal system has been written into statutes.

See 406 Why is precedent important in law?

Q 409. What is plea bargaining?

A A plea bargain is a deal between the prosecutor and a defense attorney, in which the defendant avoids standing trial on one charge by agreeing to plead guilty to a lesser charge. The prosecutor then recommends to the judge—who must agree to the plea bargain—that the defendant be given a lighter sentence or be put on probation.

A common practice in trial courts, plea bargaining offers some distinct advantages. The defendant avoids the risk of going to trial and being found guilty of a more serious charge, the prosecutor gains a conviction, and the judge helps reduce the backlog of court cases. Critics of the practice point out that under pressure of a plea bargaining offer, an innocent defendant may plead guilty to a lesser charge. Also, crime victims usually want to see longer, not shorter, sentences for their attackers.

Q 410. Do all states impose capital punishment?

A As of the mid-1990s, thirty-eight states had the option of imposing the death penalty. However, not all these states have exercised the option in recent decades, and of those that have, most have used it sparingly, in part because legal restrictions make it so costly and time consuming. In all, twelve states that have capital punishment had not executed anyone between 1976, when the U.S. Supreme Court reinstated the death penalty, and 1995. Eight other states had each put to death no more than two convicted criminals in that time period.

See 417 Which state has executed the most criminals in recent years?

411. What is the incorporation doctrine?

Provisions of the Bill of Rights in the U.S. Constitution originally were intended only for the federal government. But in recent decades the U.S. Supreme Court has ruled that the Fourteenth Amendment clause on due process of the law actually "incorporates" freedoms set forth in the Bill of Rights, and so has required states to adhere to a number of its provisions. Among those the Court has applied to the states are First Amendment freedoms and some of the provisions dealing with criminal law.

▶ How does the preemption doctrine affect state laws? *See 486 What is state preemption?*

 412. How many people serve on a jury?

The number of jurors on a grand jury varies, the maximum being twenty-three and the average being twelve. On a trial jury, the number of jurors is traditionally twelve.

See 416 What was the longest jury trial?

▶ What is a pardon? *See 97 Are pardon, reprieve, and commutation of sentence the same?*

FOR THE RECORD

413. In which state was the world's first juvenile court organized?

The Chicago Juvenile Court opened its doors in Cook County, Illinois, on July 1, 1899, the first court ever with a jurisdiction limited to cases involving juveniles. From 1913, the court had a woman judge to try girls who wound up in the court.

See 367 What state had the first night court? 388 What types of specialized courts are there?

414. When was the first partisan popular election for a state court judgeship held?

Mississippi held the first in 1832. The system was originally adopted to make judges accountable to the voters, although in the early 1900s reformers became concerned about the influence of political parties in elections of officials for all branches of state government. Today judges in many states are selected through nonpartisan elections.

Q **415. Which state supreme court was first to have a majority of female justices?**

A Minnesota became the first in 1991, when the fourth female justice was appointed to serve a six-year term on the state's seven-member supreme court panel. The new appointee, Sandra Gardebring, had been a state appeals court judge. The three other female justices were Rosalie Wahl, M. Jeanne Coyne, and Esther Tomljanovich. Only two other states had two women justices in 1991—Michigan and Oklahoma—while twenty-six other states had only one.

See 115 How many women have served as governor?

Q **416. What was the longest jury trial?**

A The longest to date was a trial held in Belleville, Illinois, on liability for a toxic spill. The case dragged on for a record three years and eight months before the jury reached a decision in October 1987.

Q **417. Which state has executed the most criminals in recent years?**

A Texas put ninety-two convicted criminals to death in the eighteen years between 1977 and 1995, more than any other state that permits capital punishment. However, both Louisiana and Nevada have higher rates based on the number of executions per capita of state residents.

Overall, the rate of executions remains fairly low. In the years between 1976, when the U.S. Supreme Court reinstated the death penalty, and late 1995, a total of 313 convicted criminals were put to death.

See 410 Do all states impose capital punishment?

SUPREME COURT TESTS OF STATES' POWERS

Q **418. What proportion of cases the Supreme Court decides affect states?**

A About half of all cases the U.S. Supreme Court has ruled on in recent years have concerned state and local government. Decisions ranged from the controversial *Roe v. Wade* case, which overturned state laws banning abortion, to seemingly more mundane rulings, such as the decision about whether the U.S. Congress has the power to impose national minimum wage standards on state governments.

See 46 What is federalism? 47 What are dual federalism and cooperative federalism? 50 Why was the Tenth Amendment to the U.S. Constitution important to states? 56 What is federal preemption?

Q 419. What did the Court rule in *Baker v. Carr?*

A This 1962 decision on reapportionment in Tennessee eventually led to the redrawing of election districts in every state but Oregon and significantly changed the makeup of state legislatures. Tennessee's election districts became an issue because the state had not conducted a reapportionment in over a half century, even though the state constitution required one every ten years.

During that time the population in cities and suburbs had grown rapidly, while rural areas had lost population. So long as there was no reapportionment, however, rural politicians continued to enjoy a disproportionately large share of power in the state legislature. For that reason they stubbornly opposed any effort to redraw election districts.

After the Tennessee state supreme court refused to consider a lawsuit to force reapportionment, a group of concerned urban citizens filed suit in federal court under the name of Shelby County chairman Charles W. Baker. Joe Carr, the target of their suit, was Tennessee's secretary of state. In 1959 the federal court dismissed the suit, though, citing an earlier Supreme Court refusal to consider a case involving congressional redistricting.

But this time the Supreme Court agreed to hear the case, and in 1962 ruled that the federal courts could decide such cases, based on a citizen's right to equal protection under the law. That sent the Tennessee case back to federal district court, and began the process of court-mandated redistricting. Another Supreme Court decision the following year, in *Gray v. Sanders,* established the "one person, one vote" test for reapportionment, which forced states to redraw state election districts so that the population was nearly equal in each.

See 171 What is reapportionment? 172 Why is redistricting important? 173 What is a gerrymander? 174 What is a majority-minority district? 175 Who actually draws up the districts? 431 What did the Court rule in Reynolds v. Sims?

Q 420. What did the Court rule in *Brown v. Board of Education?*

A This ruling in 1954 ended racial segregation in public schools and other public facilities. States, especially those in the South, were forced to reverse longstanding "separate but equal" policies in which whites and blacks went to different schools, were required to use separate public restrooms, and were expected to sit in segregated areas of buses and other public vehicles. For decades the Supreme Court had condoned the separate but equal doctrine. Facilities for blacks were often clearly inferior to those for whites, however, and the Court decided that in any event separate facilities "are inherently unequal." Blacks, the Court said, were being denied their Fourteenth Amendment right to equal protection under the law.

See 428 What did the Court rule in Missouri v. Jenkins? *434 What did the Court rule in* Swann v. Charlotte-Mecklenburg County Board of Education?

Q **421. What did the Court rule in *Chisholm v. Georgia?***

A The Court's decision in this case, concerning a lawsuit against a state by the citizen of another state, provoked such an uproar that the Eleventh Amendment to the U.S. Constitution was written and ratified just two years later in 1795 to keep such suits out of federal courts.

In Chisholm, the heirs of a pro-British loyalist brought suit to recover land the state of Georgia had confiscated during the American Revolution. But payment for all the confiscated property of loyalists would probably have ruined Georgia's finances, and many other states had good reason to worry about this problem as well. Georgia simply refused to allow the suit, in part because the heirs lived outside the state.

In its 1793 decision, the Supreme Court claimed federal courts had jurisdiction over suits by citizens of one state against another state, under Article III, Section 2, of the Constitution. This meant suits such as that upheld in Chisholm could be brought in federal courts. Threatened with financial ruin, the states protested vigorously, and Congress quickly passed the Eleventh Amendment to reverse the Supreme Court's ruling. It took less than one year for three-quarters of the states to ratify the amendment.

▶ What did the Court rule in *Elrod v. Burns? See 312 How did the Supreme Court decision in* Elrod v. Burns *affect state parties?*

▶ What did the Court rule in *Escobedo v. Illinois? See 423 What did the Court rule in* Gideon v. Wainwright?

▶ What did the Court rule in *Garcia v. San Antonio Metropolitan Transit Authority? See 430 What did the Court rule in* National League of Cities v. Usery?

Q 422. What did the Court rule in *Gibbons v. Ogden?*

A This 1824 decision in favor of the federal government curbed state powers in two ways. In the first place, the Supreme Court established a very broad definition of "commerce among the states," which the U.S. Constitution empowered the federal government to regulate. The Court held that the national government not only had authority over commerce across state lines, but also could regulate, in certain circumstances, the movement of goods and people inside state borders.

The second important aspect of the ruling concerned the supremacy of federal laws. Here the Court articulated the *preemption doctrine* for the first time, holding that whenever federal and state laws conflict, federal laws invalidate the conflicting state laws.

In the case of *Gibbons v. Ogden,* Gibbons had gotten a federal permit to operate a ferryboat serving New York City, while New York State had granted Ogden a monopoly on the ferryboats to and from the city. By the preemption doctrine, the Court invalidated the New York State license.

Q 423. What did the Court rule in *Gideon v. Wainwright?*

A Reversing an earlier ruling, the Court here decided that all indigent criminal defendants had a right to court-appointed legal counsel. Previously, states had been required to furnish indigent defendants with legal counsel only in cases of serious crimes, such as murder.

In 1961 Clarence Earl Gideon was found guilty of breaking and entering a poolroom in Florida. Too poor to afford a lawyer, he asked the court for an attorney, but was refused because the charge was not serious enough. Gideon defended himself at the trial and lost, but while serving his sentence studied law and petitioned federal courts to overturn his conviction. In 1963 the Supreme Court unanimously agreed with his argument that the Florida court had violated his Sixth Amendment right to counsel. Gideon, represented by a lawyer, was granted a new trial and this time won an acquittal.

A year after *Gideon,* the Court expanded its ruling in *Escobedo v. Illinois.* In this case the justices held that a suspect in custody was also entitled to legal counsel during police interrogation.

See 411 What is the incorporation doctrine? 427 What did the Court rule in Miranda v. Arizona?

Q 424. What did the Court rule in *Goldberg v. Kelly*?

A By this 1970 ruling, the Supreme Court ordered the holding of formal hearings before a welfare recipient's benefits could be cut off. The case involved a New York welfare recipient whose benefits had been terminated. Procedures in New York allowed only a written protest against the termination—not a formal hearing—and the welfare recipient sued.

The Supreme Court ruled that a hearing, complete with lawyers (if the recipient desires) and cross-examination of witnesses must be held before benefits can be terminated. Otherwise the recipient's Fourteenth Amendment (due process) rights would be violated. The hearing need not be a judicial hearing, however.

Q 425. What did the Court rule in *Harper v. Virginia State Board of Elections*?

A The Supreme Court struck down poll taxes in federal elections in 1964, but several southern states tried to continue collecting the tax for state elections. The Court finally ruled against this practice as well two years later in *Harper,* deciding that the poll taxes amounted to a denial of the Fourteenth Amendment right to equal protection under the law.

In Virginia, prospective voters not only had been required to pay the tax, but also had to produce tax receipts for three years prior to the election.

See 273 What is a poll tax?

Q 426. What did the Court rule in *Mapp v. Ohio*?

A In this case the Supreme Court extended federal rules on excluding illegally obtained evidence (and confessions) to criminal trials in state courts. The Court originally created the "exclusionary rule" in 1914 for federal criminal proceedings, but did not apply it to the states. It was not until the 1961 Mapp ruling that states were finally ordered to follow the federal rules.

See 411 What is the incorporation doctrine?

Q 427. What did the Court rule in *Miranda v. Arizona*?

A One of the Court's most controversial rulings concerning defendants' rights, the 1966 Miranda decision forced police to read suspects their rights before questioning them. Suspects had to be advised, the Court said, of their right to remain silent, that anything they say can be used against them, and that they have the right to legal counsel. Otherwise any evidence obtained from the suspect was inadmissible in court.

Critics argued the new rules would make getting confessions much harder, and later decisions by the Court allowed some exceptions for special circumstances. But the Miranda rule has for the most part become settled law.

Q 428. What did the Court rule in *Missouri v. Jenkins?*

A In this 1990 decision, the Court revealed a willingness to use federal judicial power to intrude directly in local affairs. The Court ruled that federal courts have the power to order local government officials to correct a violation of the U.S. Constitution.

The *Missouri* suit charged that Kansas City, Missouri, was illegally maintaining segregated schools. The Court-approved solution was a sweeping and costly desegregation plan, and it ordered the local government to double property taxes to pay for it, despite the fact voters had already rejected referenda on the plan six times. Critics attacked the ruling as "taxation without representation," but it was not the first time the Court had issued a ruling of this type. In the 1974 decision on *Milliken v. Bradley,* the Supreme Court approved a federal court order forcing a school district to set up and fund remedial education programs.

Q 429. What did the Supreme Court decide in *McCulloch v. Maryland?*

A The Court's decision, handed down in 1819, established the doctrine of implied powers. This meant the federal government not only had those powers specifically enumerated in the U.S. Constitution, but it also had other unspecified powers "necessary and proper" to execute the enumerated powers.

The case arose when Maryland and several other states tried to oppose the chartering of national bank branches within their borders. The branch manager in Baltimore, James McCulloch, took Maryland to court over the state's attempt to tax the bank out of existence. Citing the Constitution's necessary and proper clause, the Supreme Court ruled against Maryland and opened the way for a significant expansion of federal powers, often at the expense of states.

Q 430. What did the Court rule in *National League of Cities v. Usery?*

A This 1976 ruling temporarily reversed the dismantling of the Tenth Amendment guarantee reserving unenumerated powers for the states. *National League* struck down a federal law extending federal minimum wage and maximum hour rules to state and local government employees. Past Supreme Court rulings—especially since the 1930s—had found in favor of expanding the federal government's implied powers at the expense of state sovereignty (mainly through ever looser interpretations of the Constitution's commerce clause). But in this 1976 ruling, the Court unexpectedly ruled against amendments to the federal Fair Labor Standards Act, which applied federal work rules to state and local employees.

The change was short-lived, though. In 1985 the Court reversed itself in *Garcia v. San Antonio Metropolitan Transit Authority* and approved the extension of federal work rules to state and local employees. It ruled the *National League* decision was "inconsistent with established principles of federalism" and effectively bowed out of federal-state controversies over federal powers under the commerce clause. The Constitution, the Court said, did not set aside areas of state sovereignty that Congress could not displace in the exercise of its delegated powers.

See 42 Do states have any powers under the U.S. Constitution? 46 What is federalism? 50 Why was the Tenth Amendment to the U.S. Constitution important to states? 433 What did the Court rule in South Carolina v. Baker?

▶ *What did the Court rule in* Planned Parenthood v. Casey? *See 432 What did the Court rule in* Roe v. Wade?

Q 431. What did the Court rule in *Reynolds v. Sims?*

A Coming on the heels of the *Baker v. Carr* decision, this controversial ruling in 1964 extended the one person, one vote principle and became a key part of the Court's effort to reform the reapportionment of election districts in the states. In *Reynolds*, the Court ordered states to draw election districts with equal populations for all seats in both houses of their legislatures. Some states had sought to apportion districts for one of the two houses on a basis other than population (as in the U.S. Senate, where there are just two senators for every state).

The equal population rule was extended to local legislative districts in 1968. While the Court refused to allow much variation in population between congressional districts, in 1973 it did uphold a plan for reapportioning Virginia's state legislative districts, which had deviations of over 16 percent from the equal population rule (*Mahan v. Howell*).

See 171 What is reapportionment? 172 Why is redistricting important? 173 What is a gerrymander? 174 What is a majority-minority district? 175 Who actually draws up the districts? 419 What did the court rule in Baker v. Carr?

Q 432. What did the Court rule in *Roe v. Wade*?

A One of the most controversial Supreme Court rulings in recent times, this 1973 decision overturned state laws banning abortions and declared women had a right to decide to abort a pregnancy, based on their constitutional right to privacy. The Court did allow states some latitude for regulation, though, and sanctioned a ban on abortions in the later months of pregnancy.

An effort to ban abortions by constitutional amendment failed, and in the years following *Roe* the Court struck down a number of state laws that attempted to make it more difficult for women to get abortions. It did, however, uphold a Connecticut ban on using Medicaid to pay for abortions, except in the case of medical necessity *(Maher v. Roe,* 1977). In the 1989 *Webster v. Reproductive Health Services* decision, the Court let stand restrictions on abortions imposed by a Missouri abortion law (banning use of public facilities or public employees in abortions). Three years later, in *Planned Parenthood of Southeastern Pennsylvania v. Casey* (1992), the Court declared that state regulations would be permissible, unless they placed an "undue burden" on a woman seeking an abortion. At the same time, though, the Court reaffirmed the "essential holding" of its 1973 ruling in *Roe v. Wade.*

▶ What did the Court rule in *Rutlan v. Republican Party? See 312 How did the Supreme Court decision in* Elrod v. Burns *affect state parties?*

Q 433. What did the Court rule in *South Carolina v. Baker*?

A This 1988 decision served to reinforce the Court's ruling in *Garcia v. San Antonio Metropolitan Area Transit Authority.* The case itself involved the right of the federal government to tax interest on state and local government bonds. The Court upheld the federal government's position and affirmed the 1985 *Garcia* ruling by saying the Constitution does not reserve elements of state sovereignty that cannot be displaced by Congress.

The Court further noted that states should not try using the courts to establish judicially defined "spheres of unregulable state activity." Instead, they should work through the national political process to find protections from the expansion of congressional regulation.

Previously, in the *National League of Cities v. Usery* (1976) decision, the Court had tried to establish a limit to federal encroachment on state powers—the "traditional" state functions test. But that test proved unworkable, and the Court abandoned it over a decade later in *Garcia.*

See 42 Do states have any powers under the U.S. Constitution? 46 What is federalism? 50 Why was the Tenth Amendment to the U.S. Constitution important to states? 430 What did the Court rule in National League of Cities v. Usery?

Q 434. What did the Court rule in *Swann v. Charlotte-Mecklenburg County Board of Education?*

A By this controversial 1971 ruling, the Supreme Court approved school busing to redress de jure segregation (school segregation maintained by law or by sanction of local officials). The Court distinguished between de jure and de facto segregation, however. It held that de facto segregation, caused by residence patterns, economic status, and the like, was not covered by the equal protection clause of the Fourteenth Amendment. In any case, court-ordered busing proved a contentious issue, and in some cities, Boston among them, it provoked violent protests.

In its 1974 *Milliken v. Bradley* ruling, the Court held to the distinction between de jure and de facto segregation when it struck down a court-ordered plan to bus students between downtown Detroit and its suburbs. Controversial school desegregation issues also reached the Court in the 1990s. The Court upheld the right of lower courts to order local officials to increase property taxes to pay for school desegregation in *Missouri v. Jenkins* (1990), a major encroachment upon state and local powers. But in 1991 and 1992 the Court seemed to back away from tighter controls over school districts. In *Board of Education of Oklahoma City v. Dowell,* the Court approved a neighborhood schools concept, and in *Freeman v. Pitts* ruled that school districts do not have to address racial imbalances caused by housing segregation and other demographic factors.

See 428 What did the Court rule in Missouri v. Jenkins?

Q 435. What did the Court rule in *University of California Regents v. Bakke?*

A The Bakke ruling in 1978 struck down a University of California affirmative action program that set racial quotas for admissions. A prospective medical student, Allan Bakke, challenged the quota system after being turned down twice for admission to the medical school at the University of California at Davis. The school had a quota system that reserved sixteen seats for minority students out of the one hundred for each medical school class. While ruling against the quota system, the Court did say that race could be included as a factor in admissions decisions.

Q 436. What did the Court rule in *United States v. Darby Lumber Co.?*

A By this ruling in 1941, the Court broadened federal commerce powers at the expense of state powers and effectively repudiated the doctrine of dual federalism in favor of federal supremacy. The case itself involved an expansion of worker protections passed by Congress in 1938 under the Fair Labor Standards Act. It imposed a forty-hour work week, a minimum wage, and restrictions on child labor. The act barred interstate commerce of goods produced by businesses that did not comply.

The Court held that Congress had the power to regulate commerce by barring shipment of goods, and in overturning an earlier ruling on child labor, found that the Tenth Amendment did not restrict expansion of federal commerce powers.

See 46 What is federalism? 47 What are dual federalism and cooperative federalism?

Q 437. What did the Court rule in *United States v. Lopez?*

A Handed down in 1995, the *Lopez* ruling invalidated the federal Gun-Free School Zones Act of 1990, which made possession of a gun near a school a federal offense. The Court said that keeping guns away from schools was a state responsibility and noted that many states already had such laws. More importantly, though, the Court said Congress had overstepped its bounds, declaring the Gun-Free School Zones Act had nothing to do with the Constitution's commerce clause. For decades Congress has relied on very loose interpretations of the clause, which allows it to regulate interstate commerce, to expand its powers over many state activities. It was in 1936 that the Court last struck down a federal law because Congress had overstepped the boundaries of the commerce clause.

See 46 What is federalism? 47 What are dual federalism and cooperative federalism? 422 What did the Court rule in Gibbons v. Ogden?

▶ What did the Court rule in *Webster v. Reproductive Health Services? See 432 What did the Court rule in* Roe v. Wade?

WHERE CAN I FIND . . .

Sources described below provide more detailed information on topics discussed in this chapter.

Civil Jury Cases and Verdicts in Large Counties: Civil Justice Survey of State Courts, 1992.
Carol J. DeFrances, et al. Washington, D.C.: U.S. Department of Justice, Office of
Justice Programs, Bureau of Justice Statistics, 1995.

One of a series of useful government pamphlets published by the Bureau of Justice Statistics, this issue contains recent statistics on jury-award winners and losers
in civil suits, product liability cases in state courts, and related topics.

CQ's Guide to the U.S. Supreme Court, 3d ed. Joan Biskupic and Elder Witt. Washington,
D.C.: Congressional Quarterly Inc., 1997.

This two-volume set contains history and analysis of all Supreme Court decisions
rendered through the July 1996 term, including those affecting the states, states'
rights, and state government.

"Doing Justice" in the People's Court: Sentencing by Municipal Court Judges. Jon'a Meyer
and Paul Jesilow. Albany, N.Y.: State University of New York Press, 1997.

An academic study of the municipal court justice system, including analysis
of the judges, defendants' actions, and judicial bias in court proceedings and
sentencing.

Great American Trials. Edward W. Knappman, ed. Detroit: Gale Research, 1994.

Hundreds of trials are covered in this interesting reference book. Coverage of
each trial includes basic information, a synopsis, and excerpts from trial testimony.
Coverage ends with the 1992 Mike Tyson trial.

Historic U.S. Court Cases, 1690–1990: An Encyclopedia. John W. Johnson. New York:
Garland Publishing, 1992.

Treatment of cases usually runs several pages in this one-volume encyclopedia.
Most are Supreme Court cases, but notable state court decisions are also included.

Judicial Policymaking and the Modern State: How the Courts Reformed America's Prisons.
Malcolm M. Freely and Edward L. Rubin. New York: Cambridge University Press,
1998.

This book covers the theory and practice of court-ordered prison reform since
the 1960s, and includes an assessment of what the courts actually accomplished.

Judicial Process in America, 4th ed. Robert A. Carp and Ronald Stidham. Washington,
D.C.: CQ Press, 1998.

Covering both state and federal courts, the book examines the roles of lawyers
and judges in the judicial process.

Oxford Companion to the Supreme Court of the United States. Kermit L. Hall. New York: Oxford University Press, 1992.

A one-volume encyclopedia, it provides A to Z coverage of the Court, including many clear, concisely written entries on Supreme Court rulings.

The Politics of State Courts. Harry P. Stumpf and John H. Culver. New York: Longman, 1992.

This book gives an in-depth look at the politics of judicial selection, the effect of lawyers on judicial politics, and the politics of both the criminal and civil judicial processes.

Property and Freedom: the Constitution, the Courts, and Land-use Regulation. Bernard H. Siegan. New Brunswick, N.J.: Transaction Publishers, 1997.

With an emphasis on pivotal cases, this book examines basic property rights, land takings, zoning laws, and the effects of environmental concerns on property rights.

Sourcebook of Criminal Justice Statistics. Bureau of Justice Statistics. Washington, D.C.: U.S. Government Printing Office, annual.

Also available on CD-ROM, this book contains a wealth of useful tables and statistics on crimes, cases in courts, sentencing data, and so on. Many, but not all, tables are organized by state.

State and Local Government. 2d ed. Ann Bowman and Richard Kearney. Boston: Houghton Mifflin Company, 1993.

General readers will find this textbook gives a clear and useful introduction to the history and mechanics of state courts and the criminal justice system.

State Constitutions and Criminal Justice. Barry Latzer. New York: Greenwood Press, 1991.

An in-depth look at fundamental issues in criminal justice, this book covers such topics as search and seizure, Miranda rights and self-incrimination, the right to counsel, and double jeopardy. It describes the current thinking on these issues and traces the history of court decisions related to them.

State Court Organization 1993, 3d ed. David B. Rottman, Carol R. Flango, and R. Shedine Lockley. Washington, D.C.: U.S. Department of Justice, Office of Justice Programs, Bureau of Justice Statistics, 1995.

Primarily a book of tables, it contains a wide range of state-by-state information on judicial selection, judicial qualifications, court organization, and the like.

State Government: CQ's Guide to Current Issues and Activities, 1999–2000. Thad Beyle. Washington, D.C.: Congressional Quarterly Inc., 1999.

This collection includes a number of readings on current issues, including those relating to the courts.

The Supreme Court A to Z: CQ's Ready Reference Encyclopedia of American Government, 2d ed. Kenneth Jost, ed. Washington, D.C.: Congressional Quarterly Inc., 1999.

While this book focuses on the U.S. Supreme Court, it contains clear and concise entries on federal-state relations and on Court decisions affecting the states.

Supreme Court Yearbook. Kenneth Jost. Washington, D.C.: Congressional Quarterly Inc., annual.

A good source for recent Supreme Court cases affecting states, this book provides both case summaries and a review of the Court's term.

VI
STATE OF THE STATES

IN GENERAL

Q **438. How do population growth and decline affect the states?**

A Rapid growth of population in a state tends to create new business, a growing economy, and an increase in tax revenues, but it also strains the state's infrastructure. The new residents demand more housing, roads, schools, police and fire departments, and other public facilities that most people take for granted. While there are more people paying taxes, it takes time to build new roads and schools, and the costs are very high.

Declining populations pose the opposite problem. Businesses close and the economy slumps. With fewer people paying taxes, state revenues decline, and the demand for schools and other public services shrinks. States can raise taxes to compensate for declining revenues, but only so far. Higher taxes can cause even more people to leave the state.

Q **439. Which states are projected to show the biggest population gains in the census for the year 2000?**

A Nevada will likely finish out the century with a 40 percent increase in population since the 1990 census, the largest percentage gain of all the states. Florida, California, and Texas also are expected to post big increases, somewhere in the neighborhood of 18 percent over their 1990 populations. For California, that will be a gain of five million new residents. Industrial states in the North are projected to grow, but by something less than 5 percent.

440. Have population shifts between states affected national politics?

Yes, thanks to the general migration in recent decades from northern states to the Sunbelt, Sunbelt states now dominate national politics. That is because as states gain a greater share of the overall population, the number of seats they have in the U.S. Congress also increases. In 1992, for example, nineteen seats in Congress changed hands as a result of congressional redistricting (the total number of seats is fixed at 435). California, Texas, and Florida got fourteen of those seats, and all other gainers (except Washington) were in the Sunbelt, too. States losing seats were all in the North and Midwest, where population growth has been slow at best.

Looked at over a longer period, the shift is even more dramatic. Between 1960 and 1992, New York lost ten congressional seats and California picked up twenty-two. Florida, another big gainer, wound up with eleven more congressional seats.

441. Which states have the highest and lowest population densities?

New Jersey is the most densely populated of all the states. An average of 1,077 people per square mile lived in New Jersey as of 1996. Rhode Island had the second-highest density with an average of 948 people per square mile, and Massachusetts was third with 777 per square mile.

Alaska was the most sparsely populated, with an average of just 1 person per square mile. Wyoming had 5, and Montana 6.

442. Do more Americans live in big cities or towns?

As of the early 1990s, more people lived in small towns than in cities with populations of over five hundred thousand. In fact, the percentage of people living in the biggest cities (over one million residents) has been declining since 1930. Most of that change has been due to increased growth of suburban towns outside the cities, which has created a ring of less congested, but fast-growing metropolitan villages around them.

443. Which states have large black populations? Hispanic and other minorities?

Mississippi, Louisiana, and South Carolina all have black populations that are over 30 percent of the total state population. As of 1994, there were an estimated 958,000 black people living in Mississippi. That was far less than the 3.18 million living in

New York State, for example, but Mississippi nevertheless had the highest percentage of any state—35.9 percent. Louisiana had 1.36 million blacks in 1994, or 31.6 percent of its population, and South Carolina had 1.1 million, or 30.1 percent. California, Florida, and Texas each had black populations of over 2 million, but the percentage of the overall population was much lower (about 8–15 percent).

States with black populations over 1 million are:

Alabama	Maryland	Ohio
California	Michigan	Pennsylvania
Florida	New Jersey	South Carolina
Georgia	New York	Texas
Illinois	North Carolina	Virginia
Louisiana		

By percentage of total state population, New Mexico had the largest Hispanic population—39.1 percent—in 1994. The state's Hispanic population numbered nearly 646,000, but that was far less than California's, which had 8.9 million (just over 28 percent of its population). Texas had 5.02 million Hispanics for a total of 27 percent of its population, and New York had almost 2.5 million, or nearly 14 percent. Vermont had the smallest Hispanic population in 1994, 3,900, followed by North Dakota with 5,200.

States with Hispanic populations over 1 million are:

California	Illinois	Texas
Florida	New York	

Q 444. Do any states have large numbers of elderly residents?

A Given Florida's history as a mecca for retirees, it should come as no surprise that the state had the highest percentage of people over age sixty-five—18.5 percent—as of 1996. But surprisingly, its total of 2.66 million seniors is substantially less than that of California, which had 3.5 million (11 percent of its population). And it was also only slightly ahead of New York, which had 2.4 million residents over sixty-five (13.4 percent).

Alaska had the fewest seniors, only 31,000. Wyoming (54,000), Vermont (71,000), North Dakota (93,000), and Delaware (93,000) also had small elderly populations.

States with over 1 million people over age sixty-five in 1996 were:

California	Michigan	Ohio
Florida	New Jersey	Pennsylvania
Illinois	New York	Texas

Q 445. Where have the majority of recent immigrants settled in this country?

A Just six states have become home for about 75 percent of immigrants arriving in this country since the early 1980s (mostly Latin Americans and Southeast Asians). California, Florida, Illinois, New Jersey, New York, and Texas have received the bulk of legal immigrants and refugees during the period. In addition, however, they have also became the destination for large numbers of illegal immigrants. California for example is estimated to have about 2 million illegal immigrants (as of 1996). Texas has some 700,000, and New York about 540,000.

Q 446. Why did California voters approve Proposition 187?

A In the past, many California public services, including schooling and medical care for the indigent, had been provided to illegal aliens. But with an illegal alien population estimated at 2 million, the strain on the state's social services became an issue in the early 1990s, a problem Proposition 187 was intended to solve.

Passed by voters in late 1994, the ballot initiative denied all benefits to undocumented aliens and required doctors, social workers, and even teachers to report illegal aliens. But the proposition, like others before it, quickly became the object of a court test and was struck down by the courts.

See 354 Are propositions more common today?

Q 447. Why is statistical sampling for the census such a controversial issue?

A According to sampling by the Census Bureau, the 1990 census did not count about four million people. The sampling further purported to show that black and Hispanic men were missed at twice the rate for the nation as a whole. Since everything from representation in Congress to formulas for federal and state grants is based on the Census Bureau's population counts, states and their cities where undercounting was said to be heaviest were put at a political and economic disadvantage.

Ultimately the government decided not to adjust the census, which by law is supposed to actually count individuals, and in 1996 the Supreme Court ruled against a suit to adjust the census by adding five million people. If the Court had ruled in favor, Pennsylvania and Wisconsin both would have lost a seat in Congress, while Arizona and California would have gained one each.

More recently, the Clinton administration sought approval to use controversial sampling methods for the 2000 census to make up for another expected undercount. In mid-1998, however, a federal court ruled against using sampling methods for the census.

A Based on the annual index of state economic momentum, Nevada, Utah, Oregon, Washington, and Arizona make up the top five for 1997. The index, compiled from three measures of economic growth, compares state economic growth with that of the nation as a whole. Thus Nevada's index of 3.41 means the state's economy grew at a rate 3.41 percent higher than the national average. And Alaska's economy, with an index of -1.96, performed 1.96 percent below the national average. Alaska's index was the lowest of all fifty state indexes for 1997, followed by Hawaii's (-1.72) and Wyoming's (-1.17).

The state-by-state figures for economic momentum in 1997 are listed below.

State	Economic momentum index	State	Economic momentum index
Alabama	−0.53	Massachusetts	0.50
Alaska	−1.96	Michigan	−0.34
Arizona	1.10	Minnesota	0.06
Arkansas	−0.15	Mississippi	−0.81
California	0.41	Missouri	−0.43
Colorado	0.80	Montana	−0.10
Connecticut	−0.30	Nebraska	0.07
Delaware	0.70	Nevada	3.41
Florida	0.43	New Hampshire	0.39
Georgia	0.20	New Jersey	−0.33
Hawaii	−1.72	New Mexico	−0.68
Idaho	−0.01	New York	−0.82
Illinois	−0.68	North Carolina	0.83
Indiana	−0.44	North Dakota	−0.04
Iowa	−0.52	Ohio	−0.87
Kansas	0.27	Oklahoma	0.12
Kentucky	0.26	Oregon	1.45
Louisiana	−0.61	Pennsylvania	−0.37
Maine	−0.10	Rhode Island	−0.77
Maryland	−0.23	South Carolina	−0.13

(table continues)

State	Economic momentum index	State	Economic momentum index
South Dakota	−0.06	Virginia	0.09
Tennessee	−0.05	Washington	1.24
Texas	0.63	West Virginia	−0.70
Utah	2.20	Wisconsin	−0.48
Vermont	−0.88	Wyoming	−1.17

Source: Kendra A. Hovey and Harold A. Hovey, *CQ's State Fact Finder: Rankings Across America 1998* (Washington, D.C.: Congressional Quarterly, 1998).

Q 449. What are states doing to attract new businesses?

A States today focus a considerable amount of time and money on convincing new businesses to locate within their borders, and competition between states has been intense at times. States use a variety of *incentive packages* to attract the businesses and the jobs they create. Every state has at least one grant or loan program for businesses, but states can and have offered a wide range of other perks for new business, including job training, regulatory breaks, industrial revenue bonds, tax breaks, new roads, and other infrastructure improvements the business may need to operate. The incentives can amount to tens of millions of dollars—for example, Kentucky anted up a $325 million incentive package to convince Toyota to locate an assembly plant there in 1987. But the reward in new jobs, economic growth, new tax revenue, and voter approval is often seen as outweighing the costs.

By the early 1990s, a number of states had also established programs to encourage communities and even special companies to develop infrastructure that would encourage businesses to relocate to the state. States also have set up programs to provide transportation sector incentives, including tax breaks to railroads and trucking companies.

Q 450. In which states does the federal government have the largest and smallest land holdings?

A Federal land holdings are highest in western states where vast park and forest preserves account for tens of thousands of acres that would otherwise be available for states to use. Of all the states, the federal government controls far and away the largest amount of land in Alaska, at least in terms of total acres—248,021 acres, or

67.9 percent of the entire state. Nevada ranks first by percentage because 82.9 percent of its land is under federal control (58,265 acres total).

The federal government also controls large parts of the land in California (44,707 acres for 44.6 percent), Arizona (34,308 acres for 47.2 percent), Utah (33,661 acres for 63.9 percent), Idaho (32,614 for 61.6 percent), and Oregon (32,291 for 52.4 percent).

Rhode Island has the smallest amount of federal landholdings, just 2 acres, followed by Connecticut (6 acres) and Delaware (27 acres). *See also individual state profiles in Chapter 7.*

See 485 Which state has devoted the most acreage to state parks?

BUSINESS AND LABOR

Q 451. What is the dominant sector in my state's economy?

A Whereas manufacturing was once the single most important sector in this country, twenty-four states now have economies that are dominated by the services and other sectors. Business services, tourism, motion pictures, and gambling all fall under the general heading of services. Another important sector today is finance, insurance, and real estate (abbreviated below as "financial"). The country's long-time financial capital, New York, has been joined by Idaho, Nebraska, North Dakota, and South Dakota—states that have adopted regulations favoring the financial and insurance industries. Following is a list of the business sectors that predominated in each of the fifty states as of the mid-1990s.

State	Sector	State	Sector
Alabama	manufacturing	Hawaii	services
Alaska	mining	Idaho	financial
Arizona	services	Illinois	services
Arkansas	manufacturing	Indiana	manufacturing
California	services	Iowa	manufacturing
Colorado	services	Kansas	manufacturing
Connecticut	financial	Kentucky	manufacturing
Delaware	financial	Louisiana	manufacturing
Florida	services		
Georgia	manufacturing		*(table continues)*

(Continued)

State	Sector	State	Sector
Maine	manufacturing	Ohio	manufacturing
Maryland	services	Oklahoma	manufacturing
Massachusetts	services	Oregon	manufacturing
Michigan	manufacturing	Pennsylvania	services
Minnesota	manufacturing	Rhode Island	financial
Mississippi	manufacturing	South Carolina	manufacturing
Missouri	manufacturing	South Dakota	financial
Montana	services	Tennessee	manufacturing
Nebraska	financial	Texas	manufacturing
Nevada	services	Utah	services
New Hampshire	manufacturing	Vermont	manufacturing
New Jersey	services	Virginia	services
New Mexico	services	Washington	manufacturing
New York	financial	West Virginia	manufacturing
North Carolina	manufacturing	Wisconsin	manufacturing
North Dakota	financial	Wyoming	manufacturing

Source: Virginia Gray and Herbert Jacob, *Politics in the American States: A Comparative Analysis,* 6th ed. (Washington, D.C.: CQ Press, 1996).

▶ How fast is my state's economy growing? *See 448 Which states have the highest and lowest economic growth rates?*

Q **452. How many union members are there in my state?**

A As of 1997, there were about 16.1 million union members nationwide, or about 14.1 percent of all workers. New York was the most heavily unionized of all states—26.3 percent of all workers belonged to unions. But in Alaska, Hawaii, Michigan, New Jersey, and Washington, unions also claimed 20 percent or more of workers as members. Union membership in the states in 1997 was as follows:

State	Union members (thousands)	Percentage of workers	State	Union members (thousands)	Percentage of workers
Alabama	184.5	10.2	Arkansas	59.4	5.9
Alaska	50.1	20.0	California	2,066.7	16.0
Arizona	131.7	7.0		*(table continues)*	

(Continued)

State	Union members (thousands)	Percentage of workers	State	Union members (thousands)	Percentage of workers
Colorado	174.2	9.6	New Hampshire	55.6	10.2
Connecticut	247.8	16.9	New Jersey	802.1	22.0
Delaware	39.2	11.7			
Florida	403.0	6.8	New Mexico	55.6	8.4
Georgia	238.1	7.1	New York	1,949.4	26.3
			North Carolina	126.2	3.8
Hawaii	126.7	26.3	North Dakota	23.9	8.6
Idaho	43.4	8.5	Ohio	931.3	18.9
Illinois	970.8	18.5			
Indiana	398.6	14.6	Oklahoma	109.5	8.4
Iowa	172.4	13.2	Oregon	242.2	17.6
			Pennsylvania	866.0	17.1
Kansas	86.9	7.8	Rhode Island	80.9	18.7
Kentucky	193.1	12.2	South Carolina	61.3	3.7
Louisiana	118.7	7.0			
Maine	72.0	13.5	South Dakota	21.0	6.9
Maryland	348.7	14.9	Tennessee	192.9	8.6
			Texas	538.6	6.4
Massachusetts	423.1	15.1	Utah	74.0	8.3
Michigan	969.0	23.1	Vermont	21.8	8.5
Minnesota	436.1	19.9			
Mississippi	57.5	5.4	Virginia	192.6	6.5
Missouri	359.3	14.6	Washington	508.2	20.5
			West Virginia	105.6	15.6
Montana	47.3	13.8	Wisconsin	468.0	18.8
Nebraska	68.8	9.3	Wyoming	18.7	9.3
Nevada	147.1	19.1			

Source: U.S. Census Bureau, *Statistical Abstract of the United States: 1998* (Washington, D.C.: Government Printing Office, 1998). Census Bureau obtained data from Barry Hirsch and David Macpherson, *Union Membership and Earnings Data Book: Compilations from the Current Population Survey,* 1998 ed. (Washington, D.C.: Bureau of National Affairs, 1998).

453. How people are working in my state?

Of the fifty states, California has the most people working, a total of almost 14.9 million. Texas ranks second with almost 9.4 million people working, and New York is third with over 8.2 million. Employment in each state for 1997, and the growth in employment from 1996 to 1997, was as follows:

State	Jobholders (thousands)	Growth (%)	State	Jobholders (thousands)	Growth (%)
Alabama	2,009	0.9	Mississippi	1,211	0.2
Alaska	300	0.1	Missouri	2,748	1.9
Arizona	2,185	4.3	Montana	437	1.0
Arkansas	1,179	0.8	Nebraska	900	1.6
California	14,890	2.7	Nevada	862	6.5
			New Hampshire	636	1.3
Colorado	2,100	1.7	New Jersey	3,934	1.4
Connecticut	1,663	1.7			
Delaware	374	2.1	New Mexico	772	1.6
Florida	6,814	3.6	New York	8,216	1.0
Georgia	3,699	1.2	North Carolina	3,667	2.0
			North Dakota	339	2.7
Hawaii	560	-0.5	Ohio	5,490	0.9
Idaho	610	1.6			
Illinois	5,857	0.9	Oklahoma	1,542	2.6
Indiana	3,020	1.1	Oregon	1,616	3.7
Iowa	1,558	1.6	Pennsylvania	5,692	2.1
			Rhode Island	476	0.3
Kansas	1,338	2.8	South Carolina	1,817	0.7
Kentucky	1,827	2.1			
Louisiana	1,878	1.1	South Dakota	381	1.1
Maine	634	1.4	Tennessee	2,621	0.8
Maryland	2,645	1.4	Texas	9,393	2.6
			Utah	1,019	4.2
Massachusetts	3,110	2.2	Vermont	317	1.2
Michigan	4,672	1.3	Virginia	3,385	2.2
Minnesota	2,585	2.1	Washington	2,839	3.9

(table continues)

(Continued)

State	Jobholders (thousands)	Growth (%)	State	Jobholders (thousands)	Growth (%)
West Virginia	753	1.5	Wyoming	246	0.0
Wisconsin	2,820	1.8			

Source: Kendra A. Hovey and Harold A. Hovey, *CQ's State Fact Finder: Rankings Across America 1998* (Washington, D.C.: Congressional Quarterly, 1998).

Q 454. How many people work for state and local governments?

A As of the mid-1990s, California had 1.48 million state and local government employees, more than any other state. Both New York and Texas also had over 1 million employees as well. Vermont had the fewest, just under 34,000.

State and local employment in the states was as follows in 1995:

State	State employees	Local employees	State	State employees	Local employees
Alabama	81	165	Maryland	81	172
Alaska	22	24	Massachusetts	82	220
Arizona	58	161	Michigan	141	324
Arkansas	48	90	Minnesota	73	196
California	338	1,141	Mississippi	50	122
Colorado	57	148	Missouri	79	192
Connecticut	63	102	Montana	18	38
Delaware	22	19	Nebraska	30	76
Florida	175	534	Nevada	21	53
Georgia	115	333	New Hampshire	17	38
Hawaii	51	14	New Jersey	125	312
Idaho	21	46	New Mexico	42	68
Illinois	141	444	New York	257	856
Indiana	89	217	North Carolina	115	281
Iowa	53	116	North Dakota	16	22
Kansas	48	118	Ohio	143	425
Kentucky	73	133	Oklahoma	68	129
Louisiana	93	171	Oregon	52	114
Maine	21	45	Pennsylvania	152	369

(table continues)

(Continued)

State	State employees	Local employees	State	State employees	Local employees
Rhode Island	20	29	Vermont	13	21
South Carolina	78	135	Virginia	116	247
South Dakota	14	27	Washington	96	188
Tennessee	84	188	West Virginia	35	60
Texas	268	858	Wisconsin	64	201
Utah	42	63	Wyoming	11	27

Source: U.S. Census Bureau, *Statistical Abstract of the United States: 1998* (Washington, D.C.: Government Printing Office, 1998).

See 472 Which state has the largest number of education employees?

Q **455. Which states had the highest employment growth in a recent year?**

A Nevada led all other states with a 6.5 percent increase in general employment between mid-1996 and mid-1997. Arizona posted a 4.3 percent gain, followed closely by Utah with 4.2. Average employment growth was 2.9 percent.

Hawaii lost jobs—employment declined 0.05 percent—the worst performance among the states. Wyoming had no employment growth at all, and Alaska and Mississippi posted only slight gains (0.1 and 0.2 percent, respectively). The District of Columbia, which is not a state, had a decline in employment of 0.09 percent.

Q **456. What was the unemployment rate in my state?**

A Alaska had the highest unemployment rate in the country during 1997 (7.2 percent), but it was California that had the largest number of unemployed—a total of 973,000 against Alaska's 23,000. The reason of course is California has a much larger population than Alaska, and while California's percentage of unemployed was lower than Alaska's, the overall total of jobless persons was far greater.

Nebraska posted the lowest unemployment rate, 2.4 percent. The unemployment rate and number of jobless in the states during 1997 was as follows:

State	Rate (%)	Jobless (thousands)	State	Rate (%)	Jobless (thousands)
Alabama	4.7	99	Montana	5.1	23
Alaska	7.2	23	Nebraska	2.4	22
Arizona	4.1	94	Nevada	4.4	40
Arkansas	5.5	68	New Hampshire	3.0	20
California	6.1	973	New Jersey	5.4	223
Colorado	3.1	66	New Mexico	6.4	53
Connecticut	4.8	83	New York	6.4	561
Delaware	4.3	17	North Carolina	3.7	142
Florida	4.6	329	North Dakota	2.6	9
Georgia	4.3	168	Ohio	4.2	240
Hawaii	6.2	37	Oklahoma	3.8	60
Idaho	4.9	32	Oregon	5.3	90
Illinois	4.6	284	Pennsylvania	5.3	317
Indiana	3.2	99	Rhode Island	5.5	28
Iowa	2.6	42	South Carolina	4.6	87
Kansas	3.9	54	South Dakota	2.7	11
Kentucky	5.3	101	Tennessee	5.5	152
Louisiana	6.3	127	Texas	5.4	540
Maine	5.0	34	Utah	3.0	31
Maryland	4.7	131	Vermont	3.8	13
Massachusetts	3.9	125	Virginia	4.2	148
Michigan	3.8	186	Washington	4.7	141
Minnesota	3.1	82	West Virginia	6.7	54
Mississippi	5.0	64	Wisconsin	3.8	111
Missouri	3.6	102	Wyoming	4.9	13

Source: Kendra A. Hovey and Harold A. Hovey, *CQ's State Fact Finder: Rankings Across America 1998* (Washington, D.C.: Congressional Quarterly, 1998).

Q 457. Who usually heads the state's law enforcement programs?

A In nearly all states, the attorney general is the state's top law enforcement officer. Although law enforcement is only part of the attorney general's job (he or she is the state's top legal counsel and head of the justice department as well), it is a source of enormous political power. That is because the attorney general has the power to initiate high profile criminal prosecutions and lawsuits, which usually command considerable media attention and help build the attorney general's reputation among voters.

See 144 What does the attorney general do?

Q 458. How much do state and local governments spend on law enforcement?

A Law enforcement spending includes funding for both police and corrections facilities by state and local governments. The bigger states with large populations generally spend larger amounts on law enforcement, and in 1994 California ($11.6 billion), New York ($7.5 billion), and Texas ($5.1 billion) were the top three in terms of total dollars. North Dakota ($71 million) and Vermont ($86 million) spent the least. Law enforcement spending by state in 1994 is listed below.

State	Spending (in millions)	State	Spending (in millions)
Alabama	753	Hawaii	291
Alaska	283	Idaho	223
Arizona	1,183	Illinois	3,079
Arkansas	372	Indiana	967
California	11,609	Iowa	460
Colorado	937	Kansas	528
Connecticut	971	Kentucky	594
Delaware	187	Louisiana	1,003
Florida	4,648	Maine	196
Georgia	1,760	Maryland	1,553
			(table continues)

(Continued)

State	Spending (in millions)	State	Spending (in millions)
Minnesota	956	Oregon	777
Mississippi	337	Pennsylvania	2,599
Missouri	947	Rhode Island	251
		South Carolina	788
Montana	137		
Nebraska	273	South Dakota	120
Nevada	529	Tennessee	1,024
New Hampshire	213	Texas	5,093
New Jersey	2,611	Utah	366
		Vermont	86
New Mexico	433		
New York	7,483	Virginia	1,597
North Carolina	1,750	Washington	1,384
North Dakota	71	West Virginia	194
Ohio	2,573	Wisconsin	1,265
		Wyoming	111
Oklahoma	554		

Source: Kendra A. Hovey and Harold A. Hovey, *CQ's State Fact Finder: Rankings Across America 1998* (Washington, D.C.: Congressional Quarterly, 1998).

Q 459. Which states spent the most and least on their prison systems?

A California spent more than any other state on corrections, almost $3.8 billion in fiscal 1996. As might be expected, the two other largest states, Texas and New York, were not far behind with spending of about $2.4 billion each. North Dakota had the smallest outlay, just $17 million, followed by Wyoming ($32 million) and Vermont ($43 million). Spending on corrections by individual states was as follows in fiscal 1996:

State	Prison spending (in millions)	State	Prison spending (in millions)
Alabama	220	Arkansas	171
Alaska	150	California	3,843
Arizona	499	*(table continues)*	

(Continued)

State	Prison spending (in millions)	State	Prison spending (in millions)
Colorado	353	New Hampshire	62
Connecticut	465	New Jersey	875
Delaware	113		
Florida	1,647	New Mexico	175
Georgia	817	New York	2,377
		North Carolina	873
Hawaii	106	North Dakota	17
Idaho	98	Ohio	1,144
Illinois	873		
Indiana	378	Oklahoma	296
Iowa	184	Oregon	291
		Pennsylvania	1,077
Kansas	195	Rhode Island	116
Kentucky	226	South Carolina	391
Louisiana	384		
Maine	64	South Dakota	44
Maryland	743	Tennessee	445
		Texas	2,351
Massachusetts	729	Utah	158
Michigan	1,241	Vermont	43
Minnesota	302		
Mississippi	230	Virginia	809
Missouri	312	Washington	497
		West Virginia	82
Montana	66	Wisconsin	513
Nebraska	94	Wyoming	32
Nevada	151		

Source: U.S. Census Bureau, *Statistical Abstract of the United States: 1998* (Washington, D.C.: Government Printing Office, 1988).

A Big increases in the violent crime rate (crimes per one hundred thousand people) during the early 1990s, but for the 1996–1997 period most states posted declines. The states with the largest increases in 1996–1997, for example, were Iowa (13.8 percent) and South Dakota (11.4 percent).

Montana and the District of Columbia, on the other hand, had the biggest drop—18 percent each—and Colorado posted a decrease of 10.2 percent. The average change nationwide was a decrease of 4 percent in the violent crime rate.

The number of violent crimes committed per one hundred thousand people in 1997, and the percentage change in the crime rate between 1996 and 1997, are shown below for each state.

State	Crimes per 100,000	Percentage change, 1996–1997	State	Crimes per 100,000	Percentage change, 1996–1997
Alabama	564.5	−0.2	Minnesota	337.8	−0.3
Alaska	701.1	−3.7	Mississippi	469.0	−4.0
Arizona	623.7	−1.2	Missouri	577.4	−2.3
Arkansas	526.9	0.5	Montana	132.1	−18.0
California	798.3	−7.5	Nebraska	438.4	0.9
Colorado	363.2	−10.2	Nevada	798.7	−1.6
Connecticut	390.9	−5.1	New Hampshire	113.2	−4.2
Delaware	677.9	1.4	New Jersey	492.6	−7.3
Florida	1,023.6	−2.6	New Mexico	853.3	1.5
Georgia	606.6	−5.0	New York	688.6	−5.3
Hawaii	277.9	−1.0	North Carolina	607.0	3.2
Idaho	256.8	−3.9	North Dakota	87.2	3.8
Illinois	861.4	−3.3	Ohio	435.4	1.6
Indiana	514.6	−4.2	Oklahoma	559.5	−6.3
Iowa	310.0	13.8	Oregon	444.4	−4.0
Kansas	409.2	−1.1	Pennsylvania	442.1	−8.0
Kentucky	316.9	−1.1	Rhode Island	333.5	−3.9
Louisiana	855.9	−7.9	South Carolina	990.3	−0.7
Maine	120.8	−3.3	South Dakota	197.4	11.4
Maryland	846.6	−9.1	Tennessee	789.7	2.0
Massachusetts	644.2	0.3	Texas	602.5	−6.5
Michigan	590.0	−7.1			*(table continues)*

(Continued)

State	Crimes per 100,000	Percentage change, 1996–1997	State	Crimes per 100,000	Percentage change, 1996–1997
Utah	334.0	0.6	West Virginia	218.7	4.1
Vermont	119.7	−1.2	Wisconsin	270.6	7.1
Virginia	345.2	1.1	Wyoming	255.2	2.2
Washington	440.7	2.2			

Source: U.S. Department of Justice, *Crime in the United States, 1997* (Washington, D.C.: Government Printing Office, 1998).

Q 461. What factors contribute to the crime rate?

A Experts do not know what causes people to commit crimes, but they can point to a number of factors that are associated with at least some criminal behavior. Young males, for example, are far more likely to commit crimes. Males under age twenty account for about half of all those arrested for significant crimes. Drug and alcohol abuse, unemployment, and poverty also are factors that contribute to crime. One recent survey showed fully 80 percent of all prisoners in jail had been convicted for crimes related in some way to substance abuse. Another factor experts point to is population density. Cities generally have higher crime rates than rural areas, perhaps in part because there are more opportunities to commit crimes in the first place.

▶ Which states have a death penalty? *See 410 Do all states impose capital punishment?*
▶ Can the governor pardon criminals? *See 97 Are pardon, reprieve, and commutation of sentence the same?*

Q 462. What percentage of cases result in an arrest? A conviction?

A Arrest rates vary considerably according to the type of crime involved. Police clear about three-quarters of all murder cases with arrests, for example, and about three-fifths of assault cases. The rate is lower for rapes and robberies, one-half and one-quarter, respectively, and lower still for property crimes, such as larceny, burglary, auto theft, and arson. Property crime cases are cleared by arrests in only about a fifth of the cases.

Getting convictions in these cases is another matter, however. Overall only about one-third of all arrests police make result in a conviction, but here there are clear regional differences. Courts in southern states are tougher on criminals, for example, and tend to convict defendants in felony cases at double the rate outside the region.

Q 463. Why have state prison populations increased in recent years?

A Several factors are involved here, including a general rise in population, a rising crime rate, and the effort to get tough on crime by imposing stiffer sentences. For example, as the general population increases in size, one can reasonably expect to see an increase in the total number of criminals in the prison population, too.

Since the 1960s, however, the crime rate has also increased dramatically. The crime rate is the number of crimes committed per one hundred thousand in population (of a state or the United States as a whole). Between 1960 and 1980 the violent crime rate for the United States increased threefold, which meant that many more crimes were being committed than would be expected, given the increase in population during that time.

By the 1980s the crime wave forced a dramatic change in the courts' sentencing policy—one that kept criminals in jail longer and so increased prison populations. Previously judges had considerable leeway in sentencing offenders—called *indeterminate sentencing*—and rules for parole often released criminals convicted of serious crimes from prison after only a few years.

Under the new policy, called *determinate sentencing,* offenders must serve out their full sentence without possibility of parole. (Sentences can be reduced by a set amount for convicts who keep out of trouble in prison, however.) The stiffer penalties under determinate sentencing help keep criminals off the street, but they also contribute substantially to the sharp rise in prison populations.

Q 464. Are there more blacks and Hispanics than whites in prisons?

A Yes, black inmates in state and federal prisons outnumbered whites for the first time in 1994. Blacks and Hispanics starting prison sentences that year accounted for almost 75 percent of the new inmates entering prison.

Q 465. Which states have the highest and lowest incarceration rates?

A The top three are Texas, Louisiana, and Oklahoma. Measured in terms of the number of prisoners per one hundred thousand in state population (the incarceration rate), Texas had the highest rate of the three and locked up almost 75 percent more criminals than the 1996 national average of 394 prisoners per one hundred thousand people. At the other end of the spectrum, North Dakota imprisoned only 101 criminals per one hundred thousand. Prison populations and incarceration rates (per one hundred thousand people) by state for 1996 were as follows:

State	Prisoners	Incarceration rate (per 100,000)	State	Prisoners	Incarceration rate (per 100,000
Alabama	21,760	492	Nebraska	3,275	194
Alaska	3,706	379	Nevada	8,215	502
Arizona	22,573	481	New Hampshire	2,071	177
Arkansas	9,407	357	New Jersey	27,490	343
California	147,712	451			
			New Mexico	4,724	251
Colorado	12,438	322	New York	69,709	261
Connecticut	15,007	314	North Carolina	30,701	379
Delaware	5,110	428	North Dakota	722	101
Florida	63,763	439	Ohio	46,174	413
Georgia	35,139	462			
			Oklahoma	19,593	591
Hawaii	4,011	249	Oregon	8,661	226
Idaho	3,834	319	Pennsylvania	34,537	286
Illinois	38,852	327	Rhode Island	3,271	205
Indiana	16,960	287	South Carolina	20,446	532
Iowa	6,342	222			
			South Dakota	2,064	281
Kansas	7,756	301	Tennessee	15,626	292
Kentucky	12,910	331	Texas	132,383	686
Louisiana	26,779	615	Utah	3,939	194
Maine	1,476	112	Vermont	1,125	137
Maryland	22,050	412			
			Virginia	27,655	404
Massachusetts	11,790	302	Washington	12,527	224
Michigan	42,349	440	West Virginia	2,754	150
Minnesota	5,158	110	Wisconsin	12,854	230
Mississippi	14,292	498	Wyoming	1,483	307
Missouri	22,003	409			
Montana	2,073	235			

Source: Kendra A. Hovey and Harold A. Hovey, *CQ's State Fact Finder: Rankings Across America 1998* (Washington, D.C.: Congressional Quarterly, 1998).

Q 466. How much does it cost to keep a criminal in prison?

A States must pay to feed, cloth, shelter, and keep watch over inmates, all of which can amount to a considerable sum. The average daily cost of keeping a criminal behind bars is highest in Alaska, $106.63. Maine pays $83.15 per day and Minnesota $82.24 per day. Alabama's $25.10 is the lowest, about half the national average of $53.85 per day. The average per diem cost for each state in 1996 was as follows:

State	Daily cost per prisoner	State	Daily cost per prisoner
Alabama	$25.10	Missouri	28.18
Alaska	106.63		
Arizona	44.79	Montana	41.29
Arkansas	34.84	Nebraska	45.64
California	59.26	Nevada	38.76
		New Hampshire	47.00
Colorado	58.64	New Jersey	70.15
Connecticut	63.19		
Delaware	51.46	New Mexico	76.89
Florida	42.51	New York	76.57
Georgia	48.91	North Carolina	63.53
		North Dakota	50.60
Hawaii	78.56	Ohio	40.70
Idaho	48.31		
Illinois	43.18	Oklahoma	37.19
Indiana	45.17	Oregon	53.73
Iowa	48.40	Pennsylvania	60.46
		Rhode Island	79.00
Kansas	51.17	South Carolina	36.00
Kentucky	37.30		
Louisiana	34.52	South Dakota	37.47
Maine	83.15	Tennessee	50.80
Maryland	50.00	Texas	44.40
		Utah	54.22
Massachusetts	81.37	Vermont	74.38
Michigan	51.74		
Minnesota	82.24	Virginia	46.39
Mississippi	33.28	(table continues)	

(Continued)

State	Daily cost per prisoner	State	Daily cost per prisoner
Washington	63.53	Wisconsin	55.24
West Virginia	43.84	Wyoming	49.40

Source: Kendra A. Hovey and Harold A. Hovey, *CQ's State Fact Finder: Rankings Across America 1998* (Washington, D.C.: Congressional Quarterly, 1998).

Q **467. What did the infamous Willie Horton case reveal about the politics of early release programs?**

A Faced with overcrowded prisons and court orders limiting the number of inmates in prison facilities, state officials found obvious advantages to early release programs. Cell space can be freed up by shortening prisoners' sentences, and the state saves money that it otherwise would have had to pay for keeping the inmate in prison. The problem with early release, and liberal parole policies of years past, is that some criminals go right back to committing crimes after they get out of jail.

When that happens public outrage can be politically damaging for elected officials. Willie Horton was a case in point. Horton, a convicted murderer, disappeared while on a weekend furlough from a Massachusetts prison. While on the loose he raped a woman and stabbed a man before being caught again. His vicious acts might well have been forgotten had not presidential candidate George Bush made an issue of the Horton case in the 1988 campaign. Bush used Horton as evidence that his rival, Massachusetts governor Michael Dukakis, was soft on criminals and that such a policy could have serious consequences for innocent victims. In fact, other states at the time also had prison furlough programs, and the Massachusetts program had been in place when Dukakis took office. But the Horton incident occurred during Dukakis's administration and he paid a price for it.

Q **468. What percentage of arrests are for "victimless" crimes?**

A As many as half of all arrests in urban areas are for so-called victimless crimes, such as illegal gambling, pornography, prostitution, and the sale and possession of illegal drugs. The volume of cases has strained the criminal justice system, and according to some, has made criminals out of many people unnecessarily. They argue for decriminalization of these offenses, because they believe those who engage in gambling, prostitution, and drug use harm no one but themselves. But as opponents of decriminalization point out, drug use and other "victimless" crimes can and do destroy individual lives and tear apart their families as well.

And although there may not be a direct link between substance abuse and criminal behavior, a U.S. Justice Department report earlier in this decade found that of the men arrested for serious crimes in various cities, anywhere from half to three-quarters of them tested positive for drug use. Another more recent study showed that 80 percent of all inmates had been convicted of crimes related in some way to substance abuse.

EDUCATION

Q 469. Who runs the public schools?

A State government has overall responsibility for the schools, but in forty-nine states local governments have been given the authority to handle daily operations of primary and secondary schools, including management, hiring and firing of teachers, and some aspects of budgeting. Hawaii has a centralized school system that is under state control.

In the forty-nine states, the state government is mainly concerned with matters of education policy, including such fundamental decisions as teacher-student ratios, curriculum requirements, and number of days in the school year. In recent years, states have become more directly involved, though, in response to pressure to improve the quality of education. Some states have even taken direct control of especially troubled local schools.

470. Who pays for them?

 Until fairly recently, public schools were funded almost entirely by local property taxes. During the 1970s, though, state funding for school districts grew rapidly, and by 1979 had become the major source. As of 1994, state funding remained about even with the local share. The federal government share was about 6 percent.

See 474 What did the federal Elementary and Secondary Education Act of 1965 do?

Q **471. Which state spends the most for education, in totai dollars and on a per student basis? The least?**

A In terms of total dollars, the three largest states spent the most on state and local education in the school year ending in 1997—California spent $34.1 million, New York, $27.6 million, and Texas, $24.5 million. Wyoming spent the least, $695,000, followed by South Dakota, $730,000.

On a per pupil basis, though, the top three in spending were Alaska ($10,393), New Jersey ($9,455), and New York ($8,564). At $3,837, Utah's per pupil spending was the lowest in the nation.

State spending in dollars per pupil for 1997 was as follows:

State	Spending per pupil	State	Spending per pupil
Alabama	$5,478	Massachusetts	$7,628
Alaska	10,393	Michigan	7,318
Arizona	4,777	Minnesota	6,529
Arkansas	4,498	Mississippi	4,351
California	5,327	Missouri	5,375
Colorado	5,550	Montana	6,006
Connecticut	8,845	Nebraska	5,636
Delaware	8,098	Nevada	5,384
Florida	5,988	New Hampshire	6,557
Georgia	6,459	New Jersey	10,284
Hawaii	6,066	New Mexico	5,457
Idaho	4,794	New York	9,628
Illinois	6,048	North Carolina	5,623
Indiana	6,411	North Dakota	5,016
Iowa	5,546	Ohio	6,132
Kansas	6,157	Oklahoma	4,486
Kentucky	5,959	Oregon	6,602
Louisiana	5,092	Pennsylvania	7,568
Maine	6,775	Rhode Island	8,030
Maryland	7,052	South Carolina	5,357

(table continues)

(Continued)

State	Spending per pupil	State	Spending per pupil
South Dakota	$4,990	Virginia	$6,370
Tennessee	5,268	Washington	6,084
Texas	6,041	West Virginia	6,769
Utah	3,822	Wisconsin	6,999
Vermont	7,561	Wyoming	6,541

Source: U.S. Census Bureau, *Statistical Abstract of the United States: 1998* (Washington, D.C.: Government Printing Office, 1998). Data collected from Estimates of School Statistics Database, National Education Association, Washington, D.C.

Q 472. Which state has the largest number of education employees?

A Texas had 521,993 state and local education employees as of the mid-1990s, more than any other state. California employed the second-largest number at 495,587, and New York the third at 380,411. Delaware had the fewest, just 14,008, although three other states also had fewer than 15,000 education employees—North Dakota (14,045), Wyoming (14,558), and Alaska (14,776).

Education employment by state, as of 1995, was:

State	Education employees	State	Education employees
Alabama	90,597	Illinois	215,474
Alaska	14,776	Indiana	127,817
Arizona	85,974	Iowa	67,764
Arkansas	61,417		
California	495,587	Kansas	65,575
		Kentucky	94,715
Colorado	77,245	Louisiana	105,840
Connecticut	69,792	Maine	32,259
Delaware	14,008	Maryland	98,057
Florida	255,627		
Georgia	186,396	Massachusetts	130,278
		Michigan	184,756
Hawaii	23,365		
Idaho	26,706	*(table continues)*	

(Continued)

State	Education employees	State	Education employees
Minnesota	107,641	Oregon	61,922
Mississippi	65,400	Pennsylvania	203,093
Missouri	114,866	Rhode Island	19,209
		South Carolina	83,245
Montana	27,225		
Nebraska	41,964	South Dakota	17,273
Nevada	27,427	Tennessee	102,810
New Hampshire	24,987	Texas	521,993
New Jersey	187,442	Utah	39,915
		Vermont	16,947
New Mexico	41,809		
New York	380,411	Virginia	151,882
North Carolina	152,039	Washington	87,730
North Dakota	14,045	West Virginia	42,406
Ohio	209,908	Wisconsin	106,434
		Wyoming	14,558
Oklahoma	81,669		

Source: Kendra A. Hovey and Harold A. Hovey, *CQ's State Fact Finder: Rankings Across America 1998* (Washington, D.C.: Congressional Quarterly, 1998).

See 454 How many people work for state and local governments?

473. What percentage of teachers are women?

The teaching field traditionally has been dominated by women, and despite growing opportunities in other fields, women still make up the bulk of public school teachers. As of the mid-1990s, about 70 percent of all public school teachers were women.

474. What did the federal Elementary and Secondary Education Act of 1965 do?

Prior to the 1960s the federal government played only a small role in primary and secondary education. The Elementary and Secondary Education Act of 1965 changed that, however, by providing a direct federal subsidy to school districts nationwide. The federal money went to pay for teachers' aides, textbooks, library books, and special programs for poor children, the mentally retarded, and people with disabilities.

Between 1960 and 1980, at the end of the Carter administration, federal spending on education increased from 4.4 percent of total school spending to 9 percent. Along with that came greater federal involvement in primary and secondary school policy, however.

During the 1980s the Reagan administration cut back federal payments to states for education and other programs, so that by 1990 the federal share of total education spending had fallen to 6 percent. Total federal outlays for education increased during both the Bush and Clinton administrations. Currently, about 90 percent of all school districts receive federal money under the Elementary and Secondary Education Act.

Q 475. Do states attempt to equalize funding for poorer school districts?

A Every state has tried in one way or another to adjust its school finance system to provide extra funding for school districts with a low property tax base. In fact, efforts at equalizing funding for school districts has gone hand in hand with the increase in state funding for schools in recent years.

But even though states have directed extra monies to poorer school districts, disparities between rich and poor districts still exist. That is because poor school districts, while better off with extra state funds, still cannot raise as much from property taxes as wealthier districts can.

Q 476. Is there a link between higher spending for education and better academic performance?

A Strange as it may seem, scores of studies have shown there is not. Sociologist James S. Coleman first uncovered this seemingly unlikely fact in a 1966 study of thousands of schools. Contrary to popular belief, he found that such things as class size, school facilities, spending, and even the curriculum did not significantly improve overall academic achievement. Instead it was the family and socioeconomic background that counted in student performance.

Q 477. What is the most powerful education interest group in state politics?

A Teachers are, particularly where they are represented by unions and professional organizations such as the American Federation of Teachers and the National Education Association. Since the late 1960s especially, teachers' groups have become much more influential in state politics.

See 254 What are the most influential lobbying groups?

Q 478. Who sets state education policy?

A The state superintendent of schools (also called the commissioner of education) traditionally has served as the executive head of the state board of education and has overall responsibility for local school standards, teacher certification, and other state policy matters. However, in recent years, both the state governor and state legislature have played a more dominant role in setting education policy in many states.

State superintendents of education are appointed by the state board of education in twenty-nine states. Fifteen states elect their superintendents by popular ballot. Governors in six states have the power appoint them to office.

Q 479. How are state education board members selected?

A Depending on the state, education board members are chosen by voters, appointed by the governor, elected by the legislature or by local school boards, or chosen by a multiphase procedure. Voters in ten states elect board members on statewide popular ballots, while governors in thirty-two other states are empowered to appoint board members. State legislatures in two states elect them, and in one state local school boards have that power. Five other states use multiphase procedures.

The number of members on the state education board varies by state, from as few as six to as many as twenty-three.

ENVIRONMENT

Q 480. How do the states and federal government divide up responsibilities for environmental protection?

A The federal government, through the offices of the Environmental Protection Agency (EPA), sets national goals and standards for such things as allowable levels of air and water pollution, disposal of hazardous wastes, and restrictions on the use of wetlands and other ecologically sensitive areas. States take care of designing programs, as well as monitoring environmental quality and enforcing the EPA rules, for which it receives EPA grants to help defray costs. The EPA also funds the majority of research work.

Some states have gone a step further by imposing more stringent environmental regulations and taking a greater share of the costs of implementing environmental policies.

Q 481. Do tough environmental regulations hurt the economy?

A Very strict environment regulations can hurt state and local economies by forcing companies to lay off workers and by raising costs of doing business beyond a point where they can remain competitive in the marketplace. For example, one estimate held the 1990 amendments to the Clean Air Act would cost American industries an additional $21.5 billion per year—plus fifteen thousand coal workers were expected to lose their jobs.

When setting environmental standards, federal and state governments usually must balance the need for a cleaner, healthier environment against the necessity of providing jobs and keeping the economy growing.

Q 482. How many states have recycling laws?

A As of the early 1990s, statewide recycling laws had been adopted in thirty-four states. The idea here was to reduce the amount of solid waste that must be incinerated or dumped in landfills by reusing at least a portion of it. One estimate, for example, calculated that 37 percent of municipal waste was paper, 18 percent was debris from yards, and 10 percent was metals. In theory, at least, much of the waste could be recycled—even the yard waste could be reused as mulch or compost.

Citizen participation is a problem, however—an average of only about 40 percent participate when programs are not mandatory—and the supply of recycled materials generally exceeds the markets for them.

Q 483. How many hazardous waste sites are there in my state?

A The Environmental Protection Agency (EPA) has designated hundreds of hazardous waste sites nationwide for cleanup because of chemical and other pollution. A number have been cleaned up under the Superfund program, but many others remain to be done. New Jersey, with 110 remaining sites, has the most of any state. Pennsylvania is not far behind with 99 sites, and California has 94. North Dakota is the only state that does not have any hazardous waste sites. Hazardous waste sites still on the EPA's list as of 1997 were:

State	Hazardous waste sites	State	Hazardous waste sites
Alabama	13	Montana	9
Alaska	7	Nebraska	10
Arizona	10	Nevada	1
Arkansas	11	New Hampshire	18
California	94	New Jersey	110
Colorado	17	New Mexico	10
Connecticut	14	New York	80
Delaware	17	North Carolina	23
Florida	54	North Dakota	0
Georgia	16	Ohio	37
Hawaii	4	Oklahoma	11
Idaho	9	Oregon	11
Illinois	41	Pennsylvania	99
Indiana	30	Rhode Island	12
Iowa	17	South Carolina	26
Kansas	11	South Dakota	2
Kentucky	16	Tennessee	16
Louisiana	17	Texas	27
Maine	12	Utah	16
Maryland	16	Vermont	8
Massachusetts	31	Virginia	25
Michigan	74	Washington	47
Minnesota	28	West Virginia	7
Mississippi	3	Wisconsin	39
Missouri	22	Wyoming	3

Source: U.S. Environmental Protection Agency, National Priorities List.

A By one measure anyway, air pollution emissions, Texas was the nation's leading polluter in 1995. The EPA estimated emissions of five basic pollutants in the state amounted to 17,760,000 short tons for the year. (A short ton is 2,000 pounds.) California was not far behind with 13,916,000 short tons, followed by Florida and Ohio. Rhode Island and Hawaii did the least polluting during 1995, with estimated emissions at 369,000 short tons and 409,000 short tons, respectively. EPA estimates of air pollution emissions for each state in 1995 were:

State	Emissions (short tons)	State	Emissions (short tons)
Alabama	4,982,000	Michigan	6,088,000
Alaska	834,000	Minnesota	3,778,000
Arizona	2,932,000	Mississippi	3,628,000
Arkansas	2,376,000	Missouri	5,523,000
California	13,916,000		
		Montana	2,325,000
Colorado	2,742,000	Nebraska	1,891,000
Connecticut	1,300,000	Nevada	993,000
Delaware	557,000	New Hampshire	640,000
Florida	8,857,000	New Jersey	3,260,000
Georgia	6,810,000		
		New Mexico	2,799,000
Hawaii	409,000	New York	6,926,000
Idaho	1,791,000	North Carolina	5,597,000
Illinois	7,504,000	North Dakota	1,582,000
Indiana	6,578,000	Ohio	8,447,000
Iowa	2,768,000		
		Oklahoma	4,851,000
Kansas	3,102,000	Oregon	2,923,000
Kentucky	3,807,000	Pennsylvania	7,528,000
Louisiana	5,219,000	Rhode Island	369,000
Maine	794,000	South Carolina	3,370,000
Maryland	2,583,000		
		South Dakota	1,054,000
Massachusetts	2,712,000	Tennessee	4,781,000

(table continues)

(Continued)

State	Emissions (short tons)	State	Emissions (short tons)
Texas	17,760,000	West Virginia	2,936,000
Utah	1,611,000	Wisconsin	3,795,000
Vermont	422,000	Wyoming	1,613,000
Virginia	4,255,000		
Washington	4,203,000		

Source: Kendra A. Hovey and Harold A. Hovey, *CQ's State Fact Finder: Rankings Across America 1998* (Washington, D.C.: Congressional Quarterly, 1998).

Q 485. Which state has devoted the most acreage to state parks?

A Alaska has far and away more land devoted to state parks than any other state—3.25 million acres. California has the second-largest state park system with 1.35 million acres, and Texas has the third-largest with 669,000 acres. Rhode Island has the tiniest with just 9,000 acres in state parks. Park lands in the states as of 1996 were:

State	Park acreage (1,000)	State	Park acreage (1,000)
Alabama	50	Indiana	175
Alaska	3,250	Iowa	63
Arizona	46		
Arkansas	51	Kansas	29
California	1,345	Kentucky	43
		Louisiana	39
Colorado	347	Maine	567
Connecticut	176	Maryland	249
Delaware	17		
Florida	454	Massachusetts	276
Georgia	67	Michigan	266
		Minnesota	247
Hawaii	25	Mississippi	24
Idaho	42	Missouri	137
Illinois	408	*(table continues)*	

(Continued)

State	Park acreage (1,000)	State	Park acreage (1,000)
Montana	49	Rhode Island	9
Nebraska	133	South Carolina	82
Nevada	149		
New Hampshire	154	South Dakota	93
New Jersey	327	Tennessee	134
		Texas	669
New Mexico	91	Utah	114
New York	261	Vermont	65
North Carolina	143		
North Dakota	20	Virginia	66
Ohio	204	Washington	260
		West Virginia	196
Oklahoma	71	Wisconsin	140
Oregon	92	Wyoming	120
Pennsylvania	283		

Source: U.S. Census Bureau, *Statistical Abstract of the United States: 1998* (Washington, D.C.: Government Printing Office, 1998). Data appeared originally in *1997 Annual Information Exchange* (Tucson, Ariz.: National Association of State Park Directors, 1997).

See 450 In which states does the federal government have the largest and smallest land holdings?

Q **486. What is state preemption?**

A Under this policy, state governments exercise their authority over localities and decide where to site hazardous waste facilities in the state. Most localities would rather not have one of these sites located in their vicinity, which is why the facilities are classified as a "locally unwanted land use," or LULU. But the state has an overriding need to provide a place to dispose of hazardous wastes and so preempts the local opposition.

Twenty states have adopted this policy for siting hazardous waste facilities. But others, especially southern and western states, allow localities the option of vetoing a new site.

Q **487. Which state developed the first hazardous waste reduction program?**

A New York became the first in 1981, with North Carolina and Minnesota following suit over the next three years. The idea behind the waste reduction programs was simple enough—cut down on the amount of wastes manufacturers produced as byproducts of production processes. Less waste in the first place meant less of a waste disposal problem. But that also meant redesigning the production processes, something that could be quite costly. The trade-off then became increased manufacturing costs (and higher prices) against the decreased costs of disposing of the wastes.

Q **488. What are interstate compacts?**

A By the federal Low-Level Radioactive Waste (LLW) Policy Act of 1980, each state is responsible for LLW waste that is generated commercially within its borders. However, the act does allow states two options: one, dispose of LLW at their own in-state sites; or two, join an *interstate compact* in which two or more states agree to dump their LLW at an agreed upon host site. Most states have chosen the regional approach to LLW disposal.

As of 1996, thirty-nine had joined one of the nine interstate compacts formed over the years. Among the unaligned were Massachusetts and New York, both of which produce large quantities of LLW. The other unaligned states are Maine, Michigan, New Hampshire, Rhode Island, and Vermont.

The regional compacts have made little headway on actually opening waste sites, however. Texas did open an LLW facility in 1997, the first new facility opened in decades.

The interstate compacts and their members are:

Appalachian:
    Delaware
    Maryland
    Pennsylvania
    West Virginia

Northwest:
    Idaho
    Montana
    Oregon
    Utah
    Washington

Central Midwest:
    Illinois
    Kentucky

Rocky Mountain:
    Colorado
    Nevada
    New Mexico
    Wyoming

Central States:
    Arkansas
    Kansas
    Louisiana

Nebraska
Oklahoma

Southeast:
Alabama
Florida
Georgia
Mississippi
North Carolina
Minnesota
Virginia

Midwest:
Indiana

Iowa
Tennessee
Missouri
Ohio
Wisconsin

Southwest:
Arizona
California
North Dakota
South Dakota

Northeast:
Connecticut

FEDERAL AID TO STATES

Q **489. What is the primary way states get money from the federal government?**

A The federal government uses grants in aid as the primary means to transfer money to the states for such things as health care, road building, and education. While these grants funnel much needed funds to the states, they usually are structured so that states must provide at least some matching funds. For example, grants from the interstate highway program require that states spend one dollar for every ten the federal government provides. And federal grants to states for Medicaid cover only about 57 percent of what states pay out for this rapidly growing entitlement program.

Grants do help set minimum standards nationwide for such things as education and health care, and they also work to transfer funds from wealthier states to poorer ones. In addition, they encourage local initiative in policy matters as well. But grant money often comes with strings attached—policy decisions made by the federal government that states must accept in order to receive the funds.

See 57 How has the federal government used grants to increase its control over the states? 64 When did the federal government begin funneling money to the states through grant programs? 182 What are federal mandates?

Q **490. Which state received the most in federal grants in a recent year?**

A California received the largest amount in total dollars during the 1996 fiscal year—$26.4 billion—but when figured on a per capita basis, the amount of grants it got was only slightly more than the national average of $823 per capita. New York, on the other hand, received about $24.6 billion, or $528 more than the national average on a per capita basis. Texas, which had the third highest total amount, $13.3 billion, actually got $128 less than the national average on a per capita basis. The following table gives state-by-state figures for the total amount of federal state and local grants in 1996 and the per capita amounts for each.

State	Total grants (millions)	Grants per capita	State	Total grants (millions)	Grants per capita
Alabama	$3,325	$778	Michigan	$7,194	$750
Alaska	1,051	1,731	Minnesota	3,535	759
Arizona	3,095	699	Mississippi	2,754	1,014
Arkansas	2,131	849	Missouri	4,091	763
California	26,413	829			
			Montana	964	1,097
Colorado	2,410	630	Nebraska	1,232	746
Connecticut	3,080	941	Nevada	876	547
Delaware	600	828	New Hampshire	890	766
Florida	8,442	586	New Jersey	6,506	814
Georgia	5,359	729			
			New Mexico	1,942	1,134
Hawaii	1,126	951	New York	24,560	1,351
Idaho	887	746	North Carolina	5,227	714
Illinois	9,229	779	North Dakota	734	1,140
Indiana	3,657	626	Ohio	8,776	785
Iowa	2,030	712			
			Oklahoma	2,435	738
Kansas	1,700	661	Oregon	2,797	873
Kentucky	3,355	864	Pennsylvania	10,117	839
Louisiana	4,734	1,088	Rhode Island	1,176	1,188
Maine	1,389	1,117	South Carolina	3,032	820
Maryland	3,544	699			
			South Dakota	867	1,184
Massachusetts	6,813	1,118		*(table continues)*	

(Continued)

State	Total grants (millions)	Grants per capita	State	Total grants (millions)	Grants per capita
Tennessee	$4,476	$841	Washington	$4,152	$750
Texas	13,297	695	West Virginia	2,088	1,144
Utah	1,446	723	Wisconsin	3,679	713
Vermont	641	1,088	Wyoming	708	1,473
Virginia	3,403	510			

Source: Kendra A. Hovey and Harold A. Hovey, *CQ's State Fact Finder: Rankings Across America 1998* (Washington, D.C.: Congressional Quarterly, 1998).

Q 491. Has the portion of federal grant money in state budgets been rising or falling?

A Though it varies from state to state, federal grant money usually amounts to about 20 to 25 percent of state revenues. The flow of grant money to states had increased rapidly during the 1960s and 1970s. During the 1980s the rate of growth stalled as the Reagan administration sought to downsize the federal government and reduce the budget deficit. The end of the revenue sharing program in the late 1980s accounted for much of the decline in federal grant money (see next question). By the early 1990s, however, the percentage of state revenues derived from federal grants had again begun to rise.

Q 492. How do the basic types of grants differ?

A The two basic types of grants are *block grants* and *categorical grants.* They differ primarily in the amount of flexibility the state or locality receiving the money has in spending it. Block grants allow states and localities to decide what to spend the money on within a broad area, such as transportation or secondary education. Funds from categorical grants, on the other hand, can be spent only for a specific project or program, such as building a sewage treatment plant.

Block grants are awarded on a formula basis. States or localities get the money automatically in amounts that depend on preset guidelines for the grant, such as the rate of unemployment in the state or the number of elementary school students attending classes. Categorical grants can awarded by formula or on a project-by-project basis. For project-based grants, the federal agency issuing the grant decides which state or local programs will be funded. The agency makes its decision based on program proposals that have been submitted by applicants. In the past, up to about 80 percent of categorical grants have been awarded on a project-by-project basis. Since Republicans gained control of Congress in the mid-1990s, however, there has been a greater emphasis on block grants. As of 1995 there were fifteen block grant programs in effect.

Until the late 1980s, states and localities also received *revenue-sharing grants* from the federal government. The revenue-sharing program, begun by President Richard Nixon, sent lump sum grants to states and localities. Recipient governments were free to spend the money as they saw fit. Revenue-sharing grants were sharply reduced and finally halted altogether in the 1980s as the federal government sought to cut the budget deficit.

See 57 How has the federal government used grants to increase its control over the states? 64 When did the federal government begin funneling money to the states through grant programs? 182 What are federal mandates?

Q 493. Why are set-asides included in grant provisions?

A Set-asides are special spending requirements that the federal government attaches to block grants. A set-aside specifies that a part of the grant money, say 30 percent of it, must be spent on a specific program or purpose. States have objected to the use of set-asides as another instance of the federal government's dictating policy to the states. State officials also argue that circumstances vary from state to state and that they are in a better position to determine where the money should be spent.

See 57 How has the federal government used grants to increase its control over the states? 182 What are federal mandates?

Q 494. How do federal grants affect state budgets?

A Since most federal grants require states to put up matching funds, accepting the grant can have a significant impact on state spending. If the program the grant is intended to fund is large and costly, for example, the amount the state must spend in matching funds may force it to divert funds from other programs. In the end, the grant funds can give states a needed financial boost, but they also can alter the state's spending priorities as well.

See 57 How has the federal government used grants to increase its control over the states? 182 What are federal mandates?

 495. What is the estimated number of jobs created locally by $1 billion in federal defense spending?

A According to estimates made in the late 1980s, every billion dollars of federal defense spending created about thirty-five thousand jobs in local economies. Unfortunately, the reverse was also true. Defense cutbacks of the 1990s cost thousands of workers their jobs, and to one degree or another hurt state and local economies where defense spending had been heavy (California, Florida, Massachusetts, New York, Ohio, Pennsylvania, Texas, and Virginia).

HEALTH AND WELFARE

Q **496. How many doctors and community hospitals are there in my state?**

A California had the largest corps of doctors among the states as of the mid-1990s, as well as the largest network of community hospitals. However, when the number of doctors per one hundred thousand in population is taken into account, California is just slightly above the national average of 236 doctors per one hundred thousand. Interestingly, the District of Columbia, which is not a state, has the highest number of doctors per one hundred thousand population in the nation—662, or almost three times the national average. The total number of doctors practicing in the states and the number of community hospitals in each in 1995 were:

State	Doctors	Hospitals	State	Doctors	Hospitals
Alabama	7,814	115	Delaware	1,546	8
Alaska	890	17	Florida	31,053	212
Arizona	8,315	61	Georgia	13,984	160
Arkansas	4,246	85			
California	75,496	424	Hawaii	2,812	21
			Idaho	1,583	41
Colorado	8,425	69	Illinois	28,765	207
Connecticut	10,919	34	Indiana	10,426	115

(table continues)

State	Doctors	Hospitals	State	Doctors	Hospitals
Iowa	4,703	116	North Carolina	15,159	119
			North Dakota	1,291	43
Kansas	4,961	132	Ohio	24,402	180
Kentucky	7,416	104			
Louisiana	9,604	130	Oklahoma	5,203	110
Maine	2,449	39	Oregon	6,648	64
Maryland	17,463	50	Pennsylvania	32,919	225
			Rhode Island	2,942	11
Massachusetts	23,471	96	South Carolina	6,904	66
Michigan	20,061	167			
Minnesota	11,007	142	South Dakota	1,206	50
Mississippi	3,703	97	Tennessee	11,846	126
Missouri	11,594	126	Texas	35,100	416
			Utah	3,766	42
Montana	1,569	55	Vermont	1,577	14
Nebraska	3,236	91			
Nevada	2,391	20	Virginia	14,676	96
New Hampshire	2,451	29	Washington	12,032	88
New Jersey	21,895	92	West Virginia	3,582	59
			Wisconsin	10,903	127
New Mexico	3,320	36	Wyoming	716	25
New York	65,299	230			

Source: U.S. Census Bureau, *State and Metropolitan Area Databook, 1997–1998 (Washington, D.C.: Government Printing Office, 1997).*

Q **497. Which state has the most Social Security recipients?**

A California had more people receiving Social Security benefits than did any other state in the nation in 1996. With just over 4 million recipients, it was well ahead of Florida, which had over 3 million, and New York, which had just under 3 million. Alaska (46,000) and Wyoming (72,000) had the fewest Social Security recipients. State-by-state totals for 1996 were:

State	Recipients (in thousands)	State	Recipients (in thousands)
Alabama	787	Montana	153
Alaska	46	Nebraska	282
Arizona	720	Nevada	241
Arkansas	507	New Hampshire	188
California	4,023	New Jersey	1,314
Colorado	505	New Mexico	262
Connecticut	569	New York	2,968
Delaware	124	North Carolina	1,255
Florida	3,034	North Dakota	116
Georgia	1,027	Ohio	1,910
Hawaii	169	Oklahoma	580
Idaho	181	Oregon	548
Illinois	1,827	Pennsylvania	2,332
Indiana	967	Rhode Island	189
Iowa	539	South Carolina	638
Kansas	436	South Dakota	135
Kentucky	720	Tennessee	940
Louisiana	701	Texas	2,498
Maine	242	Utah	228
Maryland	685	Vermont	100
Massachusetts	1,052	Virginia	965
Michigan	1,598	Washington	802
Minnesota	715	West Virginia	386
Mississippi	498	Wisconsin	884
Missouri	977	Wyoming	72

Source: U.S. Census Bureau, *Statistical Abstract of the United States: 1998* (Washington, D.C. Government Printing Office, 1998).

498. How many people receive Medicare and Medicaid in the states?

A About 37 million Americans nationwide received Medicare payments in 1996 as part of their Social Security coverage. About 35 million needy persons across the country had their medical bills paid by the Medicaid program in 1996. California, which has the largest number of seniors, had nearly 3.7 million enrolled in the Medicare program, about a million more than Florida and New York. California also had more Medicaid recipients than any other state—over 5 million. That was almost 2 million more than New York and 2.5 million more than Texas. The following table gives the total amounts spent by each state on Medicare and Medicaid in 1996.

State	Medicare	Medicaid	State	Medicare	Medicaid
	(in thousands)			*(in thousands)*	
Alabama	651	539	Michigan	1,361	1,168
Alaska	35	68	Minnesota	636	473
Arizona	614	494	Mississippi	402	520
Arkansas	427	353	Missouri	838	695
California	3,690	5,017			
			Montana	132	99
Colorado	432	294	Nebraska	250	168
Connecticut	506	380	Nevada	202	105
Delaware	103	79	New Hampshire	159	97
Florida	2,655	1,735	New Jersey	1,177	790
Georgia	849	1,147			
			New Mexico	216	287
Hawaii	153	52	New York	2,653	3,035
Idaho	153	115	North Carolina	1,049	1,084
Illinois	1,623	1,552	North Dakota	103	61
Indiana	830	559	Ohio	1,676	1,533
Iowa	475	304			
			Oklahoma	492	394
Kansas	385	256	Oregon	472	452
Kentucky	596	641	Pennsylvania	2,078	1,230
Louisiana	586	785	Rhode Island	169	135
Maine	205	153	South Carolina	520	496
Maryland	610	414			
			South Dakota	117	74
Massachusetts	942	728	Tennessee	783	1,466

(table continues)

(Continued)

State	Medicare (in thousands)	Medicaid (in thousands)	State	Medicare (in thousands)	Medicaid (in thousands)
Texas	2,117	2,562	Washington	699	639
Utah	191	160	West Virginia	331	389
Vermont	84	100	Wisconsin	767	460
			Wyoming	61	51
Virginia	833	681			

Source: U.S. Census Bureau, *State and Metropolitan Area Databook, 1997–1998 (Washington, D.C.: Government Printing Office, 1997).*

Q 499. What are the birth and death rates in the states?

A Birth and death rates for a particular state—the births or deaths per one thousand in population—can be affected by various factors. Certainly the size of younger and older age groups in the state's population is an important one. Birth rates are likely to be higher where a larger percentage of the population falls in the childbearing years, for example. But age is not the only factor. Poorer, less educated couples generally tend to have more children, so that a state with a higher percentage of people living in poverty may have a higher birth rate. Religious background may also affect people's decisions on the number of children they have.

Whatever the reason, Utah had by far the highest birth rate of any state, 20.7, and one of the lowest death rates, 5.5. At 18 births per one thousand, Arizona was also well above the national average of 14.8 births per one thousand. Alaska, which has relatively few seniors, had a death rate of just 4.3, less than half the national average of 8.8. Following are the birth and death rates for each state as of 1996.

State	Birth rate (per 1,000)	Death rate (per 1,000)	State	Birth rate (per 1,000)	Death rate (per 1,000)
Alabama	14.4	10.0	Colorado	14.6	6.8
Alaska	16.7	4.3	Connecticut	13.5	9.0
Arizona	18.0	8.8	Delaware	14.1	9.0
Arkansas	14.5	10.6			
California	16.9	7.2		*(table continues)*	

(Continued)

State	Birth rate (per 1,000)	Death rate (per 1,000)	State	Birth rate (per 1,000)	Death rate (per 1,000)
Florida	13.2	10.7	New Jersey	14.3	9.0
Georgia	15.6	8.0	New Mexico	15.9	7.3
			New York	14.9	8.9
Hawaii	15.5	6.7	North Carolina	14.4	9.1
Idaho	16.0	7.3	North Dakota	13.0	9.3
Illinois	15.6	9.0			
Indiana	14.3	9.3	Ohio	13.7	9.4
Iowa	13.0	9.7	Oklahoma	14.0	10.0
			Oregon	13.6	9.0
Kansas	15.4	9.3	Pennsylvania	12.4	10.7
Kentucky	13.6	9.6	Rhode Island	12.6	9.6
Louisiana	15.2	9.3	South Carolina	13.7	9.3
Maine	11.1	8.9			
Maryland	13.7	8.2	South Dakota	14.3	9.3
			Tennessee	13.9	9.7
Massachusetts	13.2	9.1	Texas	17.1	7.2
Michigan	14.3	8.7	Utah	20.7	5.5
Minnesota	13.7	8.0	Vermont	11.5	8.3
Mississippi	15.3	9.8			
Missouri	13.8	10.1	Virginia	13.8	7.9
			Washington	14.5	7.6
Montana	12.2	8.7	West Virginia	11.3	11.2
Nebraska	14.1	9.4	Wisconsin	13.0	8.7
Nevada	16.2	8.2	Wyoming	13.1	7.5
New Hampshire	12.5	8.1			

Source: State and Metropolitan Area Databook, 1997–1998.

Q 500. How many AIDS patients are there in the states?

A By 1996 the total number of reported AIDS cases in the United States had reached 562,196. New York and California together reported just over 36 percent of all the AIDS cases. Large numbers of cases were also reported in Florida, Texas, and New Jersey, however. As of the end of 1996, total reported AIDS cases in the states were:

State	AIDS cases	State	AIDS cases
Alabama	4,266	Montana	227
Alaska	363	Nebraska	789
Arizona	5,038	Nevada	3,068
Arkansas	2,158	New Hampshire	712
California	98,157	New Jersey	32,926
Colorado	5,755	New Mexico	1,442
Connecticut	8,517	New York	106,897
Delaware	1,777	North Carolina	7,313
Florida	58,911	North Dakota	78
Georgia	17,004	Ohio	8,743
Hawaii	1,993	Oklahoma	2,731
Idaho	366	Oregon	3,862
Illinois	18,571	Pennsylvania	17,423
Indiana	4,424	Rhode Island	1,590
Iowa	983	South Carolina	6,273
Kansas	1,846	South Dakota	118
Kentucky	2,224	Tennessee	5,536
Louisiana	9,126	Texas	39,871
Maine	755	Utah	1,385
Maryland	15,298	Vermont	298
Massachusetts	12,067	Virginia	9,104
Michigan	8,366	Washington	7,591
Minnesota	2,991	West Virginia	745
Mississippi	2,861	Wisconsin	2,786
Missouri	7,259	Wyoming	140

Source: U.S. Census Bureau, *State and Metropolitan Area Databook, 1997–1998* (Washington, D.C.: Government Printing Office, 1997).

Q 501. What is the median household income in my state?

A Oil-rich Alaska had the highest median household income in 1996, $52,779. New Jersey, which has benefited from the exodus of corporations out of New York City in recent years, posted the second-highest median household income with $47,468. Connecticut ($42,119) and Maryland ($43,993) followed in the top bracket. The state with the lowest median income was West Virginia ($24,247). Income in Mississippi was slightly higher at $26,667. Median household incomes in 1996 for each state are listed below. Dollar figures have not been adjusted for inflation.

State	Median household income	State	Median household income
Alabama	30,302	Mississippi	26,677
Alaska	52,779	Missouri	34,265
Arizona	31,637		
Arkansas	27,123	Montana	28,684
California	38,812	Nebraska	34,014
		Nevada	38,540
Colorado	40,950	New Hampshire	39,407
Connecticut	42,119	New Jersey	47,468
Delaware	39,309		
Florida	30,641	New Mexico	25,086
Georgia	32,496	New York	35,410
		North Carolina	35,601
Hawaii	41,772	North Dakota	31,470
Idaho	34,709	Ohio	34,070
Illinois	39,554		
Indiana	35,147	Oklahoma	27,437
Iowa	33,209	Oregon	35,492
		Pennsylvania	34,899
Kansas	32,585	Rhode Island	36,986
Kentucky	32,413	South Carolina	34,665
Louisiana	30,262		
Maine	34,696	South Dakota	29,526
Maryland	43,993	Tennessee	30,790
		Texas	33,072
Massachusetts	39,494	Utah	37,038
Michigan	39,225	Vermont	32,358
Minnesota	40,991		

(table continues)

(Continued)

State	Median household income	State	Median household income
Virginia	39,211	Wisconsin	40,001
Washington	36,676	Wyoming	30,953
West Virginia	25,247		

Source: U.S. Census Bureau, *Statistical Abstract of the United States: 1998* (Washington, D.C.: Government Printing Office, 1998).

Q 502. Which states have the largest number of people living below the poverty line?

A As of 1996, California had about 5.5 million people living below the poverty line, more than any other state. Surprisingly, oil-rich Texas had the next-highest number of impoverished citizens, about 3.2 million, which was just ahead of New York's 3 million. Alaska had the fewest, 54,000, followed by Wyoming (58,000) and Delaware (63,000). State-by-state totals for 1996 were as follows:

State	Population below poverty line (thousands)	State	Population below poverty line (thousands)
Alabama	595	Illinois	1,429
Alaska	54	Indiana	428
Arizona	980	Iowa	279
Arkansas	449		
California	5,472	Kansas	287
		Kentucky	658
Colorado	412	Louisiana	873
Connecticut	392	Maine	135
Delaware	63	Maryland	522
Florida	2,037		
Georgia	1,097	Massachusetts	622
		Michigan	1,068
Hawaii	142	Minnesota	458
Idaho	140		

(table continues)

State	Population below poverty line (thousands)	State	Population below poverty line (thousands)
Mississippi	575	Oregon	382
Missouri	500	Pennsylvania	1,374
		Rhode Island	104
Montana	155	South Carolina	482
Nebraska	169		
Nevada	133	South Dakota	82
New Hampshire	73	Tennessee	878
New Jersey	726	Texas	3,180
		Utah	153
New Mexico	472	Vermont	74
New York	3,058		
North Carolina	885	Virginia	795
North Dakota	69	Washington	666
Ohio	1,424	West Virginia	323
		Wisconsin	460
Oklahoma	556	Wyoming	58

Source: U.S. Census Bureau, *Statistical Abstract of the United States: 1998* (Washington, D.C.: Government Printing Office, 1998).

STATE AID TO LOCALITIES

Q 503. What percentage of state spending goes to localities?

A States send about 33 percent of all the money they spend to cities, counties, and townships to help pay for such things as schools, social welfare programs, roads, and hospitals.

Q 504. How much did states send to localities in a recent year?

A States together sent a total of about $226 billion to their local governments for education and other spending needs in 1994. Education represented the biggest single expenditure, almost $136 billion.

As to the amounts sent to localities by individual states, California ranked first in total dollars— $44.5 billion in these intergovernmental expenditures, followed by New York ($24.6 billion) and Texas ($11 billion). Listed below are the state-by-state totals for 1994, along with amounts states sent to localities for education, highways, and health care.

	State spending on local government			
State	Total*	Education	Highways	Health
	(all in thousands)			
Alabama	$2,349,153	$1,867,737	$172,485	$16,084
Alaska	1,246,725	682,818	32,552	73,035
Arizona	3,577,730	1,946,153	394,064	107,710
Arkansas	1,547,294	1,211,656	117,237	75,991
California	44,456,355	18,670,739	1,350,221	3,333,519
Colorado	2,553,610	1,650,878	217,897	34,943
Connecticut	2,256,866	1,629,061	22,797	15,888
Delaware	419,704	329,239	6,209	12,933
Florida	10,236,796	7,364,614	186,351	125,351
Georgia	4,473,816	4,027,000	8,658	293,010
Hawaii	142,404	0	0	19,207
Idaho	858,750	656,212	82,884	7,275
Illinois	7,412,264	4,520,124	471,185	64,584
Indiana	4,594,808	2,689,576	500,166	47,115
Iowa	2,461,697	1,691,094	285,968	76,492
Kansas	2,114,401	1,725,640	127,451	63,959
Kentucky	2,581,409	2,178,258	98,235	115,091
Louisiana	2,844,099	2,316,600	51,438	2,957
Maine	738,961	590,945	21,072	5,842
Maryland	2,804,841	1,898,973	319,669	248,859
Massachusetts	4,451,132	2,004,190	110,302	0
Michigan	8,864,360	4,698,172	857,434	1,164,267
Minnesota	5,378,559	3,191,961	382,803	126,991
Mississippi	2,070,637	1,363,741	102,094	34,341
Missouri	3,250,024	2,588,094	197,213	11,153
Montana	675,772	525,596	16,787	18,470
Nebraska	1,087,419	678,732	127,686	95,469

(table continues)

State	State spending on local government			
	Total*	Education	Highways	Health
	(all in thousands)			
Nevada	1,277,353	791,216	43,830	2,983
New Hampshire	368,587	155,542	21,935	50,164
New Jersey	8,269,624	4,845,313	25,617	73,199
New Mexico	1,821,635	1,307,504	15,421	50
New York	24,641,493	11,641,994	72,475	639,932
North Carolina	6,589,994	4,889,120	156,634	400,300
North Dakota	422,452	281,094	45,732	22,232
Ohio	8,531,560	4,820,077	804,680	480,955
Oklahoma	2,388,001	1,927,974	211,196	67,146
Oregon	2,261,202	1,560,502	322,264	184,219
Pennsylvania	8,683,499	4,802,254	378,890	749,592
Rhode Island	444,141	388,062	0	0
South Carolina	2,203,683	1,709,282	1,439	27,566
South Dakota	300,224	228,909	18,322	695
Tennessee	2,998,831	1,982,914	262,796	2,455
Texas	11,091,281	9,503,732	15,686	424,273
Utah	1,302,964	1,110,074	56,096	57,851
Vermont	301,624	234,435	24,869	50
Virginia	3,861,915	2,764,375	166,951	18,577
Washington	5,049,189	4,030,382	310,973	64,798
West Virginia	1,249,440	1,182,776	0	7,032
Wisconsin	5,327,881	2,568,294	376,361	343,525
Wyoming	684,195	437,396	29,924	22,624

Source: Council of State Governments, *The Book of the States, 1996–97* (Washington, D.C.: Council of State Governments, 1996).

*Totals include spending not only on local education, highways, and health, but also on other local needs.

TAXES AND SPENDING

Q **505. Where do states get their revenue from?**

A States collect revenue from three basic sources—taxes, transfer payments from the federal government, and fees and other charges. Tax revenues come mainly from sales and gross receipts taxes (about 21 percent of all state revenues) and from personal income taxes (about 14 percent of all revenues). Transfer payments, mainly federal grants, are another important revenue source (about 22 percent of all revenue). Fees and other miscellaneous charges amount to about 15 percent of revenue, and income from insurance trust revenue, almost 19 percent of revenue.

Q **506. How much tax revenue does my state take in?**

A The amount of taxes collected varies widely between states. On a per capita basis, people living in Hawaii paid the most in 1996—$2,592 per person—and those in New Hampshire paid the least—just $720 per person. Of course when it comes to the total of tax collections, big states like California ($57.7 billion), New York ($34.2 billion), and Texas ($21.3 billion) top the list. Tax revenues by state for 1996 were as follows:

State	Tax revenue (millions)	Taxes per capita (dollars)	Rank
Alabama	$5,258	$1,230	45
Alaska	1,519	2,503	2
Arizona	6,409	1,447	29
Arkansas	3,709	1,478	26
California	57,747	1,811	11
Colorado	4,820	1,261	44
Connecticut	7,830	2,392	3
Delaware	1,688	2,329	4
Florida	19,699	1,368	40
Georgia	10,292	1,400	36
Hawaii	3,069	2,592	1

(table continues)

State	Tax revenue (millions)	Taxes per capita (dollars)	Rank
Idaho	$1,857	$1,562	19
Illinois	17,277	1,458	27
Indiana	8,437	1,444	30
Iowa	4,441	1,557	20
Kansas	3,979	1,547	22
Kentucky	6,489	1,671	15
Louisiana	4,906	1,128	47
Maine	1,897	1,526	24
Maryland	8,167	1,610	17
Massachusetts	12,455	2,044	6
Michigan	19,129	1,994	7
Minnesota	10,243	2,159	5
Mississippi	3,861	1,422	34
Missouri	7,210	1,362	41
Montana	1,256	1,429	32
Nebraska	2,369	1,434	31
Nevada	2,889	1,802	12
New Hampshire	837	720	50
New Jersey	14,385	1,801	13
New Mexico	3,061	1,787	14
New York	34,150	1,878	9
North Carolina	11,882	1,623	16
North Dakota	985	1,530	23
Ohio	15,649	1,401	35
Oklahoma	4,618	1,399	37
Oregon	4,416	1,378	39
Pennsylvania	18,729	1,553	21

(table continues)

State	Tax revenue (millions)	Taxes per capita (dollars)	Rank
Rhode Island	$1,549	$1,565	18
South Carolina	5,113	1,382	38
South Dakota	730	998	49
Tennessee	6,185	1,163	46
Texas	21,271	1,111	48
Utah	2,914	1,457	28
Vermont	841	1,428	33
Virginia	8,900	1,333	42
Washington	10,586	1,913	8
West Virginia	2,771	1,517	25
Wisconsin	9,586	1,864	10
Wyoming	626	1,301	43

Source: U.S. Census Bureau, *Statistical Abstract of the United States: 1998* (Washington, D.C.: Government Printing Office, 1998).

▶ How much state revenue comes from federal grants? *See 490 Which state received the most in federal grants in a recent year?*

▶ What was revenue sharing? *See 492 How do the basic types of grants differ?*

Q 507. What part of state revenues comes from property taxes?

A About three-quarters of all local revenue comes from taxes on personal and corporate property, but most states take in very little from these taxes—only about 1 to 2 percent of their revenues on average. Instead they rely on sales tax and income tax revenues, among other sources.

See 505 Where do states get their revenue from?

Q 508. When was the first state income tax enacted?

A State income taxes have been around since 1911, when Wisconsin became the first to enact one (even before the federal government did). Today, just seven states do not collect any income tax at all, while Tennessee and New Hampshire tax only personal income from dividends, interest, and capital gains. Four states do not tax corporate income. *(See next question.)*

Q 509. How much does my state collect in income tax revenue?

A About 15 percent of state revenues come from personal income taxes, in those states that have the tax. Only about 6 percent comes from corporate income taxes. California and New York collected the largest dollar amounts in 1996, $20.8 billion and $17.4 billion, respectively. Alaska, Florida, Nevada, South Dakota, Texas, Washington, and Wyoming do not tax personal income. State tax revenues collected from personal and corporate income taxes in 1996 were the following:

State	Personal tax	Corporate tax
	(all in millions)	
Alabama	$1,578	$218
Alaska	—	326
Arizona	1,494	448
Arkansas	1,162	229
California	20,760	5,831
Colorado	2,274	206
Connecticut	2,614	641
Delaware	632	166
Florida	—	1,008
Georgia	4,244	719
Hawaii	1,000	66
Idaho	655	153
Illinois	5,781	1,621
Indiana	3,478	894
Iowa	1,588	203
Kansas	1,377	255
Kentucky	2,075	285
Louisiana	1,160	328

(table continues)

(Continued)

State	Personal tax	Corporate tax
	(all in millions)	
Maine	$709	$71
Maryland	3,485	331
Massachusetts	6,707	1,228
Michigan	5,868	2,190
Minnesota	4,136	703
Mississippi	742	202
Missouri	2,741	426
Montana	383	76
Nebraska	840	127
Nevada	—	—
New Hampshire	52	180
New Jersey	4,734	1,155
New Mexico	643	163
New York	17,399	2,730
North Carolina	4,929	939
North Dakota	152	74
Ohio	5,903	807
Oklahoma	1,512	164
Oregon	2,823	300
Pennsylvania	5,214	1,504
Rhode Island	581	87
South Carolina	1,813	251
South Dakota	—	38
Tennessee	114	534
Texas	—	—
Utah	1,139	177
Vermont	281	45

(table continues)

State	Personal tax	Corporate tax
	(all in millions)	
Virginia	$4,301	$363
Washington	—	—
West Virginia	751	235
Wisconsin	4,151	621
Wyoming	—	—

Source: U.S. Census Bureau, *State and Metropolitan Area Databook, 1997–1998* (Washington, D.C.: Government Printing Office, 1997).

Q **510. Which state was first to adopt a sales tax?**

A With state income tax revenues falling off sharply during the depression, Mississippi adopted the sales tax in 1932 to provide a new revenue source. Twenty states followed suit in the next few years (Arizona, Arkansas, California, Colorado, Hawaii, Illinois, Indiana, Iowa, Michigan, Missouri, New Mexico, North Carolina, North Dakota, Ohio, Oklahoma, South Dakota, Utah, Washington, West Virginia, and Wyoming). Today just five states do not have a general sales tax, and sales tax revenues account for an average of nearly 21 percent of state revenues. Sales tax collections represent one of the largest revenue sources in states that have the tax.

Q **511. How much does my state collect in sales taxes?**

A California posted far and away the highest total in general sales tax collections for 1996—a total of $18.98 billion. Florida and Texas followed with $11.4 and $10.8 billion, respectively. Alaska, Delaware, Montana, New Hampshire, and Oregon do not have general sales taxes, although they (and all other states) do collect gasoline, liquor, tobacco, and some other specific sales taxes. Total general sales tax revenue by state in 1996 was as follows:

State	General sales tax revenue *(in millions)*	State	General sales tax revenue *(in millions)*
Alabama	$1,439	Arkansas	$1,376
Alaska	—	California	18,980
Arizona	2,720		*(table continues)*

(Continued)

State	General sales tax revenue (in millions)	State	General sales tax revenue (in millions)
Colorado	$1,322	New Hampshire	—
Connecticut	2,445	New Jersey	$ 4,318
Delaware	—	New Mexico	1,284
Florida	11,429	New York	6,963
Georgia	3,824	North Carolina	2,971
Hawaii	1,432	North Dakota	282
Idaho	600	Ohio	4,991
Illinois	5,057	Oklahoma	1,210
Indiana	2,868	Oregon	—
Iowa	1,456	Pennsylvania	5,701
Kansas	1,401	Rhode Island	465
Kentucky	1,784	South Carolina	1,919
Louisiana	1,622	South Dakota	383
Maine	658	Tennessee	3,537
Maryland	2,000	Texas	10,811
Massachusetts	2,610	Utah	1,710
Michigan	6,587	Vermont	183
Minnesota	2,900	Virginia	1,996
Mississippi	1,832	Washington	6,182
Missouri	2,465	West Virginia	797
Montana	—	Wisconsin	2,708
Nebraska	815	Wyoming	211
Nevada	1,572		

Source: U.S. Census Bureau, *Statistical Abstract of the United States: 1998* (Washington, D.C.: Government Printing Office, 1998).

Q 512. When were state lotteries first adopted?

A First established in the 1600s, lotteries were operated throughout this country in the 1800s to raise funds for building roads, bridges, and schools. But there were problems with lottery management, and a wave of scandals finally forced states across the country to shut down the lotteries toward the end of the century. In 1963 New

Hampshire became the first state to hold lotteries since 1895, and four years later New York State followed suit. Numerous other states have set up lotteries since then, and today only thirteen states do not permit them (see list below). Lottery revenues and costs in each of the states (in millions), as of 1995, were as follows:

State	Gross lottery revenue	Prizes awarded	Administrative costs	Balance for state
Alabama	—	—	—	—
Alaska	—	—	—	—
Arizona	$269	$151	$27	$91
Arkansas	—	—	—	—
California	2,025	1,081	182	762
Colorado	330	201	28	101
Connecticut	636	386	28	224
Delaware	109	56	9	44
Florida	2,126	1,128	122	876
Georgia	1,292	694	97	1,001
Hawaii	—	—	—	—
Idaho	88	53	16	19
Illinois	1,468	859	59	549
Indiana	563	350	30	183
Iowa	186	113	25	49
Kansas	163	92	19	51
Kentucky	480	303	30	147
Louisiana	279	152	19	108
Maine	153	89	17	48
Maryland	984	545	42	397
Massachusetts	2,629	1,938	72	619
Michigan	1,272	699	50	523
Minnesota	318	196	59	63
Mississippi	—	—	—	—
Missouri	387	222	35	131
Montana	31	16	6	8
Nebraska	79	39	16	24
Nevada	—	—	—	—
New Hampshire	132	85	6	42
New Jersey	1,491	799	47	645
New Mexico	—	—	—	—
New York	2,774	1,471	68	1,235
North Carolina	—	—	—	—

(table continues)

(Continued)

State	Gross lottery revenue	Prizes awarded	Administrative costs	Balance for state
North Dakota	—	—	—	—
Ohio	$2,049	$1,237	$86	$726
Oklahoma	—	—	—	—
Oregon	885	580	190	135
Pennsylvania	1,488	813	55	620
Rhode Island	287	207	5	75
South Carolina	—	—	—	—
South Dakota	84	19	9	56
Tennessee	—	—	—	—
Texas	2,743	1,694	53	996
Utah	—	—	—	—
Vermont	72	42	5	25
Virginia	880	487	79	314
Washington	401	208	55	139
West Virginia	155	85	16	54
Wisconsin	492	299	32	162
Wyoming	0	0	0	0
U.S. Total	$29,799	$17,368	$1,690	$11,241

Source: U.S. Census Bureau, *Statistical Abstract of the United States: 1998* (Washington, D.C.: Government Printing Office, 1998).

— = not applicable, no state lottery

▶ Where does the state's budget come from? *See 79 Who prepares the state budget?*

Q **513. How much does my state spend in a year?**

A As states have shouldered increasing responsibilities for social welfare and health care programs in recent years, overall spending has increased sharply. In 1996 the fifty states paid out upwards of three-quarters of a trillion dollars. A substantial part of that money came from the federal government in the form of grants in aid, but revenues from state sales and income taxes financed the majority of the spending. State-by-state spending totals for fiscal 1996 were:

State	Total spending (in millions)	State	Total spending (in millions)
Alabama	$12,127	Montana	$3,136
Alaska	5,630	Nebraska	4,490
Arizona	11,898	Nevada	4,831
Arkansas	7,050	New Hampshire	3,240
California	113,361	New Jersey	32,315
Colorado	10,612	New Mexico	6,740
Connecticut	13,530	New York	82,420
Delaware	3,248	North Carolina	21,221
Florida	36,454	North Dakota	2,064
Georgia	20,013	Ohio	35,517
Hawaii	5,947	Oklahoma	9,265
Idaho	3,501	Oregon	11,858
Illinois	34,111	Pennsylvania	38,699
Indiana	15,368	Rhode Island	4,016
Iowa	8,853	South Carolina	12,400
Kansas	7,276	South Dakota	1,975
Kentucky	11,842	Tennessee	13,829
Louisiana	14,030	Texas	46,082
Maine	4,240	Utah	6,172
Maryland	15,554	Vermont	2,061
Massachusetts	24,950	Virginia	17,717
Michigan	35,080	Washington	21,086
Minnesota	17,325	West Virginia	6,972
Mississippi	8,217	Wisconsin	16,990
Missouri	12,841	Wyoming	2,062
		United States	$859,959

Source: U.S. Census Bureau, *Statistical Abstract of the United States: 1998* (Washington, D.C.: Government Printing Office, 1998).

Q 514. When were federal highway grants first established?

A The federal government established the grant program to help states build and maintain highways in 1916. To receive aid, the state was required to have a highway department, and by 1917 every state had organized one. The new federal highway legislation contained some now familiar provisions for federal grants, including formulas for distributing the funds among the states and the system of matching grants. Federal grants pay for about 30 percent of what states spend on highways and mass transit.

Q 515. Who decides where highways and state roads will go?

A State and local officials usually confer on proposals to build new roads and expand existing ones. Plans are often adjusted to take into account local preferences, but state officials do not necessarily need local approval when it comes to routing and expanding roads.

Q 516. How many miles of roads are there in my state, and how many cars are on them?

A As of 1996, there were an incredible 3.9 million miles of roads in the United States, including interstate highways, other major arteries and collector roads, and local roads. Of that, 46,286 miles were interstate highways, but local roads made up the bulk of the mileage—2.7 million miles. Texas had more road mileage than any other state—296,259 miles—and Hawaii the least, just 4,142. Total mileage in 1996 for each state, along with the number of registered cars and trucks, was as follows:

State	Miles of roads	Vehicles (in thousands)
Alabama	93,340	3,324
Alaska	13,255	531
Arizona	54,895	2,983
Arkansas	77,746	1,633
California	170,506	25,214

(table continues)

(Continued)

State	Miles of roads	Vehicles (in thousands)
Colorado	84,797	3,433
Connecticut	20,600	2,609
Delaware	5,715	593
Florida	114,422	10,889
Georgia	111,746	6,283
Hawaii	4,142	786
Idaho	59,674	1,061
Illinois	137,577	8,817
Indiana	92,970	5,216
Iowa	112,708	2,869
Kansas	133,386	2,110
Kentucky	73,158	2,696
Louisiana	60,667	3,318
Maine	22,577	959
Maryland	29,680	3,635
Massachusetts	34,725	4,702
Michigan	117,620	8,010
Minnesota	130,613	3,861
Mississippi	73,202	2,182
Missouri	122,746	4,350
Montana	69,809	973
Nebraska	92,805	1,479
Nevada	45,039	1,096
New Hampshire	15,106	1,112
New Jersey	35,924	5,822
New Mexico	59,455	1,545
New York	112,347	10,636
North Carolina	97,509	5,759
North Dakota	86,808	679

(table continues)

State	Miles of roads	Vehicles (in thousands)
Ohio	114,642	9,770
Oklahoma	112,664	3,082
Oregon	83,190	2,851
Pennsylvania	118,952	8,640
Rhode Island	6,001	696
South Carolina	64,359	2,791
South Dakota	83,375	751
Tennessee	85,795	4,830
Texas	296,259	13,487
Utah	41,718	1,445
Vermont	14,192	503
Virginia	69,384	5,576
Washington	79,555	4,603
West Virginia	35,130	1,406
Wisconsin	111,435	3,972
Wyoming	34,115	562
United States	3,933,985	206,365

Source: U.S. Census Bureau, *Statistical Abstract of the United States: 1998* (Washington, D.C.: Government Printing Office, 1998).

Q 517. How many traffic fatalities were there in my state?

A A total of 41,967 people were killed in traffic accidents in 1997, a drop of just under 3,000 deaths from seven years earlier. Fatalities in alcohol-related crashes were lower by a greater margin, down from 22,084 in 1990 to 16,189 in 1997. As you might expect, the largest states—where more people are driving more miles—have more traffic fatalities. California and Texas had the highest numbers, followed by Florida. Rhode Island and Alaska had the fewest. Total traffic deaths and alcohol-related fatalities in the states for 1997 were as follows:

State	Total traffic deaths	Alcohol-related traffic deaths
Alabama	1,189	473
Alaska	77	41
Arizona	951	433
Arkansas	660	193
California	3,688	1,314
Colorado	613	218
Connecticut	338	152
Delaware	143	61
Florida	2,782	934
Georgia	1,577	578
Hawaii	131	59
Idaho	259	102
Illinois	1,395	587
Indiana	935	308
Iowa	468	174
Kansas	481	142
Kentucky	857	279
Louisiana	913	421
Maine	192	64
Maryland	608	221
Massachusetts	442	209
Michigan	1,446	558
Minnesota	600	193
Mississippi	861	344
Missouri	1,192	509
Montana	265	120
Nebraska	302	105
Nevada	347	160
New Hampshire	125	60
New Jersey	774	282

(table continues)

(Continued)

State	Total traffic deaths	Alcohol-related traffic deaths
New Mexico	484	220
New York	1,643	449
North Carolina	1,483	528
North Dakota	105	50
Ohio	1,441	476
Oklahoma	838	302
Oregon	523	228
Pennsylvania	1,557	631
Rhode Island	75	41
South Carolina	903	318
South Dakota	148	61
Tennessee	1,223	496
Texas	3,510	1,748
Utah	366	75
Vermont	96	34
Virginia	984	383
Washington	676	300
West Virginia	379	146
Wisconsin	725	329
Wyoming	137	43
Total United States	41,967	16,189

Source: National Highway Traffic Safety Commission, *Traffic Safety Facts, 1997.*

WHERE CAN I FIND. . .

Sources described below provide more detailed information on topics discussed in this chapter. Both the Census Bureau Web site *(http://www.census.gov)* and the Bureau of Labor Statistics Web site *(http://stats.bls.gov)* provide numerous tables with current data.

The Book of the States, 1996–1997. Lexington, Ky.: Council of State Governments, 1997.

An annual compilation of tables presenting comparative information about each of the states, this book has sections on state finances, employment, education, crime, the environment, highways, federal aid to the states, and other topics.

CQ's State Fact Finder: Rankings Across America, 1999. Kendra A. Hovey and Harold A. Hovey. Washington, D.C.: Congressional Quarterly Inc., 1999.

Up to date and easy to use, this book of lists presents both data and state rankings.

Governing's *State and Local Sourcebook.* Washington, D.C.: *Governing* Magazine, annual.

The book, compiled by the editors of *Governing* magazine, focuses on current comparative information for states, including data on education, transportation, crime, the environment, and revenue. The *Sourcebook* also has a contact list for state, county, and city officials.

Politics in the American States: A Comparative Analysis, 7th ed. Virginia Gray, Russell Hanson, and Herbert Jacob. Washington, D.C.: Congressional Quarterly Inc., 1999.

Based on surveys and other sources of interest to political scientists, this book provides an in-depth analysis of the workings and policy concerns of state governments. There are chapters on crime, education, health and welfare, economic development, environmental concerns, and the politics of family policy.

Sourcebook of Criminal Justice Statistics. Bureau of Justice Statistics. Washington, D.C.: U.S. Government Printing Office, annual.

Also available on CD-ROM, this book contains a wealth of useful tables and statistics on crimes, cases in courts, sentencing, and related topics. Many, but not all, tables are organized by state.

State and Local Government, 2d ed. Ann Bowman and Richard Kearney. Boston: Houghton Mifflin Company, 1993.

General readers will find this textbook gives a clear and useful introduction to the mechanics of state government, as well as policy concerns. There are chapters on state and local government relations, finance and economic development, education policy, the environment, and criminal justice.

State and Local Government: Politics and Public Policies. David Saffell and Harry Basehart. Boston: McGraw-Hill, 1998.

This book covers both the basics of state and local government and current policy concerns. Among the chapters relevant here are the ones on policymaking (education, economic development, the environment, and social welfare) and criminal justice.

State and Metropolitan Area Data Book, 1997–1998. U.S. Bureau of the Census. Lanham, Md.: Bernan Associates.

Contains a wealth of statistical information for states and metropolitan areas nationwide—everything from election data to traffic fatalities.

The State of the States. Carl E. Van Horn, ed. Washington, D.C.: Congressional Quarterly Inc., 1996.

A compilation of writings on current issues and trends in state government, this book includes chapters on state budgeting, education policy, and welfare policy.

Statistical Abstract of the United States: 1998. U.S. Census Bureau. Washington, D.C.: Government Printing Office, 1998.

Another book of tables, the *Statistical Abstract* has many that are organized by state. It may be downloaded from the Census Bureau's Web site *(http://www.census.gov)*.

VII
What About My State?
—The State Profiles

Q 518 **ALABAMA**

Home page: www.alaweb.asc.edu

Capital: Montgomery

Land area: 50,750 sq. miles

Land area (rank): 28th

Population: 4,273,000

Percentage of national population: 1.6

Population growth (percent, 1981–1996): 8.8

Population density (per square mile): 84

Largest cities: Birmingham, Mobile, Montgomery, Huntsville

Federally owned land (percent): 3.3

Representatives in U.S. House: 7

State motto: *Aldemus Jura Nostra Defendere* (We Dare Defend Our Rights)

Song: "Alabama"

Flower: Camellia

Bird: Yellowhammer

Tree: Southern pine

Insect: Monarch butterfly

Rock: Marble

Nickname: Heart of Dixie

Executive Branch

Governor: Donald Siegelman (D)

Governor's term ends: 2003

Lt. Governor: Steve Windom (R)

Attorney General: Bill Pryor (R)

Treasurer: Lucy Baxley

Legislature

Upper chamber: Senate

Lower chamber: House of Representatives

Members: Senate, 35; House, 105

Legislative session begins: January

Elections

Eligible voters: 3,218,000

Eligible voters, percentage registered: 77

Governor's party: D

Senate/House majority (1998): D/D *(see question 233)*

Vote in 1996 presidential election (percent): 43.2 D, 50.1 R

Economics

Index of economic momentum (1997): -0.53 *(see question 448)*

State spending (1996): $11.6 billion

Federal spending in state: $23.4 billion

State employment (1997): 2,009,000

State employment growth (percent, 1996–1997): 0.9 *(see question 453)*

Major industry: Manufacturing *(see question 451)*

History

Joined Union: December 14, 1819

Name origin: "Alba ayamule" (Choctaw: I open the thicket) *(see questions 9–10)*

Adopted current constitution: 1901

Governors since 1900:

William J. Samford (D)	1900–1901
William D. Jelks (D)	1901–1904
Russell M. Cunningham (D)	1904–1905
William D. Jelks (D)	1905–1907
Braxton B. Comer (D)	1907–1911
Emmet O'Neal (D)	1911–1915
Charles Henderson (D)	1915–1919
Thomas E. Kilby (D)	1919–1923
William W. Brandon (D)	1923–1927
D. Bibb Graves (D)	1927–1931
Benjamin M. Miller (D)	1931–1935
D. Bibb Graves (D)	1935–1939
Frank M. Dixon (D)	1939–1943
Chauncey M. Sparks (D)	1943–1947
James E. Folsom (D)	1947–1951
Gordon Persons (D)	1951–1955
James E. Folsom (D)	1955–1959
John M. Patterson (D)	1959–1963
George C. Wallace, Jr. (D)	1963–1967
Lurleen B. Wallace (D)	1967–1968
Albert P. Brewer (D)	1968–1971
George C. Wallace, Jr. (D)	1971–1979
Forrest James, Jr. (D)	1979–1983
George C. Wallace, Jr. (D)	1983–1987
Guy Hunt (R)	1987–1993
James E. Folsom, Jr. (D)	1993–1995
Fob James, Jr. (R)	1995–1999
Donald Siegelman (D)	1999–

Q 519 ALASKA

Home page: *www.state.ak.us/*

Capital: Juneau

Land area: 570,374 sq. miles

Land area (rank): 1st

Population: 607,000

Percentage of national population: 0.2

Population growth (percent, 1981–1996): 45.9

Population density (per square mile): 1

Largest cities: Anchorage, Fairbanks, Juneau

Federally owned land (percent): 67.9

Representatives in U.S. House: 1

State motto: North to the Future

Song: "Alaska's Flag"

Flower: Forget-me-not

Bird: Willow ptarmigan

Tree: Sitka spruce

Mineral: Gold

Fish: King salmon

Fossil: Woolly mammoth

Sport: Dog mushing

Gem: Jade

Nickname: The Last Frontier

Executive Branch

Governor: Tony Knowles (D)

Governor's term ends: 2002

Lt. Governor: Fran Ulmer (D)

Attorney General: Bruce M. Botelho (D)

Comptroller: Ross Kinney

Legislature

Upper chamber: Senate

Lower chamber: House of Representatives

Members: Senate, 20; House, 40

Legislative session begins: January

Elections

Eligible voters: 425,000

Eligible voters, percentage registered: 98

Governor's party: D

Senate/House majority (1998): R/R *(see question 233)*

Vote in 1996 presidential election (percent): 33.3 D, 50.8 R

Economics

Index of economic momentum (1997): -1.96 *(see question 448)*

State spending (1996): Not available

Federal spending in state: $4.3 billion

State employment (1997): 300,000

State employment growth (percent, 1996–1997): 0.1 *(see question 453)*

Major industry: Mining *(see question 451)*

History

Joined Union: January 3, 1959

Name origin: "Alayeksa" (Eskimo: great land) *(see questions 9–10)*

Adopted current constitution: 1956

Governors since statehood:

William A. Egan (D)	1959–1966
Walter J. Hickel (R)	1966–1969
Keith H. Miller (R)	1969–1970
William A. Egan (D)	1970–1974
Jay S. Hammond (R)	1974–1982
William Sheffield (D)	1982–1986
Steve Cowper (D)	1986–1990
Walter J. Hickel (Indep.)	1990–1994
Tony Knowles (D)	1994–

Q 520 ARIZONA

Home page: *www.state.az.us/*

Capital: Phoenix

Land area (rank): 6th

Land area: 113,642 sq. miles

Population: 4,428,000

Percentage of national population: 1.7

Population growth (percent, 1981–1996): 57.8

Population density (per square mile): 39

Largest cities: Phoenix, Tucson, Flagstaff

Federally owned land (percent): 47.2

Representatives in U.S. House: 6

State motto: *Ditat Deus* (God Enriches)

Songs: "Arizona March Song" and "Arizona"

Flower: Saguaro cactus blossom

Bird: Cactus wren

Tree: Palo verde

Gemstone: Turquoise

Official neckwear: Bolo tie

Nickname: Grand Canyon State

Executive Branch

Governor: Jane Dee Hull (R)

Governor's term ends: 2003

Attorney General: Janet Napolitano (D)

Treasurer: Carol Springer

Legislature

Upper chamber: Senate

Lower chamber: House of Representatives

Members: Senate, 30; House, 60

Legislative session begins: January

Elections

Eligible voters: 3,094,000

Eligible voters, percentage registered: 72

Governor's party: R

Senate/House majority (1998): R/R *(see question 233)*

Vote in 1996 presidential election (percent): 46.5 D, 44.3 R

Economics

Index of economic momentum (1997): 1.10 *(see question 448)*

State spending (1996): $12.7 billion

Federal spending in state: $21.8 billion

State employment (1997): 2,185,000

State employment growth (percent, 1996–1997): 4.3 *(see question 453)*

Major industry: Services *(see question 451)*

History

Joined Union: February 14, 1912

Name origin: "Aleh-zon" (Papago: place of the small spring) *(see questions 9–10)*

Adopted current constitution: 1911

Governors since statehood:

George W. P. Hunt (D)	1912–1917
Thomas E. Campbell (R)	1917
George W. P. Hunt (D)	1917–1919
Thomas E. Campbell (R)	1919–1923
George W. P. Hunt (D)	1923–1929
John C. Phillips (R)	1929–1931
George W. P. Hunt (D)	1931–1933
B. B. Moeur (D)	1933–1937
R. C. Stanford (D)	1937–1939
Robert T. Jones (D)	1939–1941
Sidney P. Osborn (D)	1941–1948
Dan E. Garvey (D)	1948–1951
Howard Pyle (R)	1951–1955
Ernest W. McFarland (D)	1955–1959
Paul J. Fannin (R)	1959–1965
Samuel P. Goddard (D)	1965–1967
J. R. ("Jack") Williams (R)	1967–1975
Raul H. Castro (D)	1975–1977
Wesley Bolin (D)	1977–1978
Bruce Babbitt (D)	1978–1987
Evan Mecham (R)	1987–1988
Rose Mofford (R)	1988–1991
Fife Symington (R)	1991–1997
Jane Dee Hull (R)	1997–

Ⓠ 521 ARKANSAS

Home page: www.state.ar.us/

Capital: Little Rock

Land area (rank): 27th

Land area: 52,075 sq. miles

Population: 2,510,000

Percentage of national population: 0.9

Population growth (percent, 1981–1996): 9.1

Population density (per square mile): 48

Largest cities: Little Rock, Fort Smith, Pine Bluff

Federally owned land (percent): 8.2

Representatives in U.S. House: 4

State motto: *Regnat Populus* (The People Rule)

Song: "Arkansas"

Flower: Apple blossom

Bird: Mockingbird

Tree: Pine

Gem: Diamond

Nickname: The Natural State

Executive Branch

Governor: Mike Huckabee (R)

Governor's term ends: 2003

Lt. Governor: Winthrop Rockefeller (R)

Attorney General: Mark Pryor (D)

Treasurer: Jimmie Lou Fisher

General Assembly

Upper chamber: Senate

Lower chamber: House of Representatives

Members: Senate, 35; House, 100

Legislative session begins: January

Elections

Eligible voters: 1,860,000

Eligible voters, percentage registered: 73

Governor's party: R

Senate/House majority (1997): D/D *(see question 233)*

Vote in 1996 presidential election (percent): 53.7 D, 36.8 R

Economics

Index of economic momentum (1997): -0.15 *(see question 448)*

State spending (1996): $7.6 billion

Federal spending in state (millions): $12,076

State employment (1997): 1,179,000

State employment growth (percent, 1996–1997): 0.8 *(see question 453)*

Major industry: Manufacturing *(see question 451)*

History

Joined Union: June 15, 1836

Name origin: From the French for "Kansas," the Algonkian name for the Quapaw tribe *(see questions 9–10)*

Adopted current constitution: 1874

Governors since 1900:

Dan W. Jones (D)	1897–1901
Jeff Davis (D)	1901–1907
John S. Little (D)	1907
John I. Moore (D)	1907
Xenophon O. Pindall (D)	1907–1909
Jesse M. Martin (D)	1909
George W. Donaghey (D)	1909–1913
Joe T. Robinson (D)	1913
William K. Oldham (D)	1913
J. M. Futrell (D)	1913
George W. Hays (D)	1913–1917
Charles H. Brough (D)	1917–1921
Thomas C. McRae (D)	1921–1925
Thomas J. Terral (D)	1925–1927
John E. Martineau (D)	1927–1928
Harvey Parnell (D)	1928–1933
J. M. Futrell (D)	1933–1937
Carl E. Bailey (D)	1937–1941
Homer M. Adkins (D)	1941–1945
Ben Laney (D)	1945–1949
Sid McMath (D)	1949–1953
Francis Cherry (D)	1953–1955
Orval E. Faubus (D)	1955–1967
Winthrop Rockefeller (R)	1967–1971
Dale Bumpers (D)	1971–1975
Robert Riley (D)	1975
David H. Pryor (D)	1975–1979
Joe Purcell (D)	1979
Bill Clinton (D)	1979–1981
Frank D. White (R)	1981–1983
Bill Clinton (D)	1983–1992
Jim Guy Tucker (D)	1992–1996
Mike Huckabee (R)	1996–

Q 522 CALIFORNIA

Home page: www.ca.gov/s/

Capital: Sacramento

Land area (rank): 3d

Land area: 155,973 sq. miles

Population: 31,878,000

Percentage of national population: 12

Population growth (percent, 1981–1996): 31.4

Population density (per square mile): 204

Largest cities: Los Angeles, San Diego, San Francisco, San Jose

Federally owned land (percent): 44.6

Representatives in U.S. House: 52

State motto: *Eureka* (I Have Found It)

Song: "I Love You, California"

Flower: Golden poppy

Bird: California valley quail

Tree: California redwood

Animal: Grizzly bear

Fossil: Saber-toothed cat

Nickname: Golden State

Executive Branch

Governor: Gray Davis (D)

Governor's term ends: 2003

Lt. Governor: Cruz Bustamante (D)

Attorney General: Bill Lockyer (D)

Treasurer: Philip Angelides

Legislature

Upper chamber: Senate

Lower chamber: Assembly

Members: Senate, 40; Assembly, 80

Legislative session begins: January

Elections

Eligible voters: 23,133,000

Eligible voters, percentage registered: 62

Governor's party: D

Senate/Assembly majority (1998): **D/D** *(see question 233)*

Vote in 1996 presidential election (percent): 51.1 D, 38.2 R

Economics

Index of economic momentum (1997): 0.41 *(see question 448)*

State spending (1996): $94.1 billion

Federal spending in state: $157.4 billion

State employment (1997): 14,890,000

State employment growth (percent, 1996–1997): 2.7 *(see question 453)*

Major industry: Services *(see question 451)*

History

Joined Union: September 9, 1850

Name origin: From the Spanish for "an earthly paradise" *(see questions 9–10)*

Adopted current constitution: 1879

Governors since 1900:

Henry T. Gage (R)	1899–1903
George C. Pardee (R)	1903–1907
James N. Gillett (R)	1907–1911
Hiram W. Johnson (R)	1911–1917
William D. Stephens (R)	1917–1923
Friend W. Richardson (R)	1923–1927
Clement C. Young (R)	1927–1931
James Rolph, Jr. (R)	1931–1934
Frank F. Merriam (R)	1934–1939
Culbert L. Olson (D)	1939–1943
Earl Warren (R)	1943–1953
Goodwin J. Knight (R)	1953–1959
Edmund G. Brown, Sr. (D)	1959–1967
Ronald Reagan (R)	1967–1975
Edmund G. Brown, Jr. (D)	1975–1983
George Deukmejian (R)	1983–1991
Pete Wilson (R)	1991–1999
Gray Davis (D)	1999–

523 COLORADO

Home page: *www.state.co.us/*

Capital: Denver

Land area (rank): 8th

Land area: 103,729 sq. miles

Population: 3,823,000

Percentage of national population: 1.4

Population growth (percent, 1981–1996): 28.1

Population density (per square mile): 37

Largest cities: Denver, Colorado Springs, Pueblo, Fort Collins

Federally owned land (percent): 36.3

Representatives in U.S. House: 6

State motto: *Nil Sine Numine* (Nothing Without Providence)

Song: "Where the Columbines Grow"

Flower: Blue columbine

Bird: Lark bunting

Tree: Blue spruce

Animal: Bighorn sheep

Fossil: Stegosaurus

Gemstone: Aquamarine

Nickname: Centennial State

Executive Branch

Governor: Bill Owens (R)

Governor's term ends: 2003

Lt. Governor: Joe Rogers (R)

Attorney General: Ken Salazar (D)

Treasurer: Mike Coffman (R)

General Assembly

Upper chamber: Senate

Lower chamber: House of Representatives

Members: Senate, 35; House, 65

Legislative session begins: January

Elections

Eligible voters: 2,843,000

Eligible voters, percentage registered: 80

Governor's party: R

Senate/House majority (1998): R/R *(see question 233)*

Vote in 1996 presidential election (percent): 44.4 D, 45.8 R

Economics

Index of economic momentum (1997): 0.80 *(see question 448)*

State spending (1996): $8.7 billion

Federal spending in state: $20 billion

State employment (1997): 2,100,000

State employment growth (percent, 1996–1997): 1.7 *(see question 453)*

Major industry: Services *(see question 451)*

History

Joined Union: August 1, 1876

Name origin: From the Spanish for "red," meaning "red land" *(see questions 9–10)*

Adopted current constitution: 1876

Governors since 1900:

Charles S. Thomas (D)	1899–1901
James B. Orman (D)	1901–1903
James H. Peabody (R)	1903–1905
Alva Adams (D)	1905
James H. Peabody (R)	1905
Jesse F. McDonald (R)	1905–1907
Henry A. Buchtel (R)	1907–1909
John F. Shafroth (D)	1909–1913
Elias M. Ammons (D)	1913–1915
George A. Carlson (R)	1915–1917
Julius C. Gunter (D)	1917–1919
Oliver H. Shoup (R)	1919–1923
William E. Sweet (D)	1923–1925
Clarence J. Morley (R)	1925–1927
William H. Adams (D)	1927–1933
Edwin C. Johnson (D)	1933–1937
Ray H. Talbot (D)	1937
Teller Ammons (D)	1937–1939
Ralph L. Carr (R)	1939–1943
John C. Vivian (R)	1943–1947
William Lee Knous (D)	1947–1950

Walter W. Johnson (D)	1950–1951
Dan Thornton (R)	1951–1955
Edwin C. Johnson (D)	1955–1957
Stephen L. R. McNichols (D)	1957–1963
John A. Love (R)	1963–1973
John D. Vanderhoof (R)	1973–1975
Richard D. Lamm (D)	1975–1987
Roy Romer (D)	1987–1999
Bill Owens (R)	1999–

Ⓠ 524 CONNECTICUT

Home page: www.state.ct.us.index.asp

Capital: Hartford

Land area (rank): 48th

Land area: 4,845 sq. miles

Population: 3,274,000

Percentage of national population: 1.2

Population growth (percent, 1981–1996): 4.8

Population density (per square mile): 676

Largest cities: Bridgeport, Hartford, New Haven, Waterbury

Federally owned land (percent): 0.2

Representatives in U.S. House: 6

State motto: *Qui Transtulit Sustinet* (He Who Transplanted Still Sustains)

Song: "Yankee Doodle"

Flower: Mountain laurel

Bird: American robin

Tree: White Oak

Animal: Sperm whale

Mineral: Garnet

Insect: European praying mantis

Nicknames: Constitution State; Nutmeg State

Executive Branch

Governor: John G. Rowland (R)

Governor's term ends: 2003

Lt. Governor: M. Jodi Rell (R)

Attorney General: Richard Blumenthal (D)

Treasurer: Denise Nappier (D)

General Assembly

Upper chamber: Senate

Lower chamber: House of Representatives

Members: Senate, 36; House, 151

Legislative session begins: January

Elections

Eligible voters: 2,468,000

Eligible voters, percentage registered: 80

Governor's party: R

Senate/House majority (1998): D/D (*see question 233*)

Vote in 1996 presidential election (percent): 52.8 D, 37.4 R

Economics

Index of economic momentum (1997): -0.30 (*see question 448*)

State spending (1996): $13.1 billion

Federal spending in state: $17.9 billion

State employment (1997): 1,663,000

State employment growth (percent, 1996–1997): 1.7 (*see question 453*)

Major industry: Finance, insurance, and real estate (*see question 451*)

History

Joined Union: January 9, 1788

Name origin: "Quinnehtukqut" (Mohican: beside the long tidal river) (*see questions 9–10*)

Adopted current constitution: 1965

Governors since 1900:

George E. Lounsbury (R)	1899–1901
George P. McLean (R)	1901–1903
Abiram Chamberlain (R)	1903–1905

Henry Roberts (R) 1905–1907
Rollin S. Woodruff (R) 1907–1909
George L. Lilley (R) 1909
Frank B. Weeks (R) 1909–1911
Simeon E. Baldwin (D) 1911–1915
Marcus H. Holcomb (R) 1915–1921
Everett J. Lake (R) 1921–1923
Charles A. Templeton (R) 1923–1925
Hiram Bingham (R) 1925
John H. Trumbull (R) 1925–1931
Wilbur L. Cross (D) 1931–1939
Raymond E. Baldwin (R) 1939–1941
Robert A. Hurley (D) 1941–1943
Raymond E. Baldwin (R) 1943–1946
Wilbert Snow (D) 1946–1947
James L. McConaughy (R) 1947–1948
James C. Shannon (R) 1948–1949
Chester Bowles (D) 1949–1951
John Lodge (R) 1951–1955
Abraham Ribicoff (D) 1955–1961
John Dempsey (D) 1961–1971
Thomas J. Meskill (R) 1971–1975
Ella T. Grasso (D) 1975–1980
William A. O'Neill (D) 1980–1991
Lowell Weicker (I) 1991–1995
John G. Rowland (R) 1995–

525 DELAWARE

Home page: www.state.de.us/

Capital: Dover
Land area (rank): 49th
Land area: 1,955 sq. miles
Population: 725,000
Percentage of national population: 0.3
Population growth (percent, 1981–1996): 21.2

Population density (per square mile): 371
Largest city: Wilmington
Federally owned land (percent): 2.2

Representatives in U.S. House: 1

State motto: Liberty and Independence
Song: "Our Delaware"
Flower: Peach blossom
Bird: Blue hen chicken
Tree: American holly
Fish: Sea trout
Nickname: First State; Diamond State

Executive Branch
Governor: Tom Carper (D)
Governor's term ends: 2001
Lt. Governor: Ruth Ann Minner (D)
Attorney General: M. Jane Brady (R)
Treasurer: Jack Markell (D)

General Assembly
Upper chamber: Senate
Lower chamber: House of Representatives
Members: Senate, 21; House, 41
Legislative session begins: January

Elections
Eligible voters: 547,000
Eligible voters, percentage registered: 77
Governor's party: D
Senate/House majority (1998): D/R *(see question 233)*
Vote in 1996 presidential election (percent): 49.5 D, 55.6 R

Economics
Index of economic momentum (1997): 0.70 *(see question 448)*
State spending (1996): $3.7 billion

Federal spending in state: $3.3 billion

State employment (1997): 374,000

State employment growth (percent, 1996–1997): 2.1 (see question 453)

Major industry: Finance, insurance, and real estate (see question 451)

History

Joined Union: December 7, 1787

Name origin: Named for the governor of Virginia, Baron De la Warr (see questions 9–10)

Adopted current constitution: 1897

Governors since 1900:

Ebe W. Tunnell (D)	1897–1901
John Hunn (R)	1901–1905
Preston Lea (R)	1905–1909
Simeon S. Pennewill (R)	1909–1913
Charles R. Miller (Repub.-Progressive)	1913–1917
John G. Townsend, Jr. (R)	1917–1921
William D. Denney (R)	1921–1925
Robert P. Robinson (R)	1925–1929
C. Douglass Buck (R)	1929–1937
Richard C. McMullen (D)	1937–1941
Walter W. Bacon (R)	1941–1949
Elbert N. Carvel (D)	1949–1953
James Caleb Boggs (R)	1953–1960
David P. Buckson (R)	1960–1961
Elbert N. Carvel (D)	1961–1965
Charles L. Terry (D)	1965–1969
Russell W. Peterson (R)	1969–1973
Sherman W. Tribbitt (D)	1973–1977
Pierre S. duPont (R)	1977–1985
Michael N. Castle (R)	1985–1992
Dale E. Wolf (R)	1993
Thomas Carper (D)	1993–

526 FLORIDA

Home page: www.dos.state.fl.us/fgils/

Capital: Tallahassee

Land area (rank): 26th

Land area: 53,997 sq. miles

Population: 14,400,000

Percentage of national population: 5.4

Population growth (percent, 1981–1996): 41.2

Population density (per square mile): 267

Largest cities: Jacksonville, Miami, Tampa, St. Petersburg

Federally owned land (percent): 9

Representatives in U.S. House: 23

State motto: In God We Trust

Song: "The Swannee River (Old Folks at Home)"

Flower: Orange blossom

Bird: Mockingbird

Tree: Sabal palmetto palm

Animal: Florida panther

Saltwater mammal: Porpoise

Shell: Horse conch

Nickname: Sunshine State

Executive Branch

Governor: Jeb Bush (R)

Governor's term ends: 2003

Lt. Governor: Frank Brogan (R)

Attorney General: Bob Butterworth (D)

Treasurer: Bill Nelson (D)

Legislature

Upper chamber: Senate

Lower chamber: House of Representatives

Members: Senate, 40; House, 120

Legislative session begins: February

Elections

Eligible voters: 11,043,000

Eligible voters, percentage registered: 75

Governor's party: R

Senate/House majority (1997): R/R *(see question 233)*

Vote in 1996 presidential election (percent): 48 D, 42.3 R

Economics

Index of economic momentum (1997): 0.43 *(see question 448)*

State spending (1996): $39.4 billion

Federal spending in state: $79.1 billion

State employment (1997): 6,814,000

State employment growth (percent, 1996–1997): 3.6 *(see question 453)*

Major industry: Services *(see question 451)*

History

Joined Union: March 3, 1845

Name origin: From the Spanish for "land of the flowers" *(see questions 9–10)*

Adopted current constitution: 1968

Governors since 1900:

William D. Bloxham (D)	1897–1901
William S. Jennings (D)	1901–1905
Napoleon B. Broward (D)	1905–1909
Albert W. Gilchrist (D)	1909–1913
Park N. Trammell (D)	1913–1917
Sidney J. Catts (Indep. Dem.)	1917–1921
Cary A. Hardee (D)	1921–1925
John W. Martin (D)	1925–1929
Doyle E. Carlton (D)	1929–1933
David Sholtz (D)	1933–1937
Frederick P. Cone (D)	1937–1941
Spessard L. Holland (D)	1941–1945
Millard F. Caldwell (D)	1945–1949
Fuller Warren (D)	1949–1953
Dan McCarty (D)	1953
Charley E. Johns (D)	1953–1955
T. LeRoy Collins (D)	1955–1961
C. Farris Bryant (D)	1961–1965
Haydon Burns (D)	1965–1967
Claude R. Kirk, Jr. (R)	1967–1971
Reubin O. Askew (D)	1971–1979
Robert Graham (D)	1979–1987
John W. Mixon (D)	1987
Bob Martinez (R)	1987–1991
Lawton Chiles (D)	1991–1999
Jeb Bush (R)	1999–

ℚ 527 GEORGIA

Home page: www.state.ga.us/

Capital: Atlanta

Land area (rank): 21st

Land area: 57,919 sq. miles

Population: 7,353,000

Percentage of national population: 2.8

Population growth (percent, 1981–1996): 32

Population density (per square mile): 127

Largest cities: Atlanta, Columbus, Macon, Savannah

Federally owned land (percent): 4

Representatives in U.S. House: 11

State motto: Wisdom, Justice and Moderation

Song: "Georgia On My Mind"

Flower: Cherokee rose

Bird: Brown thrasher

Tree: Live oak

Butterfly: Tiger swallowtail

Insect: Honeybee

Fish: Largemouth bass

Nickname: Empire State of the South

Executive Branch

Governor: Roy Barnes (D)
Governor's term ends: 2003
Lt. Governor: Pierre Howard (D)
Attorney General: Thurbert Baker (R)
Treasurer: Dan Ebersole

General Assembly

Upper chamber: Senate
Lower chamber: House of Representatives
Members: Senate, 56; House, 180
Legislative session begins: January

Elections

Eligible voters: 5,396,000
Eligible voters, percentage registered: 71
Governor's party: D
Senate/House majority (1998): D/D *(see question 233)*
Vote in 1996 presidential election (percent): 45.8 D, 47 R

Economics

Index of economic momentum (1997): 0.20 *(see also question 448)*
State spending (1996): $18.8 billion
Federal spending in state: $34.7 billion
State employment (1997): 3,699
State employment growth (percent, 1996–1997): 1.2 *(see question 453)*
Major industry: Manufacturing *(see question 451)*

History

Joined Union: See January 2, 1788
Name origin: Named for England's King George II *(see questions 9–10)*
Adopted current constitution: 1982
Governors since 1900:

Allen D. Candler (D)	1898–1902
Joseph M. Terrell (D)	1902–1907
Hoke Smith (D)	1907–1909
Joseph M. Brown (D)	1909–1911
Hoke Smith (D)	1911
John M. Slaton (D)	1911–1912
Joseph M. Brown (D)	1912–1913
John M. Slaton (D)	1913–1915
Nathaniel E. Harris (D)	1915–1917
Hugh M. Dorsey (D)	1917–1921
Thomas W. Hardwick (D)	1921–1923
Clifford Walker (D)	1923–1927
Lamartine G. Hardman (D)	1927–1931
Richard B. Russell, Jr. (D)	1931–1933
Eugene Talmadge (D)	1933–1937
Eurith D. Rivers (D)	1937–1941
Eugene Talmadge (D)	1941–1943
Ellis G. Arnall (D)	1943–1947
Melvin E. Thompson (D)	1947–1948
Herman E. Talmadge (D)	1948–1955
S. Marvin Griffin (D)	1955–1959
Samuel E. Vandiver, Jr. (D)	1959–1963
Carl E. Sanders (D)	1963–1967
Lester G. Maddox (D)	1967–1971
James Carter (D)	1971–1975
George D. Busbee (D)	1975–1983
Joe Frank Harris (D)	1983–1991
Zell Miller (D)	1991–1999
Roy Barnes (D)	1999–

528 HAWAII

Home page: www.hawaii.gov/

Capital: Honolulu
Land area (rank): 47th
Land area: 6,423 sq. miles
Population: 1,184,000
Percentage of national population: 0.4
Population growth (percent, 1981–1996): 20.8

Population density (per square mile): 184

Largest city: Honolulu

Federally owned land (percent): 15.5

Representatives in U.S. House: 2

State motto: *Ua Mau Ke Ea O Ka Aina I Ka Pono* (The Life of the Land Is Perpetuated in Righteousness)

Song: "Hawaii Ponoi"

Flower: Hibiscus

Bird: Hawaiian goose

Tree: Kukui tree (candlenut)

Nickname: Aloha State

Executive Branch

Governor: Benjamin J. Cayetano (D)

Governor's term ends: 2002

Lt. Governor: Mazie Hirono (D)

Attorney General: Margery S. Bronster (D)

Director of Finance: Earl Anzai

Legislature

Upper chamber: Senate

Lower chamber: House of Representatives

Members: Senate, 25; House, 51

Legislative session begins: January

Elections

Eligible voters: 882,000

Eligible voters, percentage registered: 71

Governor's party: D

Senate/House majority (1998): D/D *(see question 233)*

Vote in 1996 presidential election (percent): 57 D, 32 R

Economics

Index of economic momentum (1997): -1.72 *(see question 448)*

State spending (1996): $6.3 billion

Federal spending in state: $8 billion

State employment (1997): 560,000

State employment growth (percent, 1996–1997): -0.5 *(see question 453)*

Major industry: Services *(see question 451)*

History

Joined Union: August 21, 1959

Name origin: "Hawaiki" (Hawaiian: homeland) *(see questions 9–10)*

Adopted current constitution: 1950

Governors since statehood:

William F. Quinn (R)	1959–1962
John A. Burns (D)	1962–1974
George R. Ariyoshi (D)	1974–1986
John Waihee (D)	1986–1994
Ben J. Cayetano	1994–

ⓠ 529 IDAHO

Home page: www2.state.id.us/

Capital: Boise

Land area (rank): 11th

Land area: 82,751 sq. miles

Population: 1,189,000

Population (percentage of national population): 0.4

Population growth (percent, 1981–1996): 23.2

Population density (per square mile): 14

Largest cities: Boise, Pocatello, Idaho Falls

Federally owned land (percent): 61.6

Representatives in U.S. House: 2

State motto: *Esto Perpetua* (Let It Be Perpetual)

Song: "Here We Have Idaho"

Flower: Syringa

Bird: Mountain bluebird

Tree: Western white pine

Horse: Appaloosa

Gemstone: Idaho start garnet

Executive Branch

Governor: Dirk Kempthorne (R)

Governor's term ends: 2003

Lt. Governor: C. L. "Butch" Otter (R)

Attorney General: Alan Lance (R)

Treasurer: Ron Crane

Legislature

Upper chamber: Senate

Lower chamber: House of Representatives

Members: Senate, 35; House, 70

Legislative session begins: January

Elections

Eligible voters: 845,000

Eligible voters, percentage registered: 76

Governor's party: R

Senate/House majority (1998): R/R *(see question 233)*

Vote in 1996 presidential election (percent): 33.6 D, 52.2 R

Economics

Index of economic momentum (1997): -0.01 *(see question 448)*

State spending (1996): $2.9 billion

Federal spending in state: $5.5 billion

State employment (1997): 610,000

State employment growth (percent, 1996–1997): 1.6 *(see question 453)*

Major industry: Finance, insurance, and real estate *(see question 451)*

History

Joined Union: July 3,1890

Name origin: Artificial Indian name, made up by George M. Willing *(see questions 9–10)*

Adopted current constitution: 1889

Governors since statehood:

George L. Shoup (R)	1890
Norman B. Willey (R)	1890–1893
William J. McConnell (R)	1893–1897
Frank Steunenberg (D)	1897–1901
Frank W. Hunt (D)	1901–1903
John T. Morrison (R)	1903–1905
Frank R. Gooding (R)	1905–1909
James H. Brady (R)	1909–1911
James H. Hawley (D)	1911–1913
John M. Haines (R)	1913–1915
Moses Alexander (D)	1915–1919
D. W. Davis (R)	1919–1923
C. C. Moore (R)	1923–1927
H. C. Baldridge (R)	1927–1931
C. Benjamin Ross (D)	1931–1937
Barzilla W. Clark (D)	1937–1939
C. A. Bottolfsen (R)	1939–1941
Chase A. Clark (D)	1941–1943
C. A. Bottolfsen (R)	1943–1945
Charles C. Gossett (D)	1945
Arnold Williams (D)	1945–1947
C. A. Robins (R)	1947–1951
Len B. Jordan (R)	1951–1955
Robert E. Smylie (R)	1955–1967
Don Samuelson (R)	1967–1971
Cecil D. Andrus (D)	1971–1977
John V. Evans (D)	1977–1987
Cecil D. Andrus (D)	1987–1995

Philip E. Batt (R) 1995–1999
Dirk Kempthorne (R) 1999–

▣ 530 ILLINOIS

Home page: www.state.il.us/

Capital: Springfield
Land area (rank): 24th
Land area: 55,593 sq. miles
Population: 11,847,000
Population (percentage of national population): 4.5
Population growth (percent, 1981–1996): 3.2
Population density (per square mile): 213
Largest cities: Chicago, Peoria, Rockford, Springfield
Federally owned land (percent): 2.7

Representatives in U.S. House: 20

Song: "Illinois"
Flower: Native violet
Bird: Cardinal
Tree: White oak
Animal: White-tailed deer
Mineral: Flourite
Fish: Bluegill
Nickname: The Prairie State

Executive Branch

Governor: George Ryan (R)
Governor's term ends: 2003
Lt. Governor: Corinne G. Wood (R)
Attorney General: Jim Ryan (R)
Treasurer: Judith Topinka (R)

General Assembly

Upper chamber: Senate
Lower chamber: House of Representatives
Members: Senate, 59; House, 118
Legislative session begins: January

Elections

Eligible voters: 8,764,000
Eligible voters, percentage registered: 76
Governor's party: R
Senate/House majority (1998): R/D *(see question 233)*
Vote in 1996 presidential election (percent): 54.3 D, 36.8 R

Economics

Index of economic momentum (1997): -0.68 *(see question 448)*
State spending (1996): $27.1 billion
Federal spending in state: $51.2 billion
State employment (1997): 5,857,000
State employment growth (percent, 1996–1997): 0.9 *(see question 453)*
Major industry: Services *(see question 451)*

History

Joined Union: December 3, 1818
Name origin: "Illini" (Illinois tribe: man or warrior) *(see questions 9–10)*
Adopted current constitution: 1970
Governors since 1900:

John R. Tanner (R)	1897–1901
Richard Yates, Jr. (R)	1901–1905
Charles S. Deneen (R)	1905–1913
Edward F. Dunne (D)	1913–1917
Frank O. Lowden (R)	1917–1921
Len Small (R)	1921–1929
Louis L. Emmerson (R)	1929–1933
Henry Horner (D)	1933–1940
John H. Stelle (D)	1940–1941
Dwight H. Green (R)	1941–1949
Adlai E. Stevenson (D)	1949–1953

William G. Stratton (R)	1953–1961
Otto Kerner (D)	1961–1968
Samuel H. Shapiro (D)	1968–1969
Richard B. Ogilvie (R)	1969–1973
Daniel Walker (D)	1973–1977
James R. Thompson (R)	1977–1991
Jim Edgar (R)	1991–1999
George Ryan (R)	1999–

ⓠ 531 INDIANA

Home page: www.state.in.us/

Capital: Indianapolis

Land area (rank): 38th

Land area: 35,870 sq. miles

Population: 5,841,000

Population (percentage of national population): 2.2

Population growth (percent, 1981–1996): 6.4

Population density (per square mile): 163

Largest cities: Indianapolis, Fort Wayne, Gary, Evansville

Federally owned land (percent): 1.7

Representatives in U.S. House: 10

State motto: Crossroads of America

Song: "On the Banks of the Wabash, Far Away"

Flower: Peony

Bird: Cardinal

Tree: Tulip poplar

Stone: Limestone

Nickname: Hoosier State

Executive Branch

Governor: Frank O'Bannon (D)

Governor's term ends: 2001

Lt. Governor: Joseph Kerman (D)

Attorney General: Jeff Modisett (D)

Treasurer: Tim Berry

General Assembly

Upper chamber: Senate

Lower chamber: House of Representatives

Members: Senate, 50; House, 100

Legislative session begins: January

Elections

Eligible voters: 4,369,000

Eligible voters, percentage registered: 80

Governor's party: D

Senate/House majority (1998): R/D *(see question 233)*

Vote in 1996 presidential election (percent): 41.6 D, 47.1 R

Economics

Index of economic momentum (1997): -0.44 *(see question 448)*

State spending (1996): $13.2 billion

Federal spending in state: $24.2 billion

State employment (1997): 3,020,000

State employment growth (percent, 1996–1997): 1.1 *(see question 453)*

Major industry: Manufacturing *(see question 451)*

History

Joined Union: December 11, 1816

Name origin: Coined by Congress in 1800 (by adding an "a" to Indian, for "land of the Indians") *(see questions 9–10)*

Adopted current constitution: 1851

Governors since 1900:

James A. Mount (R)	1897–1901
Winfield T. Durbin (R)	1901–1905
J. Frank Hanly (R)	1905–1909

Thomas R. Marshall (D)	1909–1913
Samuel M. Ralston (D)	1913–1917
James P. Goodrich (R)	1917–1921
Warren T. McCray (R)	1921–1924
Emmett F. Branch (R)	1924–1925
Ed Jackson (R)	1925–1929
Harry G. Leslie (R)	1929–1933
Paul V. McNutt (D)	1933–1937
M. Clifford Townsend (D)	1937–1941
Henry F. Schricker (D)	1941–1945
Ralph F. Gates (R)	1945–1949
Henry F. Schricker (D)	1949–1953
George N. Craig (R)	1953–1957
Harold W. Handley (R)	1957–1961
Matthew E. Welsh (D)	1961–1965
Roger D. Branigin (D)	1965–1969
Edgar D. Whitcomb (R)	1969–1973
Otis R. Bowen (R)	1973–1981
Robert D. Orr (R)	1981–1988
Evan Bayh III (D)	1989–1997
Frank O'Bannon (D)	1997–

532 IOWA

Home page: www.state.ia.us/

Capital: Des Moines

Land area (rank): 23d

Land area: 55,875 sq. miles

Population: 2,852,000

Population (percentage of national population): 1.1

Population growth (percent, 1981–1996): 2.3

Population density (per square mile): 51

Largest cities: Des Moines, Cedar Rapids, Davenport

Federally owned land (percent): 0.9

Representatives in U.S. House: 5

State motto: Our Liberties We Prize and Our Rights We Will Maintain

Song: "The Song of Iowa"

Flower: Wild rose

Bird: Eastern goldfinch

Tree: Oak

Stone: Geode

Nickname: Hawkeye State

Executive Branch

Governor: Tom Vilsack (D)

Governor's term ends: 2003

Lt. Governor: Sally Pederson (D)

Attorney General: Tom Miller (D)

Treasurer: Michael Fitzgerald

General Assembly

Upper chamber: Senate

Lower chamber: House of Representatives

Members: Senate, 50; House, 100

Legislative session begins: January

Elections

Eligible voters: 2,138,000

Eligible voters, percentage registered: 81

Governor's party: D

Senate/House majority (1998): R/R *(see question 233)*

Vote in 1996 presidential election (percent): 50.3 D, 39.9 R

Economics

Index of economic momentum (1997): -0.52 *(see question 448)*

State spending (1996): $8.7 billion

Federal spending in state: $13.4 billion

State employment (1997): 1,558,000

State employment growth (percent, 1996–1997): 1.6 *(see question 453)*

Major industry: Manufacturing *(see question 451)*

History

Joined Union: December 28, 1846

Name origin: "Ayuxwa" (Iowa tribe: one who puts to sleep) *(see questions 9–10)*

Adopted current constitution: 1857

Governors since 1900:

Leslie M. Shaw (R)	1898–1902
Albert B. Cummins (R)	1902–1908
Warren Garst (R)	1908–1909
Beryl F. Carroll (R)	1909–1913
George W. Clarke (R)	1913–1917
William L. Harding (R)	1917–1921
Nathan E. Kendall (R)	1921–1925
John Hammill (R)	1925–1931
Daniel W. Turner (R)	1931–1933
Clyde L. Herring (D)	1933–1937
Nelson G. Kraschel (D)	1937–1939
George A. Wilson (R)	1939–1943
Bourke B. Hickenlooper (R)	1943–1945
Robert D. Blue (R)	1945–1949
William S. Beardsley (R)	1949–1954
Leo Elthon (R)	1954–1955
Leo A. Hoegh (R)	1955–1957
Herschel C. Loveless (D)	1957–1961
Norman A. Erbe (R)	1961–1963
Harold E. Hughes (D)	1963–1969
Robert D. Fulton (D)	1969
Robert D. Ray (R)	1969–1983
Terry E. Branstad (R)	1983–1999
Tom Vilsack (D)	1999–

Ⓠ 533 KANSAS

Home page: www.state.ks.us/

Capital: Topeka

Land area (rank): 13th

Land area: 81,823 sq. miles

Population: 2,572,000

Population (percentage of national population): 1

Population growth (percent, 1981–1996): 7.6

Population density (per square mile): 31

Largest cities: Wichita, Kansas City, Topeka

Federally owned land (percent): 0.8

Representatives in U.S. House: 4

State motto: *Ad Astra Per Aspera* (To the Stars Through Difficulties)

Song: "Home on the Range"

Flower: Wild native sunflower

Bird: Western meadowlark

Tree: Cottonwood

Animal: American buffalo

Reptile: Ornate box turtle

Insect: Honeybee

Nickname: Sunflower State

Executive Branch

Governor: Bill Graves (R)

Governor's term ends: 2003

Lt. Governor: Gary Sherrer (R)

Attorney General: Carla Stovall (R)

Treasurer: Tim Shallenburger (R)

Legislature

Upper chamber: Senate

Lower chamber: House of Representatives

Members: Senate, 40; House, 125

Legislative session begins: January

Elections

Eligible voters: 1,898,000

Eligible voters, percentage registered: 76

Governor's party: R

Senate/House majority (1998): R/R *(see question 233)*

Vote in 1996 presidential election (percent): 36.1 D, 54.3 R

Economics

Index of economic momentum (1997): 0.27 *(see question 448)*

State spending (1996): $7.9 billion

Federal spending in state: $12.4 billion

State employment (1997): 1,338,000

State employment growth (percent, 1996–1997): 2.8 *(see question 453)*

Major industry: Manufacturing *(see question 451)*

History

Joined Union: January 29, 1861

Name origin: "Kanze" (Kansas tribal name: south wind) *(see questions 9–10)*

Adopted current constitution: 1859

Governors since 1900:

William E. Stanley (R)	1899–1903
Willis J. Bailey (R)	1903–1905
Edward W. Hoch (R)	1905–1909
Walter R. Stubbs (R)	1909–1913
George H. Hodges (D)	1913–1915
Arthur Capper (R)	1915–1919
Henry J. Allen (R)	1919–1923
Jonathan M. Davis (D)	1923–1925
Ben S. Paulen (R)	1925–1929
Clyde M. Reed (R)	1929–1931
Harry H. Woodring (D)	1931–1933
Alfred M. Landon (R)	1933–1937
Walter A. Huxman (D)	1937–1939
Payne H. Ratner (R)	1939–1943
Andrew F. Schoeppel (R)	1943–1947
Frank Carlson (R)	1947–1950
Frank L. Hagaman (R)	1950–1951
Edward F. Arn (R)	1951–1955
Frederick L. Hall (R)	1955–1957
John McCuish (R)	1957
George Docking (D)	1957–1961
John Anderson, Jr. (R)	1961–1965
William H. Avery (R)	1965–1967
Robert B. Docking (D)	1967–1975
Robert F. Bennett (R)	1975–1979
John W. Carlin (D)	1979–1987
Mike Hayden (R)	1987–1991
Joan Finney (D)	1991–1995
Bill Graves (R)	1995–

❑ 534 KENTUCKY

Home page: www.state.ky.us/

Capital: Frankfort

Land area (rank): 36th

Land area: 39,732 sq. miles

Population: 3,884,000

Population (percentage of national population): 1.5

Population growth (percent, 1981–1996): 5.6

Population density (per square mile): 98

Largest cities: Louisville, Lexington

Federally owned land (percent): 4.2

Representatives in U.S. House: 6

State motto: United We Stand, Divided We Fall

Song: "My Old Kentucky Home"

Flower: Goldenrod

Bird: Cardinal

Tree: Tulip poplar

Animal: Gray squirrel

Fossil: Brachiopod

Fish: Kentucky bass

Nickname: Bluegrass State

Executive Branch

Governor: Paul E. Patton (D)

Governor's term ends: 1999

Lt. Governor: Stephen Henry (D)

Attorney General: Albert B. Chandler III (D)

Treasurer: John Hamilton (D)

General Assembly

Upper chamber: Senate

Lower chamber: House of Representatives

Members: Senate, 38; House, 100

Legislative session begins: January

Elections

Eligible voters: 2,924,000

Eligible voters, percentage registered: 82

Governor's party: D

Senate/House majority (1998): D/D *(see question 233)*

Vote in 1996 presidential election (percent): 45.8 D, 44.9 R

Economics

Index of economic momentum (1997): 0.26 *(see question 448)*

State spending (1996): $12.6 billion

Federal spending in state: $19.6 billion

State employment (1997): 1,827,000

State employment growth (percent, 1996–1997): 2.1 *(see question 453)*

Major industry: Manufacturing *(see question 451)*

History

Joined Union: June 1, 1792

Name origin: "Kentake" (Iroquois: meadowland) *(see questions 9–10)*

Adopted current constitution: 1891

Governors since 1900:

William S. Taylor (R)	1899–1900
William Goebel (D)	1900
J. C. W. Beckham (D)	1900–1907
Augustus C. Willson (R)	1907–1911
James B. McCreary (D)	1911–1915
Augustus O. Stanley (D)	1915–1919
James D. Black (D)	1919
Edwin P. Morrow (R)	1919–1923
William J. Fields (D)	1923–1927
Flem D. Sampson (R)	1927–1931
Ruby Laffoon (D)	1931–1935
Albert B. Chandler (D)	1935–1939
Keen Johnson (D)	1939–1943
Simeon S. Willis (R)	1943–1947
Earle C. Clements (D)	1947–1950
Lawrence W. Wetherby (D)	1950–1955
Albert B. Chandler (D)	1955–1959
Bert T. Combs (D)	1959–1963
Edward T. Breathitt (D)	1963–1967
Louis B. Nunn (R)	1967–1971
Wendell H. Ford (D)	1971–1974
Julian M. Carroll (D)	1974–1979
John Y. Brown, Jr. (D)	1979–1983
Martha Layne Collins (D)	1983–1987
Wallace G. Wilkinson (D)	1987–1991
Brereton C. Jones (D)	1991–1995
Paul E. Patton (D)	1995–

535 LOUISIANA

Home page: www.state.la.us/

Capital: Baton Rouge

Land area (rank): 33d

Land area: 43,566 sq. miles

Population: 4,351,000

Population (percentage of national population): 1.6

Population growth (percent, 1981–1996): 1.2

Population density (per square mile): 100

Largest cities: New Orleans, Baton Rouge, Shreveport

Federally owned land (percent): 2.6

Representatives in U.S. House: 7

State motto: Union, Justice and Confidence

Songs: "Give Me Louisiana"; "You Are My Sunshine"

Flower: Magnolia

Bird: Eastern brown pelican

Tree: Bald cypress

Crustacean: Crawfish

Nickname: Pelican State

Executive Branch

Governor: Mike Foster (R)

Governor's term ends: 2000

Lt. Governor: Kathleen B. Blanco (D)

Attorney General: Richard Ieyoub, Jr. (D)

Treasurer: Ken Duncan (D)

Legislature

Upper chamber: Senate

Lower chamber: House of Representatives

Members: Senate, 39; House, 105

Legislative session begins: March

Elections

Eligible voters: 3,137,000

Eligible voters, percentage registered: 81

Governor's party: R

Senate/House majority (1998): D/D *(see question 233)*

Vote in 1996 presidential election (percent): 52 D, 39.9 R

Economics

Index of economic momentum (1997): -0.61 *(see question 448)*

State spending (1996): $14.1 billion

Federal spending in state: $22.1 billion

State employment (1997): 1,878,000

State employment growth (percent, 1996–1997): 1.1 *(see question 453)*

Major industry: Manufacturing *(see question 451)*

History

Joined Union: April 30, 1812

Name origin: Named for French King Louis XIV (in 1681) *(see questions 9–10)*

Adopted current constitution: 1974

Governors since 1900:

Murphy J. Foster (Anti-Lottery Dem.)	1892–1900
William W. Heard (D)	1900–1904
Newton C. Blanchard (D)	1904–1908
Jared Y. Sanders (D)	1908–1912
Luther E. Hall (D)	1912–1916
Ruffin G. Pleasant (D)	1916–1920
John M. Parker (D)	1920–1924
Henry L. Fuqua (D)	1924–1926
O. H. Simpson (D)	1926–1928
Huey P. Long (D)	1928–1932
Alvin O. King (D)	1932
Oscar K. Allen (D)	1932–1936
James A. Noe (D)	1936
Richard W. Leche (D)	1936–1939
Earl K. Long (D)	1939–1940
Sam H. Jones (D)	1940–1944
James H. Davis (D)	1944–1948
Earl K. Long (D)	1948–1952
Robert F. Kennon (D)	1952–1956
Earl K. Long (D)	1956–1960
James H. Davis (D)	1960–1964
John J. McKeithen (D)	1964–1972
Edwin W. Edwards (D)	1972–1980
David C. Treen (R)	1980–1984
Edwin W. Edwards (D)	1984–1988
Charles E. Roemer, III (D, R)	1988–1992

| Edwin W. Edwards (D) | 1992–1996 |
| Mike Foster, Jr. (R) | 1996– |

◫ 536 **MAINE**

Home page: www.state.me.us/

Capital: Augusta
Land area (rank): 39th
Land area: 30,865 sq. miles
Population: 1,243,000
Population (percentage of national population): 0.5
Population growth (percent, 1981–1996): 9.7
Population density (per square mile): 40
Largest city: Portland
Federally owned land (percent): 0.08

Representatives in U.S. House: 2

State motto: *Dirigo* (I Direct, or I Lead)
Song: "State of Maine Song"
Flower: White pine cone
Bird: Chickadee
Tree: White pine
Animal: Moose
Mineral: Tourmaline
Fish: Landlocked salmon
Nickname: Pine Tree State

Executive Branch

Governor: Angus S. King, Jr. (Indep.)
Governor's term ends: 2003
Attorney General: Andrew Ketterer (D)
Treasurer: Dale McCormick (D)

Legislature

Upper chamber: Senate
Lower chamber: House of Representatives
Members: Senate, 35; House, 151
Legislative session begins: December

Elections

Eligible voters: 939,000
Eligible voters, percentage registered: Not available
Governor's party: Indep.
Senate/House majority (1998): D/D *(see question 233)*
Vote in 1996 presidential election (percent): 51.6 D, 30.8 R

Economics

Index of economic momentum (1997): -0.10 *(see question 448)*
State spending (1996): $4.1 billion
Federal spending in state: $6.8 billion
State employment (1997): 634,000
State employment growth (percent, 1996–1997): 1.4 *(see question 453)*
Major industry: Manufacturing *(see question 451)*

History

Joined Union: March 15, 1820
Name origin: Named after the French province of Mayne *(see questions 9–10)*
Adopted current constitution: 1819
Governors since 1900:

Llewellyn Powers (R)	1897–1901
John F. Hill (R)	1901–1905
William T. Cobb (R)	1905–1909
Bert M. Fernald (R)	1909–1911
Frederick W. Plaisted (D)	1911–1913
William T. Haines (R)	1913–1915
Oakley C. Curtis (D)	1915–1917
Carl E. Milliken (R)	1917–1921
Frederick H. Parkhurst (R)	1921
Percival P. Baxter (R)	1921–1925
Ralph O. Brewster (R)	1925–1929
William T. Gardiner (R)	1929–1933
Louis J. Brann (D)	1933–1937

Lewis O. Barrows (R)	1937–1941
Sumner Sewall (R)	1941–1945
Horace A. Hildreth (R)	1945–1949
Frederick G. Payne (R)	1949–1952
Burton M. Cross (R)	1952–1955
Edmund S. Muskie (D)	1955–1959
Robert N. Haskell (R)	1959
Clinton A. Clauson (D)	1959
John H. Reed (R)	1959–1967
Kenneth M. Curtis (D)	1967–1975
James B. Longley (Indep.)	1975–1979
Joseph E. Brennan (D)	1979–1987
John R. McKernan, Jr. (R)	1987–1995
Angus S. King, Jr. (Indep.)	1995–

537 MARYLAND

Home page: www.mec.state.md.us/mec/

Capital: Annapolis

Land area (rank): 42d

Land area: 9,775 sq. miles

Population: 5,072,000

Population (percentage of national population): 1.9

Population growth (percent, 1981–1996): 19.1

Population density (per square mile): 519

Largest cities: Baltimore, Frederick, Salisbury

Federally owned land (percent): 3

Representatives in U.S. House: 8

State motto: *Fatti Maschii, Parole Femine* (Manly Deeds, Womanly Words)

Song: "Maryland, My Maryland"

Flower: Black-eyed susan

Bird: Baltimore oriole

Tree: White oak

Boat: The skipjack

Nicknames: Old Line State; Free State

Executive Branch

Governor: Parris N. Glendening (D)

Governor's term ends: 2003

Lt. Governor: Kathleen Kennedy Townsend (D)

Attorney General: J. Joseph Curran (D)

Treasurer: Richard Dixon (D)

General Assembly

Upper chamber: Senate

Lower chamber: House of Delegates

Members: Senate, 47; House, 141

Legislative session begins: January

Elections

Eligible voters: 3,811,000

Eligible voters, percentage registered: 68

Governor's party: D

Senate/House majority (1998): D/D *(see question 233)*

Vote in 1996 presidential election (percent): 54.3 D, 38.3 R

Economics

Index of economic momentum (1997): -0.23 *(see question 448)*

State spending (1996): $14.5 billion

Federal spending in state: $37 billion

State employment (1997): 2,645,000

State employment growth (percent, 1996–1997): 1.4 *(see question 453)*

Major industry: Services *(see question 451)*

History

Joined Union: April 28, 1788

Name origin: Named by Lord Baltimore for England's Queen Mary (Henrietta Maria) *(see questions 9–10)*

Adopted current constitution: 1867

Governors since 1900:

John Walter Smith (D)	1900–1904
Edwin Warfield (D)	1904–1908
Austin L. Crothers (D)	1908–1912
Phillips Lee Goldsborough (R)	1912–1916
Emerson C. Harrington (D)	1916–1920
Albert C. Ritchie (D)	1920–1935
Harry W. Nice (R)	1935–1939
Herbert R. O'Conor (D)	1939–1947
William Preston Lane, Jr. (D)	1947–1951
Theodore R. McKeldin (R)	1951–1959
J. Millard Tawes (D)	1959–1967
Spiro T. Agnew (R)	1967–1969
Marvin Mandel (D)	1969–1977
Blair Lee, III (D)	1977–1979
Harry R. Hughes (D)	1979–1987
William Donald Schaefer (D)	1987–1995
Parris N. Glendening (D)	1995–

ⓠ 538 **MASSACHUSETTS**

Home page:
www.magnet.state.ma.us/

Capital: Boston

Land area (rank): 45th

Land area: 7,838 sq. miles

Population: 6,092,000

Population (percentage of national population): 1.3

Population growth (percent, 1981–1996): 2.3

Population density (per square mile): 777

Largest cities: Boston, Worcester, Springfield

Federally owned land (percent): 1.3

Representatives in U.S. House: 10

State motto: *Ense Petit Placidam Sub Libertate Quietem* (By the Sword We Seek Peace, But Peace Only Under liberty)

Song: "All Hail to Massachusetts"

Flower: Mayflower

Bird: Chickadee

Tree: American elm

Horse: Morgan horse

Mineral: Babingtonite

Insect: Ladybug

Nickname: Bay State

Executive Branch

Governor: Argeo Paul Cellucci (R)

Governor's term ends: 2003

Lt. Governor: Jane M. Swift (R)

Attorney General: Thomas F. Reilly (D)

Treasurer: Shannon P. O'Brien (D)

General Court (the legislature)

Upper chamber: Senate

Lower chamber: House of Representatives

Members: Senate, 40; House, 160

Legislative session begins: January

Elections

Eligible voters: 4,623,000

Eligible voters, percentage registered: 76

Governor's party: R

Senate/House majority (1998): D/D *(see question 233)*

Vote in 1996 presidential election (percent): 61.5 D, 28.1 R

Economics

Index of economic momentum (1997): 0.50
   (see question 448)

State spending (1996): $19.8 billion

Federal spending in state: $36.5 billion

State employment (1997): 3,110,000

State employment growth (percent, 1996–1997): 2.2 *(see question 453)*

Major industry: Services *(see question 451)*

History

Joined Union: February 6, 1788

Name origin: Algonquian for "big hill place," apparently in reference to Great Blue Hill, near Milton *(see questions 9–10)*

Adopted current constitution: 1780

Governors since 1900:

W. Murray Crane (R)	1900–1903
John L. Bates (R)	1903–1905
William L. Douglas (D)	1905–1906
Curtis Guild, Jr. (R)	1906–1909
Eben S. Draper (R)	1909–1911
Eugene N. Foss (D)	1911–1914
David I. Walsh (D)	1914–1916
Samuel W. McCall (R)	1916–1919
Calvin Coolidge (R)	1919–1921
Channing H. Cox (R)	1921–1925
Alvan T. Fuller (R)	1925–1929
Frank G. Allen (R)	1929–1931
Joseph B. Ely (D)	1931–1935
James M. Curley (D)	1935–1937
Charles F. Hurley (D)	1937–1939
Leverett Saltonstall (R)	1939–1945
Maurice J. Tobin (D)	1945–1947
Robert F. Bradford (R)	1947–1949
Paul A. Dever (D)	1949–1953
Christian A. Herter (R)	1953–1957
Foster Furcolo (D)	1957–1961
John A. Volpe (R)	1961–1963
Endicott Peabody (D)	1963–1965
John A. Volpe (R)	1965–1969
Francis W. Sargent (R)	1969–1975
Michael S. Dukakis (D)	1975–1979
Edward J. King (D)	1979–1983
Michael S. Dukakis (D)	1983–1991
William Weld (R)	1991–1997
Argeo Paul Cellucci (R)	1997–

Ⓠ 539 MICHIGAN

Home page: www.migov.state.mi.us/

Capital: Lansing

Land area (rank): 22d

Land area: 56,809 sq. miles

Population: 9,594,000

Population (percentage of national population): 3.6

Population growth (percent, 1981–1996): 4.2

Population density (per square mile): 169

Largest cities: Detroit, Grand Rapids, Flint, Lansing

Federally owned land (percent): 12.6

Representatives in U.S. House: 16

State motto: *Si Quaeris Peninsulam Amoenam Circumspice* (If You Seek a Pleasant Peninsula, Look About You)

Song: "My Michigan"

Flower: Apple blossom

Bird: Robin

Tree: White pine

Stone: Petoskey stone

Nickname: Wolverine State

Executive Branch

Governor: John Engler (R)

Governor's term ends: 2003

Lt. Governor: Dick Posthumus (R)

Attorney General: Jennifer Granholm (D)

Treasurer: Mark Murray

Legislature

Upper chamber: Senate

Lower chamber: House of Representatives

Members: Senate, 38; House, 110

Legislative session begins: January

Elections

Eligible voters: 7,067,000

Eligible voters, percentage registered: 94

Governor's party: R

Senate/House majority (1998): R/D *(see question 233)*

Vote in 1996 presidential election (percent): 51.7 D, 38.5 R

Economics

Index of economic momentum (1997): -0.34 *(see question 448)*

State spending (1996): $27.7 billion

Federal spending in state: $39.3 billion

State employment (1997): 4,672,000

State employment growth (percent, 1996–1997): 1.3 *(see question 453)*

Major industry: Manufacturing *(see question 451)*

History

Joined Union: January 26, 1837

Name origin: "Majigan" (Chipewa: clearing)

Adopted current constitution: 1963

Governors since 1900:

Hazen S. Pingree (R)	1897–1901
Aaron T. Bliss (R)	1901–1905
Fred M. Warner (R)	1905–1911
Chase S. Osborn (R)	1911–1913
Woodbridge N. Ferris (D)	1913–1917
Albert E. Sleeper (R)	1917–1921
Alex J. Groesbeck (R)	1921–1927
Fred W. Green (R)	1927–1931
Wilbur M. Brucker (R)	1931–1933
William A. Comstock (D)	1933–1935
Frank D. Fitzgerald (R)	1935–1937
Frank Murphy (D)	1937–1939
Frank D. Fitzgerald (R)	1939
Luren D. Dickinson (R)	1939–1941
Murray D. Van Wagoner (D)	1941–1943
Harry F. Kelly (R)	1943–1947
Kim Sigler (R)	1947–1949
G. Mennen Williams (D)	1949–1961
John B. Swainson (D)	1961–1963
George W. Romney (R)	1963–1969
William G. Milliken (R)	1969–1983
James J. Blanchard (D)	1983–1991
John Engler (R)	1991–

540 MINNESOTA

Home page: *www.state.mn.us/*

Capital: St. Paul

Land area (rank): 14th

Land area: 79,617 sq. miles

Population: 4,658,000

Population (percentage of national population): 1.8

Population growth (percent, 1981–1996): 13.2

Population density (per square mile): 59

Largest cities: Minneapolis, St. Paul, Duluth

Federally owned land (percent): 10.5

Representatives in U.S. House: 8

State motto: *L'Etoile du Nord* (The North Star)

Song: "Hail! Minnesota"

Flower: Pink and white lady-slipper

Bird: Loon

Tree: Red pine

Mushroom: Morel

Drink: Milk

Nickname: North Star State

Executive Branch

Governor: Jesse Ventura (Reform)

Governor's term ends: 2003

Lt. Governor: Mae Schunk (Reform)

Attorney General: Mike Hatch (D)

Treasurer: Carol Johnson (D)

Legislature

Upper chamber: Senate

Lower chamber: House of Representatives

Members: Senate, 67; House, 134

Legislative session begins: January

Elections

Eligible voters: 3,412,000

Eligible voters, percentage registered: 80

Governor's party: Reform

Senate/House majority (1998): Dem. Farmer Labor/R *(see question 233)*

Vote in 1996 presidential election (percent): 51.1 D, 35 R

Economics

Index of economic momentum (1997): 0.06 *(see question 448)*

State spending (1996): $14.6 billion

Federal spending in state: $18.8 billion

State employment (1997): 2,585,000

State employment growth (percent, 1996–1997): 2.1 *(see question 453)*

Major industry: Manufacturing *(see question 451)*

History

Joined Union: May 11, 1858

Name origin: "Mnishota" (Dakota Sioux: sky-tinted water) *(see questions 9–10)*

Adopted current constitution: 1857

Governors since 1900:

John Lind (D)	1899–1901
Samuel R. Van Sant (R)	1901–1905
John A. Johnson (D)	1905–1909
Adolph O. Eberhart (R)	1909–1915
Winfield S. Hammond (D)	1915
Joseph A. A. Burnquist (R)	1915–1921
Jacob A. O. Preus (R)	1921–1925
Theodore Christianson (R)	1925–1931
Floyd B. Olson (Farmer Lab.)	1931–1936
Hjalmar Peterson (Farmer Lab.)	1936–1937
Elmer A. Benson (Farmer Lab.)	1937–1939
Harold E. Stassen (R)	1939–1943
Edward J. Thye (R)	1943–1947
Luther W. Youngdahl (R)	1947–1951
Clyde E. Anderson (R)	1951–1955
Orville L. Freeman (Dem. Farmer Lab.)	1955–1961
Elmer L. Andersen (R)	1961–1963
Karl F. Rolvaag (Dem. Farmer Lab.)	1963–1967
Harold LeVander (R)	1967–1971
Wendell R. Anderson (Dem. Farmer Lab.)	1971–1976
Rudolph Perpich (Dem. Farmer Lab.)	1976–1979
Albert H. Quie (R)	1979–1983
Rudolph Perpich (Dem. Farmer Lab.)	1983–1991
Arne Carlson (R)	1991–1999
Jesse Ventura (Reform)	1999–

Q 541 **MISSISSIPPI**

Home page: www.state.ms.us/

Capital: Jackson

Land area (rank): 31st

Land area: 46,914 sq. miles

Population: 2,716,000

Population (percentage of national population): 1

Population growth (percent, 1981–1996): 6.7

Population density (per square mile): 58

Largest cities: Jackson, Meridian

Federally owned land (percent): 4.3

Representatives in U.S. House: 5

State motto: *Virtute et Armis* (By Valor and Arms)

Song: "Go, Mississippi"

Flower: Magnolia

Bird: Mockingbird

Tree: Magnolia

Animal: White-tailed deer

Fish: Largemouth bass

Beverage: Milk

Nickname: Magnolia State

Executive Branch

Governor: Kirk Fordice (R)

Governor's term ends: 2000

Lt. Governor: Ronnie Musgrove (D)

Attorney General: Mike Moore (D)

Treasurer: Marshall Bennett (D)

Legislature

Upper chamber: Senate

Lower chamber: House of Representatives

Members: Senate, 52; House, 122

Legislative session begins: January

Elections

Eligible voters: 1,961,000

Eligible voters, percentage registered: 88

Governor's party: R

Senate/House majority (1998): D/D *(see question 233)*

Vote in 1996 presidential election (percent): 44.1 D, 49.2 R

Economics

Index of economic momentum (1997): -0.81 *(see question 448)*

State spending (1996): $7.3 billion

Federal spending in state: $15,184

State employment (1997): 1,211,000

State employment growth (percent, 1996–1997): 0.2 *(see question 453)*

Major industry: Manufacturing *(see question 451)*

History

Joined Union: December 10, 1817

Name origin: "Mici sibi" (Chipewa: large river) *(see questions 9–10)*

Adopted current constitution: 1890

Governors since 1900:

Anselm J. McLaurin (D)	1896–1900
Andrew H. Longino (D)	1900–1904
James K. Vardaman (D)	1904–1908
Edmond F. Noel (D)	1908–1912
Earl L. Brewer (D)	1912–1916
Theodore G. Bilbo (D)	1916–1920
Lee M. Russell (D)	1920–1924
Henry L. Whitfield (D)	1924–1927
Dennis Murphree (D)	1927–1928
Theodore G. Bilbo (D)	1928–1932
Martin S. Conner (D)	1932–1936
Hugh L. White (D)	1936–1940
Paul B. Johnson (D)	1940–1943

Dennis Murphree (D)	1943–1944
Thomas L. Bailey (D)	1944–1946
Fielding L. Wright (D)	1946–1952
Hugh L. White (D)	1952–1956
James P. Coleman (D)	1956–1960
Ross R. Barnett (D)	1960–1964
Paul B. Johnson, Sr. (D)	1964–1968
John B. Williams (D)	1968–1972
William L. Waller (D)	1972–1976
Cliff Finch (D)	1976–1980
William Winter (D)	1980–1984
Bill Allain (D)	1984–1988
Ray Mabus (D)	1988–1992
Kirk Fordice (R)	1992–

Q 542 MISSOURI

Home page: www.state.mo.us/

Capital: Jefferson City

Land area (rank): 18th

Land area: 68,898 sq. miles

Population: 5,359,000

Population (percentage of national population): 2

Population growth (percent, 1981–1996): 8.5

Population density (per square mile): 78

Largest cities: St. Louis, Kansas City, Springfield

Federally owned land (percent): 4.7

Representatives in U.S. House: 9

State motto: *Salus Populi Suprema Lex Esto* (The Welfare of the People Shall Be the Supreme Law)

Song: "Missouri Waltz"

Flower: White hawthorn

Bird: Bluebird

Tree: Flowering dogwood

Mineral: Galena

Insect: Honeybee

Nickname: Show Me State

Executive Branch

Governor: Mel Carnahan (D)

Governor's term ends: 2001

Lt. Governor: Roger Wilson (D)

Attorney General: Jeremiah W. Nixon (D)

Treasurer: Bob Holden (D)

General Assembly

Upper chamber: Senate

Lower chamber: House of Representatives

Members: Senate, 34; House, 163

Legislative session begins: January

Elections

Eligible voters: 3,980,000

Eligible voters, percentage registered: 84

Governor's party: D

Senate/House majority (1998): D/D *(see question 233)*

Vote in 1996 presidential election (percent): 47.5 D, 41.2 R

Economics

Index of economic momentum (1997): -0.43 *(see question 448)*

State spending (1996): $12.5 billion

Federal spending in state: $35.1 billion

State employment (1997): 2,748,000

State employment growth (percent, 1996–1997): 1.9 *(see question 453)*

Major industry: Manufacturing *(see question 451)*

History

Joined Union: August 10, 1821

Name origin: Algonquian, possibly the word for "big canoe people" or another for "muddy water" *(see questions 9–10)*

Adopted current constitution: 1945

Governors since 1900:

Lawrence V. Stephens (D)	1897–1901
Alexander M. Dockery (D)	1901–1905
Joseph W. Folk (D)	1905–1909
Herbert S. Hadley (R)	1909–1913
Elliot W. Major (D)	1913–1917
Frederick D. Gardner (D)	1917–1921
Arthur M. Hyde (R)	1921–1925
Samuel A. Baker (R)	1925–1929
Henry S. Caulfield (R)	1929–1933
Guy B. Park (D)	1933–1937
Lloyd C. Stark (D)	1937–1941
Forrest C. Donnell (R)	1941–1945
Phil M. Donnelly (D)	1945–1949
Forrest Smith (D)	1949–1953
Phil M. Donnelly (D)	1953–1957
James T. Blair, Jr. (D)	1957–1961
John M. Dalton (D)	1961–1965
Warren E. Hearnes (D)	1965–1973
Christopher S. Bond (R)	1973–1977
Joseph P. Teasdale (D)	1977–1981
Christopher S. Bond (R)	1981–1985
John D. Ashcroft (R)	1985–1993
Mel Carnahan (D)	1993–

Ⓠ 543 MONTANA

Home page: www.mt.gov/

Capital: Helena

Land area (rank): 4th

Land area: 145,556 sq. miles

Population: 879,000

Population (percentage of national population): 0.3

Population growth (percent, 1981–1996): 10.5

Population density (per square mile): 6

Largest cities: Billings, Great Falls, Butte

Federally owned land (percent): 28

Representatives in U.S. House: 1

State motto: *Oro y Plata* (Gold and Silver)

Song: "Montana"

Flower: Bitterroot

Bird: Western meadowlark

Tree: Ponderosa pine

Animal: Grizzly bear

Gemstones: Sapphire and agate

Fossil: Duck-billed dinosaur

Nickname: Treasure State

Executive Branch

Governor: Marc Racicot (R)

Governor's term ends: 2001

Lt. Governor: Judy Martz (R)

Attorney General: Joseph P. Mazurek (D)

Auditor: Mark O'Keefe

Legislature

Upper chamber: Senate

Lower chamber: House of Representatives

Members: Senate, 50; House, 100

Legislative session begins: January

Elections

Eligible voters: 647,000

Eligible voters, percentage registered: 91

Governor's party: R

Senate/House majority (1998): R/R *(see question 233)*

Vote in 1996 presidential election (percent): 41.3 D, 44.1 R

Economics

Index of economic momentum (1997): -0.10 *(see question 448)*

State spending (1996): $2.3 billion

Federal spending in state: $5 billion

State employment (1997): 437,000

State employment growth (percent, 1996–1997): 1.0 *(see question 453)*

Major industry: Services *(see question 451)*

History

Joined Union: November 8, 1889

Name origin: From the Spanish for "mountainous" *(see questions 9–10)*

Adopted current constitution: 1972

Governors since statehood:

Joseph K. Toole (D)	1889–1893
John E. Rickards (R)	1893–1897
Robert B. Smith (D)	1897–1901
Joseph K. Toole (D)	1901–1908
Edwin L. Norris (D)	1908–1913
Samuel V. Stewart (D)	1913–1921
Joseph M. Dixon (R)	1921–1925
John E. Erickson (D)	1925–1933
Frank H. Cooney (D)	1933–1935
William E. Holt (D)	1935–1937
Roy E. Ayers (D)	1937–1941
Samuel C. Ford (R)	1941–1949
John W. Bonner (D)	1949–1953
John Hugo Aronson (R)	1953–1961
Donald G. Nutter (R)	1961–1962
Tim M. Babcock (R)	1962–1969
Forrest H. Anderson (D)	1969–1973
Thomas Lee Judge (D)	1973–1981
Ted Schwinden (D)	1981–1989
Stan Stephens (R)	1989–1993
Marc Racicot (R)	1993–

ⓠ 544 NEBRASKA

Home page: www.state.ne.us/

Capital: Lincoln

Land area (rank): 15th

Land area: 76,878 sq. miles

Population: 1,652,000

Population (percentage of national population): 0.6

Population growth (percent, 1981–1996): 4.4

Population density (per square mile): 21

Largest cities: Omaha, Lincoln, Grand Island

Federally owned land (percent): 1.4

Representatives in U.S. House: 3

State motto: Equality Before the Law

Song: "Beautiful Nebraska"

Flower: Goldenrod

Bird: Western meadowlark

Tree: Western cottonwood

Mammal: White-tailed deer

Insect: Honeybee

Gemstone: Blue agate

Nickname: Cornhusker State

Executive Branch

Governor: Mike Johanns (R)

Governor's term ends: 2003

Lt. Governor: Dave Maurstad (R)

Attorney General: Don Stenberg (R)

Treasurer: David Heineman (R)

Legislature

Chamber (one only): Senate

Members: Senate, 49

Legislative session begins: January

Elections

Eligible voters: 1,208,000

Eligible voters, percentage registered: 85

Governor's party: R

Legislative majority (1997): Nonpartisan (see question 233)

Vote in 1996 presidential election (percent): 35 D, 53.7 R

Economics

Index of economic momentum (1997): 0.07 *(see question 448)*

State spending (1996): $4.3 billion

Federal spending in state: $7.6 billion

State employment (1997): 900,000

State employment growth (percent, 1996–1997): 1.6 *(see question 453)*

Major industry: Finance, insurance, and real estate *(see question 451)*

History

Joined Union: March 1, 1867

Name origin: "Niboathka" (Omaha tribe: river, or flat) *(see questions 9–10)*

Adopted current constitution: 1875

Governors since 1900:

William A. Poynter (Fusion)	1899–1901
Charles H. Dietrich (R)	1901
Ezra P. Savage (R)	1901–1903
John H. Mickey (R)	1903–1907
George L. Sheldon (R)	1907–1909
Ashton C. Shallenberger (D)	1909–1911
Chester H. Aldrich (R)	1911–1913
John H. Morehead (D)	1913–1917
Keith Neville (D)	1917–1919
Samuel R. McKelvie (R)	1919–1923
Charles W. Bryan (D)	1923–1925
Adam McMullen (R)	1925–1929
Arthur J. Weaver (R)	1929–1931
Charles W. Bryan (D)	1931–1935
Robert L. Cochran (D)	1935–1941
Dwight P. Griswold (R)	1941–1947
Val Peterson (R)	1947–1953
Robert B. Crosby (R)	1953–1955
Victor E. Anderson (R)	1955–1959
Ralph G. Brooks (D)	1959–1960
Dwight W. Burney (R)	1960–1961
Frank B. Morrison (D)	1961–1967
Norbert T. Tiemann (R)	1967–1971
J. James Exon (D)	1971–1979
Charles Thone (R)	1979–1983
Robert Kerrey (D)	1983–1987
Kay A. Orr (R)	1987–1991
E. Benjamin Nelson (D)	1991–1999
Mike Johanns (R)	1999–

Ⓠ 545 **NEVADA**

Home page: www.state.nv.us/

Capital: Carson City

Land area (rank): 7th

Land area: 109,806 sq. miles

Population: 1,603,000

Population (percentage of national population): 0.6

Population growth (percent, 1981–1996): 89.7

Population density (per square mile): 15

Largest cities: Las Vegas, Reno, Paradise

Federally owned land (percent): 82.9

Representatives in U.S. House: 2

State motto: All For Our Country

Song: "Home Means Nevada"

Flower: Sagebrush

Bird: Mountain bluebird

Trees: Bristlecone pine and single-leaf pinon

Animal: Desert bighorn sheep

Fossil: Ichthyosaur

Nickname: Sagebrush State

Executive Branch

Governor: Kenny Guinn (R)

Governor's term ends: 2003

Lt. Governor: Lorraine Hunt (R)

Attorney General: Frankie Sue Del Papa (D)

Treasurer: Brian Krolicki (R)

Legislature

Upper chamber: Senate

Lower chamber: Assembly

Members: Senate, 21; Assembly, 42

Legislative session begins: January

Elections

Eligible voters: 1,180,000

Eligible voters, percentage registered: 66

Governor's party: R

Senate/Assembly majority (1998): R/D (see question 233)

Vote in 1996 presidential election (percent): 43.9 D, 42.9 R

Economics

Index of economic momentum (1997): 3.41 *(see question 448)*

State spending (1996): Not available

Federal spending in state: $7.4 billion

State employment (1997): 862,000

State employment growth (percent, 1996–1997): 6.5 *(see question 453)*

Major industry: Services *(see question 451)*

History

Joined Union: October 31, 1864

Name origin: From the Spanish for "snowy" *(see questions 9–10)*

Adopted current constitution: 1864

Governors since 1900:

Reinhold Sadler (Silver Rep.)	1896–1903
John Sparks (Dem. and Silver)	1903–1908
Denver S. Dickerson (D)	1908–1911
Tasker L. Oddie (R)	1911–1915
Emmet D. Boyle (D)	1915–1923
James G. Scrugham (D)	1923–1927
Frederick B. Balzar (R)	1927–1934
Morley I. Griswold (R)	1934–1935
Richard Kirman, Sr. (D)	1935–1939
Edward P. Carville (D)	1939–1945
Vail M. Pittman (D)	1945–1951
Charles H. Russell (R)	1951–1959
F. Grant Sawyer (D)	1959–1967
Paul D. Laxalt (R)	1967–1971
Donald N. ("Mike") O'Callaghan (D)	1971–1979
Robert List (R)	1979–1983
Richard H. Bryan (D)	1983–1989
Robert Miller (D)	1989–1999
Kenny Guinn (R)	1999–

▣ 546 NEW HAMPSHIRE

Home page: *www.state.nh.us/*

Capital: Concord

Land area (rank): 44th

Land area: 8,969 sq. miles

Population: 1,162,000

Population (percentage of national population): 0.4

Population growth (percent, 1981–1996): 24.1

Population density (per square mile): 130

Largest cities: Manchester, Nashua, Concord

Federally owned land (percent): 12.7

Representatives in U.S. House: 2

State motto: Live Free or Die

Song: "Old New Hampshire"

Flower: Purple lilac

Bird: Purple finch

Tree: White birch

Animal: White-tailed deer

Insect: Ladybug

Gem: Smoky quartz

Nickname: Granite State

Executive Branch

Governor: Jeanne Shaheen (D)

Governor's term ends (2-year term): 2001

Attorney General: Philip McLaughlin (D)

Treasurer: Georgie Thomas (R)

General Court (the legislature)

Upper chamber: Senate

Lower chamber: House of Representatives

Members: Senate, 24; House, 400

Legislative session begins: January

Elections

Eligible voters: 860,000

Eligible voters, percentage registered: 82

Governor's party: D

Senate/House majority (1998): D/R (see question 233)

Vote in 1996 presidential election (percent): 49.3 D, 39.4 R

Economics

Index of economic momentum (1997): 0.39 (see question 448)

State spending (1996): $2.3 billion

Federal spending in state: $5 billion

State employment (1997): 636,000

State employment growth (percent, 1996–1997): 1.3 (see question 453)

Major industry: Manufacturing (see question 451)

History

Joined Union: June 21, 1788

Name origin: Named after Hampshire County in England (in 1622) (see questions 9–10)

Adopted current constitution: 1784

Governors since 1900:

Frank W. Rollins (R)	1899–1901
Chester B. Jordan (R)	1901–1903
Nahum J. Batchelder (R)	1903–1905
John McLane (R)	1905–1907
Charles M. Floyd (R)	1907–1909
Henry B. Quinby (R)	1909–1911
Robert P. Bass (R)	1911–1913
Samuel D. Felker (D)	1913–1915
Rolland H. Spaulding (R)	1915–1917
Henry W. Keyes (R)	1917–1919
John H. Bartlett (R)	1919–1921
Albert O. Brown (R)	1921–1923
Fred H. Brown (D)	1923–1925
John G. Winant (R)	1925–1927
Huntley N. Spaulding (R)	1927–1929
Charles W. Tobey (R)	1929–1931
John G. Winant (R)	1931–1935
H. Styles Bridges (R)	1935–1937
Francis P. Murphy (R)	1937–1941
Robert O. Blood (R)	1941–1945
Charles M. Dale (R)	1945–1949
Sherman Adams (R)	1949–1953
Hugh Gregg (R)	1953–1955
Lane Dwinell (R)	1955–1959
Wesley Powell (R)	1959–1963
John W. King (D)	1963–1969
Walter R. Peterson (R)	1969–1973
Meldrim Thompson, Jr. (R)	1973–1979
Hugh Gallen (D)	1979–1982

Vesta Roy (R)	1982–1983
John H. Sununu (R)	1983–1989
Judd Gregg (R)	1989–1993
Steve Merrill (R)	1993–1997
Jeanne Shaheen (D)	1997–

Ⓠ 547 NEW JERSEY

Home page: *www.state.nj.us/*

Capital: Trenton

Land area (rank): 46th

Land area: 7,419 sq. miles

Population: 7,988,000

Population (percentage of national population): 3

Population growth (percent, 1981–1996): 7.8

Population density (per square mile): 1,077

Largest cities: Newark, Jersey City, Paterson, Trenton

Federally owned land (percent): 3.1

Representatives in U.S. House: 13

State motto: Liberty and Prosperity

Flower: Purple violet

Bird: Eastern goldfinch

Tree: Red oak

Animal: Horse

Insect: Honeybee

Nickname: Garden State

Executive Branch

Governor: Christine T. Whitman (R)

Governor's term ends: 2002

Attorney General: Pete Verniero (R)

Treasurer: James DiEleuterio

Legislature

Upper chamber: Senate

Lower chamber: General Assembly

Members: Senate, 40; General Assembly, 80

Legislative session begins: January

Elections

Eligible voters: 6,005,000

Eligible voters, percentage registered: 72

Governor's party: R

Senate/General Assembly majority (1998): R/R *(see question 233)*

Vote in 1996 presidential election (percent): 53.7 D, 35.9 R

Economics

Index of economic momentum (1997): -0.33 *(see question 448)*

State spending (1996): $23.9 billion

Federal spending in state: $38.4 billion

State employment (1997): 3,934,000

State employment growth (percent, 1996–1997): 1.4 *(see question 453)*

Major industry: Services *(see question 451)*

History

Joined Union: December 18, 1787

Name origin: Named after England's Isle of Jersey

Adopted current constitution: 1947

Governors since 1900:

Foster M. Voorhees (R)	1899–1902
Franklin Murphy (R)	1902–1905
Edward C. Stokes (R)	1905–1908
John F. Fort (R)	1908–1911
Woodrow Wilson (D)	1911–1913
James F. Fielder (D)	1913
Leon R. Taylor (D)	1913–1914
James F. Fielder (D)	1914–1917

Walter E. Edge (R)	1917–1919
William N. Runyon (R)	1919–1920
Clarence E. Case (R)	1920
Edward I. Edwards (D)	1920–1923
George S. Silzer (D)	1923–1926
A. Harry Moore (D)	1926–1929
Morgan F. Larson (R)	1929–1932
A. Harry Moore (D)	1932–1935
Clifford R. Powell (R)	1935
Horace G. Prall (R)	1935
Harold G. Hoffman (R)	1935–1938
A. Harry Moore (D)	1938–1941
Charles Edison (D)	1941–1944
Walter E. Edge (R)	1944–1947
Alfred E. Driscoll (R)	1947–1954
Robert B. Meyner (D)	1954–1962
Richard J. Hughes (D)	1962–1970
William T. Cahill (R)	1970–1974
Brendon T. Byrne (D)	1974–1982
Thomas H. Kean (R)	1982–1990
James Florio (D)	1990–1994
Christine Todd Whitman (R)	1994–

◨ 548 NEW MEXICO

Home page: *www.state.nm.us/*

Capital: Santa Fe

Land area (rank): 5th

Land area: 121,365 sq. miles

Population: 1,713,000

Population (percentage of national population): 0.6

Population growth (percent, 1981–1996): 28.3

Population density (per square mile): 14

Largest cities: Albuquerque, Santa Fe, Las Cruces

Federally owned land (percent): 32.4

Representatives in U.S. House: 3

State motto: *Crescit Eundo* (It Grows As It Goes)

Songs: "Asi es Nuevo Mexico" and "O, Fair New Mexico"

Flower: Yucca (Our Lord's Candles)

Bird: Chaparral bird

Tree: Pinon

Animal: Black bear

Gem: Turquoise

Fossil: Coelophysis dinosaur

Nickname: Land of Enchantment

Executive Branch

Governor: Gary E. Johnson (R)

Governor's term ends: 2003

Lt. Governor: Walter Bradley (R)

Attorney General: Patricia A. Madrid (D)

Treasurer: Michael Montoya (D)

Legislature

Upper chamber: Senate

Lower chamber: House of Representatives

Members: Senate, 42; House, 70

Legislative session begins: January

Elections

Eligible voters: 1,210,000

Eligible voters, percentage registered: 69

Governor's party: R

Senate/House majority (1998): D/D (*see question 233*)

Vote in 1996 presidential election (percent): 49.2 D, 41.9 R

Economics

Index of economic momentum (1997): -0.68 (*see question 448*)

State spending (1996): $6.2 billion

Federal spending in state: $12.1 billion

State employment (1997): 772,000

State employment growth (percent, 1996–1997): 1.6 *(see question 453)*

Major industry: Services *(see question 451)*

History

Joined Union: January 6, 1912

Name origin: Named by Spanish explorers (in 1562) *(see questions 9–10)*

Adopted current constitution: 1911

Governors since statehood:

William C. McDonald (D)	1912–1917
Ezequiel C. de Baca (D)	1917
Washington E. Lindsey (R)	1917–1919
Octaviano A. Larrazolo (R)	1919–1921
Merritt C. Mechem (R)	1921–1923
James F. Hinkle (D)	1923–1925
Arthur T. Hannett (D)	1925–1927
Richard C. Dillon (R)	1927–1931
Arthur Seligman (D)	1931–1933
Andrew W. Hockenhull (D)	1933–1935
Clyde Tingley (D)	1935–1939
John E. Miles (D)	1939–1943
John J. Dempsey (D)	1943–1947
Thomas J. Mabry (D)	1947–1951
Edwin L. Mechem (R)	1951–1955
John F. Simms (D)	1955–1957
Edwin L. Mechem (R)	1957–1959
John Burroughs (D)	1959–1961
Edwin L. Mechem (R)	1961–1962
Tom Bolack (R)	1962–1963
Jack M. Campbell (D)	1963–1967
David F. Cargo (R)	1967–1971
Bruce King (D)	1971–1975
Jerry Apodaca (D)	1975–1979
Bruce King (D)	1979–1983
Toney Anaya (D)	1983–1987
Garrey E. Carruthers (R)	1987–1991
Bruce King (D)	1991–1995
Gary E. Johnson (R)	1995–

Ⓠ 549 NEW YORK

Home page: www.state.ny.us/

Capital: Albany

Land area (rank): 30th

Land area: 47,224 sq. miles

Population: 18,185,000

Population (percentage of national population): 6.9

Population growth (percent, 1981–1996): 3.6

Population density (per square mile): 385

Largest cities: New York City, Buffalo, Rochester, Syracuse

Federally owned land (percent): 0.7

Representatives in U.S. House: 31

Motto: *Excelsior* (Ever Upward)

Song (unofficial): "I Love New York"

Flower: Rose

Bird: Bluebird

Tree: Sugar maple

Animal: American beaver

Gem: Garnet

Nickname: Empire State

Executive Branch

Governor: George E. Pataki (R)

Governor's term ends: 2003

Lt. Governor: Mary O. Donohue (R)

Attorney General: Eliot Spitzer (D)

Treasurer: George H. Gasser (R)

Legislature

Upper chamber: Senate

Lower chamber: Assembly

Members: Senate, 61; Assembly, 150
Legislative session begins: January

Elections

Eligible voters: 13,579,000
Eligible voters, percentage registered: 75
Governor's party: R
Senate/Assembly majority (1998): R/D *(see question 233)*
Vote in 1996 presidential election (percent): 59.5 D, 30.6 R

Economics

Index of economic momentum (1997): -0.82 *(see question 448)*
State spending (1996): $68.7 billion
Federal spending in state: $94.7 billion
State employment (1997): 8,216,000
State employment growth (percent, 1996–1997): 1.0 *(see question 453)*
Major industry: Finance, insurance, and real estate *(see question 451)*

History

Joined Union: July 26, 1788
Name origin: Named after the Duke of York *(see questions 9–10)*
Adopted current constitution: 1894
Governors since 1900:

Theodore Roosevelt (R)	1899–1900
Benjamin B. Odell, Jr. (R)	1901–1904
Frank W. Higgins (R)	1905–1906
Charles E. Hughes (R)	1907–1910
Horace White (R)	1910
John Alden Dix (D)	1911–1912
William Sulzer (D)	1913
Martin H. Glynn (D)	1913–1914
Charles S. Whitman (R)	1915–1918
Alfred E. Smith (D)	1919–1920
Nathan L. Miller (R)	1921–1922
Alfred E. Smith (D)	1923–1928
Franklin D. Roosevelt (D)	1929–1932
Herbert H. Lehman (D)	1933–1942
Charles Poletti (D)	1942
Thomas E. Dewey (R)	1943–1954
W. Averell Harriman (D)	1955–1958
Nelson A. Rockefeller (R)	1959–1973
Malcolm Wilson (R)	1973–1974
Hugh L. Carey (D)	1975–1982
Mario M. Cuomo (D)	1983–1995
George E. Pataki (R)	1995–

Ⓠ 550 NORTH CAROLINA

Home page: www.sips.state.nc.us/

Capital: Raleigh
Land area (rank): 29th
Land area: 48,718 sq. miles
Population: 7,323,000
Population (percentage of national population): 2.8
Population growth (percent, 1981–1996): 22.9
Population density (per square mile): 150
Largest cities: Charlotte, Greensboro, Raleigh, Winston-Salem
Federally owned land (percent): 6.3
Representatives in U.S. House: 12
State motto: *Esse Quam Videri* (To Be Rather Than to Seem)
Song: "The Old North State"
Flower: Dogwood
Bird: Cardinal
Tree: Long leaf pine
Mammal: Grey squirrel
Dog: Plott hound

Beverage: Milk

Vegetable: Sweet potato

Nickname: Tar Heel State

Executive Branch

Governor: James B. Hunt, Jr. (D)

Governor's term ends: 2001

Lt. Governor: Dennis A. Wicker (D)

Attorney General: Michael F. Easley (D)

Treasurer: Harlan Boyles (D)

General Assembly

Upper chamber: Senate

Lower chamber: House of Representatives

Members: Senate, 50; House, 120

Legislative session begins: January

Elections

Eligible voters: 5,499,000

Eligible voters, percentage registered: 76

Governor's party: D

Senate/House majority (1998): D/D *(see question 233)*

Vote in 1996 presidential election (percent): 44 D, 48.7 R

Economics

Index of economic momentum (1997): 0.83 *(see question 448)*

State spending (1996): $18.2 billion

Federal spending in state: $3.6 billion

State employment (1997): 3,667,000

State employment growth (percent, 1996–1997): 2.0 *(see question 453)*

Major industry: Manufacturing *(see question 451)*

History

Joined Union: November 21, 1789

Name origin: From the Latinized version of Charles ("Carolina"), after England's King Charles II *(see questions 9–10)*

Adopted current constitution: 1970

Governors since 1900:

Daniel L. Russell (D)	1897–1901
Charles B. Aycock (D)	1901–1905
Robert B. Glenn (D)	1905–1909
William W. Kitchin (D)	1909–1913
Locke Craig (D)	1913–1917
Thomas W. Bickett (D)	1917–1921
Cameron Morrison (D)	1921–1925
Angus W. McLean (D)	1925–1929
O. Max Gardner (D)	1929–1933
J. C. B. Ehringhaus (D)	1933–1937
Clyde R. Hoey (D)	1937–1941
J. Melville Broughton (D)	1941–1945
R. Gregg Cherry (D)	1945–1949
W. Kerr Scott (D)	1949–1953
William B. Umstead (D)	1953–1954
Luther H. Hodges (D)	1954–1961
Terry Sanford (D)	1961–1965
Dan K. Moore (D)	1965–1969
Robert W. Scott (D)	1969–1973
James E. Holshouser, Jr. (R)	1973–1977
James B. Hunt, Jr. (D)	1977–1985
James G. Martin (R)	1985–1993
James B. Hunt, Jr. (D)	1993–

Ⓠ 551 NORTH DAKOTA

Home page: www.state.nd.us/

Capital: Bismarck

Land area (rank): 17th

Land area: 68,994 sq. miles

Population: 644,000

Population (percentage of national population): 0.2

Population growth (percent, 1981–1996): 2.6

Population density (per square mile): 9

Largest city: Fargo

Federally owned land (percent): 4.2

Representatives in U.S. House: 1

State motto: Liberty and Union, Now and Forever, One and Inseparable

Song: "North Dakota Hymn"

Flower: Wild prairie rose

Bird: Western meadowlark

Tree: American elm

Fossil: Teredo petrified wood

Fish: Northern pike

Nickname: Peace Garden State

Executive Branch

Governor: Edward T. Schafer (R)

Governor's term ends: 2001

Lt. Governor: Rosemarie Myrdal (R)

Attorney General: Heidi Heitkamp (D)

Treasurer: Kathi Gilmore (D)

Legislative Assembly

Upper chamber: Senate

Lower chamber: House of Representatives

Members: Senate, 49; House, 98

Legislative session begins: January

Elections

Eligible voters: 473,000

Eligible voters, percentage registered: Not available

Governor's party: R

Senate/House majority (1998): R/R (see question 233)

Vote in 1996 presidential election (percent): 40.1 D, 48.9 R

Economics

Index of economic momentum (1997): -0.04 (see question 448)

State spending (1996): $1.8 billion

Federal spending in state: $3.6 billion

State employment (1997): 339,000

State employment growth (percent, 1996–1997): 2.7 (see question 453)

Major industry: Finance, insurance, and real estate (see question 451)

History

Joined Union: November 2, 1889

Name origin: "Dakota" (Dakota tribal name: friends, allies) (see questions 9–10)

Adopted current constitution: 1889

Governors since 1900:

Frederick B. Fancher (R)	1899–1901
Frank White (R)	1901–1905
Elmore Y. Sarles (R)	1905–1907
John Burke (D)	1907–1913
Louis B. Hanna (R)	1913–1917
Lynn J. Frazier (R)	1917–1921
Ragnvald A. Nestos (R)	1921–1925
Arthur G. Sorlie (R)	1925–1928
Walter J. Maddock (R)	1928–1929
George F. Shafer (R)	1929–1933
William Langer (R)	1933–1934
Ole H. Olson (R)	1934–1935
Thomas H. Moodie (D)	1935
Walter Welford (R)	1935–1937
William Langer (Indep.)	1937–1939
John Moses (D)	1939–1945
Fred G. Aandahl (R)	1945–1951
Clarence N. Brunsdale (R)	1951–1957
John E. Davis (R)	1957–1961
William L. Guy (D)	1961–1973
Arthur A. Link (D)	1973–1981
Allen I. Olson (R)	1981–1985

| George A. Sinner (D) | 1985–1993 |
| Edward T. Schafer (R) | 1993– |

⚪ 552 **OHIO**

Home page: www.ohio.gov/ohio/

Capital: Columbus

Land area (rank): 35th

Land area: 40,953

Population: 11,173

Population (percentage of national population): 4.2

Population growth (percent, 1981–1996): 3.5

Population density (per square mile): 273

Largest cities: Cleveland, Columbus, Cincinnati, Toledo

Federally owned land (percent): 1.3

Representatives in U.S. House: 19

State motto: With God, All Things Are Possible

Song: "Beautiful Ohio"

Flower: Scarlet carnation

Bird: Cardinal

Tree: Buckeye

Animal: White-tailed deer

Stone: Ohio flint

Insect: Ladybug

Nickname: Buckeye State

Executive Branch

Governor: Bob Taft (R)

Governor's term ends: 2003

Lt. Governor: Maureen O'Connor (R)

Attorney General: Betty D. Montgomery (R)

Treasurer: Joseph Deters (R)

General Assembly

Upper chamber: Senate

Lower chamber: House of Representatives

Members: Senate, 33; House, 99

Legislative session begins: January

Elections

Eligible voters: 8,358,000

Eligible voters, percentage registered: 82

Governor's party: R

Senate/House majority (1998): R/R *(see question 233)*

Vote in 1996 presidential election (percent): 47.4 D, 41.0 R

Economics

Index of economic momentum (1997): -0.87 *(see question 448)*

State spending (1996): $30.5 billion

Federal spending in state: $50.1 billion

State employment (1997): 5,490,000

State employment growth (percent, 1996–1997): 0.9 *(see question 453)*

Major industry: Manufacturing *(see question 451)*

History

Joined Union: March 1, 1803

Name origin: "Oheo" (Iroquois: beautiful river) *(see questions 9–10)*

Adopted current constitution: 1851

Governors since 1900:

Asa S. Bushnell (R)	1896–1900
George K. Nash (R)	1900–1904
Myron T. Herrick (R)	1904–1906
John M. Pattison (D)	1906
Andrew L. Harris (R)	1906–1909
Judson Harmon (D)	1909–1913
James M. Cox (D)	1913–1915

Frank B. Willis (R)	1915–1917
James M. Cox (D)	1917–1921
Harry L. Davis (R)	1921–1923
A. Vic Donahey (D)	1923–1929
Myers Y. Cooper (R)	1929–1931
George White (D)	1931–1935
Martin L. Davey (D)	1935–1939
John W. Bricker (R)	1939–1945
Frank J. Lausche (D)	1945–1947
Thomas J. Herbert (R)	1947–1949
Frank J. Lausche (D)	1949–1957
John W. Brown (R)	1957
C. William O'Neill (R)	1957–1959
Michael V. DiSalle (D)	1959–1963
James A. Rhodes (R)	1963–1971
John J. Gilligan (D)	1971–1975
James A. Rhodes (R)	1975–1983
Richard F. Celeste (D)	1983–1991
George Voinovich (R)	1991–1999
Bob Taft (R)	1999–

Ⓠ 553 OKLAHOMA

Home page: www.oklaosf.state.ok.us/

Capital: Oklahoma City

Land area (rank): 19th

Land area: 68,679 sq. miles

Population: 3,301,000

Population (percentage of national population): 1.2

Population growth (percent, 1981–1996): 6.3

Population density (per square mile): 48

Largest cities: Oklahoma City, Tulsa

Federally owned land (percent): 1.6

Representatives in U.S. House: 6

State motto: *Labor Omnia Vincit* (Labor Conquers All Things)

Song: "Oklahoma"

Flower: Mistletoe

Bird: Scissor-tailed flycatcher

Tree: Redbud

Animal: American buffalo

Rock: Barite rose

Nickname: Sooner State

Executive Branch

Governor: Frank Keating (R)

Governor's term ends: 2003

Lt. Governor: Mary Fallin (R)

Attorney General: W. A. Drew Edmondson (D)

Treasurer: Robert Butkin (D)

Legislature

Upper chamber: Senate

Lower chamber: House of Representatives

Members: Senate, 48; House, 101

Legislative session begins: February

Elections

Eligible voters: 2,419,000

Eligible voters, percentage registered: Not available

Governor's party: R

Senate/House majority (1998): D/D *(see question 233)*

Vote in 1996 presidential election (percent): 40.4 D, 48.3 R

Economics

Index of economic momentum (1997): 0.12 *(see question 448)*

State spending (1996): $8.2 billion

Federal spending in state: $16.7 billion

State employment (1997): 1,542,000

State employment growth (percent, 1996–1997): 2.6 *(see question 453)*

Major industry: Manufacturing *(see question 451)*

History

Joined Union: November 16, 1907

Name origin: Choctaw words "ukla" and "huma" (person red, or red people) *(see questions 9–10)*

Adopted current constitution: 1907

Governors since statehood:

Charles N. Haskell (D)	1907–1911
Lee Cruce (D)	1911–1915
Robert L. Williams (D)	1915–1919
J. B. A. Robertson (D)	1919–1923
Jack C. Waltron (D)	1923
Martin E. Trapp (D)	1923–1927
Henry S. Johnston (D)	1927–1929
William J. Holloway (D)	1929–1931
William H. Murry (D)	1931–1935
Ernest W. Marland (D)	1935–1939
Leon C. Phillips (D)	1939–1943
Robert S. Kerr (D)	1943–1947
Roy J. Turner (D)	1947–1951
Johnston Murray (D)	1951–1955
Raymond Gary (D)	1955–1959
J. Howard Edmondson (D)	1959–1963
George P. Nigh (D)	1963
Henry L. Bellmon (R)	1963–1967
Dewey F. Bartlett (R)	1967–1971
David Hall (D)	1971–1975
David L. Boren (D)	1975–1979
George P. Nigh (D)	1979–1987
Henry L. Bellmon (R)	1987–1991
David Walters (D)	1991–1995
Frank Keating (R)	1995–

◼ 554 OREGON

Home page: www.state.or.us/

Capital: Salem

Land area (rank): 10th

Land area: 96,003 sq. miles

Population: 3,204,000

Population (percentage of national population): 1.2

Population growth (percent, 1981–1996): 19.9

Population density (per square mile): 33

Largest cities: Portland, Eugene, Salem

Federally owned land (percent): 52.4

Representatives in U.S. House: 5

State motto: She Flies with Her Own Wings

Song: "Oregon, My Oregon"

Flower: Oregon grape

Bird: Western meadowlark

Tree: Douglas fir

Animal: American beaver

Gemstone: Sunstone

Insect: Oregon swallowtail butterfly

Nickname: Beaver State

Executive Branch

Governor: John A. Kitzhaber (D)

Governor's term ends: 2003

Attorney General: Hardy Myers (D)

Treasurer: Jim Hill (D)

Legislative Assembly

Upper chamber: Senate

Lower chamber: House of Representatives

Members: Senate, 30; House, 60

Legislative session begins: January

Elections

Eligible voters: 2,396,000

Eligible voters, percentage registered: 82

Governor's party: D

Senate/House majority (1998): R/R *(see question 233)*

Vote in 1996 presidential election (percent): 47.2 D, 39.1 R

Economics

Index of economic momentum (1997): 1.45 *(see question 448)*

State spending (1996): $11.1 billion

Federal spending in state: $14.2 billion

State employment (1997): 1,616,000

State employment growth (percent, 1996–1997): 3.7 *(see question 453)*

Major industry: Manufacturing *(see question 451)*

History

Joined Union: February 14, 1859

Name origin: Uncertain origins, possibly from the Algonquian "wauregan" (beautiful river); the Spanish name for a tribe, "orejon" (big ear); or other sources *(see questions 9–10)*

Adopted current constitution: 1857

Governors since 1900:

Thomas T. Geer (R)	1899–1903
George E. Chamberlain (D)	1903–1909
Frank W. Benson (R)	1909–1910
Jay Bowerman (R)	1910–1911
Oswald West (D)	1911–1915
James Withycombe (R)	1915–1919
Ben W. Olcott (R)	1919–1923
Walter M. Pierce (D)	1923–1927
I. L. Patterson (R)	1927–1929
A. W. Norblad (R)	1929–1931
Julius L. Meier (I)	1931–1935
Charles H. Martin (D)	1935–1939
Charles A. Sprague (R)	1939–1943
Earl Snell (R)	1943–1947
John H. Hall (R)	1947–1949
Douglas McKay (R)	1949–1952
Paul L. Patterson (R)	1952–1956
Elmo Smith (R)	1956–1957
Robert D. Holmes (D)	1957–1959
Mark O. Hatfield (R)	1959–1967
Thomas L. McCall (R)	1967–1975
Robert W. Straub (D)	1975–1979
Victor Atiyeh (R)	1979–1987
Neil Goldschmidt (D)	1987–1991
Barbara Roberts (D)	1991–1995
John Kitzhaber (D)	1995–

Ⓠ 555 PENNSYLVANIA

Home page: www.state.pa.us/

Capital: Harrisburg

Land area (rank): 32d

Land area: 44,820 sq. miles

Population: 12,056,000

Population (percentage of national population): 4.5

Population growth (percent, 1981–1996): 1.5

Population density (per square mile): 269

Largest cities: Philadelphia, Pittsburgh, Erie, Allentown

Federally owned land (percent): 2.1

Representatives in U.S. House: 21

State motto: Virtue, Liberty and Independence

Flower: Mountain laurel

Bird: Ruffled grouse

Tree: Hemlock

Animal: White-tailed deer

Insect: Firefly

Nickname: Keystone State

Executive Branch

Governor: Tom Ridge (R)

Governor's term ends: 2003

Lt. Governor: Mark S. Schweiker (R)

Attorney General: Mike Fisher (R)

Treasurer: Barbara Hafer (R)

General Assembly

Upper chamber: Senate

Lower chamber: House of Representatives

Members: Senate, 50; House, 203

Legislative session begins: January

Elections

Eligible voters: 9,196,000

Eligible voters, percentage registered: 74

Governor's party: R

Senate/House majority (1998): R/R *(see question 233)*

Vote in 1996 presidential election (percent): 49.2 D, 40.0 R

Economics

Index of economic momentum (1997): -0.37 *(see question 448)*

State spending (1996): $32.8 billion

Federal spending in state: $64.2 billion

State employment (1997): 5,692,000

State employment growth (percent, 1996–1997): 2.1 *(see question 453)*

Major industry: Services *(see question 451)*

History

Joined Union: December 12, 1787

Name origin: Named after William Penn, founder of the colony *(see questions 9–10)*

Adopted current constitution: 1968

Governors since 1900:

William A. Stone (R)	1899–1903
Samuel W. Pennypacker (R)	1903–1907
Edwin S. Stuart (R)	1907–1911
John K. Tener (R)	1911–1915
Martin G. Brumbaugh (R)	1915–1919
William C. Sproul (R)	1919–1923
Gifford Pinchot (R)	1923–1927
John S. Fisher (R)	1927–1931
Gifford Pinchot (R)	1931–1935
George H. Earle (D)	1935–1939
Arthur H. James (R)	1939–1943
Edward Martin (R)	1943–1947
John C. Bell, Jr. (R)	1947
James H. Duff (R)	1947–1951
John S. Fine (R)	1951–1955
George M. Leader (D)	1955–1959
David L. Lawrence (D)	1959–1963
William W. Scranton (R)	1963–1967
Raymond P. Shafer (R)	1967–1971
Milton J. Shapp (D)	1971–1979
Richard Thornburgh (R)	1979–1987
Robert P. Casey (D)	1987–1995
Thomas J. Ridge (R)	1995–

Q 556 RHODE ISLAND

Home page:
www.athena.info.state.ri.us/info/

Capital: Providence

Land area (rank): 50th

Land area: 1,045 sq. miles

Population: 990,000

Population (percentage of national population): 0.4

Population growth (percent, 1981–1996): 4

Population density (per square mile): 948

Largest cities: Providence, Warwick, Cranston

Federally owned land (percent): 0.3

Representatives in U.S. House: 2

State motto: Hope

Song: "Rhode Island"

Flower: Violet

Bird: Rhode Island red

Tree: Red maple

Animal: Quahaug

Mineral: Bowenite

Nickname: Ocean State

Executive Branch

Governor: Lincoln C. Almond (R)

Governor's term ends: 2003

Lt. Governor: Charles J. Fogarty (D)

Attorney General: Sheldon Whitehouse (D)

Treasurer: Paul Tavares (D)

General Assembly

Upper chamber: Senate

Lower chamber: House of Representatives

Members: Senate, 50; House, 100

Legislative session begins: January

Elections

Eligible voters: 750,000

Eligible voters, percentage registered: 80

Governor's party: R

Senate/House majority (1998): D/D *(see question 233)*

Vote in 1996 presidential election (percent): 49.2 D, 40.0 R

Economics

Index of economic momentum (1997): -0.77 *(see question 448)*

State spending (1996): $3.5 billion

Federal spending in state: $5.7 billion

State employment (1997): 476,000

State employment growth (percent, 1996–1997): 0.3 *(see question 453)*

Major industry: Finance, insurance, and real estate *(see question 451)*

History

Joined Union: May 29, 1790

Name origin: From the Dutch "roodt eylandt" (red island) *(see questions 9–10)*

Adopted current constitution: 1842

Governors since 1900:

William Gregory (R)	1900–1901
Charles D. Kimball (R)	1901–1903
Lucius F. C. Garvin (D)	1903–1905
George H. Utter (R)	1905–1907
James H. Higgins (D)	1907–1909
Aram J. Pothier (R)	1909–1915
R. Livingston Beekman (R)	1915–1921
Emery J. San Souci (R)	1921–1923
William S. Flynn (D)	1923–1925
Aram J. Pothier (R)	1925–1928
Norman S. Case (R)	1928–1933
Theodore F. Green (D)	1933–1937
Robert E. Quinn (D)	1937–1939
William H. Vanderbilt (R)	1939–1941
J. Howard McGrath (D)	1941–1945
John O. Pastore (D)	1945–1950
John S. McKiernan (D)	1950–1951
Dennis J. Roberts (D)	1951–1959
Christopher Del Sesto (R)	1959–1961
John A. Notte, Jr. (D)	1961–1963
John H. Chaffee (R)	1963–1969
Frank Licht (D)	1969–1973
Philip W. Noel (D)	1973–1977
J. Joseph Garrahy (D)	1977–1985
Edward D. DiPrete (R)	1985–1991

Bruce Sundlun (D)   1991–1995
Lincoln C. Almond (R)   1995–

◪ 557 SOUTH CAROLINA

Home page: www.state.sc.us/

Capital: Columbia

Land area (rank): 40th

Land area: 30,111 sq. miles

Population: 3,699,000

Population (percentage of national population): 1.4

Population growth (percent, 1981–1996): 16.1

Population density (per square mile): 123

Largest cities: Columbia, Charleston, Greenville

Federally owned land (percent): 3.7

Representatives in U.S. House: 6

State motto: *Dum Spiro Spero* (While I Breathe, I Hope)

Songs: "Carolina" and "South Carolina on My Mind"

Flower: Carolina jessamine

Bird: Carolina wren

Tree: Palmetto

Animal: White-tailed deer

Fish: Striped bass

Stone: Blue granite

Nickname: Palmetto State

Executive Branch

Governor: Jim Hodges (D)

Governor's term ends: 2003

Lt. Governor: Bob Peeler (R)

Attorney General: Charles Condon (R)

Treasurer: Grady Patterson

General Assembly

Upper chamber: Senate

Lower chamber: House of Representatives

Members: Senate, 46; House, 124

Legislative session begins: January

Elections

Eligible voters: 2,777,000

Eligible voters, percentage registered: 65

Governor's party: D

Senate/House majority (1998): D/R *(see question 233)*

Vote in 1996 presidential election (percent): 44.0 D, 49.8 R

Economics

Index of economic momentum (1997): -0.13 *(see question 448)*

State spending (1996): $10.9 billion

Federal spending in state: $18.4 billion

State employment (1997): 1,817,000

State employment growth (percent, 1996–1997): 0.7 *(see question 453)*

Major industry: Manufacturing *(see question 451)*

History

Joined Union: May 23, 1788

Name origin: From the Latinized version of Charles ("Carolina"), after England's King Charles II *(see questions 9–10)*

Adopted current constitution: 1895

Governors since 1900:

Miles B. McSweeney (D)	1899–1903
Duncan C. Heyward (D)	1903–1907
Martin F. Ansel (D)	1907–1911
Coleman L. Blease (D)	1911–1915
Charles A. Smith (D)	1915
Richard I. Manning III (D)	1915–1919

Robert A. Cooper (D)	1919–1922
William G. Harvey (D)	1922–1923
Thomas G. McLeod (D)	1923–1927
John G. Richards (D)	1927–1931
Ibra C. Blackwood (D)	1931–1935
Olin D. Johnston (D)	1935–1939
Burnet R. Maybank (D)	1939–1941
Joseph E. Harley (D)	1941–1942
Richard M. Jeffries (D)	1942–1943
Olin D. Johnston (D)	1943–1945
Ransome J. Williams (D)	1945–1947
J. Strom Thurmond (D)	1947–1951
James F. Byrnes (D)	1951–1955
George B. Timmerman, Jr. (D)	1955–1959
Ernest F. Hollings (D)	1959–1963
Donald S. Russell (D)	1963–1965
Robert E. McNair (D)	1965–1971
John C. West (D)	1971–1975
James B. Edwards (R)	1975–1979
Richard W. Riley (D)	1979–1987
Carroll A. Campbell, Jr. (R)	1987–1995
David M. Beasley (R)	1995–1999
Jim Hodges (D)	1999–

ⓠ 558 SOUTH DAKOTA

Home page: www.state.sd.us/

Capital: Pierre
Land area (rank): 16th
Land area: 75,896 sq. miles
Population: 732,000
Population (percentage of national population): 0.3
Population growth (percent, 1981–1996): 5.8
Population density (per square mile): 10
Largest cities: Sioux Falls, Rapid City, Aberdeen

Federally owned land (percent): 5.7
Representatives in U.S. House: 1
State motto: Under God the People Rule
Song: "Hail, South Dakota"
Flower: Pasque flower
Bird: Ringnecked pheasant
Tree: Black Hills spruce
Animal: Coyote
Mineral: Rose quartz
Insect: Honeybee
Fish: Walleye
Nickname: Sunshine State

Executive Branch

Governor: William J. Janklow (R)
Governor's term ends: 2003
Lt. Governor: Carole Hilliard (R)
Attorney General: Mark Barnett (R)
Treasurer: Dick Butler (D)

Legislature

Upper chamber: Senate
Lower chamber: House of Representatives
Members: Senate, 35; House, 70
Legislative session begins: January

Elections

Eligible voters: 530,000
Eligible voters, percentage registered: 87
Governor's party: R
Senate/House majority (1998): R/R *(see question 233)*
Vote in 1996 presidential election (percent): 43.0 D, 46.5 R

Economics

Index of economic momentum (1997): -0.06 *(see question 448)*
State spending (1996): $1.7 billion

Federal spending in state: $3.9 billion

State employment (1997): 381,000

State employment growth (percent, 1996–1997): 1.1 *(see question 453)*

Major industry: Finance, insurance, and real estate *(see question 451)*

History

Joined Union: November 2, 1889

Name origin: "Dakota" (Dakota tribal name: friends, allies) *(see questions 9–10)*

Adopted current constitution: 1889

Governors since statehood:

Arthur C. Mellette (R)	1889–1893
Charles H. Sheldon (R)	1893–1897
Andrew E. Lee (People's, Fusion)	1897–1901
Charles N. Herreid (R)	1901–1905
Samuel H. Elrod (R)	1905–1907
Coe I. Crawford (R)	1907–1909
Robert S. Vessey (R)	1909–1913
Frank M. Byrne (R)	1913–1917
Peter Norbeck (R)	1917–1921
William H. McMaster (R)	1921–1925
Carl Gunderson (R)	1925–1927
William J. Bulow (D)	1927–1931
Warren E. Green (R)	1931–1933
Tom Berry (D)	1933–1937
Leslie Jensen (R)	1937–1939
Harlan J. Bushfield (R)	1939–1943
Merrell Q. Sharpe (R)	1943–1947
George T. Mickelson (R)	1947–1951
Sigurd Anderson (R)	1951–1955
Joseph J. Foss (R)	1955–1959
Ralph E. Herseth (D)	1959–1961
Archie M. Gubbrud (R)	1961–1965
Nils A. Boe (R)	1965–1969
Frank L. Farrar (R)	1969–1971
Richard F. Kneip (D)	1971–1978
Harvey Wollman (D)	1978–1979
William J. Janklow (R)	1979–1987
George S. Mickelson (R)	1987–1993
Walter Dale Miller (R)	1993–1995
William J. Janklow (R)	1995–

Q 559 TENNESSEE

Home page: www.state.tn.us/

Capital: Nashville

Land area (rank): 34th

Land area: 41,220 sq. miles

Population: 5,320,000

Population (percentage of national population): 2

Population growth (percent, 1981–1996): 14.7

Population density (per square mile): 129

Largest cities: Memphis, Nashville, Knoxville

Federally owned land (percent): 3.7

Representatives in U.S. House: 9

State motto: Agriculture and Commerce

Songs: "When It's Iris Time in Tennessee" (and others)

Flower: Iris

Bird: Mockingbird

Tree: Tulip poplar

Animal: Raccoon

Wildflower: Passion flower

Gem: Freshwater pearl

Nickname: Volunteer State

Executive Branch

Governor: Don Sundquist (R)

Governor's term ends: 2003

Lt. Governor: John S. Wilder (D)

Attorney General: Paul Summers (D)

State Treasurer: Stephen Adams (D)

General Assembly

Upper chamber: Senate

Lower chamber: House of Representatives

Members: Senate, 33; House, 99

Legislative session begins: January

Elections

Eligible voters: 4,021,000

Eligible voters, percentage registered: 76

Governor's party: R

Senate/House majority (1998): D/D *(see question 233)*

Vote in 1996 presidential election (percent): 48.0 D, 45.6 R

Economics

Index of economic momentum (1997): -0.05 *(see question 448)*

State spending (1996): $12.5 billion

Federal spending in state: $27.6 billion

State employment (1997): 2,621,000

State employment growth (percent, 1996–1997): 0.8 *(see question 453)*

Major industry: Manufacturing *(see question 451)*

History

Joined Union: June 1, 1796

Name origin: "Tanasi," the name of two Cherokee villages *(see questions 9–10)*

Adopted current constitution: 1870

Governors since 1900:

Benton McMillin (D)	1899–1903
James B. Frazier (D)	1903–1905
John I. Cox (D)	1905–1907
Malcolm R. Patterson (D)	1907–1911
Ben W. Hooper (R)	1911–1915
Tom C. Rye (D)	1915–1919
A. H. Roberts (D)	1919–1921
Alfred A. Taylor (R)	1921–1923
Austin Peay (D)	1923–1927
Henry H. Horton (D)	1927–1933
Hill McMaster (D)	1933–1937
Gordon Browning (D)	1937–1939
Prentice Cooper (D)	1939–1945
Jim McCord (D)	1945–1949
Gordon Browning (D)	1949–1953
Frank G. Clement (D)	1953–1959
Buford Ellington (D)	1959–1963
Frank G. Clement (D)	1963–1967
Buford Ellington (D)	1967–1971
Winfield Dunn (R)	1971–1975
Ray Blanton (D)	1975–1979
Lamar Alexander (R)	1979–1987
Ned Ray McWherter (D)	1987–1995
Don Sundquist (R)	1995–

Q 560 TEXAS

Home page: www.state.texas.gov

Capital: Austin

Land area (rank): 2d

Land area: 261,914 sq. miles

Population: 19,128,000

Population (percentage of national population): 7.2

Population growth (percent, 1981–1996): 29.6

Population density (per square mile): 73

Largest cities: Houston, Dallas, San Antonio, El Paso

Federally owned land (percent): 1.3

Representatives in U.S. House: 30

State motto: Friendship

Song: "Texas, Our Texas"

Flower: Bluebonnet

Bird: Mockingbird

Tree: Pecan

Dish: Chili

Gem: Texas blue topaz

Stone: Petrified palmwood

Nickname: Lone Star State

Executive Branch

Governor: George W. Bush (R)

Governor's term ends: 2003

Lt. Governor: Rick Perry (R)

Attorney General: John Cornyn (R)

Comptroller of Public Accounts: Carole Keeton Rylander (R)

Legislature

Upper chamber: Senate

Lower chamber: House of Representatives

Members: Senate, 31; House, 150

Legislative session begins: January

Elections

Eligible voters: 13,622,000

Eligible voters, percentage registered: 77

Governor's party: R

Senate/House majority (1998): R/D *(see question 233)*

Vote in 1996 presidential election (percent): 43.8 D, 48.8 R

Economics

Index of economic momentum (1997): 0.63 *(see question 448)*

State spending (1996): $40 billion

Federal spending in state: $86.5 billion

State employment (1997): 9,393,000

State employment growth (percent, 1996–1997): 2.6 *(see question 453)*

Major industry: Manufacturing *(see question 451)*

History

Joined Union: December 29, 1845

Name origin: "Teysha" (Caddo: Hello, friend), or the Spanish "tejas" (allies) *(see questions 9–10)*

Adopted current constitution: 1876

Governors since 1900:

Joseph D. Sayers (D)	1899–1903
Samuel W. T. Lanham (D)	1903–1907
Thomas M. Campbell (D)	1907–1911
Oscar B. Colquitt (D)	1911–1915
James E. Ferguson (D)	1915–1917
William P. Hobby (D)	1917–1921
Pat M. Neff (D)	1921–1925
Miriam A. Ferguson (D)	1925–1927
Dan Moody (D)	1927–1931
Ross S. Sterling (D)	1931–1933
Miriam A. Ferguson (D)	1933–1935
James V. Allred (D)	1935–1939
W. Lee O'Daniel (D)	1939–1941
Coke R. Stevenson (D)	1941–1947
Beauford H. Jester (D)	1947–1949
Allan Shivers (D)	1949–1957
Price Daniel (D)	1957–1963
John Connally (D)	1963–1969
Preston Smith (D)	1969–1973
Dolph Briscoe (D)	1973–1979
William Clements (R)	1979–1983
Mark White (D)	1983–1987
William Clements (R)	1987–1991
Ann Richards (D)	1991–1995
George W. Bush (R)	1995–

Q 561 UTAH

Home page: www.state.ut.us/

Capital: Salt Lake City

Land area (rank): 12th

Land area: 82,168 sq. miles

Population: 2,000,000

Population (percentage of national population): 0.8

Population growth (percent, 1981–1996): 32

Population density (per square mile): 24

Largest cities: Salt Lake City, Ogden, Provo

Federally owned land (percent): 63.9

Representatives in U.S. House: 3

State motto: Industry

Song: "Utah, We Love Thee"

Flower: Sego lily

Bird: California seagull

Tree: Blue spruce

Animal: Rocky Mountain elk

Insect: Honeybee

Fish: Rainbow trout

Nickname: Beehive State

Executive Branch

Governor: Michael O. Leavitt (R)

Governor's term ends: 2001

Lt. Governor: Olene S. Walker (R)

Attorney General: Jan Graham (D)

Treasurer: Edward Atler (R)

Legislature

Upper chamber: Senate

Lower chamber: House of Representatives

Members: Senate, 29; House, 75

Legislative session begins: January

Elections

Eligible voters: 1,323,000

Eligible voters, percentage registered: 81

Governor's party: R

Senate/House majority (1998): R/R *(see question 233)*

Vote in 1996 presidential election (percent): 33.3 D, 54.4 R

Economics

Index of economic momentum (1997): 2.20 *(see question 448)*

State spending (1996): $5.1 billion

Federal spending in state: $8.2 billion

State employment (1997): 1,019,000

State employment growth (percent, 1996–1997): 4.2 *(see question 453)*

Major industry: Services *(see question 451)*

History

Joined Union: January 4, 1896

Name origin: From the tribal name of the Ute Indians, or possibly the Apache "yuttahih" (higher up) *(see questions 9–10)*

Adopted current constitution: 1895

Governors since statehood:

Heber M. Wells (R)	1896–1905
John C. Cutler (R)	1905–1909
William Spry (R)	1909–1917
Simon Bamberger (D)	1917–1921
Charles R. Mabey (R)	1921–1925
George H. Dern (D)	1925–1933
Henry H. Blood (D)	1933–1941
Herbert B. Maw (D)	1941–1949
J. Bracken Lee (R)	1949–1957
George D. Clyde (R)	1957–1965
Calvin L. Rampton (D)	1965–1977
Scott M. Matheson (D)	1977–1985
Norman H. Bangerter (R)	1985–1993
Michael D. Leavitt (R)	1993–

Home page: *www.cit.state.vt.us/*

Capital: Montpelier

Land area (rank): 43d

Land area: 9,249 sq. miles

Population: 589,000

Population (percentage of national population): 0.2

Population growth (percent, 1981–1996): 13.9

Population density (per square mile): 64

Largest cities: Burlington, Rutland, Montpelier

Federally owned land (percent): 6

Representatives in U.S. House: 1

State motto: Freedom and Unity

Song: "Hail, Vermont!"

Flower: Red clover

Bird: Hermit thrush

Tree: Sugar maple

Animal: Morgan horse

Beverage: Milk

Insect: Honeybee

Nickname: Green Mountain State

Executive Branch

Governor: Howard Dean (D)

Governor's term ends (2-year term): 2001

Lt. Governor: Douglas A. Racine (D)

Attorney General: William Sorrell (D)

Treasurer: James Douglas (R)

General Assembly

Upper chamber: Senate

Lower chamber: House of Representatives

Members: Senate, 30; House, 150

Legislative session begins: January

Elections

Eligible voters: 441,000

Eligible voters, percentage registered: Not available

Governor's party: D

Senate/House majority (1998): D/D *(see question 233)*

Vote in 1996 presidential election (percent): 53.4 D, 31.1 R

Economics

Index of economic momentum (1997): -0.88 *(see question 448)*

State spending (1996): $1.6 billion

Federal spending in state: $2,775

State employment (1997): 317,000

State employment growth (percent, 1996–1997): 1.2 *(see question 453)*

Major industry: Manufacturing *(see question 451)*

History

Joined Union: March 4,1791

Name origin: From the French "vert" and "mont" (green mountain) *(see questions 9–10)*

Adopted current constitution: 1793

Governors since 1900:

Edward C. Smith (R)	1898–1900
William W. Stickney (R)	1900–1902
John G. McCullough (R)	1902–1904
Charles J. Bell (R)	1904–1906
Fletcher D. Proctor (R)	1906–1908
George H. Prouty (R)	1908–1910
John A. Mead (R)	1910–1912
Allen M. Fletcher (R)	1912–1915
Charles W. Gates (R)	1915–1917
Horace F. Graham (R)	1917–1919
Percival W. Clement (R)	1919–1921
James Hartness (R)	1921–1923

Redfield Proctor, Jr. (R)	1923–1925
Franklin S. Billings (R)	1925–1927
John E. Weeks (R)	1927–1931
Stanley C. Wilson (R)	1931–1935
Charles M. Smith (R)	1935–1937
George D. Aiken (R)	1937–1941
William H. Wills (R)	1941–1945
Mortimer R. Proctor (R)	1945–1947
Ernest W. Gibson (R)	1947–1950
Harold J. Arthur (R)	1950–1951
Lee E. Emerson (R)	1951–1955
Joseph B. Johnson (R)	1955–1959
Robert T. Stafford (R)	1959–1961
Frank R. Keyser, Jr. (R)	1961–1963
Philip H. Hoff (D)	1963–1969
Deane C. Davis (R)	1969–1973
Thomas P. Salmon (D)	1973–1977
Richard A. Snelling (R)	1977–1985
Madeleine Kunin (D)	1985–1991
Richard A. Snelling (R)	1991
Howard Dean (D)	1991–

⬛ 563 VIRGINIA

Home page: www.state.va.us/

Capital: Richmond

Land area (rank): 37th

Land area: 39,598 sq. miles

Population: 6,675,000

Population (percentage of national population): 2.5

Population growth (percent, 1981–1996): 22.6

Population density (per square mile): 169

Largest cities: Norfolk, Virginia Beach, Richmond, Chesapeake

Federally owned land (percent): 6.3

Representatives in U.S. House: 11

State motto: *Sic Semper Tyrannis* (Thus Always to Tyrants)

Song: "Carry Me Back to Old Virginia"

Flower: Flowering dogwood

Bird: Cardinal

Tree: Dogwood

Animal: Foxhound

Shell: Oyster

Nickname: Old Dominion

Executive Branch

Governor: James S. Gilmore, III (R)

Governor's term ends: 2002

Lt. Governor: John Hager (R)

Attorney General: Mark Earley (R)

Treasurer: Susan Dewey

General Assembly

Upper chamber: Senate

Lower chamber: House of Delegates

Members: Senate, 40; House, 100

Legislative session begins: January

Elections

Eligible voters: 5,089,000

Eligible voters, percentage registered: 65

Governor's party: R

Senate/House majority (1998): R/D *(see question 233)*

Vote in 1996 presidential election (percent): 45.1 D, 47.1 R

Economics

Index of economic momentum (1997): 0.09 *(see question 448)*

State spending (1996): $17.2 billion

Federal spending in state: $50.3 billion

State employment (1997): 3,385,000

State employment growth (percent, 1996–1997): 2.2 *(see question 453)*

Major industry: Services *(see question 451)*

History

Joined Union: June 25, 1788

Name origin: Named after England's Queen Elizabeth, who was known as the Virgin Queen, in 1607 *(see questions 9–10)*

Adopted current constitution: 1970

Governors since 1900:

James Hoge Tyler (D)	1898–1902
Andrew J. Montague (D)	1902–1906
Claude A. Swanson (D)	1906–1910
William H. Mann (D)	1910–1914
Henry C. Stuart (D)	1914–1918
Westmoreland Davis (D)	1918–1922
E. Lee Trinkle (D)	1922–1926
Harry F. Byrd (D)	1926–1930
John G. Pollard (D)	1930–1934
George C. Peery (D)	1934–1938
James H. Price (D)	1938–1942
Colgate W. Darden, Jr. (D)	1942–1946
William M. Tuck (D)	1946–1950
John S. Battle (D)	1950–1954
Thomas B. Stanley (D)	1954–1958
J. Lindsay Almond, Jr. (D)	1958–1962
Albertis S. Harrison, Jr. (D)	1962–1966
Mills E. Godwin, Jr. (D)	1966–1970
Linwood Holton (R)	1970–1974
Mills E. Godwin, Jr. (R)	1974–1978
John Dalton (R)	1978–1982
Charles S. Robb (D)	1982–1986
Gerald L. Baliles (D)	1986–1990
L. Douglas Wilder (D)	1990–1994
George F. Allen (R)	1994–1998
James S. Gilmore, III (R)	1998–

564 WASHINGTON

Home page: www.wa.gov/

Capital: Olympia

Land area (rank): 20th

Land area: 66,681 sq. miles

Population: 5,533,000

Population (percentage of national population): 2.1

Population growth (percent, 1981–1996): 30.6

Population density (per square mile): 83

Largest cities: Seattle, Spokane, Tacoma

Federally owned land (percent): 28.3

Representatives in U.S. House: 9

State motto: *Alki* (By and By)

Song: "Washington, My Home"

Flower: Coast rhododendron

Bird: Willow goldfinch

Tree: Western hemlock

Dance: Square dance

Nickname: Evergreen State

Executive Branch

Governor: Gary Locke (D)

Governor's term ends: 2001

Lt. Governor: Brad Owen (D)

Attorney General: Christine O. Gregoire (D)

Treasurer: Michael Murphy (D)

Legislature

Upper chamber: Senate

Lower chamber: House of Representatives

Members: Senate, 49; House, 98

Legislative session begins: January

Elections

Eligible voters: 4,122,000

Eligible voters, percentage registered: 75

Governor's party: D

Senate/House majority (1998): D/no majority *(see question 233)*

Vote in 1996 presidential election (percent): 49.8 D, 37.3 R

Economics

Index of economic momentum (1997): 1.24 *(see question 448)*

State spending (1996): $16.6 billion

Federal spending in state: $29.3 billion

State employment (1997): 2,839,000

State employment growth (percent, 1996–1997): 3.9 *(see question 453)*

Major industry: Manufacturing *(see question 451)*

History

Joined Union: November 11, 1889

Name origin: Named in 1853 after President George Washington *(see questions 9–10)*

Adopted current constitution: 1889

Governors since statehood:

Elisha P. Ferry (R)	1889–1893
John H. McGraw (R)	1893–1897
John R. Rogers (Pop. Dem.)	1897–1901
Henry McBride (R)	1901–1905
Albert E. Mead (R)	1905–1909
Samuel G. Cosgrove (R)	1909
Marion E. Hay (R)	1909–1913
Ernest Lister (D)	1913–1919
Louis F. Hart (R)	1919–1925
Roland H. Hartley (R)	1925–1933
Clarence D. Martin (D)	1933–1941
Arthur B. Langlie (R)	1941–1945
Mon C. Wallgren (D)	1945–1949
Arthur B. Langlie (R)	1949–1957
Albert D. Rosselini (D)	1957–1965
Daniel J. Evans (R)	1965–1977
Dixie Lee Ray (D)	1977–1981
John Spellman (R)	1981–1985
Booth Gardner (D)	1985–1993
Mike Lowry (D)	1993–1997
Gary Locke (D)	1997–

565 WEST VIRGINIA

Home page: www.state.wv.us/

Capital: Charleston

Land area (rank): 41st

Land area: 24,087 sq. miles

Population: 1,826,000

Population (percentage of national population): 0.7

Population growth (percent, 1981–1996): 6.9

Population density (per square mile): 76

Largest cities: Charleston, Huntington, Wheeling

Federally owned land (percent): 6.7

Representatives in U.S. House: 3

State motto: *Montani Semper Liberi* (Mountaineers Are Always Free)

Songs: "West Virginia, My Sweet Home"; "The West Virginia Hills"; "This is My West Virginia"

Flower: Big laurel

Bird: Cardinal

Tree: Sugar maple

Animal: Black bear

Nickname: Mountain State

Executive Branch

Governor: Cecil H. Underwood (R)

Governor's term ends: 2001

Attorney General: Darrell McGraw, Jr. (D)

Treasurer: John Perdue (D)

Legislature

Upper chamber: Senate

Lower chamber: House of Delegates

Members: Senate, 34; House, 100

Legislative session begins: February

Elections

Eligible voters: 1,414,000

Eligible voters, percentage registered: 69

Governor's party: R

Senate/House majority (1998): D/D *(see question 233)*

Vote in 1996 presidential election (percent): 51.5 D, 36.8 R

Economics

Index of economic momentum (1997): -0.70 *(see question 448)*

State spending (1996): $4.9 billion

Federal spending in state: $10.1 billion

State employment (1997): 753,000

State employment growth (percent, 1996–1997): 1.5 *(see question 453)*

Major industry: Manufacturing *(see question 451)*

History

Joined Union: June 20, 1863

Name origin: After the state of Virginia, of which it was once a part *(see questions 9–10)*

Adopted current constitution: 1872

Governors since 1900:

George W. Atkinson (R)	1897–1901
Albert B. White (R)	1901–1905
William M. O. Dawson (R)	1905–1909
William E. Glasscock (R)	1909–1913
Henry D. Hatfield (R)	1913–1917
John J. Cornwall (D)	1917–1921
E. F. Morgan (R)	1921–1925
Howard M. Gore (R)	1925–1929
William G. Conley (R)	1929–1933
Herman G. Kump (D)	1933–1937
Homer A. Holt (D)	1937–1941
Matthew M. Neely (D)	1941–1945
Clarence W. Meadows (D)	1945–1949
Okey L. Patteson (D)	1949–1953
William C. Marland (D)	1953–1957
Cecil H. Underwood (R)	1957–1961
William W. Barron (D)	1961–1965
Hulett C. Smith (D)	1965–1969
Arch A. Moore, Jr. (R)	1969–1977
John D. Rockefeller, IV (D)	1977–1985
Arch A. Moore, Jr. (R)	1985–1989
Gaston Caperton (D)	1989–1997
Cecil H. Underwood (R)	1997–

Q 566 WISCONSIN

Home page: www.state.wi.us/

Capital: Madison

Land area (rank): 25th

Land area: 54,314 sq. miles

Population: 5,160,000

Population (percentage of national population): 1.9

Population growth (percent, 1981–1996): 9.2

Population density (per square mile): 95

Largest cities: Milwaukee, Madison, Green Bay

Federally owned land (percent): 10.1

Representatives in U.S. House: 9

State motto: Forward

Song: "On, Wisconsin!"

Flower: Wood violet

Bird: Robin

Tree: Sugar maple

Animal: Badger

Mineral: Galena

Nickname: Badger State

Executive Branch

Governor: Tommy G. Thompson (R)

Governor's term ends: 2003

Lt. Governor: Scott McCallum (R)

Attorney General: Jim Doyle (D)

Treasurer: Jack Voight (R)

Legislature

Upper chamber: Senate

Lower chamber: Assembly

Members: Senate, 33; Assembly, 99

Legislative session begins: January

Elections

Eligible voters: 3,824,000

Eligible voters, percentage registered: 68

Governor's party: R

Senate/Assembly majority (1998): D/R *(see question 233)*

Vote in 1996 presidential election (percent): 48.8 D, 38.5 R

Economics

Index of economic momentum (1997): -0.48 *(see question 448)*

State spending (1996): $16.7 billion

Federal spending in state: $20 billion

State employment (1997): 2,820,000

State employment growth (percent, 1996–1997): 1.8 *(see question 453)*

Major industry: Manufacturing *(see question 451)*

History

Joined Union: May 29, 1848

Name origin: Possibly the Chipewa word for "grassy place" *(see questions 9–10)*

Adopted current constitution: 1848

Governors since 1900:

Edward Schofield (R)	1897–1901
Robert M. LaFollette (R)	1901–1906
James O. Davidson (R)	1906–1911
Francis E. McGovern (R)	1911–1915
Emanuel L. Philipp (R)	1915–1921
John J. Blaine (R)	1921–1927
Fred R. Zimmerman (R)	1927–1929
Walter J. Kohler, Sr. (R)	1929–1931
Philip F. LaFollette (R)	1931–1933
Albert G. Schmedeman (D)	1933–1935
Philip F. LaFollette (P)	1935–1939
Julius P. Heil (R)	1939–1943
Walter S. Goodland (R)	1943–1947
Oscar Rennebohm (R)	1947–1951
Walter J. Kohler, Jr. (R)	1951–1957
Vernon W. Thompson (R)	1957–1959
Gaylord A. Nelson (D)	1959–1963
John W. Reynolds (D)	1963–1965
Warren P. Knowles (R)	1965–1971
Patrick J. Lucey (D)	1971–1977
Martin J. Schrieber (D)	1977–1979
Lee Sherman Dreyfus (R)	1979–1983
Anthony S. Earl (D)	1983–1987
Tommy G. Thompson (R)	1987–

Ⓠ 567 WYOMING

Home page: *www.state.wy.us/*

Capital: Cheyenne

Land area (rank): 9th

Land area: 97,105 sq. miles

Population: 481,000

Population (percentage of national population): 0.2

Population growth (percent, 1981–1996): 2.6

Population density (per square mile): 5

Largest cities: Casper, Cheyenne

Federally owned land (percent): 48.9

Representatives in U.S. House: 1

State motto: Equal Rights

Song: "Wyoming"

Flower: Indian paintbrush

Bird: Western meadowlark

Tree: Cottonwood

Animal: Bison

Nicknames: Equality State; Cowboy State

Executive Branch

Governor: Jim Geringer (R)

Governor's term ends: 2003

Attorney General: Gay Woodhouse (R)

Treasurer: Cynthia Lummis (R)

Legislature

Upper chamber: Senate

Lower chamber: House of Representatives

Members: Senate, 30; House, 60

Legislative session begins: January

Elections

Eligible voters: 352,000

Eligible voters, percentage registered: 68

Governor's party: R

Senate/House majority (1998): R/R *(see question 233)*

Vote in 1996 presidential election (percent): 36.8 D, 49.8 R

Economics

Index of economic momentum (1997): −1.17 *(see question 448)*

State spending (1996): $1.9 billion

Federal spending in state: $2.5 billion

State employment (1997): 246,000

State employment growth (percent, 1996–1997): 0.0 *(see question 453)*

Major industry: Manufacturing *(see question 451)*

History

Joined Union: July 10, 1890

Name origin: "Meacheweaming" (Delaware Indian: at the big flats) *(see questions 9–10)*

Adopted current constitution: 1889

Governors since 1900:

DeForest Richards (R)	1899–1903
Fenimore C. Chatterton (R)	1903–1905
Bryant B. Brooks (R)	1905–1911
Joseph M. Carey (D)	1911–1915
John B. Kendrick (D)	1915–1917
Frank L. Houx (D)	1917–1919
Robert D. Carey (R)	1919–1923
William B. Ross (D)	1923–1924
Frank E. Lucas (R)	1924–1925
Nellie Tayloe Ross (D)	1925–1927
Frank C. Emerson (R)	1927–1931
Alonzo M. Clark (R)	1931–1933
Leslie A. Miller (D)	1933–1939
Nels H. Smith (R)	1939–1943
Lester C. Hunt (D)	1943–1949
Arthur G. Crane (R)	1949–1951
Frank A. Barrett (R)	1951–1953
Clifford J. Rogers (R)	1953–1955
Milward L. Simpson (R)	1955–1959
John J. Hickey (D)	1959–1961
Jack R. Gage (D)	1961–1963
Clifford P. Hansen (R)	1963–1967
Stanley K. Hathaway (R)	1967–1975
Ed Herschler (D)	1975–1987
Mike Sullivan (D)	1987–1995
Jim Geringer (R)	1995–

SUBJECT INDEX

Basic information on the states may be found in Chapter 7, "What About My State?—The State Profiles." The location of this information appears in each state's index entry under the subheading "state profiles." Included in each state profile are essential facts and figures, such as state capital, land area, population, largest cities, number of representatives in the U.S. House, state motto, executive branch officials, size of legislature, number of registered voters, major industry, date of statehood, and governors since 1900, among other important data.

Abortion, 432
Absolute pardon of convicted criminals, 97
Academic performance, education spending and, 476
Administrative cases, state courts and, 369
Affirmative action, 354
    in university admissions, 435
Age
    of average governors, 130
    of average legislators, 218
    requirements for governors, 101
Agencies, state, 183
    interest groups and, 159
AIDS patients by state, 500
Air pollution emission rates by state, 484
Alabama
    anonymous campaign contributions in, 362
    campaign contributions in, 361
    candidate nominations in, 308
    constitutional amendments in, 33
    executive branch officials, **518**
    formation of, 7
    legal requirements for state judges in, 391
    legislative session of, 208
    line-item veto in, 95
    primary runoff elections in, 304
    state constitution length, 67
    state profile, **518**

turnover rate in legislature, 223
    Web address, **518**
Alaska
    blanket primaries in, 302
    death rate in, 499
    economic growth rate of, 448
    education employees in, 472
    education spending by, 471
    elderly population of, 444
    executive branch officials, **519**
    federal land holdings in, 450
    formation of, 7
    gubernatorial campaign spending in, 316
    labor unions in, 452
    legislature of, 168
    median household income in, 501
    population density of, 441
    poverty in, 502
    sales taxes in, 511
    state parks in, 485
    state profile, **519**
    traffic fatalities in, 517
    unemployment in, 456
    Web address, **519**
    women as state representatives in, 250
Alcohol-related traffic fatalities, 517
Alien and Sedition Acts of 1798, 51
Allen, Florence Ellinwood, 396
Amendments to legislative bills, 197

Amendments to state constitutions
    states allowing citizen initiatives for, 35
    states with largest numbers of, 34
Amendments to U.S. Constitution.
    See also specific amendments
    states' initiation of, 48
    states required to ratify, 49
    submitted to states, 65
American Federation of Teachers, 477
American Samoa, 30
Appellate courts, state, 364
    cases heard in, 386
    organization of, 385
Appointment(s)
    governors' powers of, 90
    governors' removal powers after, 152
    governors' powers of, 151
Appropriations, legislative, 201
Appropriations committee, legislative, 215
Appropriations committees, District of Columbia and, 61
Arizona
    birth rate in, 499
    bolo ties and, 68
    bribery sting in, 224
    economic growth rate of, 448
    executive branch officials, **520**
    federal land holdings in, 450
    formation of, 7

Note: References point to question numbers in the text. Entries with **bold** references appear in Chapter 7.

legislature of, 168
state profile, **520**
Web address, **520**
Arkansas
  executive branch officials, **521**
  governor's salary in, 87
  legislative session of, 207
  Missouri Compromise and, 25
  population of, 2
  primary runoff elections in, 304
  state profile, **521**
  Web address, **521**
  women as state representatives in, 250
Arrest rates, 462
Articles of Confederation, grants-in-aid under, 64
Asian-American governors, 119
Assassination attempts on governors, 111
Association lobbyists, 253
Association of State Development Agencies, 52
Attack (campaign) ads, 293
Attorneys general, 144–146
  duties of, 144
  law enforcement and, 457
  legislative selection of, 145
  list of, by state, **518–567**
  popular election of, 260
  power of, 146
Auditor, state
  duties of, 150
Australian ballots, 256
  office block versus party column, 257
Authorizations, legislative, 201, 215

Backlogs in state courts, 376
Baker Island, 30
Baker v. Carr (1962), 419
Balanced budget amendment, 48
Ballots. *See also* Initiatives, citizen; Referendums; Voting machines
  Australian, 256
  first printed, 255
  office block versus party column, 257
  requirements for inclusion on, 290
Beverages, official state, 69
Bicameral legislatures, 162
  first, 163
Biennial legislative sessions, 207

Bills
  enacted as laws, 190, 191, 204
  enrolled, 200
  introducing, 189
  processing of, 197
  versus statutes, 185
Birth rates by state, 499
Black governors, 116, 117
  women as, 118
Black legislators, 236, 237
  as representatives in state houses, 249
  in senates, 242
Black populations of states, 443
Black prison inmates, 464
Black state supreme court chief justices, 397
Blanket primaries, 302
Block grants, 492
Board of Education of Oklahoma City v. Dowell (1991), 434
Bolo ties, 68
Book of the States, The, 53
British settlers, 6
Brock, Bill, 280
Brothers
  as governors, 132
  in governorship race, 345
Brown v. Board of Education (1954), 420
Budgets, state
  for courts, 375
  federal grants' effect on, 494
  federal grants-in-aid and, 491
  localities, percentage spending on, 503
  localities, spending on, 504
  preparation of, 79
  revenue sources for, 505
"Bumper-sticker" policy (campaign) ads, 293
Bureaucracy, 155–158
  governors and, 157
  legislature role in, 158
Bureaucratic discretion, 156
Business. *See also* Employment
  dominant economic sectors, 451
  unemployment rates and, 456

Cabinet
  definition and duties of, 147
  of state governments, 148
California
  AIDS patients in, 500

air pollution emission rates of, 484
black population of, 443
candidate nomination in, 308
congressional redistricting in, 440
constitutional amendments in, 34
education employees in, 472
education spending by, 471
elderly population of, 444
employment in, 453
executive branch officials, **522**
federal grants-in-aid for, 490
federal land holdings in, 450
formation of, 7
government employees in, 454
governor's salary in, 87
gubernatorial campaign spending in, 316, 334
hazardous waste sites in, 483
Hispanic population of, 443
immigrant population of (recent), 445
income tax revenues for, 509
justices' salaries in, 373
law enforcement spending in, 458
localities, spending on, 504
Medicare/Medicaid recipients in, 498
negative campaigns in, 294
population increase in, 439
population of, 2, 4
poverty in, 502
prison system spending in, 459
Proposition 13, 353
Proposition 187, 446
sales tax revenues for, 511
size of, 1
Social Security recipients in, 497
state parks in, 485
state profile, **522**
tax revenues for, 506
traffic fatalities in, 517
unaffiliated legislators in, 324
unemployment in, 456
unusual provisions of state constitution, 68
Web address, **522**
Campaign(s). *See also* Political parties; State political parties; Third party(ies)
  ad types for, 293
  Brock's changes to Republican party, 280

Note: References point to question numbers in the text. Entries with **bold** references appear in Chapter 7.

Brown's changes to Democratic party, 282
candidate-centered, 286, 309
Federal Election Campaign Act and, 283
gubernatorial, cost of, 315, 334
hard versus soft money in, 284
Kirk's changes to Democratic party, 281
legislative campaign committees for, 322
mass media in, 295
negative, 294
spending per state, 316
Campaign financing, state
anonymous donations for, 362
by corporations/labor unions, 356
election commissions and, 360
limits on contributions to, 361
PACs and, 358
public funding of, 355
reporting requirements for, 359
Candidate-centered campaigns, 286. *See also* Independent candidates
party endorsement and, 309
Capital punishment, 410, 417
Caretaker governors, 74
Categorical grants, 492
Catholic governors, 137
Catholic settlers, 6
Caucuses, party, 299
Cause lobbyists, 253
Census, statistical sampling and, 447
Ceremonial functions of governors, 76
Chairs, legislative committee, 214
Challenge primary system, 339
Checks and balances, 162
Chinese-American state court judges, 395
Chisholm v. Georgia (1793), 421
Citizen initiatives. *See* Initiatives, citizen
Citizens' Bank of New Orleans, 20
Civil cases, state courts and, 369
Civil service, 154
Civil service, patronage and, 311
Civil War
"Dixie" and, 20
federalism and, 46
Mason-Dixon line and, 17
secession rights and, 45
states seceding during, 26
West Virginia and, 27

Class-action suits, 407
Clean Air Act amendments of 1990, 481
Closed primaries, 301
Colorado
campaign contributions in, 361
candidate nomination in, 308
executive branch officials, **523**
formation of, 7
state profile, **523**
violent crime rates in, 460
Web address, **523**
"Comedy" (negative campaign) ads, 293
Commerce clause, states and, 437
Commissioner of education, 478
Commission on Intergovernmental Relations of 1955, 39
Committees, legislative, 195–197, 210–216
appropriations/authorizations, 215
chairs' powers on, 213
functions of, 210
interim, 214
number of, 212
procedures for, 197
rules and calendar, 196
seniority system and, 216
types of, 211
Common law, 408
Commonwealth status, 29
Community hospitals per state, 496
Commutation, convicted criminals' sentence, 97
Company lobbyists, 253
Conditional pardon of convicted criminals, 97
Confederacy, definition of, 46
Conference committees, legislative, 197, 211
Confessions, defendants' rights and, 427
Congress, shadow representatives in, 61
Connecticut
candidate nomination in, 308
Dominion of New England and, 8
executive branch officials, **524**
legislative session of, 208
median household income in, 501
population of, 62
primaries in, 339
settlement of, 6

state profile, **524**
Web address, **524**
women as legislators in, 235
Consecutive terms for governors, 103
Conservative party, 291
Constitution, U.S. *See also* Amendments to U.S. Constitution; Federal government
federalism and, 46
implied powers and, 429
on location of District of Columbia, 59
on relations between states, 44
state limitations by, 43
state powers under, 42
supremacy clause of, 56
Constitution(s), state. *See also* Amendments to state constitutions
changing, 32, 33
constitutional commissions and, 32, 38
constitutional conventions and, 32, 36, 37
first adoption of, 31
Kestnbaum Commission and, 39
length of, 67
model for, 40
replacing, 66
strong versus weak governorships and, 84
unusual provisions of, 68
Constitutional commissions, 32
scope for, 38
Constitutional convention(s), 32
for amending U.S. Constitution, 48
calling, 37
procedures of, 36
Constitutional initiatives, 347
states that allow, 35, 351
Constitutionally mandated referendum, 348
Constitutional referendum, 348
Contract lobbyists, 253
Conviction rates, 462
Cook County, Ill., Democratic party patronage in, 312
Cooperative federalism, 47
Coordinated Campaign, Democratic party's, 282
Corporations, campaign contributions by, 356

Council of State Governments, 52, 53
Counsel, right to, 423
Court administration, offices of, 374
Court of appeals, 363
Courts, dual system, 377
Courts, federal, 377
Courts, state. See also Judges, state court; Supreme courts, state
    administrative offices of, 374
    annual new cases for, 365
    of appeals, 364, 385, 386
    backlogs in, 376
    capital punishment and, 410
    civil, criminal, administrative cases of, 369
    class-action suits, 407
    common law versus statutory law, 408
    Dillon's Rule and, 372
    dual system and, 377
    financial support of, 375
    general trial, 387
    grand juries' functions in, 368
    highest, 363
    incorporation doctrine and, 411
    judges, salary ranges for, 373
    judges' decisions in, 371
    jurors' service for, 412
    justices of the peace and, 389
    juvenile, 364, 388, 413
    legal terms and procedures in, 406–412
    levels of, 364
    longest jury trial, 416
    magistrates and, 389
    municipal, 388
    night court sessions in, 367
    Operation Greylord and, 404
    plea bargaining in, 409
    precedents and, 406
    probate, 388
    reforms in, 370
    small claims, 364, 388
    televised verdicts from, 366
    traffic, 388
    U.S. Supreme Court standards and, 378
Courts of limited jurisdiction, 364
Cracking, redistricting and, 173
Creative federalism, 47
Crime/criminal justice, 457–468. See also Courts, state
    arrest rates, 462

early release programs, 467
    factors in rates of, 461
    incarceration rates, 465
    law enforcement, 457
    prisoner costs per capita, 466
    prison population demographics, 464
    prison population increases and, 463
    prison system spending, 459
    spending on, 458
    victimless crimes, 468
    violent crime rates, 460

Day, legislative, 208
Death penalty, 410, 417
Death rates by state, 499
Debates, legislative, 197
Deep South, 19
Defendants' rights, confessions and, 427
Defense spending, federal, 495
Delaware
    education employees in, 472
    executive branch officials, 525
    federal land holdings in, 450
    first governor of, 70
    first to ratify Constitution, 12
    gubernatorial campaign spending in, 316
    legislature of, 168
    population of, 2
    poverty in, 502
    sales taxes in, 511
    settlement of, 6
    size of, 1
    state profile, 525
    untimely death of governors in, 112
    Web address, 525
Delegates to state legislatures, 188
Democratic party
    Brown's Coordinated Campaign program for, 282
    governorship control by, 122
    gubernatorial election totals, 1998, 321
    Kirk's Election Force for, 281
    legislative control by, 233
    naming of, 343
    patronage practices, in Cook County, Ill., 312
    Ranney index and, 314
    Solid South and, 277

state campaign funding sources for, 313
    state campaign fundraising by, 296
    state legislatures controlled by, 170
    states controlled by, 262
    women as state representatives, 250
Democratic-Republican party, 341, 342
Deseret (state), 24
Determinate sentencing, 463
Dillon's Rule, 372
Direct election of U.S. senators, 48, 279
Discharge petition, 196
District of Columbia, 58–61
    home rule and, 60
    justices' salaries in, 373
    location selection of, 59
    Mason-Dixon line and, 17
    presidential elections and, 285
    representation in Congress for, 61
    statehood of, 58
    violent crime rates in, 460
Divided government, state, 128, 202, 233
Dixie, 20
Doctors, total per state, 496
Dominion of New England, 8
Drinks, official state, 69
Dual federalism, 47
    versus federal supremacy, 436
Dual system courts, 377
Dutch settlers, 6

Economic indicators, 448–451
    dominant business sectors, 451
    environmental protection and, 481
    federal land holdings and, 450
    growth rates, 448
    new business, 449
Education, 469–479
    Elementary and Secondary Education Act of 1965 and, 474
    employees for, 472
    of governors, 133
    interest groups and, 477
    of legislators, 219
    policymaking for, 478
    poor school districts and, 475

Note: References point to question numbers in the text. Entries with **bold** references appear in Chapter 7.

public schools administration, 469

public schools financing, 470

spending for, and academic performance, 476

spending on, 471

state education board member selection, 479

women teachers, 473

Election commissions for campaign finance compliance, 360

Election Force, Democratic party's, 281

Elections. *See also* Campaign(s); Primaries; Turnout

  direct primaries, 298

  Federal Election Campaign Act and, 283

  groups likeliest to vote in, 270

  gubernatorial, turnout in, 264

  highest turnouts for, 271

  judicial retention, 328

  plurality in, 269

  political party coordination of state/national, 278

  poll tax and, 273

  presidential, District of Columbia and, 285

  primary runoff, 304, 305, 306

  registration rules and turnout for, 272

  smallest unit in, 268

  of state court judges, 335, 414

  states' cycle of, 267

  statewide primaries, 297

Electoral College, 42

Elementary and Secondary Education Act of 1965, 474

Eleventh Amendment, 421

Elrod v. Burns (1976), 312

Employment, 453. *See also* Business

  in education professions, 472

  growth rates, 455

  state/local government, 454

  unemployment rates, 456

Enrolled bills, 197, 200

Environment, 480–488

  economy and, 481

  environmental protection, 480

  hazardous waste reduction programs, 487

  hazardous waste sites, 483

  interstate compacts and, 488

  pollution emission rates, 484

  preemption and, 486

  recycling laws, 482

  state parks, 485

Environmental Protection Agency (EPA), 480, 483

Escobedo v. Illinois (1964), 423

Exclusionary rule, 426

Executive amendments to state legislation, 91

Executive branch officials

  nonpartisan elections for, 265

  state elections of, 266

  ticket-splitting and, 263

Executive orders, 96

Factionalism in state legislatures, 187

Fair Labor Standards Act, 430, 436

Family background

  of legislators, 220

  of state court judges, 393

Family courts, 364

Farmer Labor party, 291

Federal aid to states, 489–495

  defense spending and, 495

  grants-in-aid, 489

  largest recipients of, 490

  state budgets and, 491

  types of, 492

Federal constitutional questions, state supreme courts and, 382

Federal Election Campaign Act (FECA), 283

Federal government. *See also* Constitution, U.S.; *specific amendments*

  governor's office and, 86

  grants to states by, 57

  nullification and, 51

  state lobbying of, 52

  supremacy clause and, 56

Federal income tax, 55

Federalism, 46, 47

  delegated powers and, 430

Federal land holdings, 450

Federal mandates, 182

Federal preemption, 56, 422

Federal supremacy, 436

"Feel-good" (campaign) ads, 293

First reading of proposed bill, 197

Fish, official state, 69

"Flip-flop" (negative campaign) ads, 293

Floor sessions, legislative, 197

Florida

  AIDS patients in, 500

  air pollution emission rates of, 484

  anonymous campaign contributions in, 362

  black population of, 443

  congressional redistricting in, 440

  elderly population of, 444

  executive branch officials, **526**

  formation of, 7

  governor's staff allowances of, 89

  Medicare/Medicaid recipients in, 498

  Missouri Compromise and, 25

  population increase in, 439

  primary runoff elections in, 304

  recent immigrant population of, 445

  sales tax revenues for, 511

  Social Security recipients in, 497

  state profile, **526**

  traffic fatalities in, 517

  Web address, **526**

Flowers, official state, 69

Force Act of 1833, 51

Formal powers, governors', 80

Fossils, official state, 69

Fourteenth Amendment, 43, 54, 424

Franklin (state), 23

Freedom party, 291

Freeman v. Pitts (1992), 434

Fundraising

  by judicial candidates, 329

  by state political parties, 296

Garcia v. San Antonio Metropolitan Transit Authority (1985), 430, 433

General referendum, 348

Georgia

  executive branch officials, **527**

  first popularly elected senator and, 279

  legislature of, 168

  line-item veto in, 125

  majority-minority districts in, 174

  population of, 62

  primary runoff elections in, 304

  settlement of, 6

  size of, 1

  state constitutions of, 66

  state profile, **527**

  voting age in, 332

  Web address, **527**

Note: References point to question numbers in the text. Entries with **bold** references appear in Chapter 7.

Gerrymander, 173
Gibbons v. Ogden (1824), 422
Gideon v. Wainwright (1963), 423
Goldberg v. Kelly (1970), 424
Government, local, 454
Government, state. *See also*
  Appointment(s)
    bureaucracy and, 155
    bureaucratic discretion and, 156
    cabinets of, 148
    civil service and, 154
    divided, 128, 202, 233
    education policymaking by, 478
    electing top officials for, 153
    employees of, 454
    functions of, 41
    reform of, 77
    salaries of top elected officials in, 129
    sunset laws and, 149
Government lobbyists, 253
Governors. *See also* Governorships;
  Gubernatorial races; National
  Governors' Association; Veto
  power in states
    after leaving office, 105
    age of, 130
    appointment powers of, 90
    Asian-American, 119
    assassination attempts on, 111
    backgrounds of, 130–137
    blacks as, 116, 117
    black women as, 118
    brothers as, 132
    caretaker versus managerial, 74
    Catholic, 137
    ceremonial functions and, 76
    consecutive terms for, 103
    convicted criminals and, 97
    death in office of, 112
    divided governments and, 128, 202, 233
    duties of, 73
    education of, 133
    election turnout for, 264
    executive orders and, 96
    federal government and, 86
    first, 70
    formal versus informal powers of, 80
    government experience of, 135
    government reform efforts and, 77

Hispanic, 119
impeachment of, 113, 127
incumbent, successful reelection of, 261
Italian-American, 120
Jewish, 137
with law degrees, 134
legal age for, 101
legislative agenda and, 82
legislative authority of, 83
legislative experience of, 136
limits on powers of, 81
list of, by state, **518–567**
longest-serving, 72
National Guard and, 98
party switching by, 121
perks for, 88
popular election of, 259
powers and privileges of, 80–99
qualifications for, 100
recall and, 108, 125
relations between states and, 85
removed by state supreme court order, 110
removed from office, 127
resignations of, 107
salaries of, 87
signature, lawmaking and, 204
staff allowances of, 89
staff duties, 75
state budgets and, 79
state bureaucracy and, 157
state political party control by, 319
term limits and, 102
terms of service for, 71
as U.S. presidents, 106
women as, 114, 115, 131
Governorships
  political control of, 122
  strong versus weak, 84
Grand juries, functions of, 368
Grants-in-aid, federal, 57, 489
  set-asides and, 493
  start of, 64
  types of, 492
Grasses, official state, 69
Gray v. Sanders (1963), 419
Great Depression, grants-in-aid programs and, 64
Guam, 30
Gubernatorial races
  brothers competing in, 345
  cycle of, 318

increased expense of, 315
most expensive, 334
political party vote tally (1998), 321
Gun-Free School Zones Act of 1990, 437

Hard money, 284
Harper v. Virginia State Board of Elections (1966), 425
Hartford Convention, 28
Hawaii, 516
  air pollution emission rates of, 484
  economic growth rate of, 448
  executive branch officials, **528**
  formation of, 7
  governorship of, 84
  labor unions in, 452
  legislature of, 168
  public schools' administration in, 469
  road miles in, 516
  state profile, **528**
  tax revenues for, 506
  Web address, **528**
Hazardous waste
  reduction programs, 487
  sites, 483
  state preemption and, 486
Health and welfare, 496–502
  AIDS patients by state, 500
  birth/death rates by state, 499
  community hospitals per state, 496
  doctors per state, 496
  median household income by state, 501
  Medicare/Medicaid recipients, 498
  poverty, 502
  Social Security recipients, 497
Hearings, legislative, 197
Highway grants, federal, 514
  state allocation of, 515
Hispanic governors, 119
Hispanic populations of states, 443
Hispanic prison inmates, 464
"Hit-and-run" (negative campaign) ads, 293
Home rule, District of Columbia and, 60
Hospitals, community, 496

Note: References point to question numbers in the text. Entries with **bold** references appear in Chapter 7.

House Government Reform
  Committee, 61
Household income (median) by
  state, 501
House of Representatives, 245–250
  blacks in, 249
  Speaker's role in, 246
  terms for, 245
  woman as Speaker of, 247
  women in, 250
Howland Island, 30
Husband and wife in state
  legislature, 221

Idaho
  campaign contributions in, 361
  executive branch officials, **529**
  formation of, 7
  gubernatorial campaign spending
    in, 316
  state profile, **529**
  Web address, **529**
Illinois
  campaign contributions in, 361
  Chicago Juvenile Court, 413
  executive branch officials, **530**
  formation of, 7
  immigrant population of
    (recent), 445
  Operation Greylord in, 404
  state profile, **530**
  turnover rate in legislature, 223
  Web address, **530**
Impeachment
  of governors, 113, 127
  Oregon provisions for, 239, 401
  of state court judges, 401
  state legislature and, 178
Implied powers, 428, 430
Incarceration rates, 465
Incentive packages, new business,
  449
Income taxes
  federal, 55
  state, 508
  state revenues in, 509
Incorporation doctrine, state courts
  and, 411
Incumbents
  in judicial campaigns, 329, 331
  successful reelection of, 261
Independence party, 291
Independent candidates, 290, 291,
  317, 321, 324

Indeterminate sentencing, 463
Indiana
  anonymous campaign
    contributions in, 362
  campaign contributions in, 361
  candidate nomination in, 308
  executive branch officials, **531**
  formation of, 7
  line-item veto and, 95
  state profile, **531**
  Web address, **531**
Informal powers, governors', 80
Initiatives, citizen, 344. *See also*
  Propositions; Referendums
  constitutional change and, 32
  factors in success of, 352
  versus referendums, 346
  states allowing constitutional, 35
  states that allow, 351
  types of, 347
Interest groups
  most influential, 254
  state agencies and, 159
Interim committees, legislative, 214
Intermediate appellate courts, 364
  organization of, 385
Interpretation of state constitutions,
  32
Interstate commerce, 422, 436
Interstate environmental compacts,
  488
Iowa
  campaign contributions in, 361
  candidate nomination in, 308
  executive branch officials, **532**
  governor's staff allowances of, 89
  legal requirements for state judges
    in, 391
  Missouri Compromise and, 25
  state profile, **532**
  violent crime rates in, 460
  Web address, **532**
Italian-American governors, 120

Jarvis Island, 30
Jewish governors, 137
Johnston Atoll, 30
Joint committees, legislative, 211
Jousting, 63
Judges, state court. *See also* Courts,
  state; Partisan judicial elections
  Chinese-American, 395
  decision-making patterns of, 371
  elections of, 325, 326

family backgrounds of, 393
first partisan popular election for,
  335, 414
impeachment of, 401
legal requirements for, 391
legislative address system for
  removing, 402
minorities among, 398
misconduct commissions and, 403
Missouri plan and, 327
political party preferences of, 330,
  394
qualifications for, 392
recall and, 403
retention elections for, 328
retirement requirements for, 405
salaries of, 373
selection methods for, 399
terms of service of, 390
women as, 398
Judicial review
  constitutional change and, 32
  state supreme court powers of,
    381
Juries
  general trial courts and, 387
  longest trial by, 416
  number of jurors on, 412
Jurisdiction, in state versus federal
  courts, 377
Justices
  of the peace, 389
  state supreme court, 383, 384
Juvenile courts, 364, 388, 413

Kansas
  candidate nomination in, 308
  executive branch officials, **533**
  state profile, **533**
  turnover rate in legislature, 223
  Web address, **533**
Kansas-Nebraska Act (1854), 342
Kentucky
  executive branch officials, **534**
  formation of, 7
  legislative session of, 207
  new business incentive packages
    of, 449
  state profile, **534**
  Web address, **534**
Kestnbaum Commission, 39

Labor unions, 452
  campaign contributions by, 356

Note: References point to question numbers in the text. Entries with **bold** references appear in Chapter 7.

Land area of states, 1
Land Ordinance Act, 64
Largest state, 1
Law(s), 185
  versus bills, 190, 191
  common versus statutory, 408
  precedents in, 406
Law degrees of governors, 134
Law enforcement, 457
  spending for, 458
Lawsuits, 365
Leadership PACs, 323
Legislation in states
  governors' and, 91
  governors' authority in, 83
  governors' influence on, 82
Legislative address system for
  removing state court judges, 402
Legislative assemblies, colonial,
  230
Legislative day, 208
Legislative experience of governors,
  136
Legislative initiatives, 347
  states that allow, 351
Legislative majority, 186
Legislative proposals for
  constitutional change, 32, 33
Legislative referendums, 349
Legislators, state
  Arizona bribery sting and, 224
  average age of, 218
  backgrounds of, 217–221
  blacks as, 236, 237, 238
  campaign committees for, 322
  education of, 219
  family background of, 220
  husband and wife as, 221
  leadership PACs and, 323
  Michigan recall of, 228
  Operation Lost Trust and, 225
  other occupations of, 217
  problems confronting, 179
  qualifications for, 222
  retirement benefits for, 229
  salaries for, 176
  setting compensation package for,
    177
  term limits for, 226, 227
  turnover rates among, 223
  types of, 188
  unaffiliated, 324
  women as, 234, 235

Legislatures, state. *See also*
  Legislative assemblies, colonial
  authorizations versus
    appropriations by, 201
  bicameral system of, 162
  bills versus statutes of, 185
  bureaucracy role for, 158
  committee role in, 195, 210–216
  common names for, 166
  divided governments and, 128,
    202, 233
  educational policy making by,
    478
  electing attorneys general, 145
  electric tote board usage by,
    194
  factionalism in, 187
  functions of, 161
  gerrymandering and, 173
  ideal size for, 180
  impeachment and, 178
  introducing bills into, 189
  largest, 168
  legislative majority in, 186
  majority leader role in, 198
  majority-minority districts and,
    174
  minority leader role in, 198
  monitoring state agencies by, 183
  nationwide seats in, 169
  political control of, 128, 202, 233
  powers of, 165
  process of, 197
  quorums in, 192
  reapportionment and, 171
  redistricting and, 172
  redrawing district lines and, 175
  representatives serving in, 231
  roll-call votes in, 193
  rules and calendar committee role
    in, 195
  senators serving in, 232
  sessions of, 206–209
  sizes of, 167
  smallest, 168
  special legislative sessions, 206,
    209
  televised hearings of, 181
  vetoes/veto overrides and, 92, 93,
    203, 204, 205
  voting in, 193, 194
  whips' role in, 199
Liberal party, 291
Libertarian party, 292

Lieutenant governors, 138–143
  duties of, 138
  list of, by state, **518–567**
  in opposite party from governor,
    142
  popular election of, 260
  salaries of, 141
  states electing on team with
    governors, 140
  states without, 139
  succession without, 143
Line-item veto power, 91
  earliest, 125
  states without, 95
Literacy tests, voter, 336
LLW (Low-Level Radioactive
  Waste) Policy Act of 1980, 488
Lobbying federal government, 52
Lobbyists, 251–254. *See also* Interest
  groups
  derivation of term, 251
  role of, 252
  teachers as, 477
  types of, 253
Localities
  state spending on, 504
  state spending percentage on, 503
Log cabins, 6
Lotteries, state, 512
Louisiana
  black population of, 443
  criminal executions in, 417
  executive branch officials, **535**
  incarceration rates in, 465
  nonpartisan primaries in, 303, 340
  origin of "Dixie" and, 20
  primaries without general
    elections in, 320
  state constitutions of, 66
  state profile, **535**
  turnover rate in legislature, 223
  Web address, **535**
Louisiana Purchase, 7
  Missouri Compromise and, 25
Low-Level Radioactive Waste
  (LLW) Policy Act of 1980, 488

Magazines, campaigns and, 295
Magistrates, state court, 389
Mahan v. Howell (1973), 431
Maher v. Roe (1977), 432
Maine
  anonymous campaign
    contributions in, 362

Note: References point to question numbers in the text. Entries with **bold** references appear in Chapter 7.

Dominion of New England and, 8
executive branch officials, **536**
formation of, 7
independent candidate
  performances in, 291
line-item veto and, 95
low-level radioactive waste and,
  488
state profile, **536**
turnover rate in legislature, 223
unaffiliated legislators in, 324
voter registration in, 337
Web address, **536**
Majority leader, 198
Majority-minority district, 174
Major trial courts, 364
Managerial governors, 74
Mapp v. Ohio (1961), 426
Marching songs, official state, 69
Maryland
  executive branch officials, **537**
  governorship of, 84
  governor's salary in, 87
  Mason-Dixon line and, 17
  median household income in, 501
  settlement of, 6
  state profile, **537**
  state sport/boat of, 63
  turnover rate in legislature, 223
  unusual provisions of state
    constitution, 68
  Web address, **537**
  women as state representatives in,
    250
Mason-Dixon line, 17
Massachusetts
  Dominion of New England and, 8
  executive branch officials, **538**
  gerrymandering in, 173
  legal requirements for state judges
    in, 391
  legislature of, 163, 168
  low-level radioactive waste and,
    488
  official state beverage, 69
  population density of, 441
  population of, 2, 62
  settlement of, 6
  state constitution of, 31
  state profile, **538**
  veto power and, 95, 124
  voter registration in, 336
  Web address, **538**
Massachusetts General Court, 163

Mass media, campaigns and, 295
McCulloch v. Maryland (1819), 429
Medicare/Medicaid recipients by
  state, 498
Merit plan
  politics and, 400
  state court judge selections and,
    399
Mexican War (1846–1848), 7
Michigan
  candidate nomination in, 308
  executive branch officials, **539**
  formation of, 7
  governor's salary in, 87
  labor unions in, 452
  legislative session of, 208
  low-level radioactive waste and,
    488
  Missouri Compromise and, 25
  recall of legislators, 228
  Republican party founding and,
    342
  state profile, **539**
  Web address, **539**
  women as state court justices in,
    415
Middle Atlantic states, 18
Midway Atoll, 30
Midwest (region), 21
Militia(s), state, 42
Miller v. Johnson (1995), 174
Milliken v. Bradley (1974), 428, 434
Minnesota
  executive branch officials, **540**
  hazardous waste reduction
    programs, 487
  legislature of, 168
  state profile, **540**
  third-party performances in, 291
  turnover rate in legislature, 223
  voter registration in, 337
  Web address, **540**
  women as state court justices in,
    415
Minority leader, 198
Miranda v. Arizona (1966), 427
Misconduct commissions for state
  court judges, 403
Mississippi
  anonymous campaign
    contributions in, 362
  black population of, 443
  campaign contributions in, 361
  executive branch officials, **541**

median household income in, 501
primary runoff elections in, 304
sales tax in, 510
state profile, **541**
turnover rate in legislature, 223
unaffiliated legislators in, 324
Web address, **541**
Missouri
  executive branch officials, **542**
  state profile, **542**
  Web address, **542**
Missouri Compromise, 25
Missouri plan, 327
  state court judge selections and,
    399
Missouri v. Jenkins (1990), 428
Model State Constitution, 40
Montana
  executive branch officials, **543**
  governor's salary in, 87
  justices' salaries in, 373
  legislative session of, 207
  population density of, 441
  population of, 2
  sales taxes in, 511
  size of, 1
  state profile, **543**
  violent crime rates in, 460
  Web address, **543**
Mormons, Deseret (state) and, 24
Mottoes, official state, 69
Municipal courts, 388
Myer's automatic ballot cabinet, 258

National Association of Attorneys
  General, 52
National Conference of State
  Legislatures, 52, 184
National Education Association, 477
National Governors' Association, 52
  role of, 78
National Guard, 42
  control over, 98
  paying for, 99
National League of Cities v. Usery
  (1976), 430, 433
National Municipal League, 40
Navassa (U.S. possession), 30
Nebraska
  campaign contributions in, 361
  executive branch officials, **544**
  legislature of, 168
  nonpartisan elections for
    executive branch officials, 265

Note: References point to question numbers in the text. Entries with **bold** references appear in Chapter 7.

primaries in, 340
state profile, **544**
unemployment in, 456
unicameral legislature and, 164
Web address, **544**
Necessary and proper clause,
  implied powers and, 428
Negative campaign ads, 293
  first state to run, 294
Neighborhood schools concept, 434
Nevada
  criminal executions in, 417
  economic growth rate of, 448
  executive branch officials, **545**
  federal land holdings in, 450
  formation of, 7
  governorship of, 84
  legal requirements for state judges
    in, 391
  legislative session of, 207, 208
  legislature of, 168
  line-item veto and, 95
  population increase in, 439
  state profile, **545**
  turnover rate in legislature, 223
  Web address, **545**
New England, 18
New federalism, 47
New Hampshire
  executive branch officials, **546**
  gubernatorial campaign spending
    in, 316
  income taxes in, 508
  legal requirements for state judges
    in, 391
  legislative session of, 208
  legislature of, 168
  line-item veto and, 95
  lottery in, 512
  low-level radioactive waste and,
    488
  sales taxes in, 511
  settlement of, 6
  state profile, **546**
  unusual provisions of state
    constitution, 68
  Web address, **546**
  women as state representatives in,
    250
New Jersey
  AIDS patients in, 500
  Dominion of New England and, 8
  education spending by, 471
  executive branch officials, **547**

governorship of, 84
hazardous waste sites in, 483
immigrant population of
  (recent), 445
justices' salaries in, 373
labor unions in, 452
median household income in, 501
population density of, 441
settlement of, 6
state profile, **547**
Web address, **547**
New Mexico
  campaign contributions in, 361
  candidate nomination in, 308
  executive branch officials, **548**
  formation of, 7
  Hispanic population of, 443
  state profile, **548**
  turnover rate in legislature, 223
  Web address, **548**
New Netherland, 6
New Orleans, La., origin of "Dixie"
  and, 20
Newspapers, campaigns and, 295
New York
  AIDS patients in, 500
  black population of, 443
  candidate nomination in, 308
  congressional redistricting in, 440
  Dominion of New England and, 8
  education employees in, 472
  education spending by, 471
  elderly population of, 444
  employment in, 453
  executive branch officials, **549**
  federal grants-in-aid for, 490
  government employees in, 454
  governorship of, 84
  governor's salary in, 87
  governor's staff of, 89
  gubernatorial race costs in, 334
  hazardous waste reduction
    programs, 487
  immigrant population of
    (recent), 445
  income tax revenues for, 509
  labor unions in, 452
  law enforcement spending in, 458
  legislature of, 168
  localities, spending on, 504
  lottery in, 512
  low-level radioactive waste and,
    488

Medicare/Medicaid recipients in,
  498
nominating conventions and, 341
population of, 2, 4
poverty in, 502
prison system spending in, 459
settlement of, 6
state profile, **549**
tax revenues for, 506
third parties in, 291
veto power in, 124
Web address, **549**
Night courts, 367
Nominating conventions, state, 308
  first, 341
Nonpartisan elections, 310
  for executive branch officials, 265
  judicial, 325, 326, 328, 329, 331
  primaries, 303
North (region)
  Mason-Dixon line and, 17
  population increase in, 439
North Carolina
  executive branch officials, **550**
  executive branch officials'
    elections in, 266
  Franklin (state) and, 23
  governorship of, 84
  hazardous waste reduction
    programs, 487
  legislative session of, 207
  line-item veto and, 95
  population of, 2
  primary runoff elections in, 304
  settlement of, 6
  state profile, **550**
  veto power in, 94
  Web address, **550**
North Dakota
  campaign contributions in, 361
  candidate nomination in, 308
  education employees in, 472
  elderly population of, 444
  executive branch officials, **551**
  executive branch officials'
    elections in, 266
  formation of, 7
  gubernatorial campaign spending
    in, 316
  hazardous waste sites in, 483
  Hispanic population of, 443
  incarceration rates in, 465
  law enforcement spending in, 458
  name change considered, 11

Note: References point to question numbers in the text. Entries with **bold** references appear in Chapter 7.

official state march of, 69
population of, 2
prison system spending in, 459
state profile, **551**
voter registration in, 337
Web address, **551**
Northern Marianas, 30
"Not-on-the-job" (negative
  campaign) ads, 293
Nullification, 51

Offices of court administration, 374
Ohio
  air pollution emission rates of,
    484
  campaign contributions in, 361
  executive branch officials, **552**
  formation of, 7
  state profile, **552**
  Web address, **552**
Oklahoma
  executive branch officials, **553**
  incarceration rates in, 465
  official state grass of, 69
  primary runoff elections in, 304
  Revolt of the T-Bar Twelve in,
    248
  state profile, **553**
  term limits in, 226
  turnover rate in legislature, 223
  unusual provisions of state
    constitution, 68
  Web address, **553**
  women as state court justices in,
    415
One person, one vote principle, 419,
  431
Open primaries, 301
Operation Greylord, 404
Operation Lost Trust, 225
Oregon
  citizen initiatives in, 344
  economic growth rate of, 448
  executive branch officials, **554**
  federal land holdings in, 450
  formation of, 7
  legislative session of, 207
  legislature of, 168
  removal of elected officials in, 239
  sales taxes in, 511
  state courts of, 378
  state profile, **554**
  Web address, **554**

Original jurisdiction of state
  supreme courts, 380
Original thirteen states, 5
  largest population among, 62
  settlement of, 6
  urban population of, 3

Palmyra Atoll, 30
Pardon of convicted criminals, 97
Partisan judicial elections, 325
Patronage, 311
  Supreme Court on, 312
Pennsylvania
  campaign contributions in, 361
  executive branch officials, **555**
  first televised political convention
    and, 276
  hazardous waste sites in, 483
  legislature of, 168
  population of, 2
  settlement of, 6
  state profile, **555**
  Web address, **555**
Perquisites
  for governors, 88
  for state legislators, 175
Petition referendums, 348
  states that allow, 350
Philadelphia, Pa., 6
Pilgrims, 6
Plains states, 21
*Planned Parenthood of Southeastern
  Pennsylvania v. Casey* (1992), 432
Plea bargaining, 409
Plurality, electoral, 269
Plymouth Colony, 6
Pocket vetoes of state legislation, 91,
  204
Police interrogation, right to
  counsel during, 423
Political action committees (PACs),
  357
  campaign contributions and, 357
  leadership, 323
Political influence on merit plans,
  400
Political parties. *See also*
  Campaign(s); State political parties
  caucuses of, 299
  governor/lieutenant governor
    from opposite, 142
  governorship control by, 122
  governors switching, 121
  hard versus soft money for, 284

legislature control by, 233
party column ballot and, 257
patronage and, 311
requirements for ballot inclusion
  for, 290
role of, 286
state court judges and, 330, 394
state/national interaction of, 278
state regulation of, 289
televised political conventions,
  276
third-party performance in states,
  291
Politicos, state legislative, 188
Poll taxes, 273, 425
Pollution emission rates, 484
Population of states, 2
  changes in, and demand for
    services, 438
  congressional redistricting and,
    440
  density variations of, 441
  elderly in, 444
  minorities in, 443
  most populous, 4
  of recent immigrants, 445
  statistical sampling and, 447
  urban populations, 3
  urban versus rural, 442
Poverty, population below, 502
Precedents, legal, 406
Precincts, 268
  county political committees and,
    287
Preemption doctrine
  federal, 56, 422
  state, 486
Presidential primaries, 274
  Super Tuesday, 275
President of state senate, 241
President pro tem of state senate,
  241
Primaries
  blanket, 302
  closed versus open, 301
  direct, 298
  first state to adopt, 338
  last state to adopt, 339
  nonpartisan, 303, 340
  party endorsement and, 309
  presidential, 274, 275
  runoff elections and, 304, 305,
    306
  statewide election, 297

Note: References point to question numbers in the text. Entries with **bold** references appear in Chapter 7.

turnout for, 300
types of, by state, 307
without general elections, 320
Prison system
early release programs and, 467
incarceration rates, 465
per capita costs for, 466
population increases, 463
spending on, 459
Privacy, right to, 432
Probate court, 388
Progressive party, 291, 324
direct primaries and, 299
Project-based grants, 492
Property taxes, 507
Propositions, 353, 354, 446. *See also*
Initiatives, citizen; Referendums
Public interest, definition of, 160
Public schools
administration, 469
financing, 470
Puerto Rico, 29

Quaker settlers, 6
Qualifications
for governorships, 100
for legislatures, 222
for state judges, 391, 392
Quorums, 192

Radio
campaigns' use of, 295
first political convention on, 276
mass media campaign ads on,
293
Ranney index, 314
Reapportionment, 171
Baker v. Carr (1962) and, 419
Reynolds v. Sims (1964) and, 431
Recall procedure, 108
of governor, 126
Michigan legislators and, 228
for state court judges, 403
state provisions for, 109
Reconstruction
black legislators in South since,
238
Republican governorships in
South since, 123
Recycling laws, 482
Redistricting, 172
Baker v. Carr (1962) and, 419
population shifts and, 440
state legislatures and, 175

statistical sampling and, 447
Referendums. *See also* Initiatives,
citizen; Propositions
factors in success of, 352
versus initiatives, 346
legislative, 349
types of, 348
Reform party, 291, 317
Registration, voter, 272, 336, 337
Relations between states, 44
governors' role in, 85
Representation in federal
government, 42
Representatives, state, 231
incumbent, successful reelection
of, 261
Reprieve of convicted criminals, 97
Republican party
Brock's changes to, 280
first negative campaign ads of,
294
first televised political convention
of, 276
founding of, 342
governorship control by, 122
gubernatorial election totals,
1998, 321
legislative control by, 233
Ranney index and, 314
southern governorships and, 123
state campaign funding sources
for, 313
state campaign fundraising by,
296
state legislatures controlled by,
170
states controlled by, 262
women as state representatives,
250
Resignations of governors, 107
Retention elections (judicial), 328,
329
incumbents in, 331
Retirement
benefits for legislators, 229
requirements for state court
judges, 405
Revenue-sharing grants, 492
Revolt of the T-Bar Twelve, 248
Reynolds v. Sims (1964), 431
Rhode Island
air pollution emission rates of,
484
Dominion of New England and, 8

executive branch officials, **556**
federal land holdings in, 450
legal requirements for state judges
in, 391
line-item veto and, 95
low-level radioactive waste and,
488
population density of, 441
population of, 2, 62
settlement of, 6
size of, 1
state parks in, 485
state profile, **556**
traffic fatalities in, 517
Web address, **556**
Right-to-Life party, 291
Road miles per state, 516
Roe v. Wade (1973), 418, 432
Roll-call votes, 193
Runoff elections, 304
divisiveness of, 305
frequency of, 306
Rutan v. Republican Party (1990),
312

"Sainthood" (campaign) ads, 293
Salaries
of governors, 87
of lieutenant governors, 141
of state court judges, 373
of state legislators, 176, 179
of top elected state officials, 129
Sales taxes, 510
state revenues in, 511
School busing, 434
Secession(s), 45
Civil War, 26
other, 28
Second reading of proposed bill,
197
Secret ballots, 256
Segregation
de jure versus de facto, 434
Fourteenth Amendment and, 43
in schools, taxation without
representation and, 428
Select committees, legislative, 211
Semi-closed primaries, 301
Semi-open primaries, 301
Senate Governmental Affairs
Committee, 61
Senates, state, 240–244
blacks in, 242
largest versus smallest, 232

Note: References point to question numbers in the text. Entries with **bold** references appear in Chapter 7.

popular election to, 48, 279
president of, 241
president pro tem of, 241
reelection of incumbents to, 261
terms, 240
women in, 243, 244
Seniority system, legislative, 216
Separate but equal doctrine, 420
Sessions, legislative, 206
  biennial, 207
  duration of, 208
  first in colonies, 230
Set-asides requirements, 493
Seventeenth Amendment, 279
Sixteenth Amendment, 55
Sixth Amendment, 423
Slaveholding, Missouri
  Compromise and, 25
Small claims courts, 364, 388
Smallest state, 1
Socialist party, 291
Social Security recipients by state,
  497
Soft money, 284
Solid South, 277
South (region)
  black legislators since
    Reconstruction in, 238
  Mason-Dixon line and, 17
  poll taxes in, 273
  primary runoff elections in, 304
  Republican governorships since
    Reconstruction in, 123
South Carolina
  black population of, 443
  candidate nomination in, 308
  constitutional amendments in, 34
  executive branch officials, **557**
  governorship of, 84
  Operation Lost Trust and, 225
  Ordinance of Nullification of, 51
  primary runoff elections in, 304
  settlement of, 6
  state constitutions of, 66
  state profile, **557**
  turnover rate in legislature, 223
  unaffiliated legislators in, 324
  Web address, **557**
South Carolina v. Baker (1988), 433
South Dakota
  anonymous campaign
    contributions in, 362
  citizen initiatives in, 344
  education spending by, 471

executive branch officials, **558**
gubernatorial campaign spending
  in, 316
official state grass of, 69
population of, 2
state profile, **558**
violent crime rates in, 460
Web address, **558**
Southwest (region), 21
Speaker of the House, 246
  T-Bar Twelve Revolt against, 248
  woman as, 247
Special legislative sessions, 206, 209
Spending, state, 513
Sport, official state, 63, 69
Staff
  governor's, 75
  legislative, 179
Standing committees, legislative,
  211
State(s). *See also* Federal
  government; Statehood; *specific
  amendments*
  campaign finance report
    requirements of, 359
  campaign financing by, 355
  Civil War secessions of, 26
  constitutional limitations on, 43
  Constitution on borders of, 16
  Constitution on powers of, 42
  Constitution ratification by, 12
  constitutions of, 31–40
  federal grants to, 57
  federalism and, 46
  federal mandates and, 182
  federal preemption and, 56, 422
  formation of, 7
  Fourteenth Amendment and, 43,
    54
  in history, 1–21
  lobbying federal government, 52,
    53
  original thirteen, 3, 5, 6
  origins of names for, 9, 10
  other secessions of, 28
  primary types in, 307
  relations between, 44, 85
  salaries of top elected officials by,
    129
  Sixteenth Amendment and, 55
  Tenth Amendment and, 42, 46,
    50
  Union and, 41–57
State aid to localities, 503–504

State education board member
  selection, 479
Statehood, 22–30
  dates of, 14
  of District of Columbia, 58
  duration between admissions to,
    15
  Missouri Compromise and, 25
  post-Civil War readmittance, 26
  process of, 22
State parks, 485
State political parties. *See also*
  Campaign(s); Third party(ies)
  candidate endorsement and, 309
  Federal Election Campaign Act
    and, 283
  funding for, 313
  fundraising of, 296
  governors' control of, 319
  interaction with national, 278
  nominating conventions of, 308,
    341
  organization of, 287
  patronage and, 311
  regulation of, 289
  requirements for ballot inclusion
    for, 290
  third-party performance of, 291
  women as head of, 288
State superintendent of schools, 478
Statutes versus bills, 185
Statutory law, 408
Succession without lieutenant
  governors, 143
Sunbelt (region), 19. *See also* South
  (region)
Sunset laws, 149, 183
Superfund program, EPA, 483
Super Tuesday, 275
Supremacy clause, U.S.
  Constitution, 56
Supreme Court, U.S., 378. *See also
  specific cases*
  on capital punishment, 417
  decisions affecting state/local
    governments by, 418–437
  on incorporation doctrine, 411
  on patronage, 312
  on redistricting, 447
  on state election poll taxes, 273
Supreme court of appeals, 363
Supreme courts, state, 363, 364,
  379–384
  black chief justices for, 397

Note: References point to question numbers in the text. Entries with **bold** references appear in Chapter 7.

federal constitutional questions and, 382
judicial review powers of, 381
justices serving on, 383
justices' terms of office for, 384
original jurisdiction for, 380
processes in, 379
women as chief justices for, 396
women as justices on, 415
Supreme judicial court, 363
Swann v. Charlotte-Mecklenburg County Board of Education (1971), 434
Swedish settlers, 6
Symbols, official (mottoes, sports, trees, etc.), 69, **518–567**

Tariff of Abominations (1828), 51
Taxation without representation, 428
Taxes, state, 505–512
  on income, 508, 509
  lotteries, 512
  on property, 507
  revenues by state, 506
  on sales, 510, 511
  school desegregation costs and, 434
  voter revolt against, 353
T-Bar Twelve Revolt, 248
Teachers, 477
Television
  campaigns and, 295
  court verdicts on, 366
  mass media campaign ads on, 293
  political conventions on, 276
  state legislatures and, 181
Tennessee
  anonymous campaign contributions in, 362
  Baker v. Carr (1962) and, 419
  brothers in gubernatorial race in, 345
  executive branch officials, **559**
  formation of, 7
  Franklin (state) and, 23
  income taxes in, 508
  state profile, **559**
  Web address, **559**
Tenth Amendment, 42, 46, 50, 430, 436
Term limits, 354

Term of office
  of governors, 103, 104
  limits for governors, 102
  limits for legislators, 226, 227
  for state House of Representatives, 245
  for state judges, 390
  for state senators, 240
  for state supreme court justices, 384
Territories, U.S., 30
"Testimonial" (campaign) ads, 293
Texas
  AIDS patients in, 500
  air pollution emission rates of, 484
  black population of, 443
  campaign contributions in, 361
  congressional redistricting in, 440
  constitution of, 67
  criminal executions in, 417
  education employees in, 472
  education spending by, 471
  employment in, 453
  executive branch officials, **560**
  federal grants-in-aid for, 490
  formation of, 7
  government employees in, 454
  governorship of, 84
  governor's staff of, 89
  gubernatorial campaign spending in, 316, 334
  Hispanic population of, 443
  immigrant population of (recent), 445
  incarceration rates in, 465
  law enforcement spending in, 458
  legislative session of, 207
  line-item veto in, 125
  localities, spending on, 504
  low-level radioactive waste, 488
  Missouri Compromise and, 25
  population increase in, 439
  population of, 2
  poverty in, 502
  primary runoff elections in, 304
  prison system spending in, 459
  road miles in, 516
  sales tax revenues for, 511
  size of, 1
  state parks in, 485
  state profile, **560**
  tax revenues for, 506

traffic fatalities in, 517
  Web address, **560**
Third party(ies)
  current most active, 292
  governors, 317
  gubernatorial election totals, 1998, 321
  state level, 291
Ticket-splitting, executive branch officials and, 263
Traffic court, 388
Traffic fatalities by state, 517
Transportation (highways/mass transit), 514–517
  cars per state, 516
  federal highway grants, 514, 515
  road miles per state, 516
  traffic fatalities by state, 517
Treasurers (state)
  list of, by state, **518–567**
  popular election of, 260
Treaties, states formation and, 7
Trees, official state, 69
Trustees, state legislative, 188
Turnout
  by eligible voters, 270
  for gubernatorial elections, 264
  highest, 271
  for nonpartisan judicial elections, 328
  for primaries, 300
  registration rules and, 272
Twenty-fourth Amendment, 273
Twenty-third Amendment, 285

Unemployment rates, 456
Unenumerated powers, 430
Unfunded Mandates Reform Act of 1995, 182
Unicameral legislature(s), 162
  in Nebraska, 164
Union. *See also* Constitution, U.S.; Federal government
  secession from, 45
  state(s) and, 41–57
Unions. *See* Labor unions
Unitary government, definition of, 46
United States v. Darby Lumber Co. (1941), 436
United States v. Lopez (1995), 437
University of California Regents v. Bakke (1978), 435

Note: References point to question numbers in the text. Entries with **bold** references appear in Chapter 7.

Unregulable state activity spheres, 433
Urban population in original thirteen states, 3
Utah
  anonymous campaign contributions in, 362
  birth/death rates in, 499
  campaign contributions in, 361
  candidate nomination in, 308
  Deseret (state) and, 24
  economic growth rate of, 448
  education spending by, 471
  executive branch officials, **561**
  federal land holdings in, 450
  state profile, **561**
  Web address, **561**

Vermont
  anonymous campaign contributions in, 362
  elderly population of, 444
  executive branch officials, **562**
  as fourteenth state, 13
  government employees in, 454
  governorship of, 84
  gubernatorial campaign spending in, 316
  Hispanic population of, 443
  law enforcement spending in, 458
  line-item veto and, 95
  low-level radioactive waste and, 488
  prison system spending in, 459
  state profile, **562**
  unaffiliated legislators in, 324
  Web address, **562**
  women as legislators in, 235
  women as state representatives in, 250
Vest pocket tickets, 255
Veto power in states, 91, 94
  after legislative session ends, 205
  line-item, 91, 95, 125
  oldest, 124
  use/overrides of, 92, 93, 203, 204
Victimless crimes, 468
Violent crime rates, 460
Virginia
  anonymous campaign contributions in, 362
  campaign contributions in, 361
  candidate nomination in, 308
  executive branch officials, **563**

line-item veto and, 95
population of, 2
settlement of, 6
size of, 1
state profile, **563**
Web address, **563**
Virgin Islands, U.S., 30
Voters, 271. *See also* Initiatives, citizen; Referendums
  in gubernatorial elections, 264
  legal age for, 332
  registration laws for, 336, 337
Voter turnout
  by eligible voters, 270
  for gubernatorial elections, 264
  highest, 271
  for nonpartisan judicial elections, 328
  for primaries, 300
  registration rules and, 272
Voting, legislative
  electric tote board usage by legislature, 194
  roll-call votes, 193
Voting machines, 258

Wake Atoll, 30
War of 1812, 28
Washington
  blanket primaries in, 302
  economic growth rate of, 448
  executive branch officials, **564**
  formation of, 7
  governor's salary in, 87
  labor unions in, 452
  state profile, **564**
  turnover rate in legislature, 223
  Web address, **564**
  women as legislators in, 235
Webster v. Reproductive Health Services (1992), 432
Welfare benefit hearings, 424
West (region), 21
  federal land holdings in, 450
West Virginia
  executive branch officials, **565**
  formation of, 26
  governorship of, 84
  median household income in, 501
  state profile, **565**
  Web address, **565**
Whips, legislative, 199
White prison inmates, 464

Wife and husband in state legislature, 221
Wisconsin
  electric tote board usage by legislature, 194
  executive branch officials, **566**
  formation of, 7
  gubernatorial campaign spending in, 316
  income taxes in, 508
  legislative session of, 208
  Missouri Compromise and, 25
  primaries in, 338
  state profile, **566**
  third-party performances in, 291
  turnover rate in legislature, 223
  voter registration in, 337
  Web address, **566**
Women
  as state court justices, 415
  as state political party committee head, 288
  as state supreme court chief justices, 396
  state voting rights for, 333
Women governors, 114, 115, 131
  black, 118
Women legislators, 234, 235
  as representatives in state houses, 250
  in senates, 243, 244
Women teachers, 473
Wrestling matches, 68
Wyoming
  anonymous campaign contributions in, 362
  economic growth rate of, 448
  education employees in, 472
  education spending by, 471
  elderly population of, 444
  executive branch officials, **567**
  formation of, 7
  governor's staff allowances of, 89
  gubernatorial campaign spending in, 316
  legislative session of, 208
  legislature of, 168
  population density of, 441
  population of, 2
  poverty in, 502
  prison system spending in, 459
  state profile, **567**
  Web address, **567**
  women's voting rights in, 333

Note: References point to question numbers in the text. Entries with **bold** references appear in Chapter 7.

NAME INDEX

Aandahl, Fred G., **551**
Adams, Alva, **523**
Adams, Sherman, **546**
Adams, Stephen, **559**
Adams, William H., **523**
Adkins, Homer M., **521**
Agnew, Spiro T., 107, **537**
Aiken, George D., **562**
Aldrich, Chester H., **544**
Alexander, Lamar, **559**
Alexander, Moses, 137, **529**
Allain, Bill, **541**
Allen, Frank G., **538**
Allen, George F., **563**
Allen, Henry J., **533**
Allen, Oscar K., **535**
Allred, James V., **560**
Almond, J. Lindsay, Jr., **563**
Almond, Lincoln C., **556**
Ammons, Elias M., **523**
Ammons, Teller, **523**
Anaya, Toney, 119, **548**
Andersen, Elmer L., **540**
Anderson, Clyde E., **540**
Anderson, Forrest H., **543**
Anderson, John, Jr., **533**
Anderson, Sigurd, **558**
Anderson, Victor E., **544**
Anderson, Wendell R., **540**
Andros, Edmund, 8
Andrus, Cecil D., **529**
Angelides, Philip, **522**
Ansel, Martin F., **557**
Anzai, Earl, **528**
Apodaca, Jerry, 119, **548**
Ariyoshi, George R., 119, **528**
Arn, Edward F., **533**
Arnall, Ellis G., **527**
Aronson, John Hugo, **543**
Arthur, Harold J., **562**
Ashcroft, John D., **542**
Askew, Reubin O., **526**
Atiyeh, Victor, **554**
Atkinson, George W., **565**
Atler, Edward, **561**

Avery, William H., **533**
Aycock, Charles B., **550**
Ayers, Roy E., **543**

Babbitt, Bruce, **520**
Babcock, Tim M., **543**
Baca, Ezequiel C. de, 119
Bacon, Walter W., **525**
Bailey, Carl E., **521**
Bailey, Thomas L., **541**
Bailey, Willis J., **533**
Baker, Charles W., 419
Baker, Samuel A., **542**
Baker, Thurbert, **527**
Baldridge, H. C., **529**
Baldwin, Raymond E., **524**
Baldwin, Simeon E., **524**
Baliles, Gerald L., **563**
Balzar, Frederick B., **545**
Bamberger, Simon, **561**
Bangerter, Norman H., **561**
Barker, Jim, 248
Barnes, Roy, **527**
Barnett, Mark, **558**
Barnett, Ross R., **541**
Barrett, Frank A., **567**
Barron, William W., **565**
Barrows, Lewis O., **536**
Barstow, William Augustus, 110
Bartlett, Dewey F., **553**
Bartlett, John H., **546**
Bashford, Coles, 110
Bass, Robert P., **546**
Batchelder, Nahum J., **546**
Bates, John L., **538**
Batt, Philip E., **529**
Battle, John S., **563**
Baxley, Lucy, **518**
Baxter, Percival P., **536**
Bayh, Evan, III, **531**
Beardsley, William S., **532**
Beasley, David M., **557**
Beckham, J. C. W., **534**
Beekman, R. Livingston, **556**
Bell, Charles J., **562**

Bell, John C., Jr., **555**
Bellmon, Henry L., **553**
Bennett, Marshall, **541**
Bennett, Robert F., **533**
Benson, Elmer A., **540**
Benson, Frank W., **554**
Berry, Tim, **531**
Berry, Tom, **558**
Beyle, Thad, 84
Bibb Graves, D., **518**
Bickett, Thomas W., **550**
Bilbo, Theodore G., **541**
Billings, Franklin S., **562**
Bingham, Hiram, **524**
Black, James D., **534**
Blackwood, Ibra C., **557**
Blaine, John J., **566**
Blair, James T., Jr., **542**
Blanchard, James J., **539**
Blanchard, Newton C., **535**
Blanco, Kathleen B., **535**
Blanton, Ray, **559**
Blease, Coleman L., **557**
Bliss, Aaron T., **539**
Blood, Henry H., **561**
Blood, Robert O., **546**
Bloxham, William D., **526**
Blue, Robert D., **532**
Blumenthal, Richard, **524**
Boe, Nils A., **558**
Boggs, James Caleb, **525**
Bolack, Tom, **548**
Bolin, Wesley, **520**
Bond, Christopher S., **542**
Bonner, John W., **543**
Booth, Newton, 119
Boren, David L., **553**
Botelho, Bruce M., **519**
Bottolfsen, C. A., **529**
Bowen, Otis R., **531**
Bowerman, Jay, **554**
Bowles, Chester, **524**
Boyle, Emmet D., **545**
Boyles, Harlan, **550**
Bradford, Robert F., **538**

> *Note:* References point to question numbers in the text. Entries with **bold** references appear in Chapter 7.

Bradley, Walter, **548**
Brady, James H., **529**
Brady, Jane M., **525**
Branch, Emmett F., **531**
Brandon, William W., **518**
Branigin, Roger D., **531**
Brann, Louis J., **536**
Branstad, Terry E., 72, **532**
Breathitt, Edward T., **534**
Brennan, Joseph E., **536**
Brewer, Albert P., **518**
Brewer, Earl L., **541**
Brewster, Ralph O., **536**
Bricker, John W., **552**
Bridges, H. Styles, **546**
Briscoe, Dolph, **560**
Brogan, Frank, **526**
Bronster, Margery S., **528**
Brooks, Bryant B., **567**
Brooks, Ralph G., **544**
Brough, Charles H., **521**
Broughton, J. Melville, **550**
Broward, Napoleon B., **526**
Brown, Albert O., **546**
Brown, Edmund G., Jr., **522**
Brown, Edmund G., Sr., **522**
Brown, Fred H., **546**
Brown, John W., **552**
Brown, John Y., Jr., **534**
Brown, Joseph M., **527**
Brown, Ron, 282
Browning, Gordon, **559**
Brucker, Wilbur M., **539**
Brumbaugh, Martin G., **555**
Brunsdale, Clarence N., **551**
Bryan, Charles W., **544**
Bryan, Richard H., **545**
Bryant, C. Farris, **526**
Buchanan, James, 24
Buchtel, Henry A., **523**
Buck, C. Douglass, **525**
Buckson, David P., **525**
Bulow, William J., **558**
Bumpers, Dale, **521**
Burke, John, **551**
Burney, Dwight W., **544**
Burnquist, Joseph A. A., **540**
Burns, Haydon, **526**
Burns, John A., **528**
Burroughs, John, **548**
Busbee, George D., **527**
Bush, George W., 132, **560**
Bush, George, 467
Bush, Jeb, 132, **526**
Bushfield, Harlan J., **558**
Bushnell, Asa S., **552**

Bustamante, Cruz, **522**
Butkin, Robert, **553**
Butler, Dick, **558**
Butterworth, Bob, **526**
Byrd, Harry F., **563**
Byrne, Brendon T., **547**
Byrne, Frank M., **558**
Byrnes, James F., **557**

Cahill, William T., **547**
Caldwell, Millard F., **526**
Campbell, Carroll A., Jr., **557**
Campbell, Jack M., **548**
Campbell, Thomas E., **520**
Campbell, Thomas M., **560**
Candler, Allen D., **527**
Caperton, Gaston, **565**
Capper, Arthur, **533**
Carey, Hugh L., **549**
Carey, Joseph M., **567**
Carey, Robert D., **567**
Cargo, David F., **548**
Carlin, John W., **533**
Carlson, Arne, **540**
Carlson, Frank, **533**
Carlson, George A., **523**
Carlton, Doyle E., **526**
Carnahan, Mel, **542**
Carper, Tom, **525**
Carr, Joe, 419
Carr, Ralph L., **523**
Carroll, Beryl F., **532**
Carroll, Julian M., **534**
Carruthers, Garrey E., **548**
Carter, Jimmy, 106, **527**
Carvel, Elbert N., **525**
Carville, Edward P., **545**
Case, Clarence E., **547**
Case, Norman S., **556**
Casey, Robert P., **555**
Castle, Michael N., **525**
Castro, Raul H., 119, **520**
Catts, Sidney J., **526**
Caulfield, Henry S., **542**
Cayetano, Benjamin J., **528**
Celeste, Richard F., **552**
Cellucci, Argeo Paul, **538**
Chafee, John H., **556**
Chamberlain, Abiram, **524**
Chamberlain, George E., **554**
Chandler, Albert B., III, **534**
Charles I, King, 6
Charles II, King, 6
Chatterton, Fenimore C., **567**
Cherry, Francis, **521**
Cherry, R. Gregg, **550**

Chiles, Lawton, **526**
Christianson, Theodore, **540**
Clark, Alonzo M., **567**
Clark, Barzilla W., **529**
Clark, Chase A., **529**
Clarke, George W., **532**
Clauson, Clinton A., **536**
Clement, Frank G., **559**
Clement, Percival W., **562**
Clements, Earle C., **534**
Clements, William, **560**
Cleveland, Grover, 106
Clinton, Bill, 106, **521**
Clinton, De Witt, 341
Clyde, George D., **561**
Cobb, William T., **536**
Cochran, Robert L., **544**
Coffman, Mike, **523**
Coleman, James P., **541**
Coleman, James S., 476
Collins, Martha Layne, **534**
Collins, T. LeRoy, **526**
Collins, Thomas, 70
Colquitt, Oscar B., **560**
Combs, Bert T., **534**
Comer, Braxton B., **518**
Comstock, William A., **539**
Condon, Charles, **557**
Cone, Frederick P., **526**
Conley, William G., **565**
Connally, John, 111, **560**
Conner, Martin S., **541**
Coolidge, Calvin, 106, 276, **538**
Cooney, Frank H., **543**
Cooper, Myers Y., **552**
Cooper, Prentice, **559**
Cooper, Robert A., **557**
Cornwall, John J., **565**
Cornyn, John, **560**
Cosgrove, Samuel G., **564**
Cowper, Steve, **519**
Cox, Channing H., **538**
Cox, James M., **552**
Cox, John I., **559**
Coyne, M. Jeanne, 415
Craig, George N., **531**
Craig, Locke, **550**
Craig, Minnie Davenport, 247
Crane, Arthur G., **567**
Crane, Ron, **529**
Crane, W. Murray, **538**
Crawford, Coe I., **558**
Crosby, Robert B., **544**
Cross, Burton M., **536**
Cross, Wilbur L., **524**
Crothers, Austin L., **537**

Cruce, Lee, **553**
Cummins, Albert B., **532**
Cunningham, Russell M., **518**
Cuomo, Mario M., 309, **549**
Curley, James M., **538**
Curran, J. Joseph, **537**
Curtis, Kenneth M., **536**
Curtis, Oakley C., **536**
Cutler, John C., **561**

Dale, Charles M., **546**
Dalton, John M., **542**
Dalton, John, **563**
Daniel, Price, **560**
Darden, Colgate W., Jr., **563**
Davey, Martin L., **552**
Davidson, James O., **566**
Davis, D. W., **529**
Davis, Deane C., **562**
Davis, Gray, 334, **522**
Davis, Harry L., **552**
Davis, James H., **535**
Davis, Jeff, **521**
Davis, Jefferson, 20
Davis, John E., **551**
Davis, Jonathan M., **533**
Davis, Westmoreland, **563**
Dawson, William M. O., **565**
de Baca, Ezequiel C., **548**
Dean, Howard, **562**
Del Papa, Frankie Sue, **545**
Del Sesto, Christopher, **556**
Dempsey, John J., **548**
Dempsey, John, **524**
Deneen, Charles S., **530**
Denney, William D., **525**
Dern, George H., **561**
Deters, Joseph, **552**
Deukmejian, George, **522**
Dever, Paul A., **538**
Dewey, Susan, **563**
Dewey, Thomas E., **549**
Dickerson, Denver S., **545**
Dickenson, Luren D., **539**
DiEleuterio, James, **547**
Dietrich, Charles H., **544**
Dillon, John F., 372
Dillon, Richard C., **548**
DiPrete, Edward D., **556**
DiSalle, Michael V., **552**
Dix, John Alden, **549**
Dixon, Frank M., **518**
Dixon, Jeremiah, 17
Dixon, Joseph M., **543**
Dixon, Richard, **537**
Dockery, Alexander M., **542**
Docking, George, **533**

Docking, Robert B., **533**
Donaghey, George W., **521**
Donahey, A. Vic, **552**
Donnell, Forrest C., **542**
Donnelly, Phil M., **542**
Donohue, Mary O., **549**
Dorsey, Hugh M., **527**
Douglas, James, **562**
Douglas, William L., **538**
Doyle, Jim, **566**
Draper, Eben S., **538**
Dreyfus, Lee Sherman, **566**
Driscoll, Alfred E., **547**
Duff, James H., **555**
Dukakis, Michael S., 467, **538**
Duncan, Ken, **535**
Dunn, Winfield, **559**
Dunne, Edward F., **530**
duPont, Pierre S., **525**
Durbin, Winfield T., **531**
Dwinell, Lane, **546**

Earl, Anthony S., **566**
Earle, George H., **555**
Earley, Mark, **563**
Easley, Michael F., **550**
Eberhart, Adolph O., **540**
Ebersole, Dan, **527**
Edgar, Jim, **530**
Edge, Walter E., **547**
Edison, Charles, **547**
Edison, Thomas, 258
Edmondson, J. Howard, **553**
Edmondson, W. A. Drew, **553**
Edwards, Edward I., **547**
Edwards, Edwin W., 107, 320, **535**
Edwards, James B., **557**
Egan, William A., **519**
Ehringhaus, J. C. B., **550**
Ellington, Buford, **559**
Elrod, Samuel H., **558**
Elthon, Leo, **532**
Ely, Joseph B., **538**
Emanuel, David A., 137
Emerson, Frank C., **567**
Emerson, Lee E., **562**
Emmerson, Louis L., **530**
Emmett, Daniel Decatur, 20
Engler, John, **539**
Erbe, Norman A., **532**
Erickson, John E., **543**
Evans, Daniel J., **564**
Evans, John V., **529**
Exon, J. James, **544**

Fallin, Mary, **553**
Fancher, Frederick B., **551**

Fannin, Paul J., **520**
Farrar, Frank L., **558**
Faubus, Orval E., **521**
Fauset, Crystal Bird, 237
Felker, Samuel D., **546**
Ferguson, James E., 113, **560**
Ferguson, Miriam Amanda, 114, 131, **560**
Fernald, Bert M., **536**
Ferris, Woodbridge N., **539**
Ferry, Elisha P., **564**
Fielder, James F., **547**
Fields, William J., **534**
Finch, Cliff, **541**
Fine, John S., **555**
Finney, Joan, **533**
Fisher, Jimmie Lou, **521**
Fisher, John S., **555**
Fisher, Mike, **555**
Fitzgerald, Frank D., **539**
Fitzgerald, Michael, **532**
Fletcher, Allen M., **562**
Florio, James, **547**
Floyd, Charles M., **546**
Flynn, William S., **556**
Fogarty, Charles J., **556**
Folk, Joseph W., **542**
Folsom, James E., **518**
Folsom, James E., Jr., **518**
Forbes, Malcolm, 181
Ford, Samuel C., **543**
Ford, Wendell H., **534**
Fordice, Kirk, **541**
Fort, John F., **547**
Foss, Eugene N., **538**
Foss, Joseph J., **558**
Foster, Murphy J., **535**
Franklin, Benjamin, 23
Frazier, James B., **559**
Frazier, Lynn J., 126, **551**
Freeman, Orville L., **540**
Fuller, Alvan T., **538**
Fulton, Robert D., **532**
Fuqua, Henry L., **535**
Furcolo, Foster, **538**
Futrell, J. M., **521**

Gage, Henry T., **522**
Gage, Jack R., **567**
Gallen, Hugh, **546**
Gardebring, Sandra, 415
Gardiner, William T., **536**
Gardner, Booth, **564**
Gardner, Frederick D., **542**
Gardner, O. Max, **550**
Garrahy, J. Joseph, **556**
Garst, Warren, **532**

Note: References point to question numbers in the text. Entries with **bold** references appear in Chapter 7.

Garvey, Dan E., **520**
Garvin, Lucius F. C., **556**
Gary, Raymond, **553**
Gasser, George H., **549**
Gates, Charles W., **562**
Gates, Ralph F., **531**
Geer, Thomas T., **554**
George II, King, 6
Geringer, Jim, **567**
Gerry, Elbridge, 173
Gibson, Ernest W., **562**
Gideon, Clarence Earl, 423
Gilchrist, Albert W., **526**
Gillett, James N., **522**
Gilligan, John J., **552**
Gilmore, James S., III, **563**
Gilmore, Kathi, **551**
Glasscock, William E., **565**
Glendening, Parris N., **537**
Glenn, Robert B., **550**
Glynn, Martin H., **549**
Goddard, Samuel P., **520**
Godwin, Mills E., Jr., **563**
Goebel, William, **534**
Goldsborough, Phillips Lee, **537**
Goldschmidt, Neil, **554**
Gooding, Frank R., **529**
Goodland, Walter S., **566**
Goodrich, James P., **531**
Gore, Howard M., **565**
Gossett, Charles C., **529**
Graham, Horace F., **562**
Graham, Jan, **561**
Graham, Robert, **526**
Granholm, Jennifer, **539**
Grasso, Ella T., 131, **524**
Graves, Bill, **533**
Green, Dwight H., **530**
Green, Fred W., **539**
Green, Theodore F., **556**
Green, Warren E., **558**
Gregg, Hugh, **546**
Gregg, Judd, **546**
Gregoire, Christine O., **564**
Gregory, William, **556**
Griffin, S. Marvin, **527**
Griswold, Dwight P., **544**
Griswold, Morley I., **545**
Groesbeck, Alex J., **539**
Gubbrud, Archie M., **558**
Guild, Curtis, Jr. **538**
Guinn, Kenny, **545**
Gunderson, Carl, **558**
Gunter, Julius C., **523**
Guy, William L., **551**

Hadley, Herbert S., **542**
Hafer, Barbara, **555**
Hagaman, Frank L., **533**
Hager, John, **563**
Haines, John M., **529**
Haines, William T., **536**
Hall, David, 107, **553**
Hall, Frederick L., **533**
Hall, John H., **554**
Hall, Luther E., **535**
Hamilton, Alexander, 59
Hamilton, John, **534**
Hammill, John, **532**
Hammond, Jay S., **519**
Hammond, Winfield S., **540**
Handley, Harold W., **531**
Hanly, J. Frank, **531**
Hanna, Louis B., **551**
Hannett, Arthur T., **548**
Hansen, Clifford P., **567**
Hardee, Cary A., **526**
Harding, William L., **532**
Hardman, Lamartine G., **527**
Hardwick, Thomas W., **527**
Harley, Joseph E., **557**
Harmon, Judson, **552**
Harriman, W. Averell, **549**
Harrington, Emerson C., **537**
Harris, Andrew L., **552**
Harris, Charles Nathan, 367
Harris, Joe Frank, **527**
Harris, Nathaniel E., **527**
Harrison, Albertis S., Jr., **563**
Hart, Louis F., **564**
Hartley, Roland H., **564**
Hartness, James, **562**
Harvey, William G., **557**
Haskell, Charles N., **553**
Haskell, Robert N., **536**
Hatch, Mike, **540**
Hatfield, Henry D., **565**
Hatfield, Mark O., **554**
Hathaway, Stanley K., **567**
Hawley, James H., **529**
Hay, Marion E., **564**
Hayden, Mike, **533**
Hayes, Rutherford, 106
Hays, George W., **521**
Heard, William W., **535**
Hearnes, Warren E., **542**
Heil, Julius P., **566**
Heineman, David, **544**
Heitkamp, Heidi, **551**
Henderson, Charles, **518**
Henry, Stephen, **534**
Herbert, Thomas J., **552**

Herreid, Charles N., **558**
Herrick, Myron T., **552**
Herring, Clyde L., **532**
Herschler, Ed, **567**
Herseth, Ralph E., **558**
Herter, Christian A., **538**
Heyward, Duncan C., **557**
Hickel, Walter J., **519**
Hickenlooper, Bourke B., **532**
Hickey, John J., **567**
Higgins, Frank W., **549**
Higgins, James H., **556**
Hildreth, Horace A., **536**
Hill, Jim, **554**
Hill, John F., **536**
Hilliard, Carole, **558**
Hinkle, James F., **548**
Hirono, Mazie, **528**
Hobby, William P., **560**
Hoch, Edward W., **533**
Hockenhull, Andrew W., **548**
Hodges, George H., **533**
Hodges, Jim, **557**
Hodges, Luther H., **550**
Hoegh, Leo A., **532**
Hoey, Clyde R., **550**
Hoff, Philip H., **562**
Hoffman, Harold G., **547**
Holcomb, Marcus H., **524**
Holden, Bob, **542**
Holden, William Woods, 127
Holland, Spessard L., **526**
Hollings, Ernest F., **557**
Holloway, William J., **553**
Holmes, Robert D., **554**
Holshouser, James E., Jr., **550**
Holt, Homer A., **565**
Holt, William E., **543**
Holton, Linwood, **563**
Hooper, Ben W., **559**
Horner, Henry, **530**
Horton, Henry H., **559**
Horton, Willie, 467
Houx, Frank L., **567**
Howard, Pierre, **527**
Huckabee, Mike, **521**
Hughes, Charles E., **549**
Hughes, Harold E., **532**
Hughes, Harry R., **537**
Hughes, Richard J., **547**
Hull, Jane Dee, **520**
Hunn, John, **525**
Hunt, Frank W., **529**
Hunt, George W. P., **520**
Hunt, Guy, 113, **518**
Hunt, James B., Jr., **550**

Note: References point to question numbers in the text. Entries with **bold** references appear in Chapter 7.

Hunt, Lester C., **567**
Hunt, Lorraine, **545**
Hurley, Charles F., **538**
Hurley, Robert A., **524**
Huxman, Walter A., **533**
Hyde, Arthur M., **542**

Ieyoub, Richard, Jr., **535**

Jackson, Andrew, 343
Jackson, Ed, **531**
James, Arthur H., **555**
James, Fob, Jr., 121, **518**
James, Forrest, Jr., **518**
James, King, 8
Janklow, William J., **558**
Jefferson, Thomas, 7, 51, 106
Jeffries, Richard M., **557**
Jelks, William D., **518**
Jennings, William S., **526**
Jensen, Leslie, **558**
Jester, Beauford H., **560**
Johanns, Mike, **544**
Johns, Charley E., **526**
Johnson, Andrew, 106
Johnson, Carol, **540**
Johnson, Edwin C., **523**
Johnson, Gary E., **548**
Johnson, Hiram W., **522**
Johnson, John A., **540**
Johnson, Joseph B., **562**
Johnson, Keen, **534**
Johnson, Leroy Reginald, 238
Johnson, Lyndon B., 47
Johnson, Paul B., **541**
Johnson, Paul B., Sr., **541**
Johnson, Walter W., **523**
Johnston, Henry S., 113, **553**
Johnston, Olin D., **557**
Jones, Brereton C., **534**
Jones, Dan W., **521**
Jones, Robert T., **520**
Jones, Sam H., **535**
Jordan, Barbara, 118
Jordan, Chester B., **546**
Jordan, Len B., **529**
Judge, Thomas Lee, **543**

Kean, Thomas H., **547**
Keating, Frank, **553**
Kelly, Harry F., **539**
Kempthorne, Dirk, **529**
Kendall, Nathan E., **532**
Kendrick, John B., **567**
Kennedy, John F., 111, 366
Kennon, Robert F., **535**
Kerman, Joseph, **531**

Kerner, Otto, 107, **530**
Kerr, Robert S., **553**
Kerrey, Robert, **544**
Ketterer, Andrew, **536**
Keyes, Henry W., **546**
Keyser, Frank R., Jr., **562**
Kilby, Thomas E., **518**
Kimball, Charles D., **556**
King, Alvin O., **535**
King, Angus S., Jr., 291, 317, **536**
King, Bruce, **548**
King, Edward J., **538**
King, John W., **546**
Kinney, Ross, **519**
Kirk, Claude R., Jr., **526**
Kirk, Paul, 281
Kirman, Richard, Sr. **545**
Kitchin, William W., **550**
Kitzhaber, John A., **554**
Kneip, Richard F., **558**
Knight, Goodwin J., **522**
Knous, William Lee, **523**
Knowles, Tony, **519**
Knowles, Warren P., **566**
Kohler, Walter J., Jr., **566**
Kohler, Walter J., Sr., **566**
Kraschel, Nelson G., **532**
Krolicki, Brian, **545**
Kump, Herman G., **565**
Kunin, Madeleine, **562**

Laffoon, Ruby, **534**
LaFollette, Philip F., **566**
LaFollette, Robert M., **566**
Lake, Everett J., **524**
Lamm, Richard D., **523**
Lance, Alan, **529**
Landon, Alfred M., **533**
Lane, William Preston, Jr. **537**
Laney, Ben, **521**
Langer, William, **551**
Langlie, Arthur B., **564**
Lanham, Samuel W. T., **560**
Larrazolo, Octaviano A., 119, **548**
Larson, Morgan F., **547**
Lausche, Frank J., **552**
Lawrence, David L., **555**
Laxalt, Paul D., **545**
Lea, Preston, **525**
Leader, George M., **555**
Leavitt, Michael O., **561**
Leche, Richard W., **535**
Lee, Andrew E., **558**
Lee, Blair, III, **537**
Lee, J. Bracken, **561**
Lehman, Herbert H., **549**
Leslie, Harry G., **531**

LeVander, Harold, **540**
Licht, Frank, **556**
Lilley, George L., **524**
Lincoln, Abraham, 26, 45
Lincoln, Enoch, 132
Lincoln, Levi, Jr., 132
Lind, John, **540**
Lindsey, Washington E., **548**
Link, Arthur A., **551**
List, Robert, **545**
Lister, Ernest, **564**
Little, John S., **521**
Locke, Gary, 119, **564**
Lockwood, Loma Elizabeth, 396
Lockyer, Bill, **522**
Lodge, John, **524**
Long, Earl K., **535**
Long, Huey P., **535**
Longino, Andrew H., **541**
Longley, James B., **536**
Loomis, Orland S., 112
Lounsbury, George E., **524**
Love, John A., **523**
Loveless, Herschel C., **532**
Lowden, Frank O., **530**
Lowry, Mike, **564**
Lucas, Frank E., **567**
Lucey, Patrick J., **566**
Lummis, Cynthia, **567**
Lungren, Daniel, 334

Mabey, Charles R., **561**
Mabry, Thomas J., **548**
Mabus, Ray, **541**
Maddock, Walter J., **551**
Maddox, Lester G., **527**
Madison, James, 51
Madrid, Patricia A., **548**
Major, Elliot W., **542**
Mandel, Marvin, 107, **537**
Mann, William H., **563**
Manning, Richard I., III, **557**
Markell, Jack, **525**
Marland, Ernest W., **553**
Marland, William C., **565**
Marshall, Thomas R., **531**
Martin, Charles H., **554**
Martin, Clarence D., **564**
Martin, Edward, **555**
Martin, James G., **550**
Martin, Jesse M., **521**
Martin, John W., **526**
Martineau, John E., **521**
Martinez, Bob, 119, **526**
Martz, Judy, **543**
Mason, Charles, 17
Mason, John, 6

Note: References point to question numbers in the text. Entries with **bold** references appear in Chapter 7.

Matheson, Scott M., **561**
Maull, Joseph, 112
Maurstad, Dave, **544**
Maw, Herbert B., **561**
Maybank, Burnet R., **557**
Mazurek, Joseph P., **543**
McBride, Henry, **564**
McCall, Samuel W., **538**
McCall, Thomas L., **554**
McCallum, Scott, **566**
McCarty, Dan, **526**
McConaughy, James L., **524**
McConnell, William J., **529**
McCord, Jim, **559**
McCormick, Dale, **536**
McCray, Warren T., **531**
McCreary, James B., **534**
McCuish, John, **533**
McCulloch, James, 428
McCullough, John G., **562**
McDonald, Jesse F., **523**
McDonald, William C., **548**
McFarland, Ernest W., **520**
McGovern, Francis E., **566**
McGrath, J. Howard, **556**
McGraw, Darrell, Jr. **565**
McGraw, John H., **564**
McKay, Douglas, **554**
McKeithen, John J., **535**
McKeldin, Theodore R., **537**
McKelvie, Samuel R., **544**
McKernan, John R., Jr., **536**
McKiernan, John S., **556**
McKinley, William, 106
McLane, John, **546**
McLaughlin, Philip, **546**
McLaurin, Anselm J., **541**
McLean, Angus W., **550**
McLean, George P., **524**
McLeod, Thomas G., **557**
McMaster, Hill, **559**
McMaster, William H., **558**
McMath, Sid, **521**
McMillin, Benton, **559**
McMullen, Adam, **544**
McMullen, Richard C., **525**
McNair, Robert E., **557**
McNichols, Stephen L. R., **523**
McNutt, Paul V., **531**
McRae, Thomas C., **521**
McSweeney, Miles B., **557**
McWherter, Ned Ray, **559**
Mead, Albert E., **564**
Mead, John A., **562**
Meadows, Clarence W., **565**
Mecham, Evan, 113, **520**

Mechem, Edwin L., **548**
Mechem, Merritt C., **548**
Meier, Julius L., **554**
Mellette, Arthur C., **558**
Merriam, Frank F., 294, **522**
Merrill, Steve, **546**
Meskill, Thomas J., **524**
Meyner, Robert B., **547**
Mickelson, George S., **558**
Mickelson, George T., **558**
Mickey, John H., **544**
Miles, John E., **548**
Miller, Benjamin M., **518**
Miller, Charles R., **525**
Miller, Keith H., **519**
Miller, Leslie A., **567**
Miller, Nathan L., **549**
Miller, Robert, **545**
Miller, Tom, **532**
Miller, Walter Dale, **558**
Miller, Zell, **527**
Milliken, Carl E., **536**
Milliken, William G., **539**
Minner, Ruth Ann, **525**
Mitchell, Charles Lewis, 237
Mixon, John W., **526**
Modisett, Jeff, **531**
Moeur, B. B., **520**
Mofford, Rose, **520**
Molleston, Henry, 112
Monroe, James, 106
Montague, Andrew J., **563**
Montgomery, Betty D., **552**
Montoya, Michael, **548**
Moodie, Thomas H., **551**
Moody, Dan, **560**
Moore, A. Harry, **547**
Moore, Arch A., Jr., **565**
Moore, C. C., **529**
Moore, Dan K., **550**
Moore, John I., **521**
Moore, Mike, **541**
Morehead, John H., **544**
Morgan, E. F., **565**
Morley, Clarence J., **523**
Morrison, Cameron, **550**
Morrison, Frank B., **544**
Morrison, John T., **529**
Morrow, Edwin P., **534**
Moses, John, **551**
Mount, James A., **531**
Murphree, Dennis, **541**
Murphy, Francis P., **546**
Murphy, Frank, **539**
Murphy, Franklin, **547**
Murphy, Michael, **564**

Murray, Johnston, **553**
Murray, Mark, **539**
Murry, William H., **553**
Musgrove, Ronnie, **541**
Muskie, Edmund S., **536**
Myers, Hardy, **554**
Myrdal, Rosemarie, **551**

Napolitano, Janet, **520**
Nappier, Denise, **524**
Nash, George K., **552**
Neely, Matthew M., **565**
Neff, Pat M., **560**
Nelson, Bill, **526**
Nelson, E. Benjamin, **544**
Nelson, Gaylord A., **566**
Nestos, Ragnvald A., 125, **551**
Neuberger, Maurine, 221
Neuberger, Richard, 221
Neville, Keith, **544**
Nice, Harry W., **537**
Nigh, George P., **553**
Nixon, Jeremiah W., **542**
Nixon, Richard, 47, 492
Noe, James A., **535**
Noel, Edmond F., **541**
Noel, Philip W., **556**
Norbeck, Peter, **558**
Norblad, A. W., **554**
Norris, Edwin L., **543**
Norton, Mary Teresa, 288
Notte, John A., Jr., **556**
Nunn, Louis B., **534**
Nutter, Donald G., **543**

O'Bannon, Frank, **531**
O'Brien, Shannon P., **538**
O'Callaghan, Donald N. "Mike," **545**
O'Connor, Maureen, **552**
O'Conor, Herbert R., **537**
O'Daniel, W. Lee, **560**
O'Keefe, Mark, **543**
O'Neal, Emmet, **518**
O'Neill, C. William, **552**
O'Neill, William A., **524**
Oddie, Tasker L., **545**
Odell, Benjamin B., Jr., **549**
Ogilvie, Richard B., **530**
Olcott, Ben W., **554**
Oldham, William K., **521**
Olson, Allen I., **551**
Olson, Culbert L., **522**
Olson, Floyd B., **540**
Olson, Ole H., **551**
Orman, James B., **523**
Orr, Kay A., **544**

Note: References point to question numbers in the text. Entries with **bold** references appear in Chapter 7.

Orr, Robert D., **531**
Osborn, Chase S., **539**
Osborn, Sidney P., **520**
Oswald, Lee Harvey, 366
Otter, C. L. "Butch," **529**
Owen, Brad, **564**
Owens, Bill, **523**

Pacheco, Romualdo, 119
Pardee, George C., **522**
Park, Guy B., **542**
Parker, John M., **535**
Parkhurst, Frederick H., **536**
Parnell, Harvey, **521**
Parsons, James Benton, 397
Pastore, John O., 120, **556**
Pataki, George E., **549**
Patterson, Grady, **557**
Patterson, I. L., **554**
Patterson, John M., **518**
Patterson, Malcolm R., **559**
Patterson, Paul L., **554**
Patteson, Okey L., **565**
Pattison, John M., **552**
Patton, Paul E., **534**
Paulen, Ben S., **533**
Payne, Frederick G., **536**
Peabody, Endicott, **538**
Peabody, James H., **523**
Peay, Austin, **559**
Pederson, Sally, **532**
Peeler, Bob, **557**
Peery, George C., **563**
Penn, William, 6
Pennewill, Simeon S., **525**
Pennypacker, Samuel W., **555**
Perdue, John, **565**
Perpich, Rudolph, **540**
Perry, Rick, **560**
Persons, Gordon, **518**
Peterson, Hjalmar, **540**
Peterson, Russell W., **525**
Peterson, Val, **544**
Peterson, Walter R., **546**
Philipp, Emanuel L., **566**
Phillips, John C., **520**
Phillips, Leon C., **553**
Pierce, Walter M., **554**
Pinchback, Pinckney Benton Stewart, 116
Pinchot, Gifford, **555**
Pindall, Xenophon O., **521**
Pingree, Hazen S., **539**
Pittman, Vail M., **545**
Plaisted, Frederick W., **536**
Pleasant, Ruffin G., **535**
Poletti, Charles, **549**

Polk, James, 106
Pollard, John G., **563**
Posthumus, Dick, **539**
Pothier, Aram J., **556**
Powell, Clifford R., **547**
Powell, Wesley, **546**
Powers, Llewellyn, **536**
Poynter, William A., **544**
Prall, Horace G., **547**
Preus, Jacob A. O., **540**
Price, James H., **563**
Proctor, Fletcher D., **562**
Proctor, Mortimer R., **562**
Proctor, Redfield, Jr. **562**
Prouty, George H., **562**
Pryor, Bill, **518**
Pryor, David H., **521**
Pryor, Mark, **521**
Purcell, Joe, **521**
Pyle, Howard, **520**

Quie, Albert H., **540**
Quinby, Henry B., **546**
Quinn, Robert E., **556**
Quinn, William F., **528**

Racicot, Marc, **543**
Racine, Douglas A., **562**
Ralston, Samuel M., **531**
Rampton, Calvin L., **561**
Ranney, Austin, 314
Ratner, Payne H., **533**
Ray, Dixie Lee, **564**
Ray, Robert D., **532**
Reagan, Ronald, 47, 106, 353, **522**
Reed, Clyde M., **533**
Reed, John H., **536**
Reilly, Thomas F., **538**
Rell, M. Jodi, **524**
Rennebohm, Oscar, **566**
Reynolds, John W., **566**
Rhodes, James A., **552**
Ribicoff, Abraham, **524**
Richards, Ann, **560**
Richards, DeForest, **567**
Richards, John G., **557**
Richardson, Friend W., **522**
Rickards, John E., **543**
Ridge, Tom, **555**
Riley, Richard W., **557**
Riley, Robert, **521**
Ritchie, Albert C., **537**
Rivers, Eurith D., **527**
Robb, Charles S., **563**
Roberts, A. H., **559**
Roberts, Barbara, **554**
Roberts, Dennis J., **556**

Roberts, Henry, **524**
Robertson, J. B. A., **553**
Robins, C. A., **529**
Robinson, Charles, 127
Robinson, Joe T., **521**
Robinson, Robert P., **525**
Rockefeller, John D., IV, **565**
Rockefeller, Nelson A., **549**
Rockefeller, Winthrop, **521**
Roemer, Charles E., III, 121, 320, **535**
Rogers, Clifford J., **567**
Rogers, Joe, **523**
Rogers, John R., 121, **564**
Rollins, Frank W., **546**
Rolph, James, Jr., **522**
Rolvaag, Karl F., **540**
Romer, Roy, **523**
Romney, George W., **539**
Roosevelt, Franklin D., 47, 64, 106, 276, **549**
Roosevelt, Theodore, 106, **549**
Ross, C. Benjamin, **529**
Ross, Nellie Tayloe, 114, 131, **567**
Ross, William B., **567**
Rosselini, Albert D., **564**
Rowland, John G., **524**
Roy, Vesta, **546**
Ruby, Jack, 366
Runyon, William N., **547**
Russell, Charles H., **545**
Russell, Daniel L., **550**
Russell, Donald S., **557**
Russell, Lee M., **541**
Russell, Richard B., Jr., **527**
Ryan, George, **530**
Ryan, Jim, **530**
Rye, Tom C., **559**
Rylander, Carole Keeton, **560**

Sadler, Reinhold, **545**
Salazar, Ken, **523**
Salmon, Thomas P., **562**
Saltonstall, Leverett, **538**
Samford, William J., **518**
Sampson, Flem D., **534**
Samuelson, Don, **529**
San Souci, Emery J., **556**
Sanders, Carl E., **527**
Sanders, Jared Y., **535**
Sanford, Terry, **550**
Sargent, Francis W., **538**
Sarles, Elmore Y., **551**
Savage, Ezra P., **544**
Sawyer, F. Grant, **545**
Sayers, Joseph D., **560**
Schaefer, William Donald, **537**
Schafer, Edward T., **551**

Note: References point to question numbers in the text. Entries with **bold** references appear in Chapter 7.

Schmedeman, Albert G., **566**
Schoeppel, Andrew F., **533**
Schofield, Edward, **566**
Schricker, Henry F., **531**
Schrieber, Martin J., **566**
Schunk, Mae, **540**
Schweiker, Mark S., **555**
Schwinden, Ted, **543**
Scott, Robert W., **550**
Scott, W. Kerr, **550**
Scranton, William W., **555**
Scrugham, James G., **545**
Seligman, Arthur, **548**
Sevier, John, 23
Sewall, Sumner, **536**
Shafer, George F., **551**
Shafer, Raymond P., **555**
Shafroth, John F., **523**
Shaheen, Jeanne, **546**
Shallenberger, Ashton C., **544**
Shallenburger, Tim, **533**
Shannon, James C., **524**
Shapiro, Samuel H., **530**
Shapp, Milton J., **555**
Sharpe, Merrell Q., **558**
Shaw, Leslie M., **532**
Sheffield, William, **519**
Sheldon, Charles H., **558**
Sheldon, George L., **544**
Sherrer, Gary, **533**
Shivers, Allan, **560**
Sholtz, David, **526**
Shoup, George L., **529**
Shoup, Oliver H., **523**
Siegelman, Donald, **518**
Sigler, Kim, **539**
Silzer, George S., **547**
Simms, John F., **548**
Simpson, Milward L., **567**
Simpson, O. H., **535**
Sinclair, Upton, 294
Sinner, George A., **551**
Slaton, John M., **527**
Sleeper, Albert E., **539**
Small, Len, **530**
Smith, Alfred E., 104, **549**
Smith, Charles A., **557**
Smith, Charles M., **562**
Smith, Edward C., **562**
Smith, Elmo, **554**
Smith, Forrest, **542**
Smith, Hoke, **527**
Smith, Hulett C., **565**
Smith, John Walter, **537**
Smith, John, 18
Smith, Nels H., **567**

Smith, Preston, **560**
Smith, Robert B., **543**
Smylie, Robert E., **529**
Snell, Earl, **554**
Snelling, Richard A., **562**
Snow, Wilbert, **524**
Sorlie, Arthur G., **551**
Sorrell, William, **562**
Sparks, Chauncey M., **518**
Sparks, John, **545**
Spaulding, Huntley N., **546**
Spaulding, Rolland H., **546**
Spellman, John, **564**
Spitzer, Eliot, **549**
Sprague, Charles A., **554**
Springer, Carol, **520**
Sproul, William C., **555**
Spry, William, **561**
Stafford, Robert T., **562**
Stanford, R. C., **520**
Stanley, Augustus O., **534**
Stanley, Thomas B., **563**
Stanley, William E., **533**
Stark, Lloyd C., **542**
Stassen, Harold E., **540**
Stelle, John H., **530**
Stenberg, Don, **544**
Stephens, Lawrence V., **542**
Stephens, Stan, **543**
Stephens, William D., **522**
Sterling, Ross S., **560**
Steunenberg, Frank, **529**
Stevenson, Adlai E., **530**
Stevenson, Coke R., **560**
Stewart, Samuel V., **543**
Stickney, William W., **562**
Stockton, Thomas, 112
Stokes, Edward C., **547**
Stone, William A., **555**
Stovall, Carla, **533**
Stratton, William G., **530**
Straub, Robert W., **554**
Stuart, Edwin S., **555**
Stuart, Henry C., **563**
Stubbs, Walter R., **533**
Sullivan, Mike, **567**
Sulzer, William, 113, **549**
Summers, Paul, **559**
Sundlun, Bruce, **556**
Sundquist, Don, **559**
Sununu, John H., **546**
Swainson, John B., **539**
Swanson, Claude A., **563**
Sweet, William E., **523**
Swift, Jane M., **538**
Symington, Fife, **520**

Taft, Bob, **552**
Talbot, Ray H., **523**
Talmadge, Eugene, 112, **527**
Tanner, John R., **530**
Tavares, Paul, **556**
Tawes, J. Millard, **537**
Taylor, Alfred A., 345, **559**
Taylor, Leon R., **547**
Taylor, Robert, 345
Taylor, William S., **534**
Teasdale, Joseph P., **542**
Temple, William, 112
Templeton, Charles A., **524**
Tener, John K., **555**
Terral, Thomas J., **521**
Terrell, Joseph M., **527**
Terry, Charles L., **525**
Thomas, Charles S., **523**
Thomas, Georgie, **546**
Thompson, James R., 72, **530**
Thompson, Meldrim, Jr. **546**
Thompson, Melvin E., **527**
Thompson, Tommy G., 93, **566**
Thompson, Vernon W., **566**
Thone, Charles, **544**
Thornburgh, Richard, **555**
Thornton, Dan, **523**
Thurmond, J. Strom, **557**
Thye, Edward J., **540**
Tiemann, Norbert T., **544**
Timmerman, George B., Jr., **557**
Tingley, Clyde, **548**
Tobey, Charles W., **546**
Tobin, Maurice J., **538**
Tomljanovich, Esther, 415
Tompkins, Daniel D., 107
Toole, Joseph K., **543**
Topinka, Judith, **530**
Townsend, John G., Jr., **525**
Townsend, Kathleen Kennedy, 537
Townsend, M. Clifford, **531**
Trammell, Park N., **526**
Trapp, Martin E., **553**
Treen, David C., **535**
Tribbitt, Sherman W., **525**
Trinkle, E. Lee, **563**
Trumbull, John H., **524**
Tuck, William M., **563**
Tucker, Jim Guy, 107, **521**
Tunnell, Ebe W., **525**
Turner, Daniel W., **532**
Turner, Roy J., **553**
Tyler, James Hoge, **563**
Tyler, John, 106

Note: References point to question numbers in the text. Entries with **bold** references appear in Chapter 7.

Ulmer, Fran, **519**
Umstead, William B., **550**
Underwood, Cecil H., **565**
Utter, George H., **556**

Van Buren, Martin, 106
Van Sant, Samuel R., **540**
Van Wagoner, Murray D., **539**
Vanderbilt, William H., **556**
Vanderhoof, John D., **523**
Vandiver, Samuel E., Jr., **527**
Vardaman, James K., **541**
Ventura, Jesse, 291, 317, **540**
Verniero, Pete, **547**
Vessey, Robert S., **558**
Vilsack, Tom, **532**
Vivian, John C., **523**
Voight, Jack, **566**
Voinovich, George, **552**
Volpe, John A., **538**
Voorhees, Foster M., **547**

Wahl, Rosalie, 415
Waihee, John, **528**
Walker, Clifford, **527**
Walker, Daniel, **530**
Walker, Edward Garrison, 237
Walker, Olene S., **561**
Wallace, George C., Jr., 111, 131, **518**
Wallace, Lurleen B., 131, **518**
Waller, William L., **541**
Wallgren, Mon C., **564**
Walsh, David I., **538**
Walters, David, **553**
Walton, John, 113
Waltron, Jack C., **553**

Warfield, Edwin, **537**
Warner, Fred M., **539**
Warren, Earl, **522**
Warren, Fuller, **526**
Washington, George, 59
Weaver, Arthur J., **544**
Weeks, Frank B., **524**
Weeks, John E., **562**
Weicker, Lowell, **524**
Weld, William, **538**
Welford, Walter, **551**
Wells, Heber M., **561**
Welsh, Matthew E., **531**
West, John C., **557**
West, Oswald, **554**
Wetherby, Lawrence W., **534**
Whitcomb, Edgar D., **531**
White, Albert B., **565**
White, Edward Douglass, 137
White, Frank D., **521**
White, Frank, **551**
White, George, **552**
White, Horace, **549**
White, Hugh L., **541**
White, Mark, **560**
Whitehouse, Sheldon, **556**
Whitfield, Henry L., **541**
Whitman, Charles S., **549**
Whitman, Christine T., **547**
Wicker, Dennis A., **550**
Wilder, John S., **559**
Wilder, L. Douglas, 117, **563**
Wilkie, Wendell, 276
Wilkinson, Wallace G., **534**
Willey, Norman B., **529**
Williams, Anthony, 60
Williams, Arnold, **529**

Williams, G. Mennen, **539**
Williams, J. R. "Jack," **520**
Williams, John B., **541**
Williams, Ransome J., **557**
Williams, Robert L., **553**
Williams, Roger, 6
Willis, Frank B., **552**
Willis, Simeon S., **534**
Wills, William H., **562**
Willson, Augustus C., **534**
Wilson, George A., **532**
Wilson, Malcolm, **549**
Wilson, Pete, **522**
Wilson, Roger, **542**
Wilson, Stanley C., **562**
Wilson, Woodrow, 106, 107, **547**
Winant, John G., **546**
Windom, Steve, **518**
Winter, William, **541**
Withycombe, James, **554**
Wolf, Dale E., **525**
Wollman, Harvey, **558**
Wong, Delbert E., 395
Wood, Corinne G., **530**
Woodhouse, Gay, **567**
Woodring, Harry H., **533**
Woodruff, Rollin S., **524**
Wright, Fielding L., **541**
Wright, Jonathan Jasper, 397

Yates, Richard, Jr., **530**
Young, Brigham, 24
Young, Clement C., **522**
Youngdahl, Luther W., **540**

Zimmerman, Fred R., **566**

Note: References point to question numbers in the text. Entries with **bold** references appear in Chapter 7.